PRICE TRENDS OF ROYAL TRIBUTE COMMODITIES IN NUEVA GALICIA, 1557–1598

Price Trends of Royal Tribute Commodities in Nueva Galicia, 1557–1598

Woodrow Borah

UNIVERSITY OF CALIFORNIA PRESS
Berkeley • Los Angeles • Oxford

UNIVERSITY OF CALIFORNIA PUBLICATIONS:
IBERO-AMERICANA

Volume 55

UNIVERSITY OF CALIFORNIA PRESS
BERKELEY AND LOS ANGELES, CALIFORNIA

UNIVERSITY OF CALIFORNIA PRESS, LTD.
OXFORD, ENGLAND

PRINTED IN THE UNITED STATES OF AMERICA

Library of Congress Cataloging-in-Publication Data

Borah, Woodrow Wilson, 1912–
Price trends of royal tribute commodities in Nueva Galicia, 1557–1598 / Woodrow Borah.
p. cm. – (University of California publications. Ibero-Americana; v. 55)
ISBN 0-520-09769-6 (paper)
1. Agricultural prices—Mexico—Nueva Galicia—History—16th century. I. Title. II. Series.
HD1792.75.B67 1991
338.1'3'097235—dc20 91-29604

The paper used in this publication meets the minimum requirements of American National Standard for Information Sciences—Permanence of Paper for Printed Library Materials, ANSI Z39.48-1984. ♾

Contents

List of Graphs and Tables

Graphs

Tables

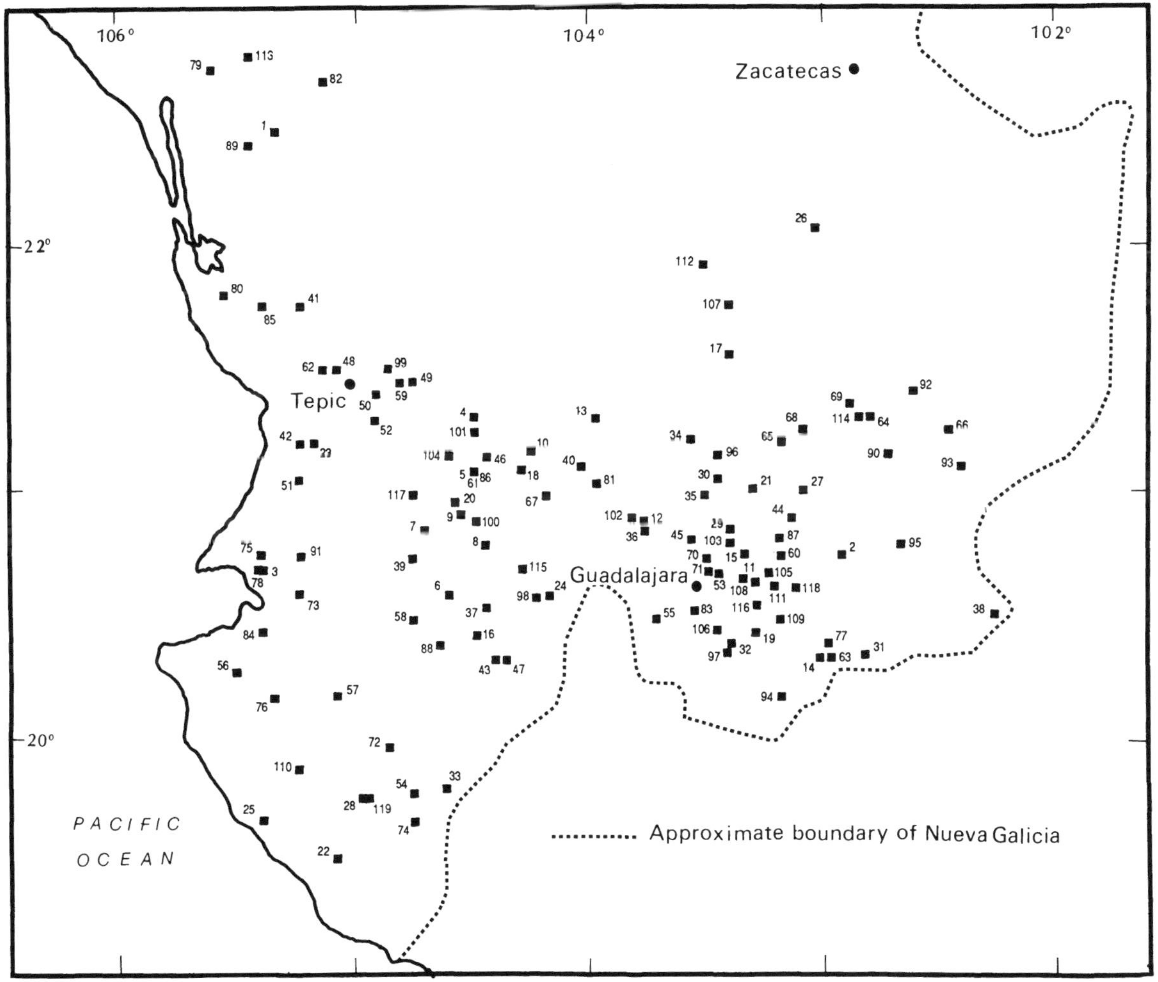

Towns of Nueva Galicia Figuring in Royal Auctions, 1557-1598

KEY TO MAP

Number on Map	Name of Town	Province
1	Acaponeta	Acaponeta
2	Acatic	Tecpatitlán
	*Acatique	Purificación
3	Acatispa	Tepic
4	Acuitlapilco, Sta. María de	Tequepexpan
	(today Santa María del Oro)	
5	Ahuacatlán	Ahuacatlán and Jala
6	Ahuisculco	Tala
	*Amaito	Purificación
7	Amatitán	Tequila
8	Amatlán (de las Cañas)	Guauchinango
9	Amaxaque	Guauchinango
10	Amaxaque	Hostotipaquillo
	*Amboquito Atengo	Purificación
11	Analco	Guadalajara
	(also as Analco y Tetlán and Analcotetlán)	
	*Apanaloa	Purificación
	*Apeque	Purificación
12	Apozol	Juchipila
13	Apozolco	Colotlán
14	Ascatlán	Tecpatitlán
15	Atemajac (del Valle)	S. Cristóbal de la Barranca
	*Atengo	Purificación
16	Atengoichán	Guauchinango
	(also Atengo and Atenguillo)	
	*Atelaco (linked with Culeque)	Purificación
	*Atetaco	Purificación
17	Atixtac, Santa Ana	Tlajomulco
	*Cacalotitlán	Purificación
18	Cacaluta	Hostotipaquillo
19	Cajititlán	Tlajomulco
20	Camotlán	Tequepexpan
21	Camotlán	S. Cristóbal de la Barranca
	Canala (with Acatispa)	Tepic
22	Chamela	Purificación
23	Chila	Tepic
24	Chistique	Guauchinango
25	Chola	Purificación
26	Colotlán	Colotlán
27	Contla	Cuquío
28	Contla	Purificación
29	Copala (linked with Quilitlán)	S. Cristóbal de la Barranca
30	Coscotitán, S. Cristóbal	S. Cristóbal de la Barranca
31	Cuitzeo	La Barca
	*Culeque	Purificación
	(also Colique and Queleque)	
	*Cusmini, S. Andrés	Purificación
	*Cuyulomitle	Purificación
32	Cuyutlán	Tlajomulco
33	Cuyutlán	Purificación
34	Cuyutlán, Sta. Maria	S. Cristóbal de la Barranca
35	Epatlán (also Ipatán)	S. Cristóbal de la Barranca
36	Los Guajes	Tequila
	(with Tequila; also Guastla)	
	*Guamuchal (with Chamela)	Purificación
37	Guauchinango, Naborias de (enter 1598 auctions)	Guauchinango
38	Guázcato	La Barca
39	Hostotipac	Hostotipac
40	Hostotipaquillo	Hostotipaquillo
	*Huelotitlán (also Velotitlán)	Purificación
	*Inrimota	Purificación
	*Iquilapique	Purificación
41	Ixcuintla (de Corzo), Santiago	Sentispac
	*Ixtapa	Acaponeta
42	Ixtapa, Sta. Maria	Tepic
43	Iximitique	Guauchinango
44	Ixtlahuacán	Cuquío
	*Ixtlahuatengo	S. Cristóbal de la Barranca
45	Ixtlán	Tala
	*Ixtlapa, Santiago	Tepic
	*Jala (with Contla)	Cuquío
46	Jala	Ahuacatlán and Jala
47	Jalacingo	Guauchinango
48	Jalcocotán	Tepic
49	Jalisco	Tepic
50	Jalisquillo	Tepic
51	Jaltemba	Tepic
52	Jaltepec	Tepic
53	Jocotlán	Tala
54	Jocotlán	Purificación
	*Jocotlán (near Chola and Quemara)	Purificación
55	Juanacatlán (also Xonacatlán)	Tecpatitlán
56	Maito	Purificación
57	Maloto	Purificación
58	Mascota	Guauchinango

* Cannot be located

cont'd

Number on Map	Name of Town	Province
59	Matacticpac	Tepic
60	Matatlán (also Matatán)	Tecpatitlán
61	Mayanalistlán, S. Pedro	Tepic
62	Mecatán	Tepic
63	Mexcala	La Barca
64	Mexticacán	Cuquío
	*Mezquititique	Purificación
	*Mezquitlán	Purificación
65	Mezquituta	Juchipila
66	Mitic	Lagos
67	Mochitiltic	Hostotipaquillo
68	Moyagua	Juchipila
69	Nochistlán	Juchipila
70	Nochistlanejo	Tala
	*Ocotique	Acaponeta ?
71	Ocotlán	Tala
72	Opono	Purificación
73	Orita	Tepic
	*Otala (with Apozolco)	Colotlán
74	Panpuchín	Purificación
75	Papachula, S. Juan	Tepic
76	Piloto	Purificación
77	Poncitlán	La Barca
78	Pontoque	Tepic
79	Quebiquinto	Acaponeta
	*Quezdaquepa (in Nayarit)	?
	*Quilapique	Purificación
	*Quilitlán	S. Cristóbal de la Barranca
	*Quilitlán	Tepic
80	S. Andrés (Amazcula)	Sentispac
81	S. Francisco	Hostotipaquillo
	*S. Miguel (with Chila and Zanatlán)	Tepic
82	S. Pedro (sujeto of Tetitlán ?)	Acaponeta
83	Sta. Fe (with Juanacatlán)	Tecpatitlán
	*Santiago Ixcuintla	Tepic
84	Sayula, S. Francisco	Acaponeta
85	Sentispac (also Centiquipaque and Senticpac)	Sentispac
	*Sila	Purificación
86	Suchipil (Otomí half o Ahuacatlán)	Ahuacatlán and Jala
87	Tacotlán (with Ixtlahuacán)	Cuquío
88	Tala	Tala
	*Talistaque	Hostotipaquillo
	*Tecametlán	Hostotipaquillo

Number on Map	Name of Town	Province
89	Tecuala	Acaponeta
90	Temacapulín	Tecpatitlán
91	Temichoque, Santiago (also Timichoc)	Tepic
	*Tena	Purificación
92	Teocaltiche	Lagos
93	Teocaltitlán, Santiago	Lagos
94	Tepacatengo	Tecpatitlán
95	Tepatitlán	Tecpatitlán
96	Tepeaca (also Tepaca)	S. Cristóbal de la Barranca
97	Tepetitlán (de los Negros), Sta. Ana	Tala
98	Tepetlatlauca	Guauchinango
99	Tepic	Tepic
100	Tepuzhuacán	Guauchinango
101	Tequepexpan	Tequepexpan
102	Tequila (with Los Guajes)	Tequila
	*Tequiltitlán	Purificación
	*Terequita (with Mezquititique)	Purificación
103	Tesistán (also Tequixixtlán)	S. Cristóbal de la Barranca
104	Tetitlán	Tequepexpan
	*Tetitlán	Acaponeta
105	Tetlán (with Analco)	Guadalajara
106	Tlajomulco	Tlajomulco
107	Tlaltenango	Tlaltenango
108	Tlaquepaque, S. Pedro (also Tlacpac, S. Pedro; with Toluquilla)	Tonalá
	*Toconis (with Tomatlán)	Purificación
109	Toluquilla (with Tlaquepaque)	Tonalá
110	Tomatlán	Purificación
111	Tonalá	Tonalá
	*Tosmotoc, S. Miguel	Tepic
112	Totatiche	Colotlán
113	Totorán (also Totorane)	Acaponeta
114	Yahualica (also Agualica)	Cuquío
	*Yegualtitlán	Purificación
115	Zacatlán	Guauchinango
116	Zalatitlán	Tonalá
117	Zanatlán (also Zanalatitlán)	Tepic
118	Zapotlán	Tecpatitlán
119	Zapotlán	Purificación

* Cannot be located

Acknowledgments

Any study of great detail and considerable complexity, carried out over a period of thirty years, requires much help and advice. This one certainly has had a great deal of both, for which I make grateful acknowledgment. A year of sabbatical leave from the University of California, Berkeley, supplemented by a John Simon Guggenheim Memorial Foundation fellowship, made it possible for me to take notes in the Archivo General de Indias, Sevilla, in the spring months of 1959. The then Director of the Archivo, José María de la Peña y Cámara, and his assistant, Rosario Parra, later his successor, afforded me free access to materials and gave much valuable advice. Later my notes were reordered in the beginnings of what is now Appendix A by two able research assistants, Gloria Grajales and J. A. Sulliger; funds for this were supplied by the Center for Latin American Studies, University of California, Berkeley, administering a grant from the Ford Foundation.

Supplementary research in Mexico, further services by research assistants, and the necessary work on a computer have been funded by the endowment of the Abraham D. Shepard Chair, Department of History, University of California, Berkeley. For guidance in the archival deposits and libraries of Guadalajara, I am deeply indebted to Dra. Carmen Castañeda, then of El Colegio de Jalisco, who unselfishly placed herself at the disposition of a visiting scholar. For advice on clearing up doubts about the names of bidders, I am indebted to Don Pedro Franco, Lic. Miguel Claudio Jiménez y Vizcarra, and Don Jorge Palomino Cañedo, all of Guadalajara. The last two, formidable genealogists, not merely provided help but also gave me copies of publications on genealogies of Jalisco notables, almost all rare and out of print. Dra. Águeda Jiménez Pelayo kindly furnished me a copy of her newly published study of haciendas and native communities in southern Zacatecas. In determining the meaning of sixteenth-century Mexican terms no longer in use, Dr. Miguel León-Portilla of the Universidad Nacional Autónoma de México, and Peter Gerhard, expert in the historical geography of Mexico, gave much-needed suggestions.

At the Computer Laboratory of the Department of Anthropology and Graduate Group in Demography, University of California, Berkeley, I was welcomed and given desperately needed guidance by Professor Eugene A. Hammel and the chief technician, Madeline Anderson, who adjusted programs and techniques to my needs, with the help of Jiang Lin and Deborah Balk. At one period of crisis, Professor John H. Rowe came to the rescue. The resulting graphs were redrawn by Mrs. Adrienne Morgan, who also prepared the map. For advice in my attempts to establish the relation, if any, of the phenomenon dubbed the Little Ice Age to the movement of commodity prices in the last decades of the sixteenth century, I turned to Professor O.E. Granger of the University of California, Berkeley, Department of Geography and Mr. Thomas H. Naylor, associated with the Laboratory of Tree-Ring Research, University of Arizona, Tucson, who placed their knowledge at my disposal.

Lastly, I have benefited greatly from the critical reading of text and suggestions for improvement of Professors James J. Parsons, Department of Geography, and Jan de Vries and Richard J. Salvucci, Department of History, University of California, Berkeley. For the typing of manuscript, text, and tables I am grateful to Mrs. Dorothy Shannon, Cathy Fallon, and Nadine Ghammache.

1

A NEGLECTED SOURCE OF PRICE DATA FOR EARLY SPANISH AMERICA

The study of Nueva Galicia in this monograph indicates a partial solution to a general problem for studies on Spanish America. Finding data in series for determining price trends in the sixteenth and early seventeenth centuries has perplexed scholars ever since the Europeans developed histories of prices for previous centuries, and especially since Earl Hamilton's well-known histories of prices for the kingdoms of Spain.[1] Occasional attempts at studies of trends in prices for parts of Latin America in the earlier colonial period have met with substantial criticism that they are unscholarly and unsound, applying oversophisticated techniques to basically unreliable data. For example, in 1958 the late Sherburne Cook and I published a study covering forty years, 1531-1570, restricted to the territory of the royal treasury district centered in Mexico City–essentially the Audiencia of Mexico less Yucatan and Tabasco.[2] Its purpose was to ascertain prices and price changes over time for the principal commodities delivered each year by Indian towns in the entire region to their Spanish

[1]Hamilton, *American Treasure and the Prize Revolution in Spain, 1501-1650*, and *War and Prices in Spain, 1651-1800*. A good summary of the history of studies of prices, down to 1967, especially for Europe and the Mediterranean, may be found in the Introduzione by Ruggiero Romano, ed., to *I prezzi in Europa*, pp. ix-xliv; a long bibliography of such studies is given on pp. 569-590. The *Prólogo* by Rolando Mellafe to Armando de Ramón and José Manuel Larraín, *Orígenes de la vida económica chilena, 1659-1808*, pp. 9-26, carries the history to 1973. It may be supplemented further by Romano, "Algunas consideraciones sobre la historia de precios en América colonial" and "Some Considerations on the History of Prices in Colonial Latin America," (essentially a somewhat revised version of the same essay); John H. Coatsworth, "Economic History and the History of Prices in Colonial Latin America"; and Woodrow Borah "Las almonedas reales como fuente de precios para el siglo XVI," a paper presented at the Simposio sobre Historia de los Precios de Alimentos y Manufacturas Novohispanos, Villahermosa, Tabasco, 27-30 June 1990, to be published in the proceedings. This last contains a survey of price studies on colonial Mexico to date.

[2]Borah and Cook, *Price Trends of Some Basic Commodities in Central Mexico, 1531-1570.*

overlords, i.e., the Crown and individual encomenderos. Behind it was the idea that we might calculate average annual prices for each tribute commodity in order to arrive at an approximate probable value in the minds of the Spanish officials who counted the population of an Indian town and recommended the annual tribute to be paid–in short, to provide the necessary basis for analyzing what we dubbed the gamma category of demographic data, *tasaciones* without known relation of amount to tributary.

Our study had specific ends and used a mix of data which distinguished it from price studies elsewhere. It contained various kinds of price data, though all exhibiting, in general, the same tendencies, and data from various parts of the region. Although it comprised all the data we could then locate, they were fewer than we should have liked, though well distributed and coherent. We did not calculate moving averages, as some critics have pointed out, since our data covered the short span of forty years, too few for moving averages to be important and sufficiently few that surrendering years at either end to create moving averages would have represented a serious truncation. We lumped together wholesale and retail prices, after careful testing, since the trend in both was approximately the same and the slope of a regression line arrived at by least squares should be valid for both. Criticism, moreover, assumed a more rigid separation of wholesale and retail markets customary in Europe and in commerce today, rather than the more flexible usage of sixteenth-century Mexico. Further, our resort to data comprising prices at tribute auctions, and to the commutations which were based on an average of preceding transactions at such auctions for the commodity and the town in question, gave rise to the charge that these were not free market values and therefore suspect. Since the commutations were based upon the auction prices of tribute commodities for each town, this objection really deals with the validity of the latter as a true value. This entire monograph handles that point. All reviewers and critics, it should be emphasized, basically accepted or did not challenge our overall findings of a steep upward trend in prices, but wished for more conventionally acceptable data and refined calculations.[3]

Since 1958 a number of studies on prices of foodstuffs and other commodities in colonial Spanish America have appeared. Virtually all concentrate upon the latter half of the colonial period; the later seventeenth and the eighteenth centuries.[4] Only three, all dealing with Chile, attempt the fuller kind of examination which

---

[3]The most extended discussion and criticism are in Enrique Florescano, *Precios del maíz y crisis agrícolas en México, 1708-1818*, pp. 8-28, which undoubtedly reflects a distillation of French comment. See also Pedro Pérez Herrero, "Comercio y precios en la Nueva España," esp. pp. 475-476; and contributions by Ruggiero Romano cited in note 1 above.

[4]The essays by Ruggiero Romano mentioned above list many of them. Those in Johnson and Tandeter, eds., *Essays on the Price History of Eighteenth-Century Latin America*, should be added; the one on Potosí by Enrique Tandeter and Nathan Wachtel is a reworking of their article, "Conjonctures inverses: Le mouvement des prix à Potosí pendant le XVIIIe siècle."

scholars have been able to carry out for Europe.[5] In general, the sixteenth century and the earlier seventeenth remain nearly as ill-covered as they had been before.

The excellent price studies on Europe have been based upon market reports of daily prices for a major center, such as Paris, which are especially good on the grains of popular consumption, like wheat, or on the records of purchases of convents, hospices and hospitals, and schools, which afford a far more varied range of prices for food, fuel, clothing, and wages.[6] From the data in the latter kind of source, scholars have been able to construct indexes of consumption in order to gain an idea of trends in real terms, i.e., commodities of all kinds relative to wages. To be sure, Europe also was developing market differentiation and structure so that the distinction between retail and wholesale, which for the eighteenth century is fairly clear, is distinctly less so the farther back one goes in time.[7] Europe, however, basically has an abundance of records, whatever the heavy losses through catastrophe and neglect.

For Spanish America the situation is different. Price data of the kind required for studies on the European model no longer exist for large areas. Civil tumult and war, fire and earthquake, neglect, and the sale of old records for wrapping, pulping, and fireworks have done away with most early records of convents, schools, hospices, hospitals, and other pious and public foundations. Similarly, municipal and royal treasury records and the data on sales at local granaries have tended to vanish. In general, a rule of recency applies to possible survival–that is, records of the sixteenth century are least likely to survive, those of the seventeenth century have a somewhat better chance, those of the eighteenth century yet better and the best for all colonial records. Thus for Mexico City, although the alhóndiga, the central municipal grain market, functioned from the last quarter of the sixteenth century, only from the eighteenth century did the survival of records enable Enrique Florescano to reconstruct a series of maize prices.[8] There are, to be sure, exceptions: In Santiago, Chile, accounts of purchases for convents and hospices survive to a much greater extent–for one convent from 1596–and have furnished the data for price studies commencing sometime in the seventeenth century and covering the later colonial period. It has even been possible to construct a consumers' price index.[9] In Lima, the major convents may still hold such records in their archives, and there remains the possibility that in highland Ecuador, Peru, Bolivia, and Colombia parts of such archives have survived, perhaps even in Mexico in the largely unexplored masses of church records confiscated in the nineteenth century–but we have almost no information on the matter.

---

[5]Marcello Carmagnani, *Les mécanismes de la vie économique dans une société coloniale: Le Chili (1680-1830)*; Ramón and Larraín, *Orígines*; and Larraín, "Gross National Product and Prices: The Chilean Case in the Seventeenth and Eighteenth Centuries" in Johnson and Tandeter.

[6]Larraín, "Movimiento de precios en Santiago de Chile, 1749-1808, pp. 199-200.

[7]See Ruggiero Romano, "Problèmes et méthodes d'histoire économique de l'Amérique Latine," stressing the differences between underdeveloped and developed countries resulting from the extent of penetration of commercialization and investment, which basically bring about more formal markets.

[8]*Precios del maíz.*

[9]Ramón and Larraín, pp. 354-355; and Larraín, "Gross National Product."

Another possible source of data has lain in the *actas de cabildo* of the various cities. Again, for many cities the earlier volumes of *actas* have disappeared, but for the major capitals, such as Mexico City and Lima, they survive and have been published.[10] From time to time the town councils set prices for basic articles of consumption within their territory, but the intervals are erratic and the prices clearly were set by the council, i.e., they hardly result from the free movement of supply and demand in a market. Theoretically they should nevertheless respond in the end to seasons of scarcity and abundance if they were to have any observance by suppliers to the public, such as bakers, who could not continue in business for long unless they could operate with some margin of profit.[11] Nevertheless, the danger inherent in the information in cabildo records may be seen in one study of Mexico City based on them, which charts a most improbable course of prices contradicted by all later studies.[12]

Yet another source of data for price series, particularly for common and skilled labor and for construction materials, should lie in business records. Unfortunately, precisely this kind of record has had the least chance of survival in early colonial Spanish America. The one exception located so far has been the records of the Cortés estate, the great entail bestowed upon the conqueror of Mexico as the Marquesado del Valle de Oaxaca by a presumably grateful Crown. A large part of the Marquesado's accounts, but far from all, survive as the Archivo del Hospital de Jesús, since that is where they were deposited, and are now in the Archivo General de la Nación in Mexico City. For the Audiencia of Mexico they afford data for reconstructing trends in wages for common labor and the prices of some construction materials. It may be that in Spain or Spanish America similar records may be found, but so far the Marquesado records remain unique.

Have we, then, to come to a counsel of despair? Must we write off as unknowable the history of prices for early colonial Spanish America before perhaps 1650? In the almost theological arguing that surrounds price studies, there will undoubtedly be some purists who will cry, yes. Still, there exists the possibility of shedding much light that may be acceptable to the majority of scholars. That lies in the records of royal auctions in each royal treasury district of commodities paid in tribute by Indian towns held by the Crown (*en cabeza real*). The data obtainable concern only tribute commodities, but those included major foodstuffs and some other materials, such as cloth and clothing. They are limited in that they cover only items delivered as tribute, so that no index of consumption can be constructed from them. Further, acceptance of the data as proper for a study of prices and trends requires that we return to the concept underlying price studies: the measure of change in value over time for a product or group of products, preferably of common consumption, through determination of the amount of money or equivalent paid for a constant unit of the product or each of the products at regular and frequent

---

[10]Mexico (City), *Actas de cabildo del ayuntamiento de México*, and Lima, *Libros de cabildo de Lima*.

[11]Ramón and Larraín, pp. 316-340, esp. 320.

[12]Chester L. Guthrie, "Colonial Economy: Trade, Industry and Labor in the Seventeenth Century."

intervals during the period involved. Ideally, the study should be able to cover a group of products of common consumption that may be assigned relative weights, in order to arrive at an index of common consumption, which could then be placed against a determination of trend in wages for the same period and so measure change in real terms, i.e., in a way that examines the earning capacity of the general population relative to changes in values set upon commodities.

For much, perhaps all, of Spanish America in the sixteenth century the ideal may be impossible, both because of the loss of records and because there were two populations with different patterns of consumption: (1) a Spanish world wishing to eat wheaten bread, oil, meat, and wine, to dress in European clothing made of wool and silk, and to live with European furniture in houses built according to European standards; as against (2) Indian worlds living on native American products such as maize and in South America manioc, potatoes, etc., wearing native American clothing of cotton, agave, and in South America wool from camellids, and living in native-style huts or houses, furnished in native fashion. Because of the differing patterns of consumption, it is highly unlikely that there existed a unified market, but rather there were different kinds of markets for each ethnic group. On the other hand, there do exist records enabling construction of price series for individual commodities in markets broad enough to cover substantial territories during much of the sixteenth and early seventeenth centuries, the particularly blank period for other records.

This source arose because Indian towns paid tribute in specie, products, and labor either to private individuals, under the system known as encomienda, or directly to the Crown, and because the Spanish royal treasury attempted to keep meticulous accounts. Each Indian town was assessed, on the basis of its population, an annual quota of specie and other commodities. Until the New Laws of 1542-1543 and somewhat later tribute reforms were implemented, the tribute might include labor and a bewildering variety of products. After the reforms the tendency was to require specie, usually expressed in the silver coins in general use, and a small number of products raised or manufactured in the town.[13] Payments of tribute to individual encomenderos have left few surviving records except for the formal summaries of assessments for most towns and the detailed records of a few great estates like the Marquesado del Valle. The towns obligated to deliver tribute to the Crown, those *en cabeza real* as they were denominated, were handled under the royal treasury system with its careful regulations and minute accounting in writing.[14] For fiscal purposes, Spanish America was divided into a series of *cajas reales* or royal treasury

---

[13]The tribute system for central Mexico is well described in José Miranda, *El tributo indígena en la Nueva España durante el siglo XVI*; that for Peru and Bolivia in Ronald Escobedo Mansilla, *El tributo indígena en el Perú: siglos XVI y XVII*. The descriptions apply in a general way to all of Spanish America.

[14]The description of the Spanish royal fiscal system in America is based upon Ismael Sánchez-Bella, *La organización financiera de las Indias (siglo XVI)*, pp. 97-109, 123-124, 142-145, 206-214, 266-269, and passim. The governing legislation is to be found in Diego de Encinas, comp., *Cedulario indiano*, 3: 243-324 and 350-355; and in Spain, Laws, *Recopilación de leyes de los reynos de las Indias, lib.* 8, *títulos* 3, 4, 6, 7, 8, 9, 25, and 29. The practice may be traced in the account books in AGI, Contaduría.

districts, at first few but gradually increasing as districts were divided. Each was administered by a board of three treasury officials—a treasurer, accountant, and business agent—each official required to keep individual records plus collective ones, and each possessing a separate key to the padlock of a large royal chest of wood and metal (the *caja real*), in which were to be kept under lock and key specie, jewels, and written instruments representing royal revenues and royal assets.

Indian tributes in specie or money could be deposited in the royal chest when it was opened, as it had to be at least once a week for counting and examining the contents in the presence of all treasury officials. Indian tributes in commodities had to be handled in another way, since the royal treasuries had no means of storing them and, in any event, they tended to deteriorate and lose value with time. Accordingly, the royal regulations ordered that, except for specie, jewels, and written instruments, all other items be sold as rapidly as possible at public auction and the yield in money deposited in the royal chest. In obedience to this regulation the royal treasury officials, with occasional exceptions because of needs of the royal administration or specific royal grants, put up for sale at auctions called for the purpose the right to receive from each royal town all or part of the non-specie tribute assessed for a specific year. At first the natives were held to carry the tribute to a Spanish city, but one of the reforms of midcentury restricted that obligation to delivery in the *cabecera* or chief settlement in the territory of the Indian town. Thereafter, the price for each item of tribute of a town contained the buyer's calculation of the cost of transportation to where he planned to use the item. That is impossible for us today to determine, but fortunately it tended to remain constant for each town, especially if the item was to be moved to the nearest Spanish city.

Auctions had to be publicly proclaimed for a period of days and held in the main square of a Spanish city, very often the one nearest to the Indian town involved. The royal treasury officials had to be present either in person or through deputies, as well as a judge of the audiencia, if the auction was held in the seat of the high court, or the local Spanish governor if in another city. The auctions were usually held after the harvest, so that the excellence or scarcity of the crop was known to the bidders. Theoretically all purchases had to be paid for in cash soon after the conclusion of the bidding, but in frontier provinces, where money was in short supply, that was obviously impossible. Accordingly, with the permission of the viceroy or the audiencia, the purchasers executed contracts agreeing to pay within a short term in a series of payments, usually a year and three installments. Everything was carefully recorded including the agreements to pay.

Royal regulations demanded detailed accounting. A formal record was to be made on the spot by a notary; the transactions were to be entered into the respective ledgers of the royal treasury officials; and the contracts for payment were also to be executed on the spot and deposited in the royal chest. At the beginning of each year, in the months of January and February, the royal treasury officials were supposed to prepare a statement of the revenues and disbursements of the year for the inspection of the audiencia, which after checking the accounts carefully was to forward them to the Council of the Indies in Spain, for further audit and inspection. After 1605 the audiencia was replaced as auditing agent by Tribunales de Cuentas in Mexico City,

Cartagena, and Lima, but detailed records were still supposed to be sent to the Council of the Indies.

The meaning of this system for price information is that detailed records of the values at which tribute commodities were successfully bid for in every treasury district should be available in Spain in the Archivo General de Indias, Sevilla, in the enormous fiscal division known as Contaduría. The theory of administrative requirement and the reality of compliance and survival do not always match, since between lie negligence, losses in transit, and destruction in the fire of November 1924, which damaged part of the records of the Caja de México; but anyone who has explored in the division of Contaduría can testify that vast masses of records are still extant. In America, the original records kept in the chief seat of each royal treasury district have run greater chances of destruction, but to the extent that they survive may be used to substitute for or fill in gaps in the duplicates sent to Spain.

Since the Spanish fiscal system was nearly uniform throughout colonial Spanish America, there is accordingly for all of the *cajas reales* from the northern frontier in what is now the United States to the southern frontier in Chile and Argentina, for each Indian town *en cabeza real* a single annual value for each commodity, set town by town through the annual public treasury auctions. The only exceptions would occur either when the towns were in rebellion, and tribute being uncollectible would not be auctioned, or when the population of an Indian town fell so low that all of its tribute was lumped together in a single sale that makes it impossible to find individual values for the various items.[15] The New Laws and subsequent tribute reform mark a division in this system, in that previously the burdens of the tribute were much more complex, including such items as delivery of labor or even slaves, and that subsequently assessments were set in the much simpler terms of a money payment and a smaller number of commodities.[16] At all times, though, the general requirement was sale at public auction of all items save specie. The time of sale of agricultural commodities came at or after the harvest, so that prospective purchasers had a good idea of the crop, whether poor, average, or excellent, and set their bids accordingly. When a bidder proved successful at the auction, he was supposed to pay the royal treasury in coin for the commodity and then arrange to collect his purchase—before the New Laws through delivery by the Indians to a Spanish settlement, after the New Laws through delivery to the *cabecera* or chief settlement of the Indian town. In many of the royal treasury districts the purchaser would not pay in cash on the spot but executed a promissory note, agreeing to pay within a year in a series of payments, usually three. The contract of sale usually set a value per unit of the commodity. Before the changes of the tribute reforms, the total amount of the commodity to be delivered by an individual town would be set as the harvest from sowing of a certain quantity of seed or the product of a certain extension of

[15]See the notations in Appendix A, summarizing the royal tribute auctions for the Audiencia of Guadalajara, 1557-1598, from data in AGI, Contaduría, legs. 850-861B.

[16]Miranda, *El tributo indígena*, pp. 99-143. The changes decreed by the New Laws were implemented at differing times in the various audiencia districts: in Nueva Galicia perhaps a decade later than in central Mexico; in Peru after the civil wars of the mid-sixteenth century.

land, the exact amount of the crop to be harvested being determined by the royal governor of the district through personal inspection just before the harvest. After the reform, the tribute assessments usually called for the delivery of a set amount of the crop, i.e., so many fanegas of maize or so many pieces of cloth of a given size.[17] Hence the calculation of trend for any commodity in a royal treasury district from data from the auctions of royal tributes will involve values for the individual towns with a mix of varying adjustments for transportation for each town, but adjustments that are the same from year to year, that is, they are held constant and may be ignored. Data should be as abundant as the number of royal towns in the district, records surviving, and may be segregated by individual towns or groups of towns for regional analysis. The wealth of documents surviving in the Archivo General de Indias indicates an equal wealth of data for price studies, to be supplemented to a meager extent by surviving documents in American archives.

Resort to the data afforded by royal treasury auctions of tribute commodities both gives rise to a series of objections and affords certain advantages. A number of the objections derive from the system itself. First is the fact of a single annual value for each commodity for each town, but as is well known prices for commodities such as maize and wheat tended to move in an annual pattern. Immediately after the harvests they were at their lowest, and slowly rose as the current crop was consumed. They tended to be at their highest point of the agricultural year when the new crop was growing but could not yet be consumed.[18] Normally the auctions of tribute commodities took place when the harvest was gathered and its quality known, i.e., at the lowest point for prices in the year. Data from these gives an indication of the trend in the lowest prices, but does not give much information on variations during the year. Second is the matter of transportation of the commodities. Until the reforms of the New Laws, the Indian towns were required to deliver the tribute to the purchaser in a Spanish city; the reform changed that to a requirement of delivery in the *cabecera* of the Indian town. Accordingly, after the reform there enters into the price an unknown element for the cost of transportation which we could adjust for only by elaborate calculation. True, it remains relatively constant for each town over the years, and in a mix of towns of varying distances from Spanish cities and other places the Spaniards might wish to use their purchases may be ignored with little effect upon the general trend. Third is the variability in the elements and nature of the tribute, for until the tribute reforms of the middle and later sixteenth century the assessments contained varying and changing requirements in the commodities demanded and in the frequency of delivery. Further, reassessments changed the amounts of tribute to be delivered according to the movement of the native population of the town involved. In addition, towns ceased to make deliveries as they rebelled or were abandoned through consolidation of the declining population into other settlements. On the other hand, towns not previously in the royal system entered it as they escheated to the Crown at the end of the grant to a family.

---

[17] See the accounts for 1558 and 1561-1564 in AGI, Contaduría, leg. 860.

[18] Borah and Cook, *Price Trends*, pp. 13-14 and 19; and Florescano, *Precios del maíz*, pp. 88-110.

These objections on the grounds of variability of elements sound more serious than they really are. True, the scholar must take care by examining the requirement current in each year. True, also, that although certain commodities show up throughout the years, others are required only for short terms of years and then disappear. True, too, that there are changes in the amount of commodities delivered by each town, usually downward, and some towns enter the rolls and some disappear. In a large mix, these factors will have little effect and can be adjusted for, if necessary. Much more serious potentially is the fourth class of objection, namely, that differences in kinds of money and in measure must be guarded against.[19] In some regions transactions proceeded in a bewildering complexity of coins of varying values relative to each other, but their relation to each other was known and stated in terms of maravedíes, the common denominator.[20] The royal accounts for many regions were kept in pesos of fine gold worth 450 maravedíes, essentially money of account, or in pesos of common gold, equivalent to eight silver reales of 34 maravedíes each.[21] Differences in the size of common measures, such as the fanega or the arroba, certainly existed and might be serious. But for each town held to tribute they would not have varied and so the differences from town to town would have remained constant.

A number of further objections have been raised by scholars of prices. One is that it is impossible to determine the nature of the transactions, since they are neither unmistakably wholesale nor retail. That is so, but the objection springs from students of areas and periods with more developed market structures when differentiation into wholesale and retail was far clearer than in medieval European transactions or those of sixteenth century America.[22] Another is that we may not be dealing with a free market, since rigging and collusion would be much easier among the small number of purchasers participating in the tribute auctions. Despite the royal regulations to prevent fraud and collusion,[23] auctions among a relatively small group of Spanish purchasers who were bound together by ties of family, origin in a common region, the Church-created relations of *compadrazgo*, and friendship could, and undoubtedly did, lead to collusion and assistance. Nevertheless, the variation from year to year in prices of the same commodities from the same towns indicates that collusion and

---

[19]Romano, "Algunas consideraciones," pp. 77 and 97-99, and "*Some Considerations*," pp. 39-41 and 57-61.

[20]See, for example, Juan de Belveder, *Libro general de las redvciones de plata.*

[21]The accounts of Yucatan during the sixteenth century were kept in pesos of fine gold, but these undoubtedly were recalculated from silver reales and pesos. See AGI, Contaduría, legs. 911A-911B.

[22]Romano, "Problèmes et méthodes."

[23]Encinas, 3:352-353 and 355, excerpting paragraphs of royal letters of 21 and 12 September 1556 ordering that nothing be sold except in public auctions; quoting a royal cédula, Madrid, 3 October 1562, ordering that the royal auctions of tributes be held with the prescribed attendance of royal officials in public places; and excerpting a paragraph of a letter to Luis de Velasco in New Spain, 1552, ordering that no royal treasury official, nor a servant nor agent of them, might buy or acquire any item in the auctions of royal tribute either directly or through intermediaries. These orders were repeated in the *Recopilación de leyes de los reynos de las Indias*, with the additional safeguard of an order of 8 May 1568, forbidding appointment to a royal treasury post of any merchant or trader (8.4.54 and 3.2.25).

rigging did not operate as major factors in setting prices. Rainfall, frost, and pestilence played a far greater role by determining scarcity or abundance of supply as did the needs of the Spanish settlers for the degree and nature of demand.[24] Another objection is that the data of the tribute auctions cannot be held to yield true prices unless the cost of labor is known as well. This objection demands the possibility of determination of real values, i.e., commodities against wages. Obviously, a value in coin for a commodity that does not also tell us how many days' wages would be needed to buy a given amount does not yield as much information as a value that does. For some regions, data on wages are obtainable; for others in sixteenth-century Spanish America they are not. Nevertheless, where they are not, values in coin for commodities, although they cannot tell us as much as we should like to know, do reveal a good deal, and this information may be all we are likely to get. Still another objection is that the price data from tribute auctions are fullest for the sixteenth century and the early seventeenth, and that thereafter they tend to diminish in abundance because of commutations of the commodity payments to coin. This is true, but for the sixteenth and early seventeenth centuries resort to the data of price auctions is usually a case of *aut hoc aut nihil*, no other way.

Of the usefulness of data from tribute auctions for price studies, there can be little question. The Spanish royal fiscal system covered all of its American possessions, so that wherever Indians paid tribute there were auctions of the commodities to be delivered. The data give an annual value for each commodity delivered by each town, except in the few instances in which the tribute for the town was sold for a lump price. The overwhelming mass of the data thus permits a determination of trend. The data constitute an abundant, readily available source through the Contaduría records in Spain that may be supplemented by surviving records in America, where there is virtually no other possible surviving record. They cover many towns and regional differences. Since the records give as well the names of the purchasers, research into them and their connections is also possible. Although the sales undoubtedly contained a mix of retail and wholesale transactions, in that some buyers used their purchases for the needs of their own households whereas others undoubtedly planned resale, the transactions as a whole probably yield wholesale prices. In an inquiry held in Guadalajara in 1550 into the precipitous rise in the cost of living, actually brought about by the silver discoveries at Zacatecas, one of the witnesses, Juana Rodríguez de Arenas, declared that tribute maize cost half as much as that bought in private purchase.[25] We have as yet no other testimony or other evidence on the relation of auction prices of tribute commodities to those sold in other markets, but the probability is that the same disparity existed and continued.

Oddly enough, analysis of the data of royal tribute auctions gives rise to a new question, for the studies to date for New Spain show a relatively uniform movement,

[24]This matter is discussed at greater length in Chapter 6, on buyers.

[25]Información hecha por el Alcalde Mayor de Guadalajara y Visitador General del Reino de la Nueva Galicia, Lic. D. Hernando Martínez de la Marcha, acerca del precio de venta de varios alimentos de primera necesidad, Guadalajara, 16 July 1550," Orozco y Jiménez, *Colección*, 5:13-14.

i.e., agreement in trend, in what presumably must have been mini-markets, separated by the high cost of moving bulk commodities by human carrier or pack animal. But that is a question for further study. Let us turn now to an examination of the prices of tribute commodities sold in royal public auctions in the Audiencia of Nueva Galicia, as an illustration of the value of data derived from such auctions and for the information it affords on west-central Mexico in the later sixteenth century.

2

NUEVA GALICIA IN THE SIXTEENTH CENTURY

A Frontier Province

Nueva Galicia as a Spanish colonial jurisdiction came into existence through the efforts of Nuño de Guzmán and his lieutenants in the 1530s. After destroying the Tarascan kingdom in Michoacán, they entered the lands lying farther north, which they conquered in an unusually brutal series of expeditions. To consolidate Spanish hold on the newly conquered area, they established Spanish settlements, including Guadalajara in its first location and, as the provincial capital, Compostela, in present-day Nayarit. In 1532 the Crown appointed three treasury officials for a caja for the province, with residence in Compostela. Legally, Nuño de Guzmán established a group of new provinces within the jurisdiction of the Audiencia of Mexico, a subordination which was reaffirmed when he was sent to Spain under arrest. The new provinces, which now constitute all or parts of the states of Jalisco, Aguascalientes, Nayarit, Zacatecas, and Sinaloa, were a remote frontier area, their natives in the west sedentary cultivators of the soil; in the east, nomadic hunters and gatherers. To the latter the Spanish applied the Aztec term "Chichimecs." They found the Chichimecs an elusive, baffling adversary whose raids interrupted supply lines and made settlement difficult. The earliest Spanish settlers lived by exacting tribute and labor from the sedentary Indian population through the assignment of the native villages in encomiendas, of which all but the richest furnished a meager livelihood to their masters. Discoveries of silver deposits soon added a major new element to the regional economy, for the mines meant a valued product and the miners a market for agricultural surpluses. Although the earliest discoveries soon petered out, in 1546 Juan de Tolosa and a group of associates stumbled upon rich, virtually inexhaustible deposits of silver ore deep in Chichimec country, near what became the city of Zacatecas. Their discoveries set off a boom that drew settlers in large numbers. Zacatecas quickly became the most populous Spanish settlement in Nueva Galicia.

The opening of the rich new mining district coincided with the decision of the Crown to give Nueva Galicia, because of its remoteness from Mexico City, a regional government of its own through the creation of an audiencia, subordinate to the Viceroy and Audiencia of Mexico but with considerable administrative and judicial autonomy. The royal order came in January 1548; the new Audiencia of Nueva Galicia took possession of its jurisdiction late in 1548 or early in 1549, with its capital at Compostela. The territory of the new audiencia was curiously truncated in favor of New Spain, through retention in the latter of Colima and the rich towns of Avalos. Within Nueva Galicia, as then defined, there were the productive Indian villages of the region around Guadalajara, the coastal districts of Purificación and Banderas, central and coastal Nayarit, the central river valleys of Sinaloa, the few Indian towns of Zacatecas, and the mines of Zacatecas and whatever discoveries might be made to the north. Much of the territory was frontier, with the Indians yet to be subdued before they could be brought to tribute.

In its first years the newly created audiencia district changed the seats of administration. In 1552 the royal treasury was moved to Zacatecas, since that was the chief source of royal revenues. In 1560, with royal consent, the audiencia shifted its capital to Guadalajara, which also had experimented with locations until finding a third and final one at Atemajac in 1542. The bishopric followed the same decision to move its see from Compostela to Guadalajara. Finally, the royal treasury officials, who found themselves uncomfortable in the dry, cold altitude of Zacatecas, won royal permission to move to the more comfortable climate of Guadalajara, but with each member of their number serving in turn for four months in Zacatecas. By 1562 the administrative predominance of Guadalajara was clearly established, but Zacatecas remained the major economic center and most populous city of Nueva Galicia.[1]

Nueva Galicia differed from the Audiencia of Mexico in that it was conquered a generation later, the sedentary Indian population was much sparser, and much more of its territory was frontier. Its later settlement meant that, although the same processes were set in motion by Spanish conquest, they moved at a pace a generation behind those in the Audiencia of Mexico. Thus contact with the Spaniards unleashed the same destruction of population as elsewhere in Mexico. We do not have clear estimates of Indian numbers when Nuño de Guzmán commenced his expeditions, but war, disease, exploitation, and the violent upsetting of Indian life must have taken heavy toll. A bitter Indian rebellion, known as the Mixtón War, brutally suppressed by the Spaniards, meant further massive loss of population and the devastation of the region north of the Santiago River as far as southern Nayarit and southwestern Zacatecas. Our first reasonably good estimates of Indian numbers are for 1548, when they had already suffered considerable diminution; they are 169,421–say 170,000–including the sedentary Indians in the Valley of Juchipila, today in southwestern Zacatecas. During the second half of the sixteenth century, numbers

---

[1]John H. Parry, *The Audiencia of New Galicia in the Sixteenth Century*, pp. 14-132; Peter J. Bakewell, *Silver Mining and Society in Colonial Mexico: Zacatecas, 1546-1700*, pp. 1-40; Ismael Sánchez-Bella, *La organización financiera de las Indias (siglo XVI)*, pp. 18-19 and 97; and Philip Wayne Powell, *Soldiers, Indians, and Silver: The Northward Advance of New Spain, 1550-1600*, pp. 3-70.

steadily decreased. By 1570, there were approximately 66,000, and by 1600, 29,000. Although the rate of decrease was slowly diminishing, decline continued until approximately 1650, when Indian numbers reached nadir at an estimated 18,500. Thereafter there began a slow but accelerating increase, which with some irregularities continues to this day as a general increase of population.

Meantime, the Spanish conquest brought the entrance of a new population as small numbers of Spaniards, Blacks, and Indian auxiliaries from New Spain settled in Nueva Galicia. They constituted a slowly increasing element of the population, creating, as well, through procreating across racial lines with or without marriage, new groups of mixed bloods, who generally adhered to Hispanic language and culture. The new racial stocks and their progeny, on the one hand, and the Indians, on the other, lived in an essentially exploitive relationship in that the people of Hispanic culture derived their livelihood from the extraction of labor, tribute, and fees from the Indians. The two principal cities, Guadalajara and Zacatecas, held the bulk of the non-Indian population, and grew fairly steadily through the second half of the sixteenth century. By 1570 Guadalajara had perhaps 50 Spanish vecinos, or heads of households. With women, children, dependents, slaves, and servants, the city held between 400 and 500 people.[2] By 1602, it had approximately 160 vecinos, who with their households might have numbered between 1,400 and 1,800 people.[3] Zacatecas, founded in 1548 in a high, arid waste, attracted population steadily, and by the earliest years of the seventeenth century, as reported by Bishop Mota y Escobar, had perhaps 300 Spanish vecinos, 60-70 sons of Spaniards born in the city, 800 slaves, 10-12 Portuguese and Italians (probably a gross underestimate of the number of foreigners), and perhaps 1,500 Indian workers, drawn by the wages which could be earned in the mines. With their wives, children, and other dependents,[4] they might have reached a total of 5,000 in an area that had had only a few nomadic Chichimecs before. Zacatecas and its mines, then, were an exception to the general rule of decline of the Indian population in the sixteenth century, in that they attracted native workers from other areas, especially the Tarascan and Nahuatl zones to the south and east.[5] The remainder of the non-Indian population of Nueva Galicia in the

[2]Sherburne F. Cook and Woodrow Borah, *Essays in Population History*, 1: 310 (Table 40a) and in general 300-375; Parry, pp. 27-28.

[3]Arturo Chávez Hayhoe, "Guadalajara de 1560 a 1600," p. 27. Chávez Hayhoe declares that half of the thousand were slaves. Juan López de Velasco, *Geografía y descripción universal de las Indias*, pp. 135-136, gives the number of vecinos in Guadalajara as 150, but his figure seems too high since in December 1586 Fray Antonio de Ciudad Real, *Relación breve y verdadera de algunas cosas de las muchas que sucedieron al Padre Fray Alonso Ponce*, 2: 27, set the number at 80 to 100.

[4]François Chevalier, *La formation des grands domaines au Mexique*, pp. 211-212, citing a report of Jerónimo Conde, alguacil mayor and regidor of Guadalajara, Guadalajara, 1 May 1602. Bishop Alonso de la Mota y Escobar *Descripción geográphica de los reynos de Galicia, Vizcaya y León*, writing slightly later, states (pp. 294-295) 173 vecinos and their families, plus 500 slaves and free people of color; see also pp. 335-338.

[5]Bakewell, pp. 128-129.

second half of the sixteenth century lived in small settlements, around mines scattered throughout the district, and on estancias.[6]

A generally poor area in the sixteenth century, Nueva Galicia could not support its Spanish settlers through grants of encomiendas. In the 1570s, López de Velasco reported that there were in the audiencia jurisdiction 50-55 encomenderos;[7] but most encomiendas, especially after the tribute reforms began to be implemented in Nueva Galicia, yielded too little to support an encomendero and his family, so that even this favored group was forced to turn to other activities for support. By the end of the century, as many ecomiendas reverted to the Crown, even the slender, partial support of Indian tributes failed this once-favored group. Many of the Spanish settlers, encomenderos or not, turned to stock-raising, for which there were vast expanses of land. A market existed for the meat and even more the fat, tallow, and hides, since the mines needed provisions, candles, grease, and leather. Others turned to raising crops in some demand, especially cacao in the coastal lowlands and wheat in the uplands. A few turned to trade, not the grand commerce carried on by merchant houses in Mexico City, but a more humble distributive function, purchasing in Mexico City and selling in the cities of Nueva Galicia. Many of the poorer Hispanic settlers and at least part of the people of mixed race associated with the Hispanic communities supported themselves by the various crafts needed in cities and settlements far from other sources of supply, such as leatherwork, metalworking, making clothing, specialized carpentry, and so on, or lived as dependents and servants in households and ranches.[8]

Most of the settlers, including those relatively far up the social scale, put their hands to whatever enterprises promised gain. Bernardo de Balbuena, the father of the famous poet and cleric of the same name, operated as notary, government official, stock-raiser, speculator in land and commodities, merchant, miner, and dealer in Indian tribute commodities. He had considerable success;[9] others far less so. In a report of 1603 to the President of the Council of the Indies, Bishop Mota y Escobar commented:

> A venido esta ciudad a menos en lo que es qualidad de vecinos principales aunque tiene algunos porque sus primeros pobladores tuuieron encomiendas de yndios, y minas con que viuian opulenta y honrradamente, y como lo vno y lo otro an faltado por muerte de los yndios, y por falta de los metales, acavaronse estas familias principales, y sus descendientes se fueron a otras prouincias, y an sucedido en su lugar nueuas gentes venidas de España, y otras partes.
>
> [This city has declined in the quality of its leading citizens, although it [still] has a few. Its first settlers had encomiendas of Indians and mines that supported them in wealth and honor. As both have failed through Indian deaths and the exhaustion of ores,

---

[6]López de Velasco, pp. 135-136; Antonio F. García-Abasolo, *Martín Enríquez y la reforma de 1568 en Nueva España*, pp. 150-151.

[7]López de Velasco, p. 133.

[8]Woodrow Borah, "Los tributos y su recaudación en la audiencia de Nueva Galicia durante el siglo XVI," pp. 40-47; Domingo Lázaro de Arregui, *Descripcíon de La Nueva Galicia*, pp. 21-22 and 62-67.

[9]José Rojas Garcidueñas, *Bernardo de Balbuena: La vida y la obra*, pp. 3-5; Matías Angel de la Mota Padilla, *Historia del reino de la Nueva Galicia en la América Septentrional*, p. 206.

these leading families faced ruin and their descendants migrated to other provinces. In their place new people have come from Spain and other places.]

Capital city though Guadalajara was, it had only three rich vecinos, with an individual wealth of barely 100,000 pesos. The rest of the vecinos were poor, save for a few merchants. The bishop set the poverty line for vecinos at possessions worth 2,000 pesos. Of the 22 merchants in the city worthy of the name, with shops dealing in Spanish and Chinese imports as well as local items, not one had wealth over 20,000 pesos; the range was from 4,000 to 20,000. The city itself consisted of unimpressive one-story adobe structures, for the area lacked stone and lime. Only the royal house, where the audiencia held its sessions, had two stories, though also of adobe.[10]

Aside from administration, the most highly regarded occupation was mining. Throughout the territory of the audiencia, small silver mines opened as Spaniards discovered deposits of ore, mined them for a time, and then, when the richer ores petered out, abandoned them. By the end of the century, most of the earlier mining sites had been abandoned.[11] The major and long-term mining centers lay in the arid eastern districts dominated by nomadic Indians. Zacatecas, the center of vast deposits, became the most populous city in the audiencia jurisdiction. The great private fortunes were held by men fortunate to own lucky strikes around Zacatecas and adjacent centers. When mercury amalgamation for extracting silver from the ores was introduced, Zacatecas began a long period of prosperity as a mining center. Peter Bakewell, in his fine study of silver mining and society in Zacatecas, 1546-1700, has charted the quinquennial totals of all silver presented for taxation at the royal treasury in Zacatecas. For the years 1560-1605, they are:

1560-1564	587,374 marks
1565-1569	675,368 "
1570-1574	766,763 "
1575-1579	716,620 "
1580-1584	582,415 " (estimate)
1585-1589	617,169 " (estimate)
1590-1594	623,866 "
1595-31 March 1600	532,138 "
31 April 1600-1605	634,575 "

(A mark is eight ounces of silver or eight pesos.)

This vast outpouring of silver brought Indians, mixed-bloods, and Spanish to the mines of Zacatecas, attracted by high wages and even the chance to become owner of a mining claim. To supply the mines, auxiliary shops, industries, and crafts arose in the area, selling foodstuffs, clothing, and supplies; manufacturing leather items, such as buckets; working metal into the tools needed in the excavations; providing lodging, food, and clothing; dealing in the silver ore; and providing the animals and

[10]Mota y Escobar, pp. 293-296.

[11]Ibid., p. 293.

their drivers for the pack trains and carts that came and went.[12] A further effect of the vast production of silver, despite drainage of most of it to Mexico City and Spain, was that supplies of specie rose relative to supplies of many basic commodities. Predictably, the prices of such commodities rose, and sharply.

Aside from mining, administration through the royal government and Church was perhaps the most highly regarded occupation in the jurisdiction. The higher officials–judges of the audiencia, the royal treasury officials, the better-paid members of their staffs, the bishop, and the cathedral chapter–were all centered in Guadalajara after 1560 and even more after 1562, when the royal treasury officials moved to Guadalajara and left only a *subcaja* in Zacatecas. According to a report made in 1602, of 160 vecinos in Guadalajara, 120 had a post in the royal government or the Church. In the lower ranks, where salaries were low, the holders of the posts had to hold several appointments or engage in other occupations for decent support. Most of the parish priests, and their vicars to the extent that they had any, found themselves in respectable poverty, from which they could only emerge through other occupations, such as mining, stock-raising, and farming, to the extent the Church permitted.

As Bishop Mota y Escobar reported, the drastic decline in Indians and the rapid exhaustion of the small silver mines in the west of the jurisdiction left most of the Spanish population with little support. By 1593, the surviving 158 Indian towns held to tribute had only 11,536½ tributaries. By then the Crown took the tribute from 6,739½ tributaries and private encomenderos, holders in second or third life, from 4,797. As more encomiendas reverted to the Crown at the end of the third life, Indian tribute as direct support for Spaniards ebbed further until, in the seventeenth century, it virtually ceased. Even in the first days of Nueva Galicia there had not been enough Indians for all deserving Spaniards to secure encomiendas, since most of the grants provided too little revenue for what a conqueror's or settler's family regarded as decent support. In a necessary effort to placate deserving claimants, the Crown granted small annual pensions of 50-100 pesos to the families descended from conquerors and early settlers it could not provide with encomiendas, and declared the male scions of such families entitled to preferment in minor royal posts, such as corregidor, alguacil, and the lesser posts associated with the royal government. Most of these appointments were annual, renewable for another year, and carried small stipends, plus the right to fees. As a result of the royal policy, during the sixteenth century an increasing Spanish population earned part of its support through posts in royal, municipal, or Church administration, and had to supplement stipends and fees by other pursuits.

In the small society of Guadalajara, close-knit with a small pool of marriage partners, dependent on government favor, and bound together by ties of blood relationship, marriage, friendship, fictive religious kinship, and patron-client relations, the influence of higher government officials and the few wealthy men loomed large. A network of patronage and favor united the bulk of the Spanish residents. Those

---

[12] Bakewell, pp. 41-80 and 241-247; the quinquennial totals are in table 5 on pp. 246-247. See also the description in Mota y Escobar, pp. 335-338.

outside it were poor, with few opportunities to support themselves, let alone better their economic position. In 1602 a complaint against Dr. Santiago de Vera, President of the Audiencia of Nueva Galicia, reported that of the 160 vecinos of Guadalajara, 37 were his relatives by blood or marriage, friends, or relatives of friends. Public office was held to be for the private good of the officeholder, his family, and people allied with him. In such circumstances, corruption was endemic.[13] The Crown could do little about it, for the salaries it paid could not provide the support for officeholders and their families deemed consonant with their position. As Viceroy Cerralvo commented in 1636, "It seems that we must either increase salaries or close our eyes." The Crown chose to close its eyes.[14]

The Nueva Galicia we are dealing with–I exclude Nueva Vizcaya (now Durango), and Sinaloa, which were forming dependent but separate entities to the north–consisted, then, of the economic territories of the two cities of Guadalajara and Zacatecas. Guadalajara, the political capital, had as its economic hinterland the poorer western reaches of the audiencia; Zacatecas, in many ways the economic capital, had as its economic territory the arid east with its rich mines and oases raising foodstuffs. Guadalajara, much the poorer and less populous city, drew its supplies from its hinterland by porters (*tamemes*) and *recuas*, trains of pack animals. Zacatecas, the more opulent and populous center, required so many supplies and services that there had developed for its needs a series of cart roads so that foodstuffs and other supplies could be shipped by cart at much lower cost.[15]

In the embryonic Hispanic society of sixteenth-century Nueva Galicia, the royal treasury loomed far larger than it would in later centuries, for a large proportion of the Hispanic settlers and their descendants drew all or part of their support from it in the form of salaries, pensions, and perquisites, legal and illegal. The twin pillars of the royal system in the sixteenth century were the revenues from mining and those from Indian tributes. Mining, although the motor of the economy and of prime concern for the royal treasury, need not concern us here. Indian tributes, whether paid to private individuals as encomenderos or to the Crown, in the earliest days provided for the bulk of the needs of the Hispanic community in foodstuffs, coarse cloth, and labor, just as did the earliest encomiendas in central Mexico. As in central Mexico, the tribute reforms of the midcentury led to the suppression of *comida*, the direct provision of foodstuffs for the household of the encomendero or in the royal towns to the highest bidders for the right to receive them. Similarly, *servicio*, teams of servants sent, in rotation, to households, and the provision of workmen for service

---

[13]Chevalier, pp. 122 and 211-212, citing a report of Jerónimo Conde, alguacil mayor and regidor, against the president of the audiencia, Guadalajara, 1 May 1604, part of which is reproduced on p. 431; Mota y Escobar, pp. 294-295; Arreguí, p. 21; report of royal treasury officials of Nueva Galicia on salaries and grants-in-aid to conquerors and their children, Mines of Zacatecas, 10 February 1563, in Paso y Troncoso, *Epistolario*, 9: 196-208. See also the following note.

[14]Chevalier, pp. 164-166; Borah, *El gobierno provincial en la Nueva España, 1570-1787*, pp. 37-50; report of the Marqués de Cerralvo, Viceroy of New Spain, to the King, Mexico City, 17 March 1636, in Vázquez de Espinosa, *Descripción de la Nueva España en el siglo XVII*, pp. 231-232 [translation mine].

[15]Mota y Escobar, p. 296; Powell, pp. 16-31.

in mines and plantations, disappeared from assessments as the tribute reforms took hold. The changes came ten to twenty years later and more slowly than in central Mexico, but by the 1560s most royal towns were assessed for tribute in payments of silver, maize, and other commodities in obedience to the royal requirement that tribute be assessed in silver coin and one or a few locally produced commodities. The Audiencia seems to have aimed at a standard basic assessment of six reales in silver, a fanega of maize, and a chicken per tributary, although it never fully implemented the idea. As in central Mexico, the basis of liability to pay tribute was the Indian couple. Widows and widowers were held to half, and the governor of the town, the aged, cripples, and certain servants of the Church were held to be exempt. These exemptions differed somewhat from the rules in central Mexico. Commutation of commodity payments to additional assessments in silver coin, a distinctive feature of the evolution of the tribute system in the Audiencia of Mexico, found little echo in the Audiencia of Nueva Galicia. Why this was so is an interesting question, since the mines of the jurisdiction were pouring out silver that was readily obtainable by the Indians in exchange for products and labor, especially at the mines themselves. The best answer at this time would seem to be that the Hispanic community, which continued to be much more dependent on direct Indian production than its counterpart in central Mexico, opposed commutation, lest it bring about even higher prices for basic commodities.[16]

To understand their hypothesized objection, we must attempt to reconstruct the distributive system of Nueva Galicia in the sixteenth century. At the lowest level lay a network of native markets in each barrio and town, linked by periodic regional markets. Guadalajara, for example, had a native *tianguis* or market at five-day intervals,[17] an interesting survival of Indian custom, since the Spanish normally changed such markets to intervals in the Christian calendar, usually a week for a local market. Such markets served for the distribution of native production, disposing of small surpluses of foodstuffs left after the needs of the Indian household had been met and selling the products of native crafts like pots, baskets, leatherwork, etc. We know virtually nothing about these markets since they have left few traces in records, but undoubtedly Indians and Spaniards resorted to them. At a perhaps higher level lay the Spanish stores, fairly numerous in Guadalajara and Zacatecas and thinning out to one or two in the smaller Spanish settlements, or even to part-time enterprises. These dealt in European commodities, imported by the great merchant houses of Mexico City via the Atlantic fleet system and resold to traders from Nueva Galicia.[18] Chinese commodities came via the Pacific ships of the Manila-Acapulco route. Whether these were controlled by the Mexico City houses or bought at Acapulco we do not know. The stores also dealt in local production of foodstuffs, clothing, leatherwork, and pottery. The smallest traders even resorted to peddling. Indian tributes entered this network in a number of ways. Individual encomenderos would dispose of surpluses beyond their needs to the merchants or in a series of deals

---

16. Borah, "Los tributos y su recaudación."
17. Mota y Escobar, p. 296.
18. Mota y Escobar, pp. 294-295; Arregui, pp. 62-67.

with private consumers. Similarly, although tributes in kind due to the Crown had to be offered at public auction, numbers of the successful bidders undoubtedly bought products for resale to other members of the Hispanic community as well as to meet the needs of their own households and the workers in their enterprises. The mining settlements in the eastern regions were able to mitigate their earlier dependence upon Indian production for tribute by developing their own agriculture in oases and moving the crops to the mines and Zacatecas by cart.[19] Whatever their efforts to encourage agriculture under Spanish management, the Hispanic communities in the western regions of the audiencia remained directly dependent upon Indian production for certain commodities, particularly maize and chickens. This dependence made it possible for the Crown to convert its large share of Indian tributes in kind, which it had no means of storing, into specie. The auctions of royal tributes in kind cannot be understood unless one visualizes them as part of a widespread and complex system of distribution.

Chapter 1 outlined the general royal regulations for the operation of the fisc in Nueva Galicia. Obviously, in practice, many modifications became necessary because of local conditions. One example will make that point plain. According to royal regulation, Indian tribute due in coin was to be paid in three installments at four-month intervals (*tercios*).[20] If one examines the royal records, one finds something less than full compliance. In 1581, 31 towns *en cabeza real* paid at one time for the entire year; 17 paid the coin due in six-month installments; 8 by the stipulated four-month intervals; and 47 made a series of payments on account at irregular intervals.[21] In effect, 45.6 percent would not or could not comply with the royal regulation, whereas 54.4 percent either complied or exceeded the compliance required. Presumably the royal treasury officials were unable to bring about fuller compliance without resort to excessively brutal measures, and the Crown was unwilling to order such measures.

In Nueva Galicia the royal treasury officials, by royal order, followed the practice of their fellow officials in Mexico City, which brought the auctions of the royal tribute in kind to an annual round in harmony with the calendar year beginning on 1 January, and with native cultivation of maize based upon the climatic regime of summer rainfall, harvest coming toward the end of the year. In Nueva Galicia rains began in May or June and continued until September or October. Maize was planted in late June, after the moisture had saturated the soil, and harvested in November or December. In the coastal lowlands a second crop of maize might be grown after the principal one of the summer.[22] When the season or seasons had ended and the

---

[19]Bakewell, pp. 58-80; López de Velasco, pp. 137-138.

[20]Cédula real of Felipe II to the royal treasury officals of Mexico City, El Pardo, July 21, 1570, in Encinas, *Cedulario indiano*, 3: 265-267. The royal instruction, which became general for Spanish America, entered the *Recopilación de leyes de los reynos de las Indias* as 8.9.3.

[21]Treasury accounts of Nueva Galicia for 1581, AGI, Contaduría, leg. 861A.

[22]Arregui, p. 17; relación de la ciudad de Compostela, 26 November 1584; relación de las minas de Xocotlán, 15 October 1584; and relación de la Villa de S. Martín, Llerena y Minas de Sombrerete, 6 February 1585, in Acuña, ed., *Relaciones geográficas*, 10: 88, 3, and 247, respectively; cédula real of Felipe II to the royal treasury officials of Mexico, El Pardo, 21 July 1570, quoting two instructions of

abundance or scarcity of the current maize harvest was known, the royal treasury officials began the procedures of selling off the right to receive portions of the royal tributes in kind. Notice of the impending auctions was proclaimed three times by the town criers in the months of October and November in Compostela, Guadalajara, Zacatecas, and Purificación. The auctions were held usually in December and January, although sometimes a few weeks earlier or later, in Guadalajara for all towns except those in the province of Purificación, where in earlier years the governor of the province acted as deputy for the royal treasury, and in Zacatecas for towns in the Tlaltenango and Juchipila basins. The actual bidding was carried out on two days of the week, usually Tuesday and Friday, and continued, for individual communities, town by town until the royal treasury officials or their deputies were satisfied that they had secured the best price possible. Occasionally, for towns whose population and the tribute based on it had shrunk to insignificance, they might lump the entire tribute of one or several towns together; and in situations of great demand, they might divide the right to the tribute of one commodity from a large town into parts, in order to satisfy as many applicants as possible. Proclamation of readiness to receive bids did not always mean getting them, or getting them at prices held to be satisfactory. The royal treasury officials sometimes had to continue the bidding until a suitable offer was made, persuade people to raise their bids, or even offer premiums to secure what they regarded as a reasonable one. Occasionally, also, since in the end all bids had to pass scrutiny by the audiencia, at its inspection bids were voided and the auction reopened. Such orders to reopen auctions explain sales in the spring, long after the normal season for the auctions.

What the successful bidder got for the price he agreed to pay was the right to receive all or part of one or more commodities due from an Indian town as part of its annual tribute. Originally, the Indians of the town were obligated to deliver the tribute in kind to the nearest Spanish settlement, but one of the reform laws of the 1540s reduced that requirement to delivery in the cabecera of the town. Transportation beyond the cabecera to wherever the Spaniard planned to use or sell the commodity became his responsibility. Accordingly, there is in each sale of a tribute commodity a buyer's calculation of probable transportation cost to the point at which he could use or sell it. We have no way of allowing for this cost except perhaps by calculating transportation to the nearest large Spanish settlement, but fortunately the cost would tend to be invariable for each town and so be held constant year after year. Our failure to know it does not affect calculations of long-term trend.

Similarly, a successful bidder might not be able to exercise his right to collect because a town was in rebellion, a circumstance particularly true at times for those in Nayarit. In such cases, if the rebellion of the town was known in advance of the auctions, the royal treasury would not sell the rights to its tribute; if the fact of

---

Viceroy Martin Enríquez, Mexico City, 18 August and 24 September 1569, in Encinas, *Cedulario indiano*, 3: 265-267, and letter of the royal treasurer of Mexico, Fernando Portugal, to the King, 1571, quoted in Sánchez-Bella, pp. 212-213, note 42.

rebellion was ascertained subsequent to a sale, the sale would be canceled and any payment refunded.

The Church's right to a tenth of Indian tribute as tithe raises an interesting aspect, which is not really a problem for our purposes. In many instances, the royal treasury officials auctioned off rights to the entire tribute in agricultural produce of the royal towns and then arranged to pay the Church officials a tenth of the proceeds. The tithe from non-agricultural items was always handled by the Church; probably the most efficient way of handling it. If the Church, however, preferred to collect its tenth of agricultural commodities directly from the towns for disposal as it might, the royal treasury does not seem to have opposed it. The royal subvention of 100 fanegas of maize to each missionary was delivered by the Indians directly but deducted from their tribute. It is specifically allowed for in the auctions.

Another non-problem concerns the diversion of some of the tribute from the auctions for royal purposes. This category really embraces few commodities. Maize was diverted to feed the Indians who gathered salt for sale as a royal monopoly to the mines. Salt was used in the patio process of reduction of ores. Cotton cloth was occasionally used for making padded armor for use by troops fighting the Chichimecs. Finally, coarser, heavier cloth might be used for sails for royal vessels.[23]

By royal regulation, purchasers of the right to receive any part of the royal tributes in kind had to pay *de contado* (in cash) within a very short period.[24] In the economic conditions of Nueva Galicia such a condition could not be enforced. So the Crown very reluctantly agreed that its treasury officials might extend credit for a limited period. Usually the successful bidder executed a note agreeing to payment in three installments at four-month intervals, the standard *tercios*. Presumably also, as in all obligations to the royal treasury, the note had to have guarantors, who in case of default could be held to payment. Most buyers of royal tribute commodities apparently did pay within the stipulated year, if one may judge from entries in the fragments of royal treasury accounts surviving in Guadalajara. A fair number paid after a longer period. The longest delay in payment recorded in the surviving records occurred when Juan Bautista de Agüero, who bid successfully for the tribute maize due for 1596 from Tetitlán, Camotlán, San Pedro, Tepequespa, and Acuitlapilco with an offer of 0/7 the fanega on 22 January 1597, finally redeemed his promissory note to the Crown on 3 January 1606–just eighteen days short of nine years later. He paid directly and in one installment. The surprising feature is that the royal treasury officials apparently did not call upon his guarantors for payment, despite the long interval of default.[25] They must always have had the difficult task of balancing

[23]Borah, "Los tributos y su recaudación," pp. 40-47; Appendix A herein; and Sánchez-Bella, p. 249.

[24]Recopilación, *8.8.4 and 8.25.6.*

[25]Royal treasury records of Nueva Galicia, AGI, Contaduría, legs. 856-861, and GBPE, Archivo de la Real Audiencia de Guadalajara, ramo fiscal, exps. 1-5. Agüero's payment is recorded in the book of accounts for 1605-1606, Cargo de Tributos de Almonedas, f. 97v. I have tried to reconcile the totals for sales of royal tributes in kind with the totals in the annual cartas-cuentas published in John J. TePaske and Herbert S. Klein, *Ingresos y egresos de la Real Hacienda de Nueva España*, cajas de Guadalajara and Zacatecas, in vols. 1 and 2 respectively, but find no correspondences. I am led

their obligations to the fisc with their desire to maintain amicable relations with the tightly-knit Hispanic community of Guadalajara. Extension of credit forced upon a reluctant Crown by the local conditions of Nueva Galicia, then, meant that in some percentage of the sales the Crown received payment at longer intervals than a year. Ultimately, it seems to have collected in all cases. On the whole, that was not a bad record.

The sales at public auction were subject to audiencia review. In some instances, the audiencia ordered the sales of the tributes of some towns canceled and the auctions reopened. As a further check on fraud and collusion, the royal treasury officials were supposed to submit their accounts for each year to audiencia audit. When approved by the audiencia, the accounts were then transcribed in full and the transcription forwarded to the Council of the Indies for further inspection. This system turned out to be cumbersome and the audits long-delayed.[26] In 1605, audit of the royal treasury accounts became the responsibility of a Tribunal de Cuentas established in Mexico City for all of the northern Spanish audiencias, the Viceroyalty of New Spain in its widest sense. Similar bodies in Lima and Bogotá bore responsibility for the audiencias of the Viceroyalty of Peru.[27]

---

to conclude that the cartas-cuentas record receipts of coin, and do not count promissory notes until paid.

[26]Sánchez-Bella, pp. 269-282.

[27]Real Cédula of Felipe III, Burgos, 24 August 1605, *Recopilación*,8.1.1 *et seq.*; Sánchez-Bella, pp. 59-68.

3

THE DATA AND THEIR TREATMENT

Gathering the basic statistical data on sales of Indian tribute in kind for Nueva Galicia during the years 1557-1598 has been tedious but relatively rapid; collecting the additional historical material necessary for understanding the fiscal system and units of measure in the data, a much lengthier process; correcting, interpreting, and analyzing the data even more time-consuming. It has, in fact, taken nearly thirty years and the labor of a number of research assistants. The basic data were collected during the early months of 1959 at the Archivo General de Indias, Sevilla. They were found in the surviving records sent by the royal treasury officials of Nueva Galicia to Spain: Contaduría, legajos 853, 856-861B, 867B, and 869A. Some of the legajos are double, the two halves being designated A and B, although each half is a full-sized bundle. In part, the legajos contain copies of the actual contracts of sale for each individual item; in part, only the account books of the treasury officials were available. The information on sales was taken off onto 4 x 6-inch cards in closely written lines across the four-inch width of each card, using both sides. In all, there are 267 cards. Each line records the date of sale, the name of the town, the commodity auctioned, the purchase price, and the name of the successful bidder. Occasionally there are further notations on the circumstances of the sale, such as the difficulty of securing bids, premiums paid in order to persuade the bidder, problems of the town or in securing tribute from it, and other uses to which the tribute was put. During those early months of 1959 I examined the other legajos in Contaduría relating to Nueva Galicia in order to understand the evolution of the system of tribute assessment and collection and the general operation of the royal fiscal system. At the starting date of 1557, the Audiencia of Nueva Galicia was well into implementing the reforms mandated by the New Laws and additional changes under way in the neighboring Audiencia of Mexico. The closing date of 1598 marks the end of free bidding for tribute maize and the resort to a system of allocation for worthy Spaniards at prices set by averaging the prices for that town during a number of previous years.[1] I examined legajos for the years after 1598, but in general those data do not enter into this study.

Records for a number of years were missing, and apparently had been missing by the later eighteenth century when the records were put in order. Data for 1579, 1588, and 1589 are completely absent, and there are some gaps within years, most notably for the towns whose tribute was auctioned in Zacatecas. A subsequent search in the fragments of royal fiscal records surviving in Guadalajara, Mexico, turned up data for the auctions of December 1580 in Zacatecas, but nothing else. The Guadalajara data were located too late for inclusion in the computer analysis but are so few, and in line with Zacatecas sales for other years, that they would not affect results.

In the years subsequent to 1959, as funds could be squeezed from other projects, the data were copied from the note cards in two different ways. One set them forth on ordinary sheets of typewriter paper by commodity and year, a separate sheet for each year. The other restated the sales in chronological form as the note cards did only in part. The second organization is reproduced here as Appendix A. Its length will give some idea of the time needed. Appendix B reproduces the data for 1580 on sales in Zacatecas, found in Guadalajara. In either form, the data were checked repeatedly against the note cards to catch possible copying errors and discrepancies.

As the data were being copied from the original note cards, a number of questions, normal in such operations, had to be resolved. One set concerned money statements in the sales; another, the meaning and interchangeability of units of measure; yet another, the meaning of various terms for commodities; others, the location of towns and differentiating between different towns of the same name; and last, the names of the buyers. Actually, the matter of money presented few difficulties, since all of the statements of price were in terms of the silver reales, pesos, and granos, which before 1557 replaced older and variant coins in common use in colonial Mexico. In 1536 Viceroy Antonio de Mendoza standardized the value of the silver real and the tomín of base gold at 34 maravedís, the legal value in Spain. Maravedís, originally silver coins, had become the common denominator in which the values of various coins could be expressed in relation to each other. The flood of silver from the newly discovered mines soon made the silver real and the silver peso of 8 reales (one ounce) the coinage of common usage, whatever the money of account in which books might be kept and contracts issued. Payment would be in silver coins of reales of 34 maravedís and pesos of 272 maravedís, calculated to the value of the money of account in terms of relative value in maravedís. Fortunately, the royal treasury in Nueva Galicia early began to keep its books in terms of the common silver coinage, and apparently all auctions of the royal treasury were conducted in terms of the same coins. In my citations and statements they are written in English fashion as pesos/reales/granos. Granos were 12 to a real. Thus 8/7/4 means eight pesos, seven reales, four granos. The number of pesos is always written as 2/ , two pesos; or 0/6, six reales. The granos are written if the price

---

[1]For a history of tributes and tribute collection in the Audiencia of Nueva Galicia, see Woodrow Borah, "Los tributos y su recaudación en la Audiencia de Nueva Galicia durante el siglo XVI."

contains them, but may be omitted if it has none. E.g., the statement 0/0/6 means six granos, or half a real. There is no evidence that granos were ever coined in colonial Mexico in any form but half and quarter reales: six and three granos, respectively. For computer calculations, all values had to be handled as granos and then converted into the appropriate number of reales and pesos. Complicated though this procedure was, it created far less trouble than figuring in coins of the varying values current in earlier New Spain or in contemporary Peru.[2]

Weights and measures in which commodities were stated constituted a much more complex problem. Those used in sixteenth-century Mexico represented an adjustment of Andalusian and Castilian units to local conditions. Nueva Galicia apparently adopted the measures common in the Audiencia of Mexico without local changes. In dry measure, the unit was the fanega, still current in Mexico, rated at 54.52 liters, or 1.55 U.S. bushels. It was closer to the fanega of Sevilla, 54.7 liters, the Andalusian standard, than to that of Ávila, 55.5 liters, common to Castile. The Andalusian origin of so many of the early conquerors and settlers perhaps explains the preference. Each fanega could be divided into 12 almudes or celemines. In liquid measure, the unit was the Castilian arroba, probably rated at 16.13 liters, or 4.26 U.S. gallons. Divisions of the arroba as liquid measure were:

4 cuartillos	=	1 azumbre
8 azumbres	=	1 arroba

Liquid measure, further, was sometimes stated in terms of cántaros, pottery jars, a variable measure, for in the tribute of some towns a cántaro of honey meant an arroba and in others a half or quarter of an arroba. In linear measure, the basic unit was the Castilian vara, or yard, of 0.84 meters, or 33 U.S. inches. Tribute cloth was delivered in mantas, generally but not always of 16 square varas. The questions of variable size and quality are discussed in the section on cloth. Weight was stated in terms of the Castilian libra or pound, weighing 460.093 grams, or slightly more than the U.S. pound of 453.54 grams. Its division and multiple for tribute purposes in Nueva Galicia were:

16 onzas	=	1 libra
25 libras	=	1 arroba as a measure of weight

Other measures of weight and volume, such as the arrelde (four pounds, a measure of meat), the carga (50 Castilian pounds for an Indian porter, or a much heavier load of 400 pounds for a pack animal); the carretada (a cartload of 30 fanegas), the braza (the fathom of 6 varas); and the Indian terms for dealing in cacao do not show up in the Nueva Galicia tribute auctions for our period, although they undoubtedly were current in trade and other usage.[3]

Terms for commodities occasionally presented difficulties, but all could be resolved by consulting dictionaries of specifically American terms in Spanish or a

---

[2]Borah and Cook, *Price Trends*, pp. 9-10; Belveder, *Libro general de las redvciones de plata,* passim.

[3]Borah and Cook, *Price Trends*, pp. 10-12. Material on Nueva Galicia is gleaned from royal fiscal records in AGI, Contaduría.

Nahuatl dictionary to trace roots in the native tongue of most common usage. The one stubborn question concerned the meaning of *mechinpuyeque*, for the word occurred in no Spanish dictionary nor one of native tongues. *Puyeque* occurs in the Santamaría *Diccionario de mejicanismos* as meaning a piece of mangrove wood, but what was *mechinpuyeque*? Inquiries sent to various experts in Indian terms in Mexican Spanish found them as puzzled as I, until Peter Gerhard suggested that the term is a compound of Spanish *mecha*, wick, and *puyeque*, a piece or length of mangrove wood, frequently used as a torch by fishermen. Such mixed forms do occur in Indian and Spanish-American usage. The term, then, evidently means torches of mangrove wood for use in fisheries or mines.

Questions relating to towns involved two different matters: identification and location. One is impressed, and perhaps annoyed, by the relative lack of variety in town names in Nueva Galicia, since in so many instances two or more of them bore the same names. The royal treasury officials found themselves in the same difficulty, which they tried to solve either by giving the location of the town or the name of its former encomendero, if it had once been held in private encomienda. These indications continued to be clues of value. A third clue lay in the fact that the royal treasury officials dealt with the towns, in the sale of their tributes, in groups. The mention of a town within a group meant that the town was situated near the others. A further aid in handling duplication of town names and an invaluable guide in finding location was afforded by the existence of a precious new tool in Peter Gerhard's *The North Frontier of New Spain*, the appearance of which in 1982 provided a remarkable compendium of information on sites and their history. Its index and maps, personally prepared by the author, contain the names and give the locations of almost all of the towns mentioned in the tribute auctions. Rather than follow Gerhard's somewhat romantic preference for archaic spelling, I have chosen to modernize the names in accordance with the orthography of the 1950 Mexican census except in the very few instances of too drastic change. That decision involved me in the shift from Nahuatl to Nahuat spelling, from the spellings used in the tribute auctions to present-day usage recorded in the 1950 Mexican census. For the town names, the shift meant dropping the letter l from many combinations of tl, and occasionally the shortening of the name.

The last set of problems concerned the names of the buyers. In the royal treasury records the names are erratically written in accordance with the casual unconcern of the sixteenth century for consistent orthography. E.g., what turned out to be the same name was written in three quite different spellings in the instance of Egurrola, whose name fortunately could be established through the fact that his brother figured in correspondence with Spain. In addition, many of the names were abbreviated in forms susceptible to a number of readings. The current reading had to be ascertained by reference to the names of Spaniards living in Nueva Galicia at that time. Still other names, spelled correctly for the epoch, involved the shift in the pronunciation of x, originally like our sh, to the Spanish j and s–particularly the difficulty with Xuárez, which today has been changed either to Juárez or Suárez. Examination of histories of Nueva Galicia and its component regions, consultation of Gerhard, extensive search in the archives and libraries of Guadalajara, and the invaluable comments of a group of distinguished genealogical scholars in Guadalajara, especially Don Jorge Palomino y Cañedo and Lic. Miguel Claudio Jiménez y Vizcarra, enabled me to straighten out the problems of all but a very few names. Names which could not be identified involved questions other than spelling–for example, Maese Pedro–and probably referred to sailors or to people from outside of Guadalajara.

The availability in our information of the names of the purchasers is somewhat unusual in price data except for retail data culled from the books of an institution such as a convent, hospital, or school. It adds considerably to the possibility of exploring the economic and social history of early Nueva Galicia. Chapter 6 is devoted to discussing the purchasers.

Once the initial transfer of the data from the note cards was completed and both transcriptions checked against them to detect errors, the next step was to transfer the data to a computer for further processing and analysis. The program chosen was GANDER, a simple and unusually flexible program devised initially for the Data General computer by anthropologists at the University of California, Berkeley. Its format was planned to record and analyze field notes, but it proved exactly right for the price data. For each sale there went into the computer the date of sale, treasury province, town, the commodity sold, the quantity, and the price per unit accepted by the royal treasury officials, expressed in the silver pesos, reales, and granos of the common colonial Mexican coinage. Commodities were stated in the appropriate unit for that product. Once all the data were entered, a printout was taken off for checking against the transcription sheets and, in instances of doubt, the original notes. Any errors noted were corrected.

A trial analysis of the data on maize in the computer disclosed that the division of the data by treasury provinces was essentially meaningless, and that a more significant division would be by coast and plateau. Accordingly, the data were rearranged–an easy matter for the computer–into two divisions according to altitude and climate. Only data from the treasury province of Zacatecas, although incorporated in the highland data, were reserved as well for additional and special treatment. The towns concerned, southwest of the city of Zacatecas, supplied the new silver mines in their first years, but by the late 1560s the prices bid for tribute commodities showed a special and unusual pattern, to be handled in the discussion of each commodity. Mezquituta in 1570 was actually transferred to the Guadalajara auctions, but for the purposes of continuity and comparison here has been retained in the Zacatecas province. A similar procedure has been followed for all commodities.

For the purpose of analysis, all statements of quantity of commodity had to be converted to the lowest unit in which each commodity was measured. Thus for maize and wheat the unit for computer calculations was almudes, 12 to a fanega, instead of fanegas. Prices were all converted into granos, 96 to a peso and 12 to a real. In this way, the computer dealt with a single form of statement in each instance.

At this point, a question arose as to the more representative value for determining trend in price. We had a unit price for almost all sales of commodities, the exceptions being the occasional sale of a number of commodities at a group price. However, the quantities sold varied considerably according to the size of the town. Basing calculation upon the total unit prices of each year would assign a perhaps excessive weight to the many little towns delivering small quantities. A weighted average derived by calculating the total amount of money and the total amount of the commodity each year in each major region and in the whole of Nueva Galicia, and dividing the first value by the second, would give due attention to the quantities involved and would allow the larger towns more influence. In the end, the decision was to calculate trends by both methods, but as a further check to separate out and calculate the trends for the individual towns of Tlaquepaque and Tepic, both close to major Spanish settlements, one on the plateau and the other on the coast, and for Mezquituta for the Zacatecas province. Where appropriate or necessary, other towns were substituted in instances in which the three selected for calculation provided no data. The additional calculations using individual towns for trend lines also furnished evidence of the extent to which adjustments for cost of transportation figured in the thinking of bidders and influenced the price paid, since Tlaquepaque lay within a half-hour's walk of Guadalajara and Tepic was next door to Spanish Tepic. In the instance of these two towns, there would be virtually no cost of transportation to the successful bidder.

Trends were calculated by least squares through use of the program called REGRESS, and through the same program the corresponding graphs were sketched upon a data plotter. To one who has been used to the tedious methods of an earlier technology, the process is little short of miraculous. The graphs were then redrawn by a technician for reproduction in this monograph.

It will be noticed that I have not resorted to rolling averages. The reasons are two. In the first place, since the term of years is fairly short, 1557-1598, resort to rolling averages would lose two years at either end of the period, a serious subtraction in view of the brevity of the period. In the second place, since the purpose has been to calculate trend, and calculation by least squares accomplishes this most elegantly, resort to rolling averages and then calculating least squares would change the trend line only to the slight extent that the lesser weight assigned to initial and terminal years might dictate.

Similarly, I have not attempted to create a consumption index as many other price studies have. The data on sales of tribute commodities do not contain information on many items that should enter into one for it to have any validity. Meat, and most items of Spanish consumption, do not occur in the data. Further, in terms of consumption, the sixteenth-century population of Nueva Galicia, like that of most of Spanish America, was divided into two quite different communities, Indians and Europeans, with widely different patterns of consumption. For the Indian population of Nueva Galicia, maize was the major foodstuff and its price close to a good index of consumption, but the Spanish population consumed large amounts of meats, fruits, vegetables, hides, local manufactures, wine, olive oil, imported cloth and silks, and local furniture and pottery, as well as imported household furnishings.[4] Any index for the Spanish community would have to take account of such items, for which we have almost no information.

---

[4]See the discussion in Borah and Cook, *Price Trends*, pp. 46-47.

Further, a careful search has located almost no information on wages in Nueva Galicia (the mines excepted) for the years of this study. The data are too scanty for reliable calculation of movement of monetary wages, and additionally of inflation in real terms, as commonly accepted by comparison of wages paid in silver with the movement of commodity values also expressed in silver. Nevertheless, the information is set forth in a section of this study and analyzed for a suggestion of trend. Perhaps some day documents may come to light that will furnish more data.

4

COMMODITIES SHOWING LONG-TERM RISE

Tribute commodities showed different trends in the forty-year period studied here. Those of consistent long-term rise–maize, beans, chickens, and turkeys–have been grouped in this chapter, the rest in the following one. The reasons for substantial differences in trend are complex, two principal ones being changing Spanish needs and the shrinking ability of the Indian towns to deliver tribute. The first century of Spanish collection of tribute, in fact, should be considered a steady interplay between these factors. Two other factors of major importance were the steady outpouring of silver from the mines of Zacatecas, bringing inflation, and the onset of the "Little Ice Age" in the last decades of the century.

MAIZE

Despite the Spanish desire for bread made from wheat flour, Indian numbers and practice made maize the staple grain of Nueva Galicia, as elsewhere in New Spain. Further, the grain, leaves, and stalks of the plant, green and dried, were widely used as fodder.[1] The prevailing pattern of summer rainfall determined that the principal crop of maize was sown at the beginning of the rains after the ground was sufficiently moist. The conventional date was the Day of St. John the Baptist, June 24, although depending on the coming of the rains and the altitude, planting might be as early as May. Harvest occurred from mid-September to December. At lower altitudes, especially on the coast, another sowing might take place from December to February, with harvest occurring in April and May. At the lower altitudes there was much

[1]Bakewell, p. 59; also, my own attempts to secure animal fodder during field expeditions.

damage by weevils and rot, explained as due to humidity. Grain did not store well on the coast, so that the two harvests really were needed.[2]

The royal auctions took place as the principal maize harvest either was about to be or had already been gathered, so that the quality and quantity of the crop were known. This time was also the low point of an annual cycle for maize prices, which usually reached a peak when stores of the previous harvest had been exhausted, just before the new crop would be gathered. With the new harvest, prices dropped to a low level and remained there for several months. They then began a slow climb as stored grain was used up, until they peaked just before the harvest of the next new crop. The royal auction values for maize thus indicate the lowest wholesale prices of the year.[3]

We have 1,996 transactions for maize in which the unit price could be identified, 1,234 for the coast and 762 for the plateau, covering a forty-two-year period. What do they show? Whether calculated in terms of unit price per fanega at each sale or the weighted average price per fanega for the year, both coast and plateau exhibit a strong upward movement of values in silver coin. Let us begin our examination with the calculations in terms of unit price for the coast and the plateau, leaving discussion of Zacatecas, including Mezquituta, for slightly later. The coast has the most data, which also show the greatest amount of dispersion. In the earliest years of our period, prices moved upward at a relatively moderate rate, but beginning in 1574 prices on the whole moved distinctly higher, a somewhat surprising development since they anticipated the great epidemic of matlazáhuatl by two years. Nevertheless, calculation by subperiods 1557-1574 and 1575-1598 demonstrates that a single trend line for the entire period expresses the trend well. The slope of the line for the entire period is 1.16. With a t value of 12.3 for 1,232 degrees of freedom, the probability that these results are due to random variation in the data is far less than one percent. (See Graph 4.1.)

Although I had separated data on unit prices for the plateau in order to test for possible difference in degree of upward movement, unit prices for the plateau (Graph 4.2) show a slope of almost the same degree as those for the coast. For the plateau, calculation of a single trend line for the 762 items entering into it yields a slope of 1.17. The difference with the coast is insignificant for the term of years. The value for t, 16.98, is even higher than that for the coast, and with 760 degrees of freedom again indicates a probability of far less than one percent that these results are due merely to random variation.

When the data for the coast and the plateau are combined, calculation of a trend line for all of Nueva Galicia yields a result that is intermediate between the slight

---

[2]Arregui, pp. 17 and 93-94; relación de la ciudad de Compostela, Compostela, 26 November 1584; relación de las minas de San Demetrio, Fresnillo, 1 January, 1585, relación de las minas del Peñol, 15 January 1585, relación de las minas del Fresnillo II, Fresnillo, 20 January 1585, and III, 7 February 1585; relación de Jérez de la Frontera, Jérez de la Frontera, 13 October 1584; relación de la villa de la Purificación, La Purificación, 12 January 1585; relación de las minas de San Martín, 6 February 1585; relación de las minas de Xocotlán, 15 October 1584; all in Acuña, ed., *Relaciones geográficas del siglo XVI*, 10:88, 104, 111, 120, 128, 211, 247, and 316, respectively.

[3]See Chapter 3 above; also Borah and Cook, *Price Trends*, pp. 13-14.

difference of the lines for the two regions, the coast having slightly greater weight because of the greater number of items; but the difference is basically insignificant. The slope is 1.14; the value for *t*, 18.5, with 1,994 degrees of freedom, is even higher. It again indicates a reliability far beyond the one-percent level. (See Graph 4.3.) These results may be taken as solidly grounded.

As a check upon the calculations in terms of unit prices, I have had the computer also calculate weighted average prices for each year–i.e., for coast, plateau, for Nueva Galicia as a whole, there would be one value each for every year, representing an average reached by multiplying for each area the total quantity of maize sold at auction and the total amount of coin involved in the transactions, and then dividing the total of coin by the total quantity of maize to arrive at a weighted average price for the year. The effect is to reduce variation markedly, entirely within the year and somewhat from year to year, although there would still be the variation caused by differences in the abundance or scarcity of the year's crop.

For the coast, with values for thirty-seven years, the slope of the trend line is raised somewhat to 1.47, and indicates a rise from approximately 0/3 to 1/0/1–that is, 2.8 times. (See Graph 4.4.) With 35 degrees of freedom, *t* at a value of 4.7 remains well beyond the one-percent level of probability that the result should be ascribed to random variation. (These are values taken from the trend line, the slope of which is influenced by high values in the 1570s and 1580s. The actual values at either terminus of the trend line are lower: for 1557-1559 an average of slightly less than 0/2/5, and for 1596-1598 an average of approximately 0/6/4, or an increase of 2.6-fold.) The difference between a calculation based upon unit prices and one based on weighted average prices suggests that the presence of numerous small towns did weight the calculation by unit price downward. Calculation in weighted average prices, by giving the larger towns greater weight, redresses the balance.

For the plateau, calculation by weighted average prices results in a trend line with a slope that is still markedly upward (1.3) but, in contrast to the coast, somewhat less so than that for unit prices. The rise was approximately from 0/3/6 to 1/0/6. With 39 annual averages entering the calculation, a value for *t* of 6.2, with 37 degrees of freedom, again indicates a reliability considerably beyond the one-percent level. (See Graph 4.5.) In terms of weighted annual average prices, tribute maize for the plateau towns sold at auction brought higher prices relative to the coastal towns in the earlier years, and lesser ones in the later ones. For the forty-two years of our period the rise for the plateau was 2.4-fold. (Again, these are calculations from the trend line. The actual values at either terminus are somewhat different: for 1557-1559, 0/2/11, and for 1596-1598, 0/7/11, or an increase of 2.7-fold.) For the plateau, calculation by annual weighted averages increases the influence of small towns and may, as well, represent the influence of another factor, the tendency in years of scarcity to divide the maize tribute of larger towns into portions for sale among several purchasers, even if this tactic meant differing prices.

Combining the data for all of Nueva Galicia in a series of annual weighted average prices yields a trend line with a slope of 1.3, slightly steeper than the trend line for all of Nueva Galicia by unit prices. (See Graph 4.6.) At a value for *t* of 6.11 with 39 degrees of freedom, the result is again well beyond the one-percent level. It is actually beyond the .001 level of probability that these values are the result of

Graph 4.1 Maize Unit Prices: Coast

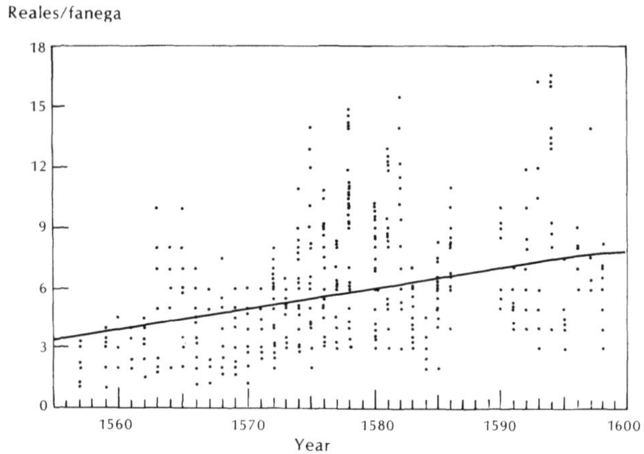

Graph 4.2 Maize Unit Prices: Plateau

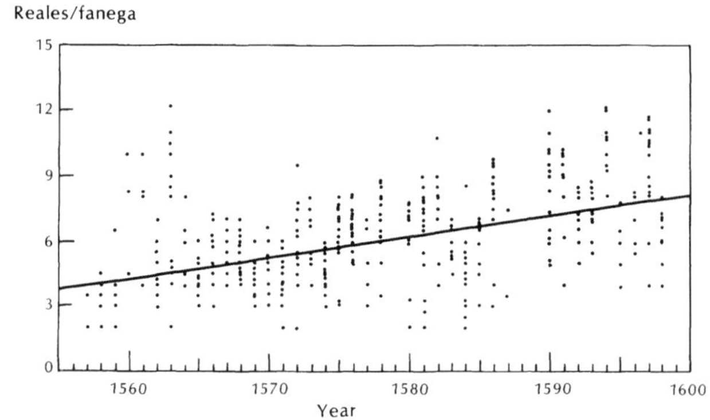

Graph 4.3 Maize Unit Prices: All Towns

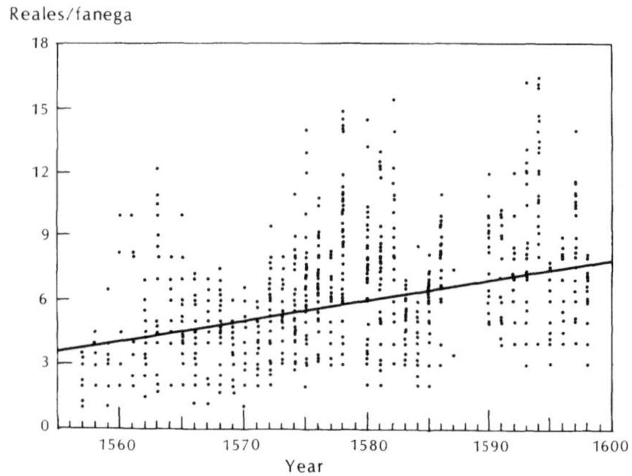

Graph 4.4 Maize Annual Average Prices: Coast

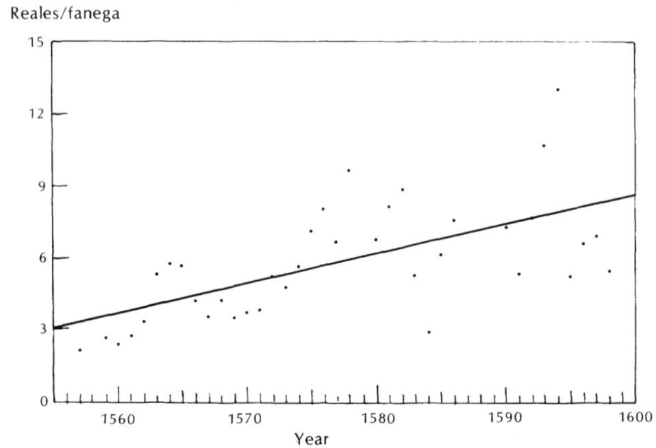

random variation, as it is with all of the values given so far. Gauged from the trend line, the rise was from 0/3/6 in 1557 to 1/0/4 in 1598, or approximately 2.2-fold. (Actual values at either terminus were somewhat different: from 0/2/11 for 1557-1559 to 0/7/4 for 1596-1598, or 2.5-fold.) Again, the influence of the higher values of the 1570s is apparent in the slope of the trend line.

Recalculating by annual weighted average prices thus confirms the general result obtained through examining in terms of unit prices, but somewhat reduces the steepness of slope of the trend line. As a further check, I had the computer sort out the data for one town in each region, a town so close to the major Spanish settlement that transportation for Spanish use could be ignored. San Pedro Tlaquepaque lay within half a league of Guadalajara, or a half-hour's walk; today it is part of the urban area of Guadalajara. Indian Tepic lay contiguous to the Spanish city at even less distance, and today forms part of the urban whole. For each town, the unit price for the year was used for the calculation by least squares of trend for the period.

For Tepic, in the coastal region, the slope of the trend line (2.01) is distinctly greater than that for the entire region, in terms both of unit prices and annual weighted average prices. (See Graph 4.7.) The rise for the period in the value of royal tribute maize secured from Tepic would be from approximately 0/4 to 1/3 on the trend line, 2.75-fold. With data for thirty-eight years, *t* at 2.0 with 36 degrees of freedom is again a highly reliable calculation well beyond the one-percent level of probability. For San Pedro Tlaquepaque, on the plateau, data for forty years yield a trend line with a slope of 1.87 and a value for *t* of 8.0, which with 38 degrees of freedom lies well beyond the one-percent level. (See Graph 4.8.) As with Tepic, the rise in prices during the period for the royal tribute maize of Tlaquepaque was steeper than the regional trend, whether calculated in terms of unit prices or annual weighted averages. The movement was from 0/3 to 1/2, or more than three fold. The values for Tlaquepaque probably represent a premium on maize in the audiencia seat, the largest Spanish settlement in the area, just as the prices for Tepic probably represents a premium on maize at the local capital.

The calculations for these two Indian towns both confirm that there was a sharp rise in the prices for maize; but in varying from other calculations, they demonstrate that the regional figures analyzed in terms of either method represent mixtures of individual town values, and the values for towns at a distance from major Spanish settlements or enterprises probably contain reductions for the cost of transportation to where the purchaser could put the maize to use or sell it. Contrary to what one might have expected at the outset, the degree of overall rise was approximately as steep on the coast as on the plateau. One might have expected a steeper rise in the former because of the more rapid decline of the Indian population in the lowlands, since that decrease meant correspondingly greater shrinkage in the amount of tribute maize entering the auctions, at the same time that the Spanish need for maize to feed workers and animals on haciendas, estancias, and other enterprises at the least was holding steady but more probably rising. Given the technology of the day and the nature of settlement in western Nueva Galicia–dirt trails serving as roads, transportation by bearer and pack animal–it was not economical to move bulky commodities like maize more than a few days' journey, so that Nueva Galicia, on both coast and plateau, really consisted of many small market areas which had to

Graph 4.5 Maize Annual Average Prices: Plateau

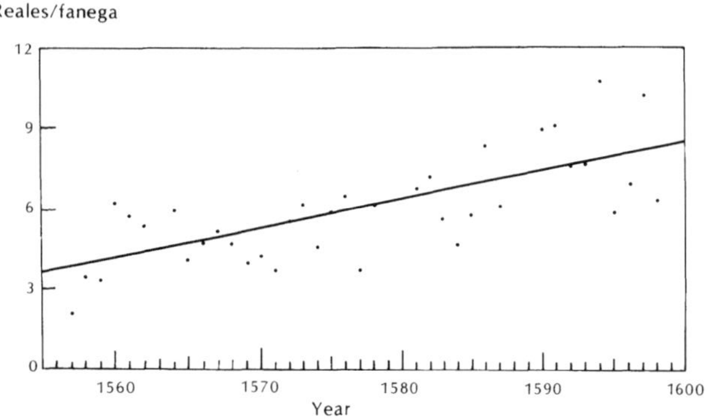

Graph 4.6 Maize Annual Average Prices: All Towns

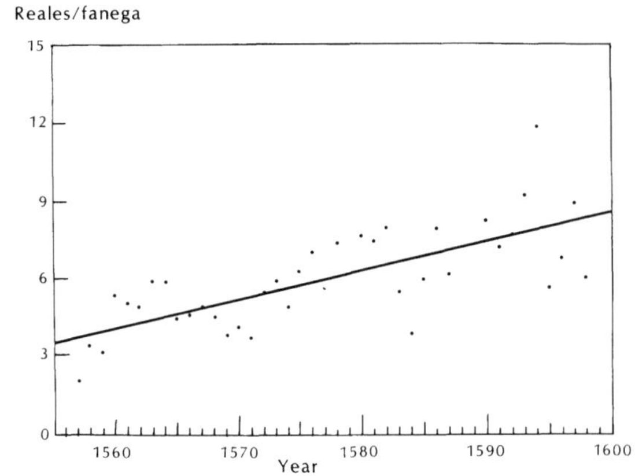

Graph 4.7 Maize Unit Prices: Tepic

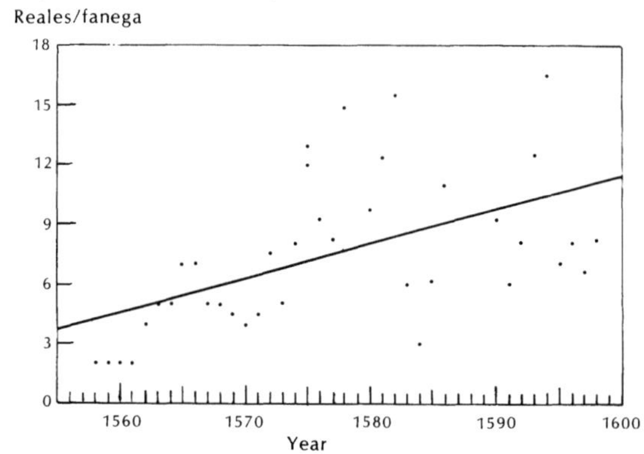

Graph 4.8 Maize Unit Prices: Tlaquepaque

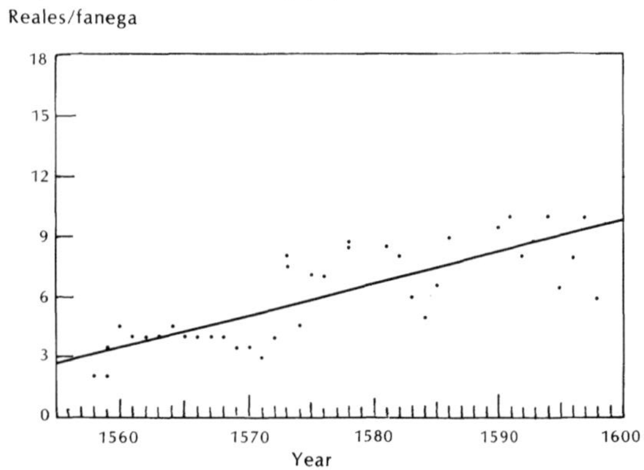

take care of their own supply of foodstuffs. We can only speculate at this stage of investigation on how the growing deficit in maize on the coast was met. The increasing availability of meat from the rapidly expanding numbers of livestock may be one explanation.

Zacatecas data present behavior that departs considerably from that of the plateau and of Nueva Galicia in general. Accordingly, although the data for Zacatecas have been included within the general calculations for the plateau, they have been segregated as well for another series of calculations. In the earlier years the prices bid for maize in the Zacatecas area were, in general, higher than those for the tribute of towns elsewhere on the plateau; in the later years, to the extent that we have data, they were lower. The towns whose tribute maize was auctioned in Zacatecas in the early years are all in the Juchipila Valley and adjacent parts of the Río Verde drainages, southwest of the mining center. Today the Juchipila Valley is mostly a southwest extension of the state of Zacatecas; the Río Verde drainage lies in Jalisco. Since the great silver strikes at Zacatecas were already under way in the early years of our period, clearly the maize was bid on for the maintenance of Indians and animals working in the mines and in ancillary operations. In fact, one of the bidders was Francisco de Ibarra, a discoverer of one of the deposits and a major mine owner. Zacatecas was then drawing food and other supplies from Michoacán and other areas in the Audiencia of Mexico. A cart road was built to facilitate transportation. With the expansion of silver mining, especially after the development and application at midcentury of the mercury amalgamation treatment of ores in the patio process, the needs of Zacatecas stimulated both an increase in supplies from the Audiencia of Mexico and local agriculture in oases near the mines on haciendas very often owned by miners.[4] Royal tribute maize thus became far less important, and the prices Zacatecas bidders were willing to pay fell accordingly. This explains the apparently aberrant behavior of the prices bid for tribute maize in the middle and later years of our period. In 1570 Mezquituta, at the southern end of the Juchipila Valley, was removed from the bidding in Zacatecas to that in Guadalajara, in recognition by the royal treasury officials of the possibilities of sale. It has been kept within the Zacatecas group in our calculations in order to permit comparison for the entire period. The maize tribute of the other towns was largely removed from the auctions in a slow, cumulative process and applied to the maintenance of the Indians who gathered salt from saline ponds and deposits for the royal monopoly, providing low-grade salt for the patio process. The only addition to the auctions in the later years was Apozol, when it escheated to the Crown in 1595, but its maize too was auctioned in Guadalajara.[5]

The aberrant behavior of maize prices for Zacatecas, relative to that of all other towns on the coast and the plateau, is clearly evident in the calculation of trend in terms of unit prices. (See Graph 4.9.) The slope is downward (-.416) on reports of

---

[4]Bakewell, pp. 58-80; Acuña, vol. 10, passim; Chevalier, pp. 216-222; Enrique Florescano, "El abasto," 14:589-600; Mota y Escobar, pp. 294-295. Ross Hassig, *Trade, Tribute, and Transportation,* pp. 200-201; López de Velasco, pp. 137-138; Powell, pp. 18-27.

[5]See Appendix A.

124 bids for the period. With a value for *t* of -2.1 with 122 degrees of freedom, the result does not have the extraordinarily high degree of validity of the previous calculations, but still lies between the two- and three-percent level of probability. The range of prices started at 0/6 but dropped to 0/4/6 in the course of the period. There is no reason to postulate that the removal of tribute maize from the auctions, for the consumption of the salt workers, lowered prices, inasmuch as the removal of maize from the market, in the absence of other supplies, would have lessened the amount for sale and ordinarily should have raised prices. The movement of prices is testimony to relative abundance of supply.

Calculation in terms of annual weighted average price confirms the conclusion based on unit prices. (See Graph 4.10.) With data for thirty-eight years, the variability is lowered so that the average price of maize begins at 0/5/6 and falls during the period to 0/5. The slope is mildly negative (-.120); with 36 degrees of freedom, the value of *t* (-.36) falls so low that the calculation must be regarded as having only minor statistical reliability. In effect, the trend is flat, or one might say that there is no trend.

An additional test in the form of calculating the trend of maize prices for Mezquituta bears out the determinations for the Zacatecas treasury province. Mezquituta royal tribute maize, it should be remembered, was auctioned in Zacatecas until 1570 and thereafter in Guadalajara. (See Graph 4.11.) We have data for thirty-six years. The slope of the trend line is mildly upward (.49), and *t*, with a value of 1.5 on 34 degrees of freedom, has relatively weak validity, since it indicates slightly better than a 10-percent level of probability, i.e., 90-percent reliability, which is weak for analysis of historical data. The trend of prices would start at 0/4/4 and finish at 0/6/6.

The Zacatecas region, then, exhibits price behavior for royal tribute maize distinctly different from that of the rest of the Audiencia of Nueva Galicia. The contrast must be ascribed to the development around the mining center of Spanish-owned haciendas raising maize and to imports from the Audiencia of Mexico. As its need for maize—always far larger than the possibilities of supply through royal tribute maize—increased steadily, Zacatecas developed its own sources of supply. In the home area, it was more efficient to employ Indians directly on haciendas than to apply more indirect methods of extraction or production. This development testifies to the strongly entrepreneurial spirit of the Spaniards in the city, who obviously examined their problems and, in terms of the resources and technology available to them, moved to a rational solution.

Taken as a whole, what does this body of data for prices of royal tribute maize in the Audiencia of Nueva Galicia indicate; what should be our interpretation of the calculations outlined thus far? First, the variability in prices within each year and between years indicates a true market. In the second place, despite the sparse population of Spaniards in some areas of the audiencia and the relatively small population of Guadalajara, Spanish society in Nueva Galicia tended to be capitalist or, if one prefers the term, commercial-precapitalist. It was oriented toward enterprise, even though much of its revenue may have come from administration and encomiendas. Many of the bidders bought maize for workmen in mines and ancillary operations. Undoubtedly, others—particularly those bidding for the tributes of the

Graph 4.9 Maize Unit Prices: Zacatecas

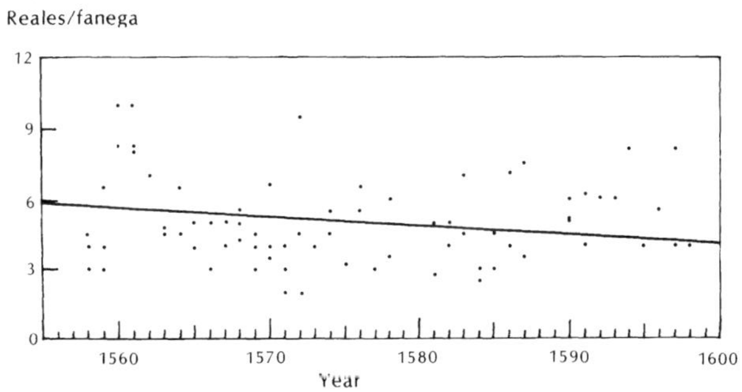

Graph 4.10 Maize Annual Average Prices: Zacatecas

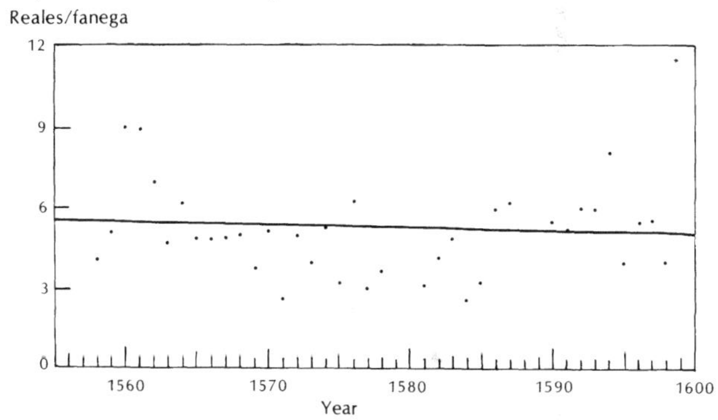

Graph 4.11 Maize Unit Prices: Mezquituta

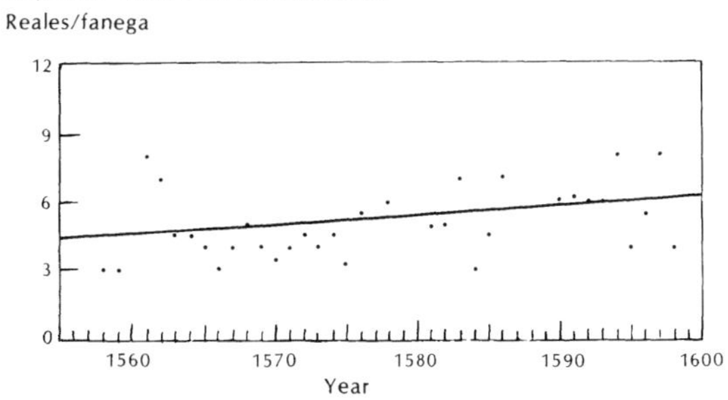

larger Indian towns—sought them for resale in smaller lots. Basically, they were acting as wholesalers acquiring a supply for the retail market. Lay and ecclesiastical officeholders, who figure prominently in the sales, may have fallen in any of these categories, their business activities being additional to their posts in the royal government or the Church.

In the third place, we should want to search for the possible influence of change in climate upon the movement of maize prices. After perhaps 1560, the weather in Mexico may have been slowly growing more severe as climate in the northern hemisphere moved into what has been called the "Little Ice Age." It should have been manifested in our area by decreasing summer temperatures and more erratic rainfall, perhaps with years of severer drought. Unfortunately, there is as yet no way of comparing our area with the fine dendrochronological readings for the Southwest of the United States. Attempts at dendrochronologies for Mexico have gone no farther south than Durango and no farther back in time than the seventeenth century. The movements of maize prices in our period would suggest—as yet no more—times of stress in 1558-1564, 1572-1583, and 1585-1593. Interestingly, the period 1572-1583 included the years of epidemic, 1576-1579, but prices indicate that trouble in supply of maize began before 1576. Years of relative respite notwithstanding, the entire period 1557-1598 was one of rising prices.[6] The question of climatic change is discussed at greater length in Chapter 7.

In the fourth place, the prices of royal tribute maize in the Audiencia of Nueva Galicia show a trend similar, though not identical, to that calculated for maize at wholesale in the Audiencia of Mexico. For this comparison I do not use the Borah and Cook study of 1958 (which, as noted in Chapter 1, has been objected to because of its use of various kinds of data), for it is limited to the period 1531-1570, so that its results would be only partially applicable. It has now been superseded as to maize prices by a new study prepared by Ulises Beltrán,[7] which assembles considerably more data and eliminates the items subject to objection in the data used by Borah and Cook. The two studies of the Audiencia of Mexico, incidentally, are in agreement as to trend, but are not directly comparable as to year-to-year values, since the Borah and Cook study was fundamentally based on auction prices of royal tribute, whereas the Beltrán presents average prices for the half year. It thus covers both highs and lows in the annual cycle of maize prices, as against the data from auctions of royal tribute maize, which give only the one annual price for each town at the low

[6]The entire question of the "Little Ice Age" in Mexico is only now coming under study. Enrique Florescano, "Una historia olvidada: la sequía en México"; Dieter Klaus, "Las fluctuaciones del clima en el valle de Puebla-Tlaxcala"; Robert H. Claxton and Alan D. Hecht, "Climatic and Human History in Europe and Latin America, pp. 197-200; H. C. Fritts, "Tree Ring Evidence for Climatic Change in Western North America" and *Tree Rings and Climate*, pp. 36-37 and 409; Susan L. Swan, "Mexico in the Little Ice Age"; Edmund Schulman, *Dendroclimatic Changes in Semiarid America*, pp. 39-41, 58-59, and 69; W. Portig, "Klimapendelungen in San Salvador"; O. E. Jáuregui, "Algunos aspectos de las fluctuaciones pluviométricos en México in los últimos cien años". A magisterial study for Switzerland by Christian Pfister, *Das Klima der Schweiz von 1525-1800*, gives a clear idea of possible meaning if we had comparable studies for Mexico and Nueva Galicia, in particular.

[7]"Evolución de los sistemas de trabajo en la Nueva España, 1521-1640."

point of the year immediately after the harvest. This same difficulty applies to direct comparison of the year-to-year values with the Nueva Galicia data. Nevertheless, the two sets of values may be compared as to trend over a term of years, since the averages resulting from the annual cycle would be driven higher or lower in response to abundance and scarcity, as well as silver inflation, just as would the prices at public auction. The Beltrán data do cover the 1580s, but not the 1590s. Table 4.1 presents the pertinent material for comparison of the trends in Nueva Galicia and the Audiencia of Mexico in terms of direct values, i.e., silver reales and decimal fractions thereof, which are not directly comparable for any one year, and of index numbers calculated upon the average prices of 1557-1559 and annual weighted averages. Rather than a single year for the base, 1557-1559 was used, to avoid stressing what might be an unusual year.

The two jurisdictions show great differences in the movement of prices in most individual years, but the trend tends to be the same. In terms of index numbers, the Audiencia of Nueva Galicia generally outstripped the Audiencia of Mexico, although not in all individual years. We are led to conclude that Nueva Galicia underwent a stiffer rise in prices than did the Audiencia of Mexico.

That rise apparently led the more prominent Spaniards in Nueva Galicia to petition the high court for relief, with the result that an order of the Audiencia of Guadalajara dated 2 February 1600 directed that the royal maize tributes of the Indian towns in Nueva Galicia be sold to deserving Spaniards at the average price received for the maize of each town in the previous five years.[8] The *beneméritos de la república* were obviously the royal and Church officials plus wealthy traders and miners, who thus gained a handsome subsidy at the cost of the royal treasury. Implemented with the tribute maize of 1599, the audiencia's order effectively ended the free market in royal tribute maize.

In the Audiencia of Mexico, there was no similar system of distribution of royal tribute maize to those deserving well of the republic. Unlike Nueva Galicia, townshere could petition and did secure commutation of their tribute in maize to silver coin at a value calculated on the price the tribute had brought in a term of preceding years. That trend toward commutation came to a climax in 1627, when the viceroy decreed commutation at 1/1 or 0/9 the fanega.[9] In Nueva Galicia, probably because of the system of supply to Spaniards, commutation was rarely granted.[10] As the increase in commutation value suggests, maize prices in the Audiencia of Mexico continued to rise until the early seventeenth century, when they reached comparative stability. It would be hazardous, however, to extrapolate the experience of the Audiencia of Mexico to Nueva Galicia in these years until we have detailed information. As to the free market in maize, which undoubtedly existed, we are faced equally with a blank.

---

[8] Accounts of 1599, AGI, Contaduría, leg. 859B.

[9] Borah and Cook, *Price Trends*, pp. 44-46.

[10] Borah, "Los tributos y su recaudación," pp. 44-46.

Table 4.1
Comparison of Average Maize Prices:
Central Mexico and Nueva Galicia

	Central Mexico		N. Galicia	
Year	R/F	Index	R/F	Index
1557	3.50	100	2.08	72
1558	3.00	86	3.45	119
1559	4.00	114	3.17	109
1560	3.00	86	5.40	186
1561	3.60	103	5.09	176
1562	4.00	114	4.97	171
1563	NA	NA	5.93	204
1564	5.00	143	5.94	204
1565	5.00	143	4.48	154
1566	NA	NA	4.66	161
1567	3.60	103	4.94	170
1568	4.95	141	4.60	159
1569	3.92	112	3.87	133
1570	3.18	91	4.15	143
1571	4.56	130	3.76	130
1572	4.86	139	5.49	189
1573	NA	NA	5.96	206
1574	NA	NA	4.95	171
1575	NA	NA	6.32	218
1576	NA	NA	7.06	243
1577	5.49	157	5.64	194
1578	5.77	165	7.43	256
1579	5.39	154	NA	NA
1580	NA	NA	7.70	266
1581	4.53	129	7.49	258
1582	9.88	282	8.02	277
1583	7.72	221	5.51	190
1584	NA	NA	3.90	134
1585	NA	NA	6.02	208
1586	NA	NA	7.99	276
1587	NA	NA	6.23	215
1588	NA	NA	NA	NA
1589	NA	NA	NA	NA
1590	5.28	151	8.23	284
1591			7.20	248
1592			7.70	266
1593			9.23	318
1594			11.85	409
1595			5.67	196
1596			6.83	236
1597			8.90	307
1598			6.03	208
[1599			2.00	69]

Base = Av. of 1557 - 1559 = 100.
Correlation of two sets of prices = .6.
Sources: Nueva Galicia: Appendix C; Central Mexico: Beltrán.

FRIJOLES

Frijoles, or kidney beans, were a staple Mesoamerican native food, one of the basic trinity of foods of the region. In the tributes of the Triple Alliance, they had a customary value approximately equal to that of maize.[11] After the conquest, the extent to which they were consumed by the Spaniards, who had a preferred but not always available equivalent in garbanzos (chickpeas), is not clear, but Indian and lower-class workmen in Spanish households, on Spanish estates, and in Spanish mines must have eaten frijoles and thus created a market. Indian tributes through the royal auctions supplied relatively small amounts to this market. For the years 1555 to 1581 we have thirty-six items; for the last seventeen years of our period, nothing, indicating that the Spanish abandoned the attempt to have the Indians supply frijoles through tributes.

In the years for which we have data, unit prices for frijoles rose steadily on the coast. The graph for the coast (see Graph 4.12), based on twelve items, has a slope of 3.40, for which *t*, with a value of 2.58 and 10 degrees of freedom, reaches a confidence level between .05 and .02. The parallel calculation for plateau towns, based on twenty-four items (see Graph 4.13), yields a negative trend line, -.84, and a value for *t* of -.82, which with 22 degrees of freedom reaches a confidence level of .4–what one might characterize as indicative but not reliable. The Zacatecas towns (see Graph 4.14), with seventeen of these items, yield a much more sharply downward trend line, -3.53, and a value for *t* of -3.12, which with 15 degrees of freedom reaches a confidence level of .01, or highly reliable. The ability of the Zacatecas mines early to arrange supplies independent of the tributes is again manifest. Calculation for all of Nueva Galicia (see Graph 4.15) yields a trend line that is a composite of these opposing tendencies. It is upward, 1.31; the value for *t* at 1.6 with 34 degrees of freedom, yields a confidence level of .1, the so-called 10-percent level. For historical data, it is indicative but not strong.

Analysis through annual weighted averages yields results which, though somewhat different, are basically the same. The coast, with data for twelve years (see Graph 4.16), shows an upward trend, 3.60, that is slightly steeper than the line for unit prices. The value for *t*, 2.40, with 9 degrees of freedom, reaches a confidence level between .02 and .01–slightly better than that for the calculation through unit prices. The plateau, with data for twenty years (see Graph 4.17), shows a more sharply descending trend line, -1.23, than that for unit prices. Its *t* value of -1.47, with 18 degrees of freedom, reaches a confidence level between .2 and .1. Zacatecas replicates its calculation for unit prices (see Graph 4.14), since only one town is involved in each annual price. For all of Nueva Galicia, we have twenty-four annual values (see Graph 4.18), which they yield a slope of 1.41, slightly steeper than that resulting from calculation of unit prices. At 22 degrees of freedom, *t* equals 1.33, between the .2 and .1 level of confidence. Again, the preponderance of the Zacatecas prices is manifest.

---

[11]Woodrow Borah and Sherburne F. Cook, *The Aboriginal Population of Mexico on the Eve of the Spanish Conquest*, p. 42.

Graph 4.12 Frijoles Unit Prices: Coast

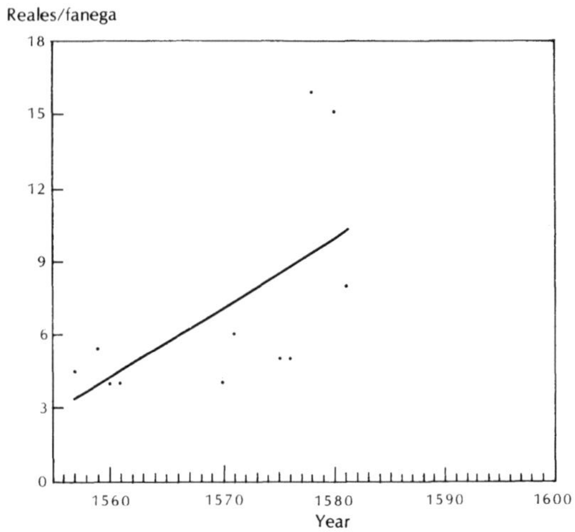

Graph 4.14 Frijoles Unit Prices: Zacatecas

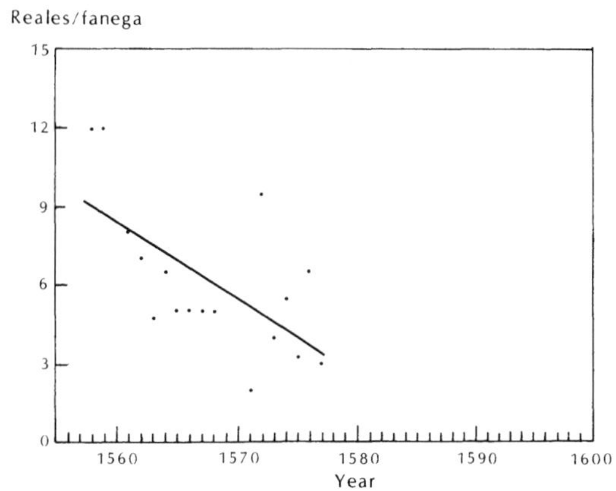

Graph 4.13 Frijoles Unit Prices: Plateau

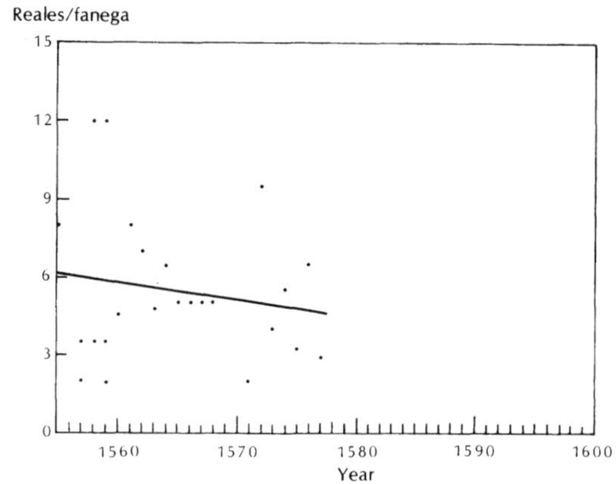

Graph 4.15 Frijoles Unit Prices: All Towns

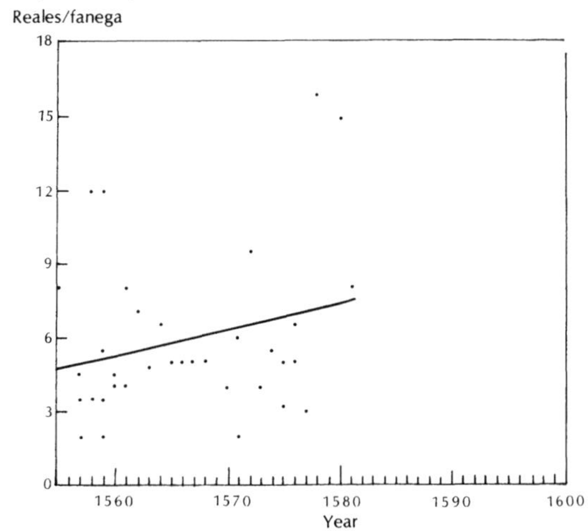

Graph 4.16 Frijoles Annual Average Prices: Coast

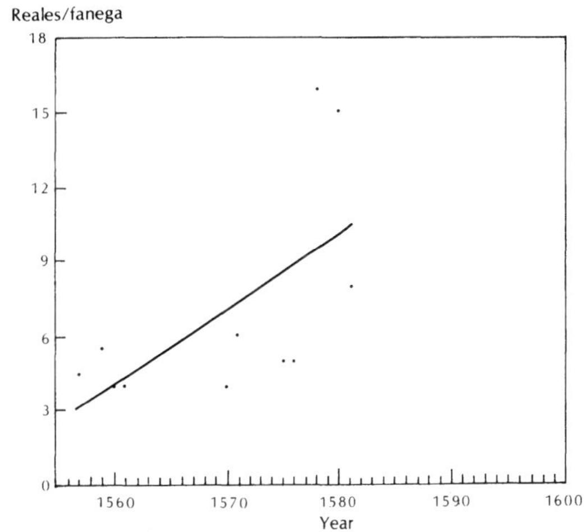

Graph 4.17 Frijoles Annual Average Prices: Plateau

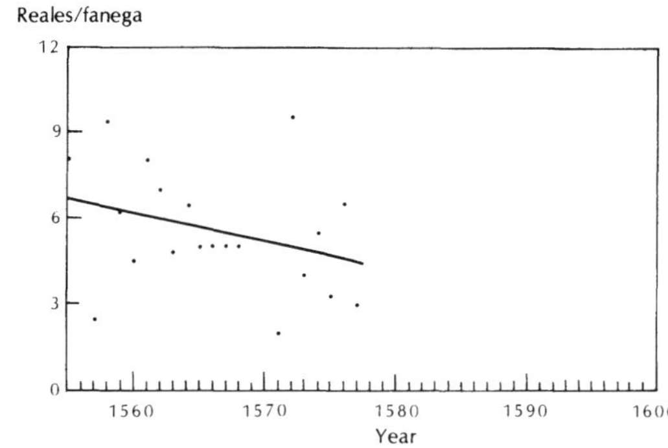

Graph 4.18 Frijoles Annual Average Prices: All Towns

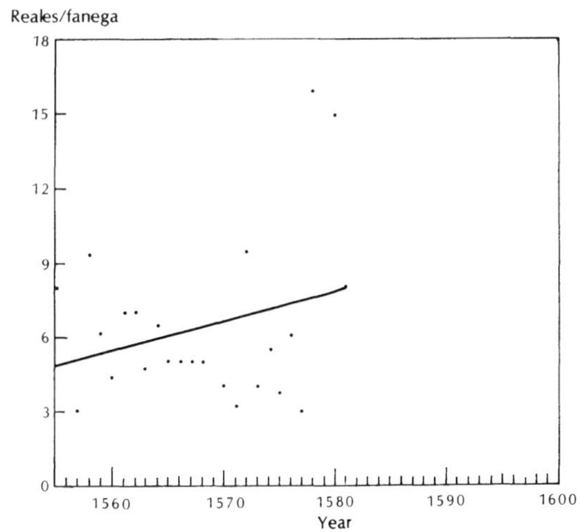

Graph 4.19 Frijoles Unit Prices: Matacticpac

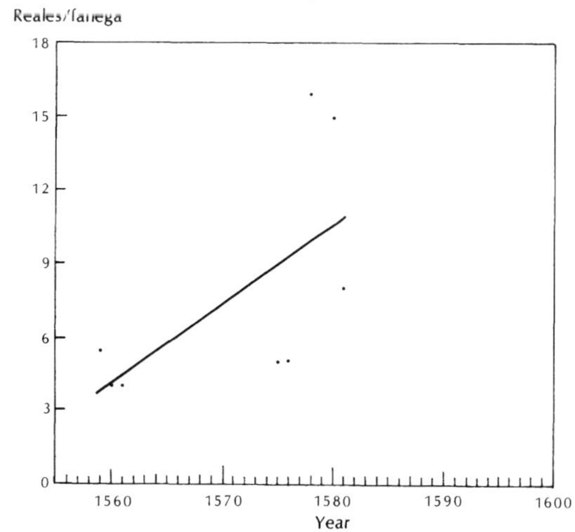

Calculation of trends for individual towns yields supportive results. Matacticpac, with data for eight years, yields a distinctly rising trend of 3.89, with a value for t of 1.99 and 6 degrees of freedom, reaching a confidence level of .1. (See Graph 4.19.) Teocaltitlán, a town in the Zacatecas auctions, with fifteen items, yields a trend line with a negative slope of -1.58; with a t of -1.41 and 13 degrees of freedom, its confidence level lies between .2 and .1, indicative rather than solidly established. (See Graph 4.20.) Since the data are annual reports for one town, the confidence level is testimony to the annual variation.

A comparison of the average prices of maize and frijoles in the Nueva Galicia royal tribute auctions is possible. In general, frijoles commanded a premium, year in and year out. (See Appendix C.) Comparison with the movement of prices in central Mexico unfortunately is not possible at this point, since no data for the latter have been assembled and made public.

CHICKENS

Chickens delivered in tribute were not native to America. When introduced from Europe, they were quickly adopted by the Indians, who at once recognized in them a cheap, convenient source of flesh and eggs, requiring little or no care, and easily available when wanted. They early became an item required in tribute, supplementing or even supplanting the native turkeys. The Spanish consumed a great many chickens. How many of these they raised themselves and how many they derived from tribute we have no means of knowing, but certainly the numbers involved in tribute assessments and the outcry by Spanish notables in later years of the sixteenth century, as the prices of the fowls rose and the supply became less, would indicate that a fair part of the supply came from tribute, either delivered to private encomenderos or bought at the public auctions of royal tribute. Under one of the Crown's reforms, transportation of the fowls from the town center to the household or point of resale was the responsibility of the encomendero or purchaser. Presumably the live fowls were trussed up for transport to a Spanish market and on to a *gallinera*, where they could forage for themselves, with some supplemental feeding, until they ended in a cooking pot or on a spit.

Like maize, the graphs for chickens show a distinct tendency toward rise for our period. In terms of unit prices, the coast, with 889 sales, shows an upward slope of .26. (See Graph 4.21.) The trend line for the plateau, based on 672 transactions, is even steeper (.36) (see Graph 4.22), and the trend line for all of Nueva Galicia, based on 1,561 transactions, is intermediate at .29. (See Graph 4.23.) With t values of 25.3, 30.8, and 36.9, respectively, all these calculations by least squares yield results beyond the one-percent level of probability, in fact beyond the .001 level. For the towns of the Zacatecas auctions, a similar calculation, based on 147 sales, yields a trend line with a slope of .27. (See Graph 4.24.) With a t value of 13.8 for 145 degrees of freedom, this result too lies beyond the .001 level.

In terms of annual weighted average prices, that is, for each year, dividing the total number of chickens sold into the total price received, calculation of the trend by least squares yields lines with somewhat higher degrees of slope. That for the coastal towns, based on thirty-four items, is .27 (see Graph 4.25); that for the plateau towns, based on thirty-five items, is .36 (see Graph 4.26); and that for all of Nueva Galicia, based on thirty-five items, is .32 (see Graph 4.27). With *t* values of 12.1, 12.0, and 13.1, respectively, all results lie beyond the .001 level of probability. For the towns of the Zacatecas auctions, calculation of trend by annual weighted averages yields a slope of .20, less steep than that calculated on unit prices, an indication of the smoothing effect of averages. (See Graph 4.28.) With a *t* value of 6.54 and 32 degrees of freedom, this result also lies beyond the .001 level of probability.

Calculation of trend for individual towns once again demonstrates that the results for regions and for all of Nueva Galicia are composites of greater variation. Tepic, with data for thirty-two years–but with forty-four prices, because of division of the tribute in some years–yields a line with a slope of .30, somewhat greater than those lines for the coast calculated on either unit prices or annual weighted averages. (See Graph 4.29.) Similarly, Tlaquepaque, with data for thirty-eight years, yields a line with a slope of .48, very much steeper that those for the plateau calculated on either basis. (See Graph 4.30.) Trend lines were calculated for Nochistlán and Mezquituta in the Zacatecas towns (see Graphs 4.31 and 4.32), with slopes of .24 and .23, respectively–much lower than the trend for the Zacatecas region calculated on the basis of unit prices, but greater than the trend calculated by annual weightedaverages. With *t* values of 7.99, 10.78, 3.9, and 6.9, respectively, all these results lie beyond the .001 level of probability.

In terms of annual weighted averages, a rise from 0/0/3.28 in 1557 to 0/1/3.5 in 1594 yields a nearly five-fold increase (4.8). The increases for the coast and the plateau were similar, particularly if one averages the initial three years–1557-1559–and the last three years–1591-1594–to smooth out a great deal of variation in the former. Prices for chickens from the towns of the Zacatecas region exhibit the least increase, since they begin in 1558 with a very high price (0/0/10.2) and end with a distinctly lower average than either coast or plateau as a whole (0/1/0). Prices for chickens for the Zacatecas towns show averages for the years 1584 to 1594 of 0/1/0 uniformly, suggesting some kind of control of the market or collusion among the buyers without opposition from the royal treasury officials or the audiencia.

The reader will notice that prices for chickens are given only to the year 1594. That was the last year of a relatively free market in chickens. The dependence of the Spanish settlers upon a supply of chickens through the royal tribute, coupled with sharply rising prices for the fowls, led the Spanish to petition for what amounted to a system of rationing and price control. In reply, an order of the viceroy, dated 22 December 1594, directed that, instead of selling chickens due as royal tribute through auction, they be distributed to royal and Church officials and the *beneméritos de la republica* at a uniform value of one real per chicken. The order did not apply to auctions in Zacatecas. This order had interesting aspects: Clearly it suspended, in regard to chickens, the royal legislation for sale of all royal tribute in kind at public auction, although it does not seem to have been so regarded by contemporaries. It opened the royal tribute in chickens to royal officials who were barred from bidding in royal tribute auctions, and so gave them direct access to a supply they could only have gotten to previously through resale or illegal collusion. In effect, the Spanish upper class, government officials included, assured its supply at prices it was prepared to pay, to the detriment of the fisc, apparently with acquiescence of the Crown. The

Graph 4.20 Frijoles Unit Prices: Teocaltitlán

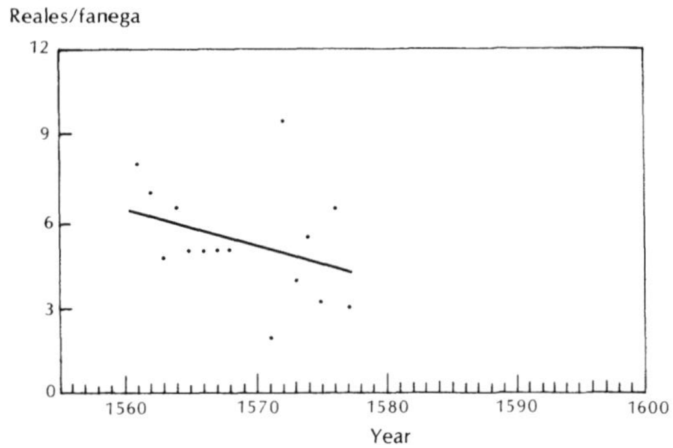

Graph 4.21 Chicken Unit Prices: Coast

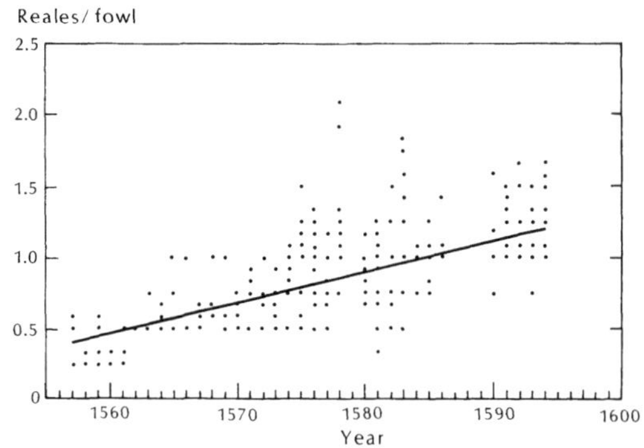

Graph 4.22 Chicken Unit Prices: Plateau

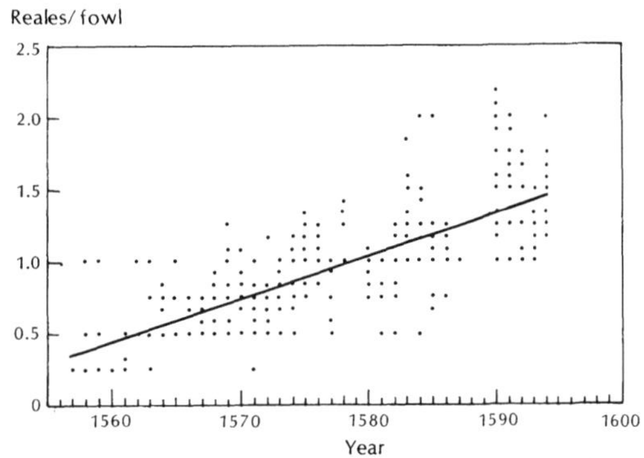

Graph 4.23 Chicken Unit Prices: All Towns

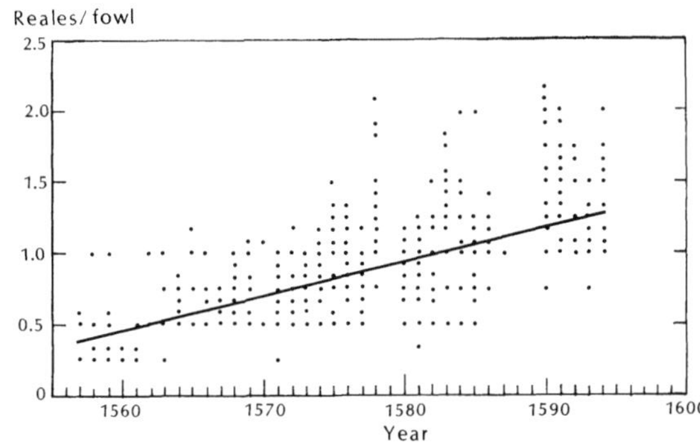

Graph 4.24 Chicken Unit Prices: Zacatecas

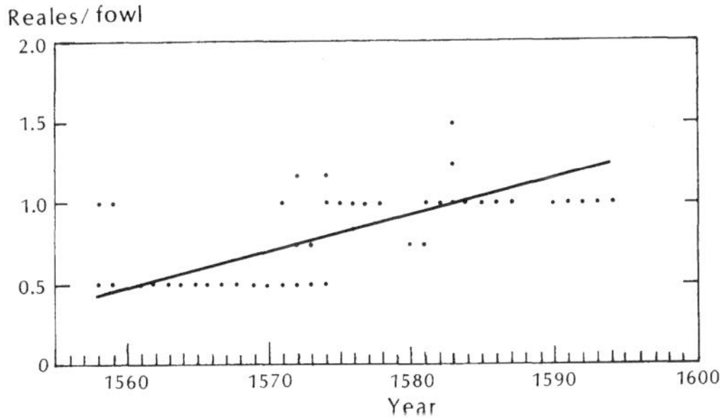

Graph 4.25 Chicken Annual Average Prices: Coast

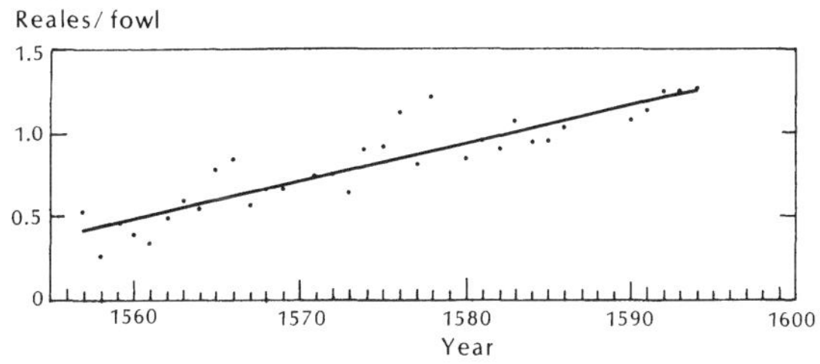

Graph 4.26 Chicken Annual Average Prices: Plateau

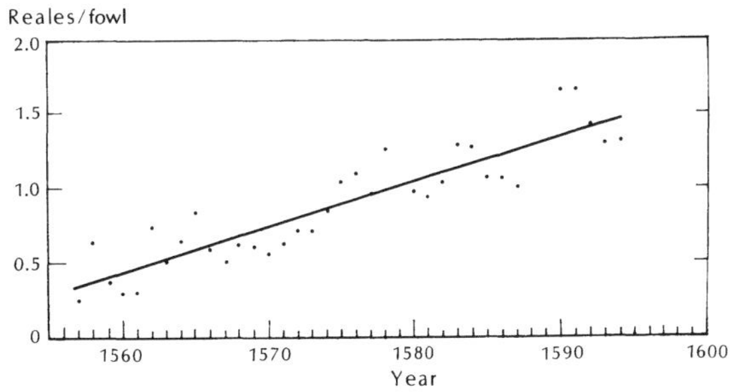

Graph 4.27 Chicken Annual Average Prices: All Towns

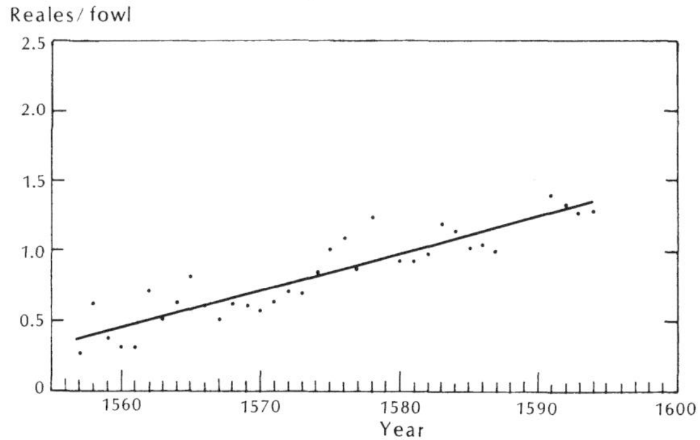

Graph 4.28 Chicken Annual Average Prices: Zacatecas

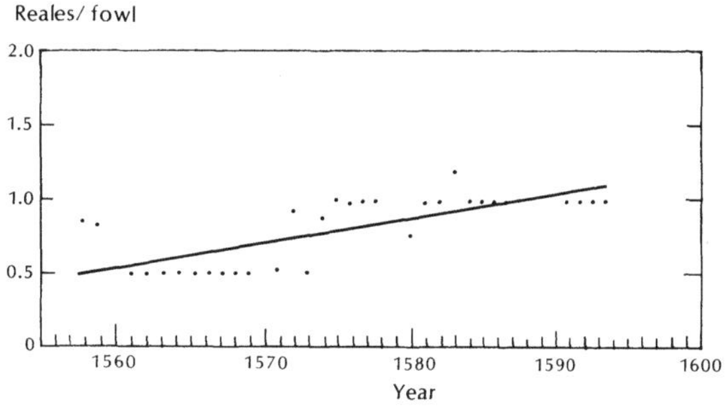

Graph 4.29 Chicken Unit Prices: Tepic

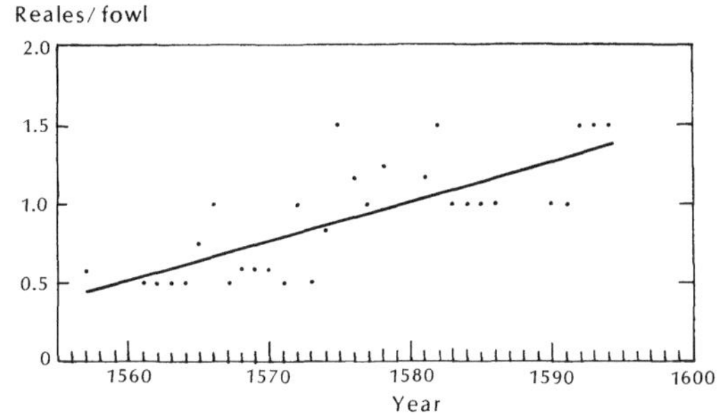

Graph 4.30 Chicken Unit Prices: Tlaquepaque

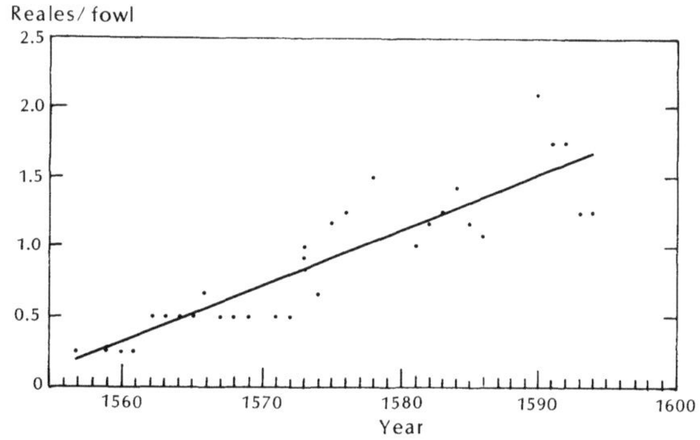

Graph 4.31 Chicken Unit Prices: Nochistlán

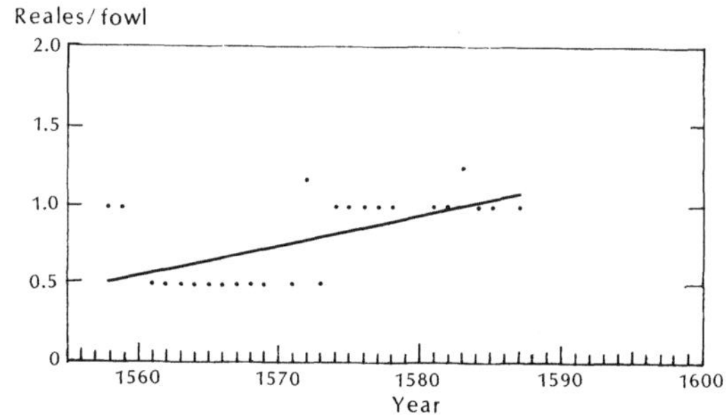

surviving books of treasury accounts in Guadalajara show entries for 1598-1599 indicating substantial distribution to the members of the audiencia. Dr. Santiago de Vera, the president, paid for 737 chickens from Analco, San Pedro Tlaquepaque, and Tonalá. The entries occur under almoneda receipts, maintaining the fiction of sale at public auction (by that fiction making clear the questionable legality of the practice).[12] The viceroy's order of 1594 preceded the distribution of maize to deserving Spaniards by five years. It was implemented for tributes due in 1595; one guesses that the order arrived in Guadalajara too late to affect the auctions for tribute due for 1594. With it, the fairly free market in royal tribute chickens came to a close.

One would like to compare the movement of prices for chickens in Nueva Galicia with that in New Spain. Unfortunately, the only data we possess to date on the value of chickens in New Spain are the few listed in Table 8 of the Borah and Cook price study.[13] No published study yet has added to that material. On the basis of the hazardous comparison possible, the data for New Spain suggest that in the Audiencia of Mexico chickens brought distinctly higher prices than in Nueva Galicia and that the upward trend continued into the seventeenth century, long after the Spanish upper class in Nueva Galicia had stabilized the price of the fowls to its members at the expense of the royal treasury.

TURKEYS

Turkeys were the domesticated fowl native to Mesoamerica, which both competed with and complemented chickens. In central Mexico, a customary relation of two-chickens-equal-one-turkey prevailed,[14] although doubtless with numerous exceptions, but in Nueva Galicia the relation varied much more, from one-to-one to as high as several chickens for one turkey. The two Spanish authors of the *relación geográfica* for the province of Tenamaztlán, dated 28 November 1579, reported that at that time, customarily,

> q[ue] dan tres gallinas ponedores por dos to[mines], y tres pollos por un tomín, muy buenos. Las gallinas desta tierra también se crian y multiplican muy bien; valen a dos reales y, los gallos, a tres.[15]
>
> [that they give three laying hens for two tomines, and three chickens for one tomin, [all] very good. Turkeys are also raised; they multiply very well. The turkey hens are worth two reales and the cocks, three.]

---

[12]Charles V and the Princess Regent, Valladolid, 12 May 1551, *Recopilación de leyes de los reynos de Indias*, 6.5.44; accounts of 1596, AGI, Contaduría, leg. 859B. The order did not include the Zacatecas towns, but the uniform price for chickens from those towns from 1584 on suggests that an earlier order had instituted the same system there, but the record is missing. GBPE, Archivo de la Real Audiencia, Ramo Fiscal, exp. 3, Cuentas 1598-1599, ff. 77f-85v.

[13]Borah and Cook, *Price Trends*, p. 79.

[14]Ibid., p. 38.

[15]Acuña, ed., *Relaciones geográficas*, 10: 289. The province of Tenamaztlán was in the Audiencia of Mexico, bordering Nueva Galicia and close to Guadalajara.

Graph 4.32 Chicken Unit Prices: Mezquituta

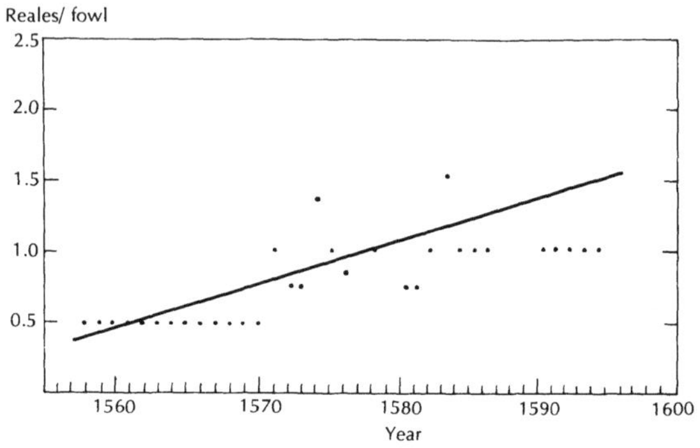

Graph 4.34 Turkey Unit Prices: Plateau

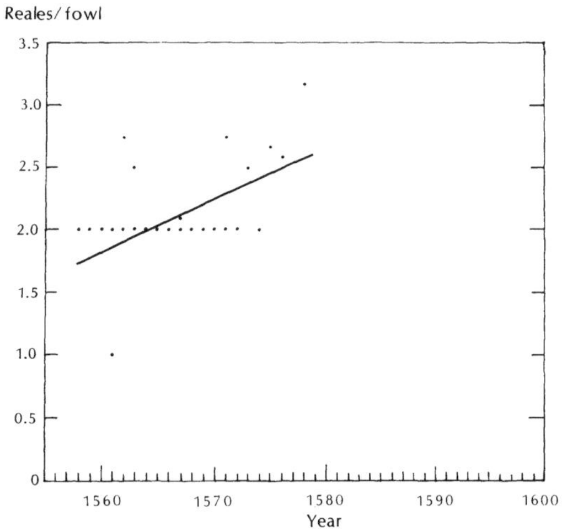

Graph 4.33 Turkey Unit Prices: Coast

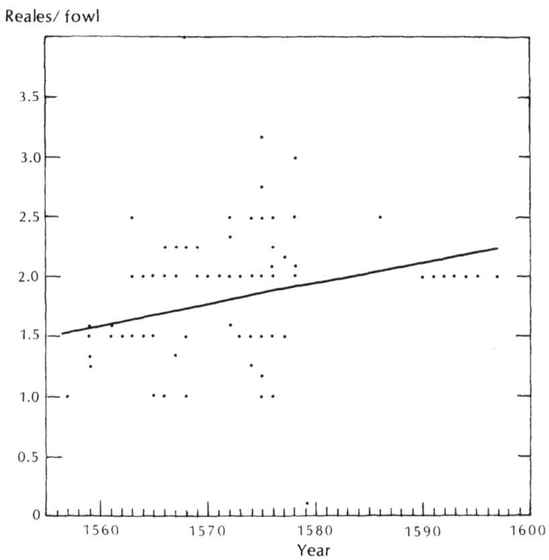

Graph 4.35 Turkey Unit Prices: All Towns

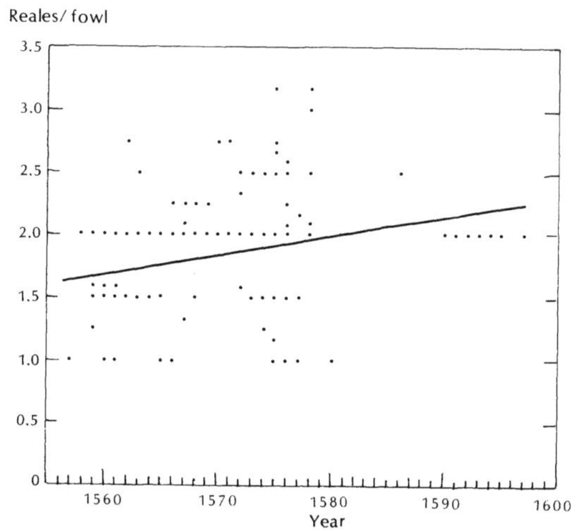

Graph 4.36 Turkey Unit Prices: Zacatecas

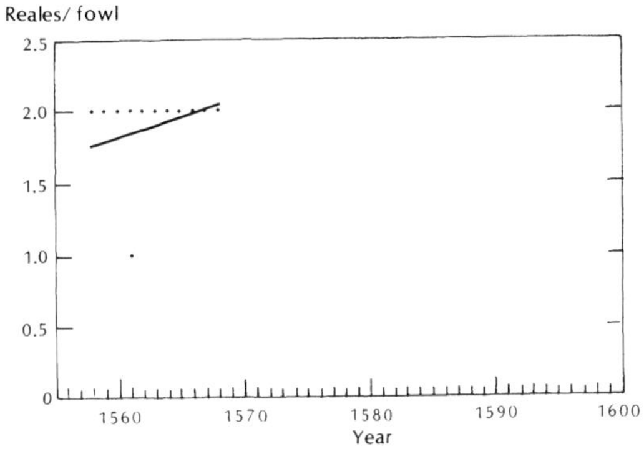

Graph 4.37 Turkey Annual Average Prices: Coast

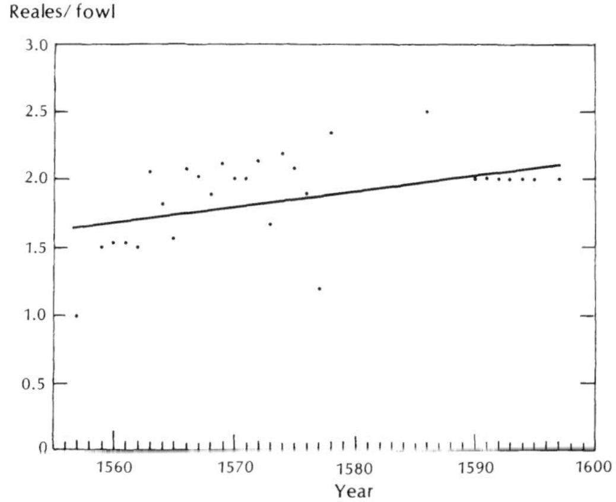

Graph 4.38 Turkey Annual Average Prices: Plateau

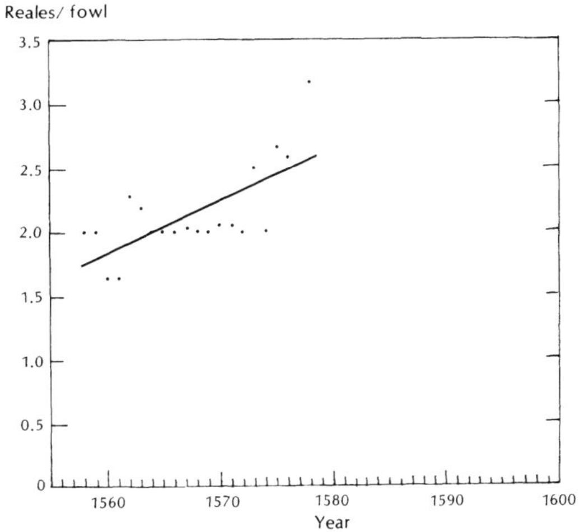

Graph 4.39 Turkey Annual Average Prices: All Towns

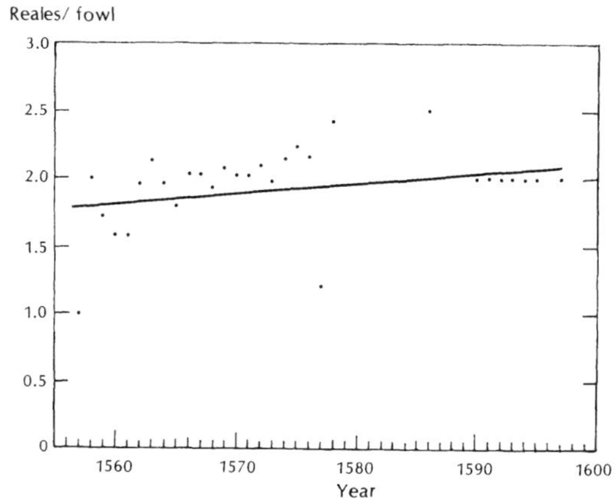

Graph 4.40 Turkey Annual Average Prices: Zacatecas

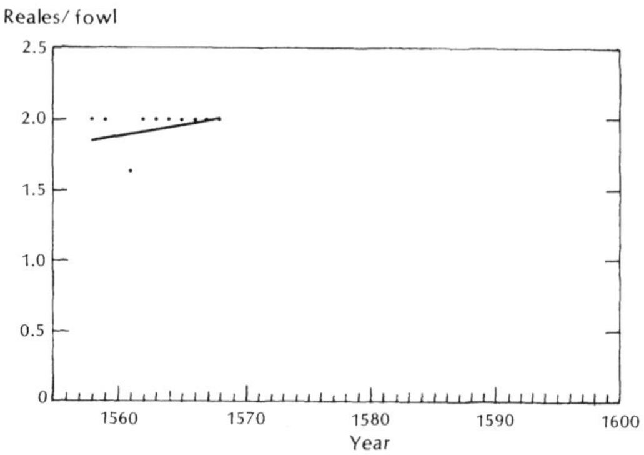

Graph 4.41 Turkey Unit Prices: Tepic

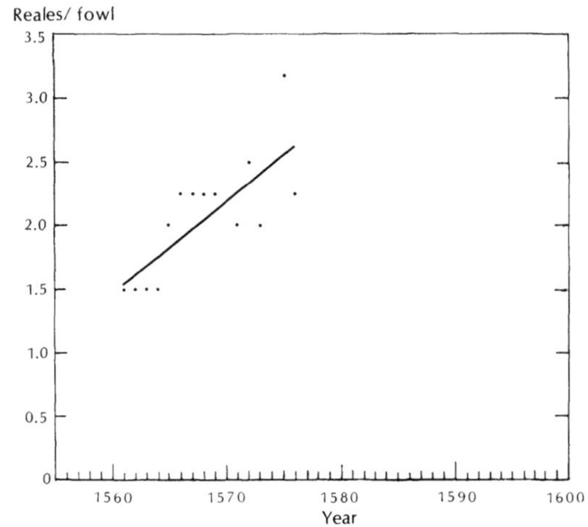

Graph 4.42 Turkey Unit Prices: Tonalá

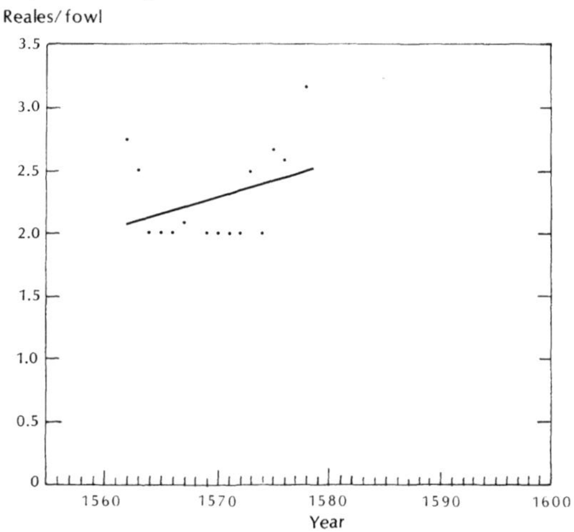

Graph 4.43 Turkey Unit Prices: Nochistlán

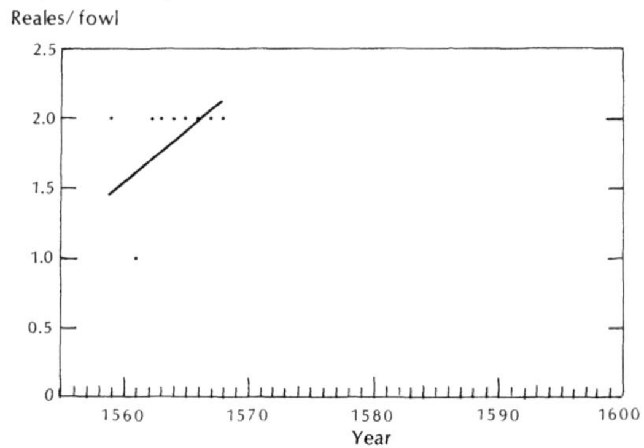

Their account works out to six chickens for a turkey hen and nine chickens for the male. How widely beyond the province this customary relation extended, we do not know.

The number of turkeys entering the royal tribute auctions annually was considerably smaller than the number of chickens. They figure far more prominently in the tributes of coastal towns than in those of the plateau. Prices paid at the auctions peaked in 1578 and 1586, with a rapidly contracting supply, but soon thereafter sank to a value of 0/2 per bird. The price became so uniform that even in the absence of other evidence, one suspects some arrangement like the set price of 0/1 per chicken instituted in 1594. If so, it would have been instituted with the turkeys due in tribute in 1590. The chicken/turkey ratio in these set prices adhered to the custom of New Spain.

Like the graphs for chickens, those for the unit prices of turkeys show a pronounced rise. The slope of the graph for the coast at .209, with 163 items (see Graph 4.33); that for the plateau at .498, with forty-two items (see Graph 4.34); and that for the whole of Nueva Galicia at .182, with 205 items (see Graph 4.35), all lie beyond the .001 percent level of confidence, with *t* values of 3.7, 8.98, and 3.5, respectively. The graph for the unit prices of turkeys for the Zacatecas towns (see Graph 4.36), based on twenty-one items, yields a slope of .339, which with a *t* value of 1.3 lies at the 20-percent level of confidence.

Calculation of trend in terms of annual weighted averages yields somewhat different results. The graph for the coast, based on thirty items (see Graph 4.37), yields a slope of .139, distinctly less than the graph for unit values, with a *t* value of 2.3, that is, with a level of confidence between .05 and .02; that for the plateau, based on twenty items (see Graph 4.38), shows a slope of .487, close to the slope of the trend line calculated by unit value, with a *t* value of 4.0, lying beyond the .001 level of confidence. That for all of Nueva Galicia, based on averages for thirty-one years (see Graph 4.39), has a slope of .088, much less steep than that calculated by unit value, with a *t* value of 1.5, or between the .2 and .1 level of confidence. The graph for Zacatecas, based on eleven years (see Graph 4.40), has a slope of .197 with a *t* value of 1.2, between the .3 and .2 level of confidence. It is based on so few years that it probably should be discarded.

The trend lines for individual towns confirm the somewhat erratic results of the graphs for regions. That for Tepic, based on data for sixteen years (see Graph 4.41), yields a slope of .881, a steep rise, with a *t* value of 4.6, which for 14 degrees of freedom lies beyond the .001 confidence level. That for Tonalá, with data for fifteen years (see Graph 4.42), has a slope of .317, much less steep, with a *t* value of 1.3, at the .2 confidence level The graph for Nochistlán (see Graph 4.43), of the Zacatecas towns, based on data for ten years, shows a slope of .873, apparently very steep, with a *t* value of 1.7, or confidence level between .2 and .1. The graph for Nochistlán is somewhat puzzling, since it is based upon two low prices at 0/1 in the early years and the rest at 0/2. The trend line should halt at 1568.

5

COMMODITIES OF MORE IRREGULAR COURSE

A number of commodities sold at the auctions of royal tribute in kind did not have the irregular but fairly steady upward rise in price shown by maize, frijoles, chickens, and turkeys. Some represented attempts by the Spanish to derive through tribute crops that were ill-suited to the localities; others, items that changes in the economy of the Spanish colony and their Indian work force rendered obsolete. Of still others I can offer no explanation, but must hope that future scholars will pierce the mystery.

WHEAT

Wheat was an Old World grain, the staple in the Mediterranean and in most of Europe. Ground into flour, mixed with water, kneaded into dough, and baked, it became bread–in most European and Mediterranean languages, including Spanish, the basic foodstuff and the symbol of food itself. To the natives of the New World, wheat was unknown until introduced by Europeans. It had the advantage that it could be grown in drier areas, in which maize required irrigation, and that it tolerated lower temperatures. On the other hand, it had substantial disadvantages relative to maize. Its cultivation required plowing and harrowing the land through use of a plow pulled by draft animals–and those, in turn, meant hiring the instruments and the animals as well as employing a Spanish master worker. Even if these disadvantages were overcome, wheat yielded considerably less than maize per fanega sown. Moreover, the grain had to be milled into flour. For the Indians, these rational considerations, as well as the weight of tradition, taste, and custom, militated against the adoption of wheat. Their conquerors, wedded to a diet of bread, wine, and oil, tried to bring the Indians to cultivate wheat for Spanish supply by requiring it as tribute.[1] In effect, the course of prices of wheat in the royal tribute auctions tells the extent of success of that endeavor.

In terms of unit prices, the trend for the coast was steeply downward (see Graph 5.1), -2.70, until 1573, when wheat ceased to be an item in the tribute of the coastal towns. Our data consist of forty-four items, which yield a *t* value of 3.82 with 42 degrees of freedom, a value beyond the level of confidence of .001–i.e., the chances that this result is due to the random movement of the items is less than one in a thousand. For the royal towns in the uplands, the trend line for unit prices is mildly upward (.24) until data cease in 1586. (See Graph 5.2.) Based upon thirty items, *t* with a value of .41 and 28 degrees of freedom yields a confidence level between .7 and .6, so low that the trend line must be regarded as unreliable, or the result testimony to extreme variability in the data. For all towns in Nueva Galicia, we have seventy-four items. The trend line is mildly negative, -.164, a compromise between coast and plateau, with the greater number of items of the coast exerting more weight. (See Graph 5.3.) The value for *t*, -.39, with 72 degrees of freedom, has a confidence level of .7, that is, the chances that the trend calculated is due to random action are 70 percent. If the number of items in our data on wheat is compared with that on maize, 74 as against 1,996, the scant success of the Spaniards in bringing the Indians to supply them with wheat is evident.

Calculation of annual weighted averages essentially corroborates the calculation by unit prices. In terms of annual weighted averages, the coastal towns, items now reduced to fifteen, show a trend line again negative at -1.59. (See Graph 5.4.) With a value of -2.0 and 13 degrees of freedom, *t* yields a confidence level between .05 and .1, still highly reliable, although somewhat less so than the calculation by unit prices. The plateau towns, with their longer period of tribute in wheat, yield twenty-nine annual weighted averages. These show a mildly upward trend of .221. (See Graph 5.5.) However, *t* is .378, which with 27 degrees of freedom lies at about the .7 level of confidence. Calculation of annual weighted averages for all of Nueva Galicia yields a trend line that is mildly upward. (See Graph 5.6.) With a value for *t* of .72and 27 degrees of freedom, the calculation lies at a confidence level of between .5 and .4.

Calculation of trend lines for data on towns, of course, bears out those of the regions. Tepic, for which we have fifteen items, shows a trend fairly steeply downward, -4.13, with a value for *t* of -2.76, which with 13 degrees of freedom stands at a confidence level of .02 or slightly better. (See Graph 5.7.) Tequila, on the plateau, with thirty items, shows a mildly upward movement, .24 (see Graph 5.8), but with a value for *t* of .41 and 28 degrees of freedom stands at a confidence level between .7 and .6, testifying to the fluctuations in annual prices.

On the whole, the data on wheat prices derived from the royal tribute auctions are too scanty for reliable statistical results. Oddly enough, the ill-fated attempts to cultivate wheat in the coastal region yield the greater number of items and the more reliable result. By 1586 the Spanish abandoned their attempt to derive a supply of

---

[1]Borah and Cook, *Price Trends*, pp. 19-21; Chevalier, pp. 58-78.

Graph 5.1 Wheat Unit Prices: Coast

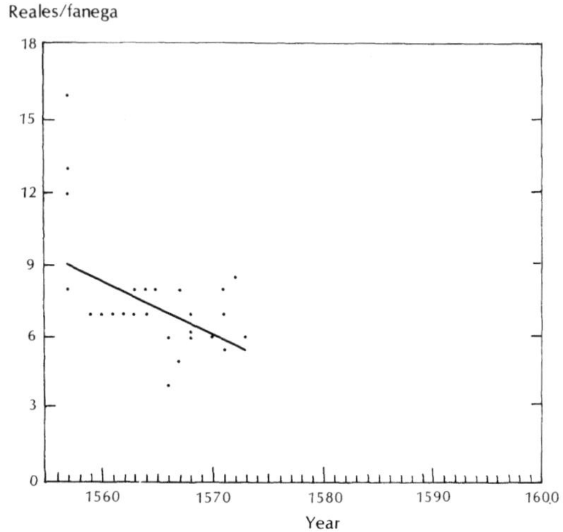

Graph 5.2 Wheat Unit Prices: Plateau

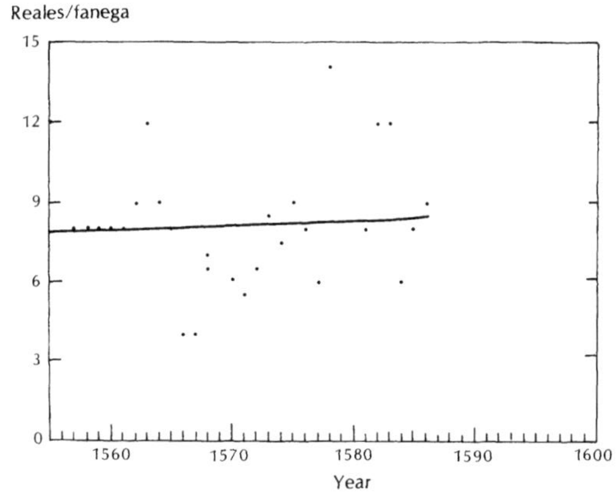

Graph 5.3 Wheat Unit Prices: All Towns

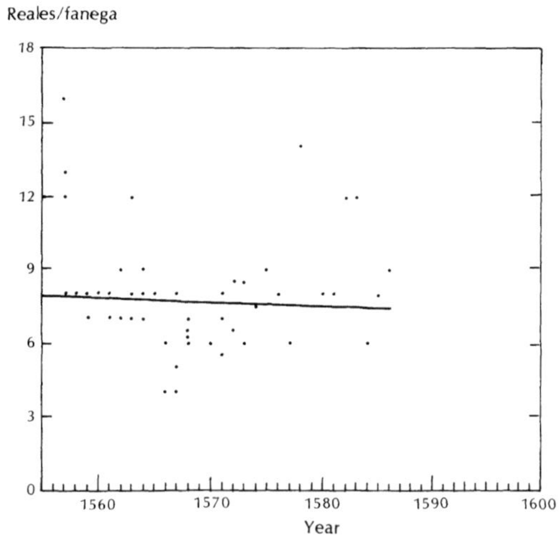

Graph 5.4 Wheat Annual Average Prices: Coast

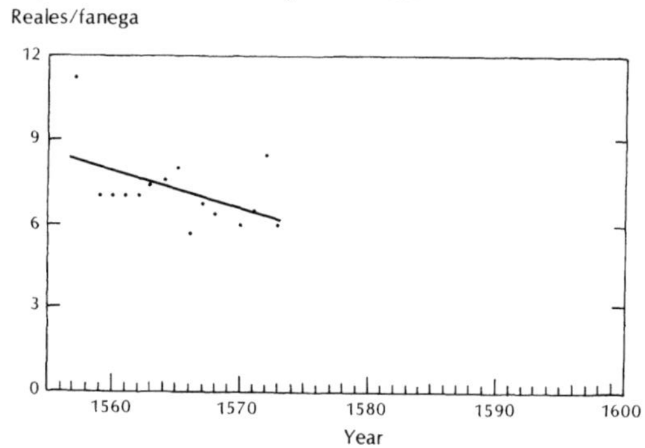

Graph 5.5 Wheat Annual Average Prices: Plateau

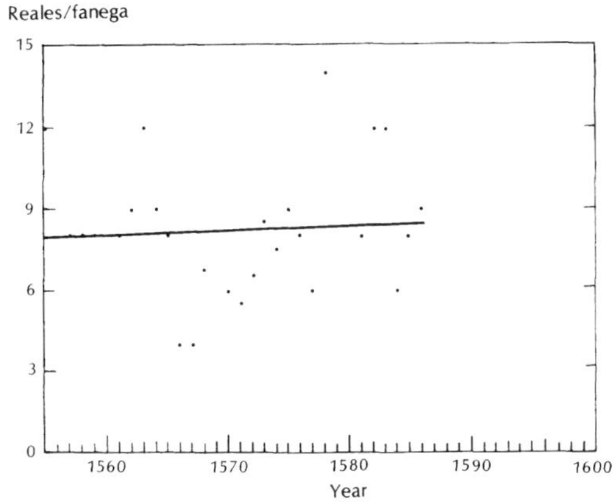

Graph 5.6 Wheat Annual Average Prices: All Towns

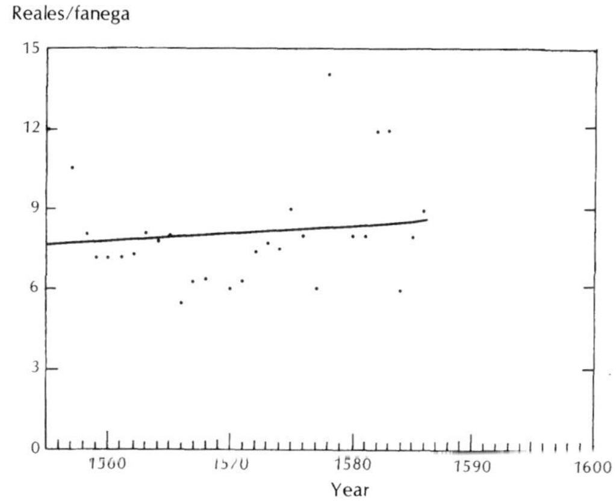

Graph 5.7 Wheat Unit Prices: Tepic

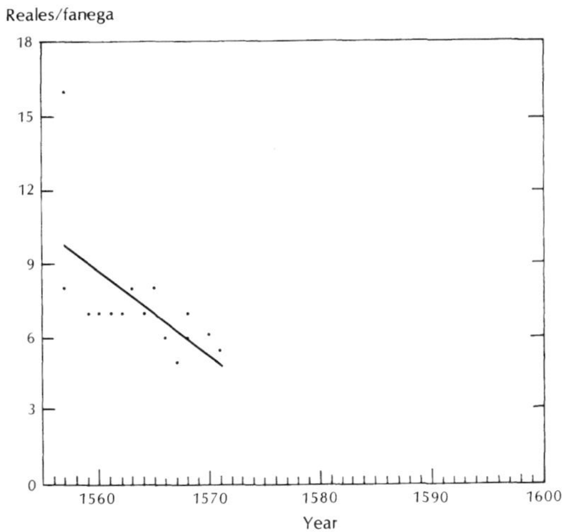

Graph 5.8 Wheat Unit Prices: Tequila

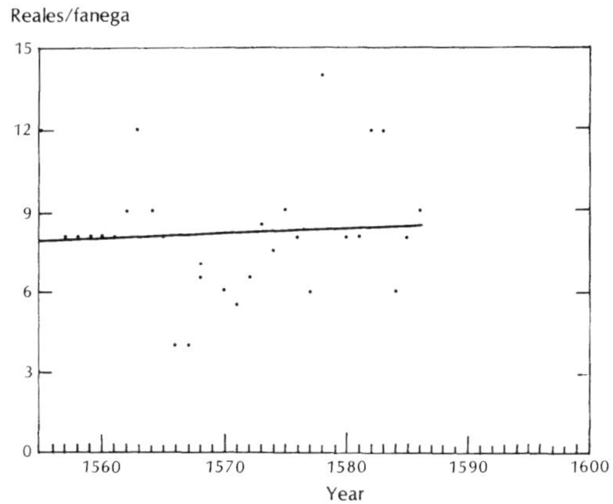

wheat from Indian tribute, if one may judge by the royal towns. Instead, they developed the cultivation of wheat on their own estates, particularly in the valley of Tlala, west of Guadalajara, which quickly became famous for an abundant and excellent supply more than sufficient for their needs.[2] Zacatecas, the greater market, never depended upon Indian tribute from Nueva Galicia for wheat but instead secured its supplies from the Audiencia of Mexico, especially Michoacán, and from estates established by its own miners and merchants in the oases near the mining *reales*. Vacant land, irrigation, and relatively cheap transportation by cart made the ventures successful.[3] The ownership of these enterprises was Spanish, the labor Indian and, in this period to a lesser extent, Black and various racial mixtures.

Comparison of prices for wheat with those of maize indicates that the two grains did not maintain a steady price ratio. In 1557, at the beginning of our period, the weighted average price of wheat was over five times that of maize, whether due to temporary shortage or some other phenomenon we do not know. From that high point, the value of wheat relative to maize quickly declined. In 1559 the ratio was 2.26/1, by 1562 a surprising 1.46/1, by 1573, 1.26/1, and by 1586, the last year from which we have wheat data, a mere 1.13/1.[4] The earlier premium on wheat was almost gone, perhaps because of the abundant supplies from Spanish enterprises.

Comparison with the course of wheat prices in central Mexico, which is possible through the Borah and Cook study of the years to 1573, indicates that the long-term trend of wheat prices in the two jurisdictions differed substantially. In central Mexico, during the years of our period, wheat prices rose fairly steadily and somewhat more rapidly than maize prices. "In 1573 the long-term value for wheat was to the long-term value for maize as 10.1:4.8, slightly higher than the 2:1 ratio used by the treasury. Equally clearly, the disparity was increasing."[5] The very different experience of Nueva Galicia testifies to the success of the Spanish in creating a source of supply that increased more rapidly than the consuming population, despite the demands of Zacatecas and its mines.

CHILE

The native American condiment chile, or ají, does not figure as an important item in the royal tributes. We have only nineteen sales, for the years 1557 to 1578, when chile ceased to show up in the tribute lists. Eighteen of the sales are for the joint tribute of two towns in the Zacatecas tribute province, Teocaltiche and Teocaltitlán. The prices tend to be erratic, but in general show a tendency to decrease. The graph for the eighteen sales from the towns in the Zacatecas province shows a fairly sharply negative slope of -3.43 (see Graph 5.9); with a *t* value of -3.28 and 16 degrees of

---

[2]Mota y Escobar, pp. 305-306; Arregui, p. 71.

[3]Bakewell, pp. 58-68; Relación de las minas del Fresnillo, 1 January-7 February 1585; Relación de las villas de San Martín y Llerena, y de su partido, 6 February 1585; in Acuña, 10: 107-109, 113, 121, 130; and 257; López de Velasco, pp. 137-138; Powell, pp. 18-27; Chevalier, pp. 216-222.

[4]See the tables of annual weighted average prices for maize and wheat in Appendix C.

[5]Borah and Cook, *Price Trends*, pp. 21-23 and 60-61.

Graph 5.9 Chile Unit Prices: Zacatecas

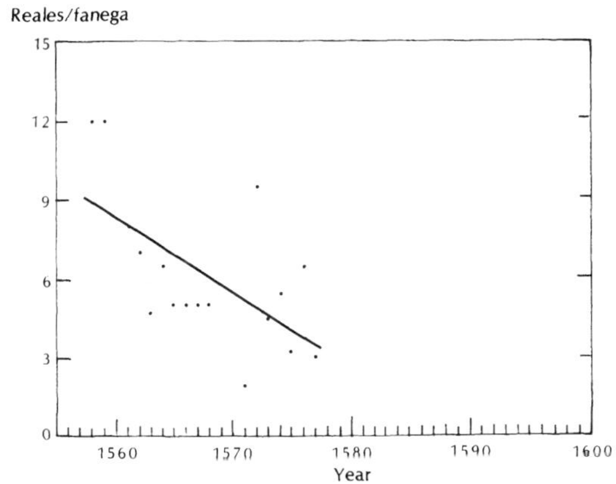

Graph 5.10 Chile Unit Prices: All Towns

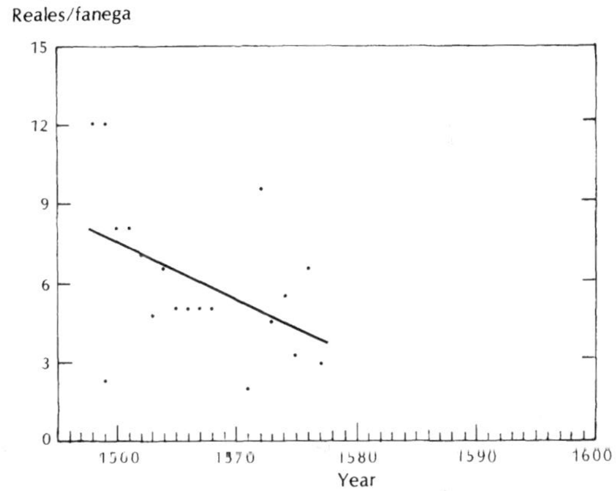

Graph 5.11 Chile Annual Average Prices: All Towns

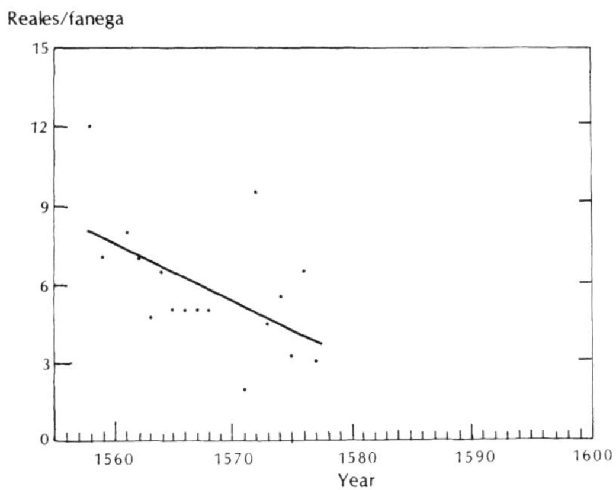

Graph 5.12 Honey Unit Prices: Coast

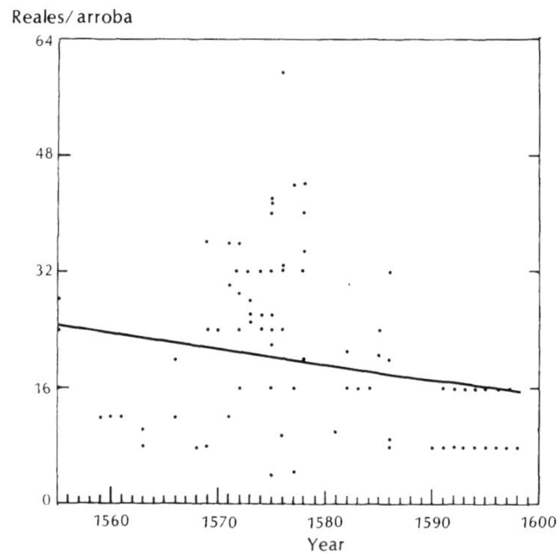

Graph 5.13 Honey Unit Prices: All Towns

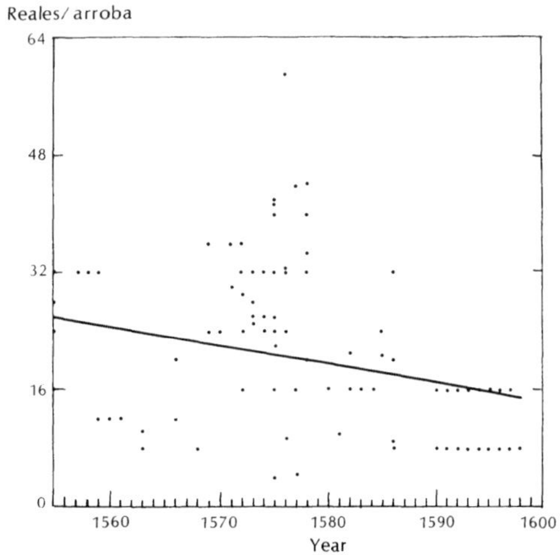

Graph 5.14 Honey Annual Average Prices: Coast

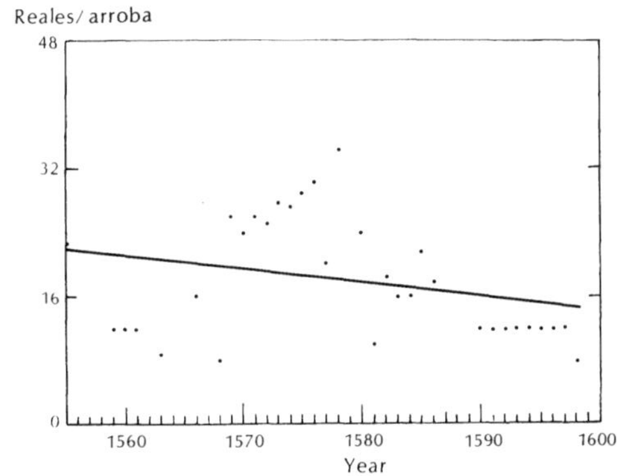

Graph 5.15 Honey Annual Average Prices: All Towns

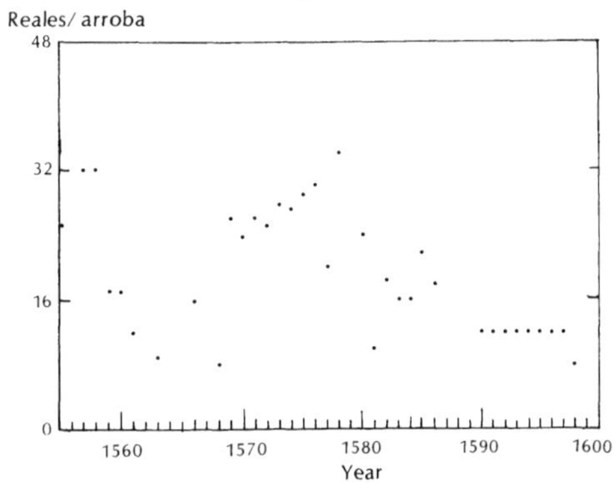

Graph 5.16 Honey Unit Prices: Quilitlán

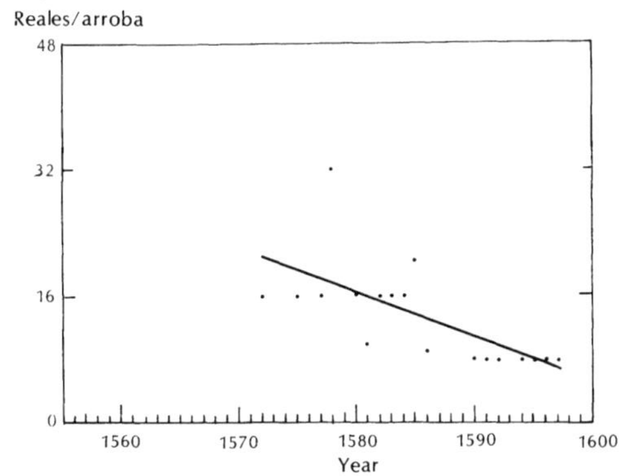

Graph 5.17 Honey Unit Prices: Papachula

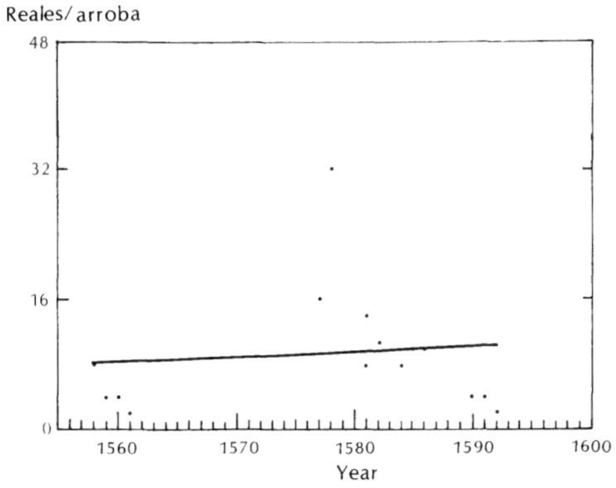

Graph 5.18 Honey Unit Prices: Tequila

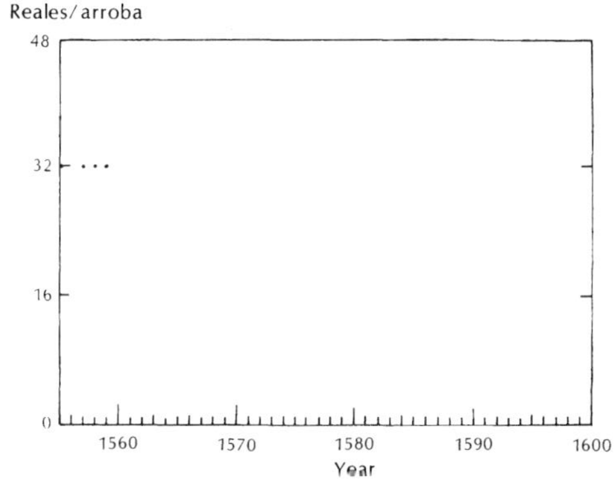

Graph 5.19 Fish Unit Prices: Coast

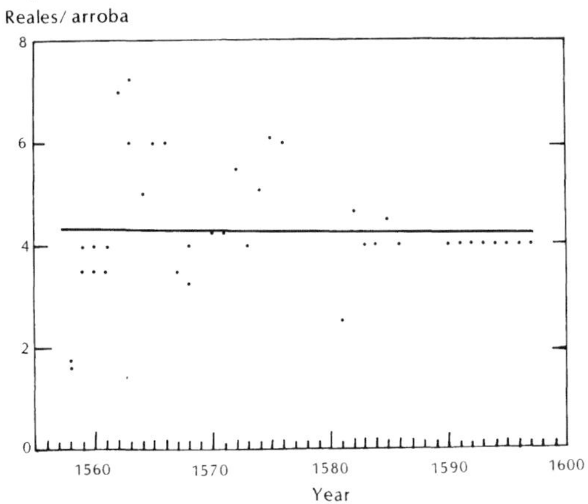

Graph 5.20 Fish Annual Average Prices: Coast

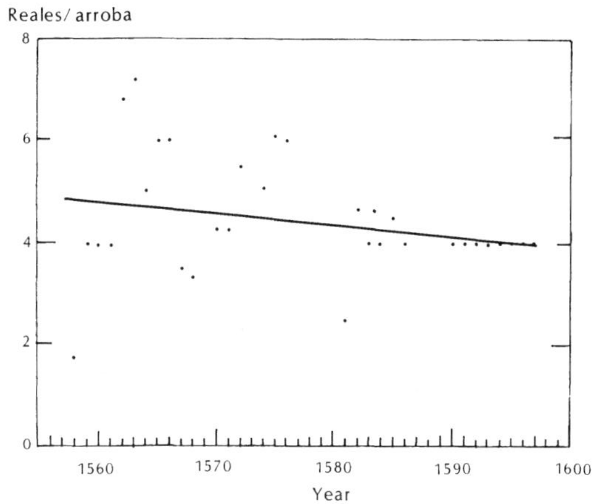

freedom, it lies at a confidence level of one percent. The graph for the unit prices in all of Nueva Galicia, which adds one more item, detracts somewhat from this result. It has a less negative slope, but still a definite one, at -2.61. (See Graph 5.10.) With a value for *t* of -2.25 and 17 degrees of freedom, it lies very near the .2 level of confidence, a somewhat less reliable result. Calculation of annual weighted averages, which only changes the value for one year, 1559, yields a result in the same general range as the others above. The trend line for all of Nueva Galicia, based on eighteen items, has a negative slope of -2.68 (see Graph 5.11); with a value for *t* of -2.8 and 16 degrees of freedom, it lies between the confidence level of .02 and .01.

On the whole, the data on chile are too few for adequate results. On the other hand, these nineteen sales are all that we have at this point for Nueva Galicia, compared to none for central Mexico.

HONEY

Honey was an important sweetener in both the Spanish and Indian diet. Its competitor, sugar, was an Old World crop, introduced by the Europeans. As the supply from sugar cultivation and manufacture gradually increased, it displaced honey for most purposes. Throughout our period the Spanish derived a supply of honey through tributes, but as the royal tribute auctions indicate, by 1598 it was diminishing into insignificance. For that year, honey from only one town figured in the royal auctions. For the entire period we have relatively abundant data: 128 prices. With the exception of five from Tequila, all come from the coast, an indication that, as an item of Indian tribute, it was a coastal product, even though beekeeping could certainly have been carried on on the plateau. It was probably produced by the native stingless bee, but in the later years may have involved the Old World stinging bee, a more prolific producer.

For the coast we have 123 prices. They reached a particularly wide dispersion in the years 1568-1578. For the forty-two years of our period, whatever annual vagaries, the general tendency of the trend line is downward. Prices reached a relative low in the 1590s, when they settled at 2/ and 1/ the arroba. The slope of the trend line is -2.49, moderately downward. (See Graph 5.12.) The value for *t*, with 121 degrees of freedom, stands at -2.45, or a confidence level of between .02 and .01, distinctly reliable. Addition to the calculation of the five prices for the plateau yields a trend line with a slightly more pronounced downward slope of -3.02 (see Graph 5.13) and a value for *t* of -3.19, which with 126 degrees of freedom yields a confidence level beyond .01.

Calculation by annual weighted averages lessens the dispersion of unit prices. For the coast, based on data for thirty-three years, the slope of the trend line is slightly less negative at -2.08 (see Graph 5.14); and a *t* value of -1.67, which with 31 degrees of freedom stands at a confidence level of .1, is indicative rather than fully reliable. Adding the plateau to the calculated averages yields a trend line for all of Nueva Galicia, based on data for thirty-five years (see Graph 5.15), with a slope of -3.46, much more sharply negative, which with a value for *t* of -3.11 for 33 degrees of freedom lies beyond the confidence level of .01.

Calculation of trends for individual towns bears out the regional calculations but again emphasizes that they are composites of individual trends. Quilitlán, with data for eighteen years, shows a very sharply downward trend, with a slope of -6.71. (See Graph 5.16.) With a value for *t* of -3.66 and 16 degrees of freedom, the calculation enjoys a confidence level beyond .01. Papachula, another coastal town, based on data for sixteen years, shows a trend line with a slope of .38, slightly upward, and contrary to the general regional tendency. (See Graph 5.17.) Its *t* value of .389 with 14 degrees of freedom, however, stands at .7, testimony to highly erratic annual variation. The one plateau town furnishing data, Tequila, with five prices for five years, all the same, shows a trend line that is absolutely flat. (See Graph 5.18.) The computer finds neither slope nor value for *t*.

Comparison with prices of honey in central Mexico is at this point impossible since the very few prices published to date are for years earlier than our period.[6]

DRIED FISH

In officially devoutly Roman Catholic Nueva Galicia, religious observance required the population to avoid eating meat on days of abstinence.[7] Accordingly, sixteenth-century tribute schedules provided that the Indians furnish as *comida* suitable foods for abstinence during such days. Although *comida* disappeared from tribute schedules in the initial years of our period,[8] dried fish and fish products remained as a requirement of annual tribute for a number of royal coastal towns until 1585. In dried and salted form, fish could be preserved safely without refrigeration (almost completely unknown) and transported to inland markets for sale. The tribute category was a general one that may have included dried seafood like shrimp. We cannot be sure.

The price data for dried fish from the royal auctions in Nueva Galicia include forty-four items, of which twenty come from Ixtapa and eighteen from Sentispac. These towns obviously were the principal suppliers. Calculation by unit price yields a slightly negative trend, with a slope of -.033. (See Graph 5.19) Dispersion of the prices is so great that the value for *t* of -.188, with 42 degrees of freedom, stands at a level of confidence between .8 and .9. Calculation of annual weighted averages, of which there are thirty-three, yields a trend line of -.259, more negative than the calculation by unit prices. (See Graph 5.20) With a value for *t* of -1.34 and 31 degrees of freedom, the calculation enjoys a confidence level somewhat better than .2.

Trend lines for the two major towns providing the dried fish show comparable results. Ixtapa, with prices for twenty years, shows a mildly positive slope of .211. (See Graph 5.21.) With a *t* value of 1.26 and 18 degrees of freedom, it stands at a confidence level between .2 and .3. Sentispac, with prices for eighteen years, yields a trend line with a much more positive upward slope of .756. (See Graph 5.22.) However, the calculation has a value for *t* of 1.06, which with 16 degrees of freedom

[6] Borah and Cook, *Price Trends*, p. 80.

[7] That is, until the papal dispensation permitting the eating of meat on most days of abstinence.

[8] Borah, "Los tributos y au recaudación," pp. 30-37.

lies below the confidence level of .3, a slightly poorer result than the calculation for Ixtapa.

Unit prices and annual weighted average prices for dried fish show very great variation from year to year. Since this was a product not dependent upon the regime of rains, although it was upon oceanic temperatures and currents and human energy, we cannot be sure of the factors involved. We have no comparable data for these years from the Audiencia of Mexico.

OYSTERS

Oysters were furnished by Sentispac alone among the royal towns. Whether in dried form or fresh we do not know, but can guess, in view of the dangers of eating raw oysters in the absence of refrigeration, that they were dried. We have, in all, prices for eighteen years, from 1558 to 1576. The trend line has a decidedly upward slope of 1.797. (See Graph 5.23.) With a value for *t* of 1.84 and 16 degrees of freedom, it has a confidence level between .1 and .05, moderately reliable, and here a testimony to consistency.

SALT

Salt received as tribute came from towns on the seashore. Part was used to season and preserve food, the latter use especially important in an age when the only way to keep foods like meat and fish edible for more than a few days was to dry them or salt them, or both. Most of the salt garnered from the sea was used in the patio process of mercury amalgamation for extracting silver from its ore. Inland, miners turned to a much less pure salt for use in the patio process, derived from salt flats and salt lagoons. In this form, salt was a Crown monopoly, gathered by Indians paid and fed by the Crown and sold to miners at a price decided upon by the royal treasury. The royal monopoly, established in the 1570s, included some gathering of salt for royal account on the coast, since the treasury records list sales of sea salt in amounts both large and small, but the operations of the royal monopoly lay outside the tribute system. Sea salt derived as tribute was sold at public auction.[9] We must keep in mind that Nueva Galicia had two additional sources of salt through tribute to encomenderos and further Indian production for sale.

We have for royal tribute salt fifty-six sales, stretching through the whole of our period, for towns on the shore. In terms of unit prices, the trend line has a slope of

[9] See, for example, accounts of the sale of salt from Piloto for 1598, in GBPE, Archivo de la Real Audiencia, Ramo Fiscal, exp. 3, Cuentas, 1598-1599, f. 100f. The poorer-grade salt was sold for 0/5 the fanega, slightly more than the 0/4 obtained at public auction for tribute salt. See Relación de la villa de la Purificación, 12 January 1585, in Acuña, 10: 215 for an interesting account of the salt monopoly on the coast and the production of two grades of salt: *sal blanca* and *sal bermeja*. See Mota y Escobar, p. 341, for an account of the inland royal salt monopoly at Peñol Blanco. According to García-Abasolo, *Martín Enríquez y la reforma de 1568*, pp. 138-139, a report to Philip II, based on books for 1563-1576, indicated a production of 25,000 fanegas a year at Santa María and Peñol Blanco of the two grades, sold at 0/4 and 1/, respectively.

Graph 5.21 Fish Unit Prices: Ixtapa

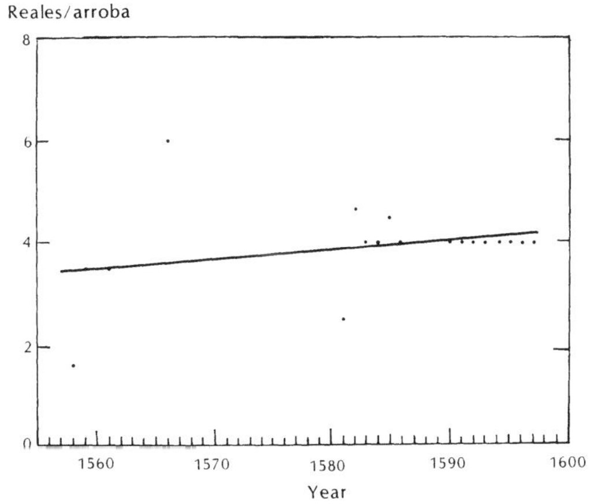

Graph 5.22 Fish Unit Prices: Sentispac

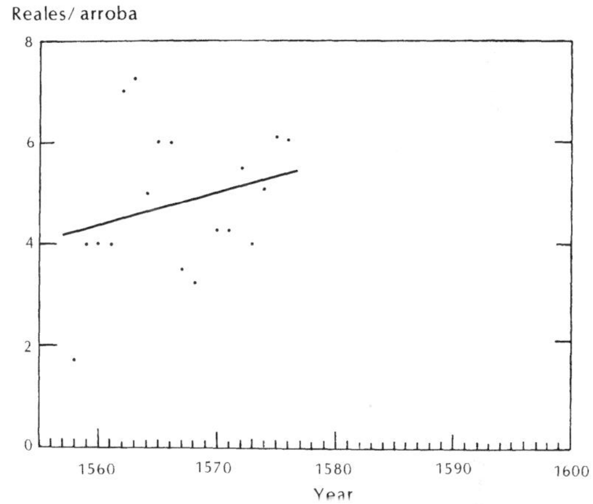

Graph 5.23 Oyster Unit Prices: Sentispac

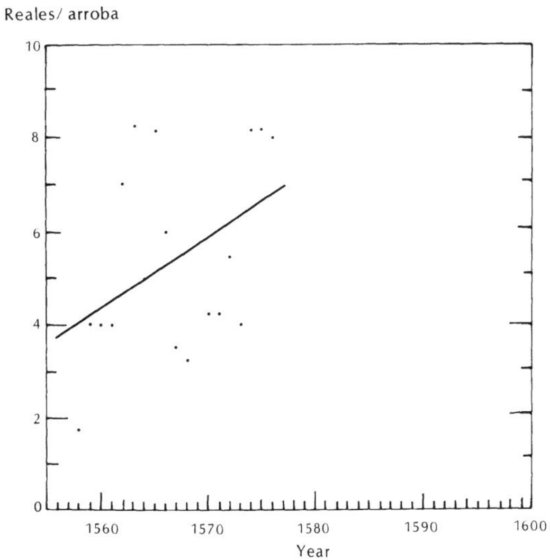

Graph 5.24 Salt Unit Prices: Coast

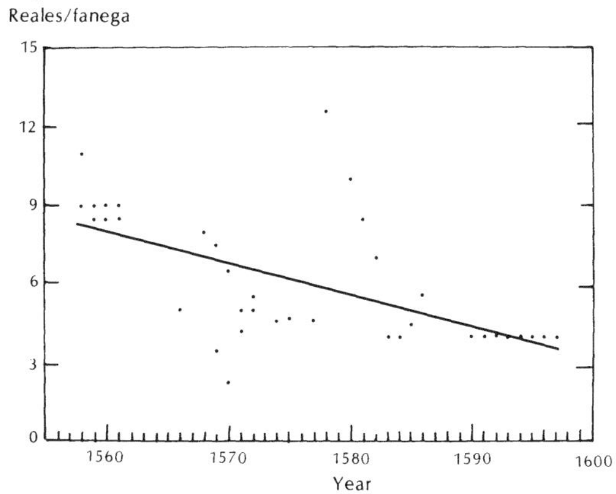

Graph 5.25 Salt Annual Average Prices: Coast

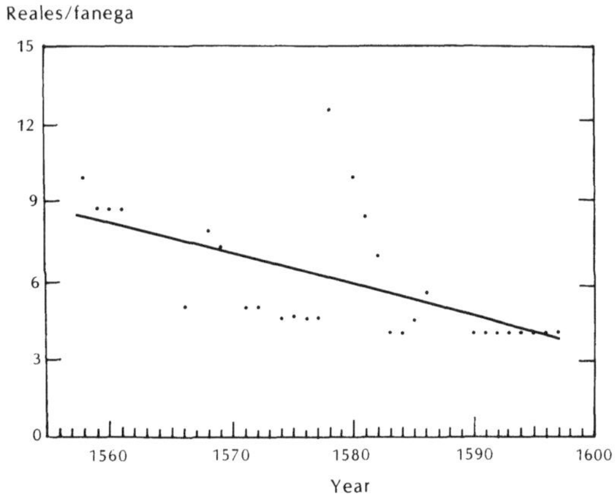

Graph 5.26 Cotton Unit Prices: Coast

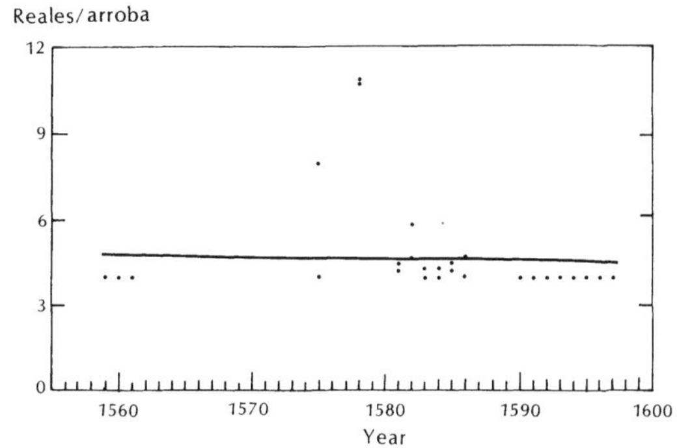

Graph 5.27 Cotton Annual Average Prices: Coast

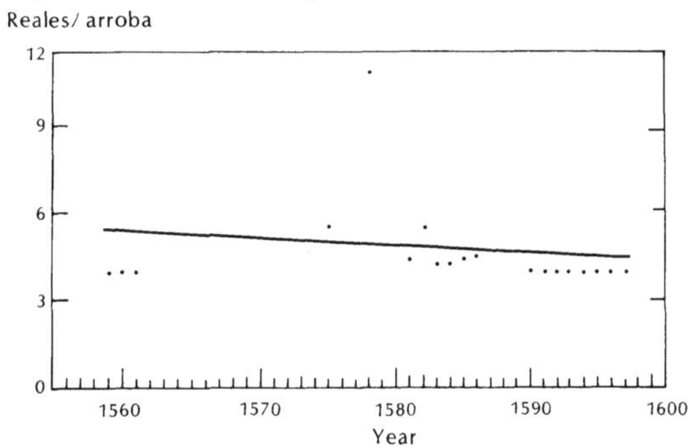

Graph 5.28 Cotton Unit Prices: Ixtapa

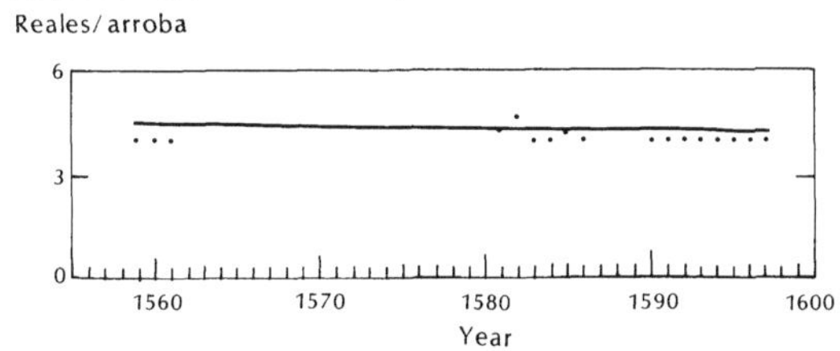

-1.437, moderately downward. (See Graph 5.24.) With a value for t of -6.14 and 54 degrees of freedom, the calculation has a confidence level of .001, extremely reliable. In the 1590s the prices at public auction were uniformly a fraction over four reales a fanega. Such regularity suggests that a customary price prevailed. Calculation by annual weighted average prices yields data for thirty years. The trend line resulting almost parallels that of unit prices (slope = -1.456). (See Graph 5.25.) The value for t of -3.97 with 28 degrees of freedom reaches a confidence level of .001, again extremely reliable. Starting at prices above a peso per fanega in the late 1550s, salt tended to fall to a uniform low price of slightly over four reales–half a peso–the fanega.

Comparison with the movement of prices of tribute sale in the Audiencia of Mexico is only possible through the scanty data in the Borah and Cook study. The highs in the Audiencia of Mexico are far higher than in Nueva Galicia, the lower prices distinctly lower.[10] Why, we simply do not know.

COTTON

Used in a number of ways–spun and woven into cloth or made into padding for protection against Indian weapons–cotton had great utility for the Spanish, who derived at least part of their supply from Indian tributes. The measure applied in the tribute schedules is the arroba of 25 Spanish pounds, slightly more than the equivalent number of pounds avoirdupois. Since the delivery was almost certainly of fiber cleaned of debris, seeds, and dirt, the tributes yielded substantial quantities for further processing. They came entirely from the coastal region, since the plateau was a less favorable area for the crop.

Our usable data on cotton prices from the royal auctions are lessened by the facts that in some years the tribute of coastal towns was sold in a lump sale, so that we cannot know the value given to individual items, and further that in other years cotton, instead of being sold, was diverted to making arms for royal troops engaged in Indian hostilities.[11] We have forty-four usable sales, covering the years 1559 to 1598. The gaps are particularly noticeable in the 1560s and 1570s. Calculation by unit prices yields a trend line which is virtually flat: slope is -.074, slightly negative but almost imperceptibly so. (See Graph 5.26.) The value for t of -.325 with 42 degrees of freedom gives a confidence level between .7 and .8, without significance. Calculation by annual weighted averages yields a result, based on values for twenty years, that is only slightly better. The trend line, with a slope of -.275, is somewhat more negative (see Graph 5.27), and the value for t of -.67 with 18 degrees offreedom stands at the confidence level of .5, more reliable than the calculation by unit values but indicative rather than conclusive.

---

[10]Borah and Cook, *Price Trends*, p. 78.

[11]Thus the auction records declare under date 14 January 1581 for Temichoque that the 5½ arrobas of cotton due, since they could not be sold, were employed in arms for use against the Chichimecs. See Appendix A under date indicated.

Graph 5.29 Cotton Unit Prices: Temichoque

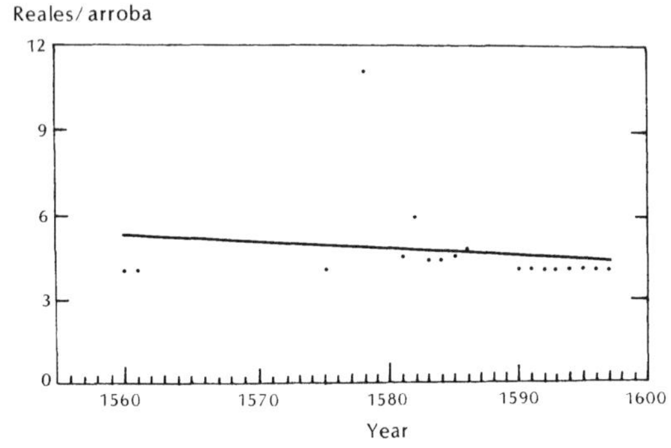

Graph 5.30 Cotton Unit Prices: Orita

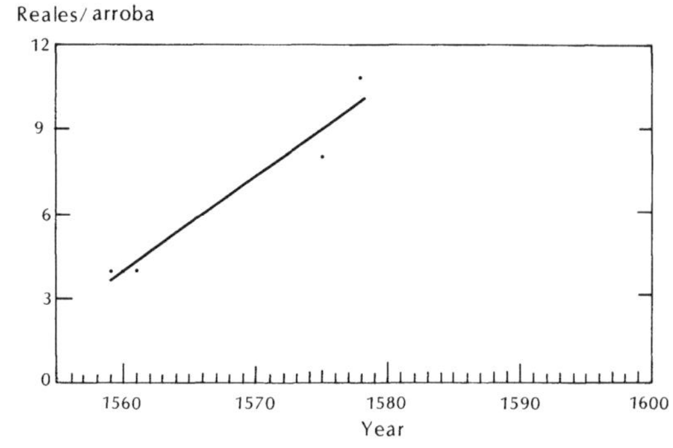

Graph 5.31 Cloth Unit Prices: Coast

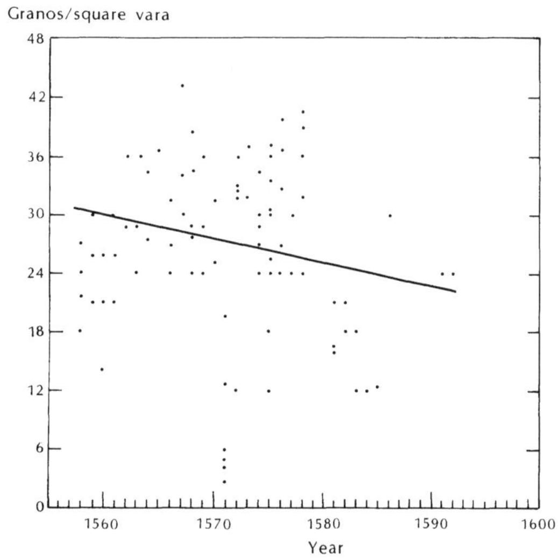

Calculations of trend for individual towns yield results that are widely disparate, demonstrating again that the trend for the region is a composite of differing trends for towns. Ixtapa, with data for eighteen years, has a trend line with a slope of -.081, slightly negative. (See Graph 5.28.) With a value for *t* of -.349 and 16 degrees of freedom, its confidence level between .7 and .8 is a testimony to the erratic annual values. Temichoque, also with data for eighteen years, has a trend line of -.313, distinctly more negative (see Graph 5.29), and a value for *t* of -.7 with 16 degrees of freedom, for a confidence level of .5. Orita, with data for only five years (see Graph 5.30), shows a trend line with a highly positive slope of 4.02 and a value for *t* of 7.65, which with 3 degrees of freedom stands at the confidence level of .01 and is the most consistent calculation of all those for cotton.

From 1590 to 1598 the price for cotton of the two royal towns still paying tribute in that commodity was 0/4. Such an invariable value again suggests some form of control of the market starting in 1590.

We have no data for our period from the Audiencia of Mexico for comparison.

COTTON CLOTH

Until perhaps 1578, one of the most important commodities that the Indians supplied to the Spaniards through tribute was cotton cloth in the form of mantas. *Manta* in common Mexican usage today means unbleached muslin, suggesting the kind and quality of cloth supplied in the sixteenth century. Natives–more usually women than men–working in time not allotted to other tasks, spun and then wove the cotton thread on a backstrap loom, such as is used even today, into strips of cloth, usually from two-thirds to seven-eighths of a Spanish vara wide (from 22 to 30 U.S. inches), but sometimes up to one vara, and of a length to suit their purpose. These strips, known as *piernas de manta*, were then sewn together along the edge to form a manta, the number and so the width varying according to the purpose. Unlike central Mexico, the tribute manta in Nueva Galicia seems to have been nearly, though not entirely, standardized at 4 x 4 varas, that is, 16 square varas. A few towns supplied larger mantas of 20 square varas; some, smaller ones of 12 square varas, and even a manta *pequeña*. Fortunately, the tribute schedules and at times the documents of sale specify the size of the manta.[12] It has been possible, therefore, to convert all prices to a value per square vara for uniform treatment. The only exceptions are the numerous sales that lumped all tribute of a town under a general price that could not be reduced to individual values, and the tribute in cloth of Sentispac. That town wove an unusually large manta of a heavy cloth like canvas, suitable for use as sails in Spanish vessels. Its mantas supplied the sails of many vessels in expeditions exploring the Pacific and those in coastwise traffic. Accordingly, they commanded special prices. For the purpose of our calculations, the Sentispac data have been segregated from those on cloth and treated separately.

---

[12]See the discussion in Borah and Cook, *Price Trends*, pp. 26-29 and 62-75; and Appendix A for Nueva Galicia. The tribute schedules occur throughout AGN, Contaduría, legs. 853, 856-861B, and 869A.

As in central Mexico, the introduction of sheep and the consequent production of wool led to the development of cloth weaving under Spanish control and an Indian shift to woolen cloth, since the plateau could produce its own supply of fiber and did not have to import it from the coast.[13] This tendency shows clearly in the number of royal towns supplying cotton cloth as tribute: by 1584 two and by 1592 one; thereafter, none.

For purposes of calculation, we have 177 prices. All are for the coast since the plateau towns produced no cotton and therefore paid no tribute in cotton cloth. All have been reduced to price per square vara. In unit terms, the trend line calculated is somewhat negative for the entire period (-.241) (see Graph 5.31), with the value for t at -3.348. With 175 degrees of freedom, this result lies at the level of confidence of .001 and must be regarded as solidly established. Our calculation in terms of unit prices is heavily influenced by the low prices from 1581 to 1592. If the calculation were for 1558 to 1578, the slope of the trend line would be upward.

Calculation of annual weighted averages confirms the calculation by unit prices. With data for thirty-one years, the slope of the trend line for the period is slightly more negative (-.311). (See Graph 5.32.) With a value for t of -2.58 and 29 degrees of freedom, the calculation stands at a confidence level between .02 and .01, still highly reliable.

Prices for cotton cloth, then, tended to rise in Nueva Galicia until 1578 and thereafter declined sharply, probably as wool became the preferred fiber for textiles. The trend in Nueva Galicia was similar to that in the Audiencia of Mexico, so far as the Borah and Cook data go—that is, to 1573. Our data for the years 1581 to 1592, showing the rapid decline of prices for cotton cloth in Nueva Galicia, would suggest that one should look for a somewhat similar development in the Audiencia of Mexico. The rise in price in the initial period may have been somewhat steeper in Nueva Galicia, since our data indicate an average value for a square vara of cotton cloth of 34.5 granos in 1570, whereas the Borah and Cook data for the Audiencia of Mexico indicate an average value there of 28 granos per square vara.[14] In Nueva Galicia the average price of a square vara of manta fell to a low of 12 granos in 1584, and thereafter rose to a final price of 24 granos in the years 1590-1592.[15]

SENTISPAC'S COTTON CLOTH

The town of Sentispac, on the coast of Nayarit, paid as tribute an unusually heavy, canvas-like cloth in large mantas, suitable for use as sails. As such, the cloth was sometimes reserved from auction for the use of royal expeditions, sometimes used for armor against hostile Indians, and sometimes sold to private purchasers. Because of its unusual character, data on cloth from Sentispac are not comparable to other data on tribute in cotton cloth and have been kept entirely separate for purposes of calculation. We have data only to 1581, when Sentispac ceased to pay tribute in

[13] Borah and Cook, *Price Trends*, p. 26.

[14] Ibid., pp. 31-34 and 62-75.

[15] See Appendix C.

Graph 5.32 Cloth Annual Average Prices: Coast

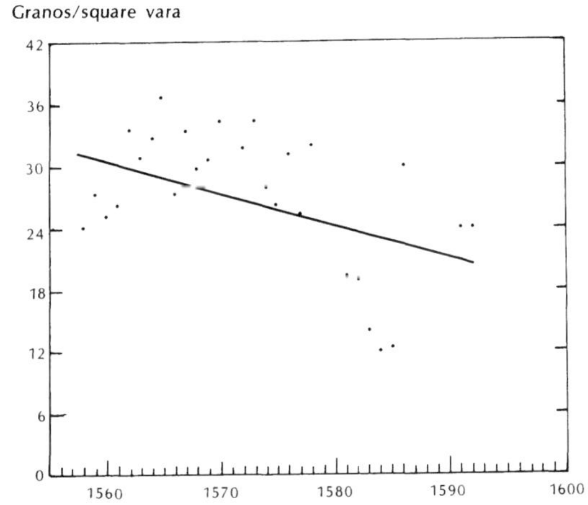

Graph 5.33 Cloth Unit Prices: Sentispac

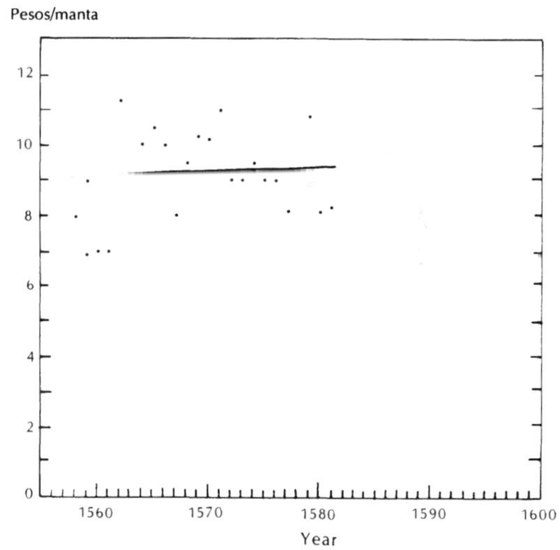

heavy cloth.[16] Since the Spanish need for sails for ships increased rather than decreased, the reason perhaps lay in loss of population and Indian disaffection in northern Nayarit.

We have prices for the cloth tribute of Sentispac for twenty-five years. The slope of the trend line is mildly upward (1.04). (See Graph 5.33.) With a value for *t* of .24 and 23 degrees of freedom, it stands at a confidence level between .02 and .05–testimony to the variation from year to year. Despite erratic ups and downs, the price of the Sentispac manta tended to rise somewhat. In 1579 it stood at one of the highest prices of the period, 10/6/6, but thereafter fell sharply in 1580 to a final value in 1581 of 8/1. That year the Indians of Sentispac were permitted to buy back their tribute in maize because of their need.[17]

---

[16]Ibid. Under date of 19 January 1581, the last sale of Sentispac cloth in the surviving records states that the mantas were bid in "*por armas de su Magestad.*"

[17]Under date of January 11, 1581; see Appendix A.

6

THE BUYERS

We are fortunate in that the Contaduría records of royal tribute auctions in Nueva Galicia in the Archivo General de Indias in Sevilla give the names of the buyers. They are not unique in this, since institutional records of purchases obviously indicate the buyers, and municipal records of sales in granaries and markets may contain such names as well, but not much use can be made of the identity of a single institutional buyer and, in the latter instance, scholars have not bothered to take off the names nor analyze them. The auction records for Nueva Galicia lack completely the years 1579, 1588, and 1589, and occasionally parts of the transactions of other years. These gaps are remarkably small for a run of sixteenth-century fiscal accounts, so that the information may be regarded as unusually full.

Transcribing the names from sixteenth-century script and abbreviations and the distortions introduced by copyists at the time as they prepared duplicates and triplicates for audit and transmission has been a difficult task, not made easier by finding the same name spelled in a number of quite different ways. The name Pedro de Egurrola, for example, was spelled in three quite different ways—all misleading—and only the suggestion of a kindly genealogist of Guadalajara, Don Jorge Palomino y Cañedo, plus finding traces of the man's brother in filmed correspondence from Spain, established the true form. Similarly, Don Alonso de Rubalcava occurred in a number of variants, none of them correct, yet the man is well known in the history of Guadalajara as the architect and master builder of the second cathedral of the city.[1] Still unidentified is a S^{e} Juan, Interprete, doubtless known to the royal treasury officials but not, alas, to us. He may have been Señor Juan, interpreter, a man too humble for further trace. The remarkable aspect of these searches is that with the one exception of S^{e} Juan, Interprete, all of the other

[1]Palomino y Cañedo, *Los protocolos*, p. 263.

names were identified as to correct form today. They are transcribed in Appendix A in modernized spelling.

Furthermore, a good deal of information has been found on most of the people. On wealthy, prominent figures–like Luis de Ahumada, Diego and Francisco de Ibarra, and Diego de Colio el Viejo–there is a plethora of material. On most of the others, encomendero lists, official correspondence, notarial records to the extent that they survive, and histories of the Church in Guadalajara provide a considerable amount of information. Surprisingly, except for the most important miners, data on figures in Zacatecas are scarce, since even fewer of the sixteenth-century notarial and municipal records survive for that city than for Guadalajara.

Virtually all the buyers were what one might call vecinos of the jurisdiction, residents in one town or another, although not all held formal vecindad, that is, admission by a town council to citizenship. A few were estantes–people spending longer or shorter periods of time in the jurisdiction, but having residence outside it. Such might be merchants, carters, and sailors. They would, of course, have to be known in the jurisdiction in order to find bondsmen to serve as guarantors of their promissory notes.

The buyers operated in a rudimentary but complex series of markets and in an economy undergoing substantial structural change. Immediately after the conquest of Nueva Galicia, the Spanish community depended upon Indian tributes for most of its supplies. At the beginning of our period, in 1559, forty-eight towns furnished 13,640 fanegas of maize through the royal auctions. By the end of our period, even though escheatment of private encomiendas to the Crown added tributes paid by the Indians of those encomiendas to the royal auctions, the disastrous melting away of the native population and subsequent revisions of tribute schedules to reflect the declining population meant that in 1598, the last year of a relatively free market in auctions of royal tribute maize, seventy-two towns delivered 3,169 fanegas of maize.[2] The royal government, to be sure, was diverting some tribute maize to Indians working in the royal salt monopoly, but those amounts should be balanced against the large number of towns absorbed in consolidations and *congregación*. The seventy-two towns of 1598 represented a total swelled by the addition of escheatments but greatly reduced by the disappearance of some upland and most coastal towns. In consequence, during the sixteenth century the Spanish communities were forced to develop sources of production under their own control and independent of the Indian tributes. In part, they used Indian labor recruited from those towns, augmented by Indian and mixed-blood immigrants from other areas. They were most successful in wheat and in livestock. A rapid development of Spanish estates in the desert oases and valleys near Zacatecas augmented the supply of the mines to an extent that tributes became far less important there by 1570. The Spanish estates raised enormous numbers of cattle, sheep, and other livestock on the scrublands, and wheat and maize on irrigated farms drawing water from springs and diversion ditches. Similarly, the western part of the audiencia district–essentially Guadalajara, its hinterland, and the coast–became independent of Indian tributes for wheat, but

---

[2]See Appendix C.

continued to rely upon them for at least a substantial part of its supply of maize and fowls.[3]

Royal auctions of tributes in kind constituted only one of a number of markets in operation simultaneously, but changing during the period in relative weight. On their nature and what went on in them we can only conjecture, since little information survives. The Indians undoubtedly held daily markets and at less frequent intervals local and regional markets for the exchange of surpluses and specialty wares, such as pottery and cloth, manufactured locally by artisans. These constituted what one might call the tianguis network. The Spaniards must have resorted to it for some items they needed. A Spanish network of markets and stores, however, constituted the main means of exchange among the Hispanized communities. Larger-scale merchants imported European and Asiatic wares and foodstuffs for sale in their stores, which handled some local products as well. Further distribution occurred through peddlers and smaller stores,[4] which purchased from the merchants and picked up Indian and local Spanish production. Some kind of market must have existed through which encomenderos with surplus tributes to dispose of could sell them, either through private transactions direct to users or through merchants and peddlers who, in turn, acted as distributors. At first a considerable source of supply for the Spanish communities, sales of surplus by encomenderos trailed off as the Indian population shrank, with consequent diminution of tributes, and encomiendas escheated to the Crown on the death of the holder in third life.

Yet another source of supplies either fed the existing network of Spanish markets or became another market within it. That was the sale by the Church of tithes in kind that it collected directly and those assembled by tithe farmers who bought the right of collection. Non-Indians had to pay on all agricultural products, although not always at the rate of a tenth; Indians were liable to tithe only on products introduced from the Old World, like wheat and livestock. In the course of the sixteenth century, the Church, which at first was willing to have royal treasury officials handle much of the tithes, increasingly assumed control of them.[5] By the end of the century, the tithes amounted to much larger amounts, which attracted buyers. Thomas Calvo has sketched the life of Maese de Campo don Francisco de Pareja y Rivera, son of a judge of the Audiencia of Guadalajara, who became wealthy through buying cattle delivered to the Church as its tenth of increase, pasturing them under lease to others, fattening, and driving them to Mexico City for sale. He held little land, but did have a general store.[6] Dealing in tithe commodities and animals must have been a profitable enterprise for a number of Spaniards in the Diocese of Guadalajara and have constituted a further part of the Spanish network of markets. Ordinary Spaniards could supply themselves to the extent that they had the means from any part of these networks as well as the sale of royal tributes in kind at the public

[3]Mota y Escobar, passim; López de Velasco, pp. 137-138; Guillermo Porras Muñoz, *El nuevo discubrimiento de San Josę del Parral*, p. 20; Chevalier, pp. 197-206 and 209-228.

[4]Mota y Escobar, p. 295.

[5]John Frederick Schwaller, *Origins of Church Wealth in Mexico*, pp. 19-27, 42-43, 47-48, and 50-53.

[6]Calvo, "Un extraño señor de ganados."

auctions, but the royal treasury officials and the judges of the audiencia, who were formally forbidden to buy in the royal auctions, had to resort to the private networks, unless they were prepared to break the law. They had substantial households, which required large amounts of foodstuffs and other supplies, and in turn necessitated purchases in quantity. Only the permission in the 1590s to buy royal tribute chickens and maize at set prices permitted them legally to buy royal tributes openly.

The motives that led Spaniards to bid for royal tributes in kind in the auctions must have varied greatly, although all were attracted by a relatively abundant supply, prices that ran below those prevailing in private markets,[7] and sale on credit for up to a year. One major reason for entering the auctions was supply of household. Spanish establishments tended to be large, with members of the immediate family, relatives, dependents, servants and, in larger establishments, slaves and dependents of servants. They would need substantial supplies of foodstuffs for the people in the household and for animal fodder. We may judge the requirements of the larger establishments by the allocations of maize and chickens under the system of sale at set prices to *beneméritos de la república*, initiated for chickens with the tributes of 1595 and for maize with those of 1599. The largest household was probably that of Dr. Santiago de Vera, the president of the audiencia. In 1598 he received and paid for 737 chickens from Analco, San Pedro Tlaquepaque, and Tonalá. The next year he received and paid for 786½ chickens from the same towns. Other judges and officials of the audiencia bought in numbers usually hovering around 200. Don Francisco Martínez, the precenter of the cathedral chapter, bought 150 chickens from Sentispac. One wonders how he transported them to Guadalajara. Private citizens ranged in their allotments from 50 to 200. Doña Isabel de Tovar's allotment for 1598 ran to 102 chickens from Tepic and Analco Tepic; Don Alvaro de Bracamonte, of a wealthy landholding family, was granted an allotment of 148 chickens from the partido of Sentispac. For 1598 the royal treasury officials received and paid for 45 chickens from Contla. Since they received the allotment *en bloc*, it presumably was for joint meals. Chickens, of course, were paid for at the set rate of a real per fowl, regardless of the distance they had to be transported for the use of the Spanish household. Maize was paid for at varying rates based on the average of previous sales for the town, those prices in turn being very much affected by the distance the maize had to be moved for use. The proportions of maize to fowls can be judged by the allotment of Lic. Andrés Ramírez de Alarcón, son of a judge of the audiencia and a prominent and wealthy man in his own right. For 1599 he received and paid for 77 chickens from Cuitzeo and Poncitlán and 50 fanegas of maize from the district of Poncitlán. The price of the maize was set at 0/8/9 the fanega.[8] The quantities given above will serve as measure, but hardly an exact one, for determining whether purchases in the auctions were for household supply or for other reasons. It should

[7]Testimony of Juana Rodríguez de Arenas in the inquiry into the rise in the cost of basic foodstuffs, made by Lic. D. Hernando Martínez de la Marcha, Guadalajara, 16 July 1550, in Orozco y Jiménez, *Colección*, 5: 13-14.

[8]GBPE, Archivo de la Real Audiencia, Ramo Fiscal, exp. 3, Cuentas 1598-1599, Receipts for Almonedas de Tributos, ff. 77f-85v; exp. 3a, Cuentas 1599, ff. 90v-98f; exp. 4, Cuentas 1605-1606, ff. 90f-108v.

be emphasized that allotment for the supply of households applied only to the *beneméritos de la república*. Spaniards of lesser degree, such as artisans, people of mixed genetic stock, free Blacks, and Hispanized Indians–the so-called meaner sort who probably comprised the major part of the population of the Spanish towns--unless they were dependents in upper-class households, would have had to purchase their supplies in private markets. Of course, such households were usually smaller and consumed less.

Another motive for bidding in the auctions of royal tribute commodities, closely allied to that of supply of households, was supply of enterprises. Mining, an important activity much favored by the Crown because it yielded the coveted silver and handsome revenues and stimulated other economic activity, not merely created large consuming centers in Zacatecas and the oases of the eastern part of the audiencia district, but also many smaller sites in the western parts. Almost all of the western mining sites flourished for a while, then were abandoned when ore ran out or costs proved too great.[9] All of the sites, while exploited, needed considerable supplies of foodstuffs, cloth, leather, and metal for their workers; fodder, including grain for the animals that provided tractive power and transport; and fuel, salt, mercury, and iron and copper pyrites for extracting silver from the ores. Foodstuffs from royal tributary towns near the mining site provided a solution to part of the problem of supply, particularly prominent in the earlier history of Zacatecas and in mining activity in the west of the audiencia district throughout the period. In 1566 Juanes de Tolosa, one of the four partners who founded Zacatecas and a close associate of Diego de Ibarra, bought the tribute commodities due from Teocaltiche, Teocaltitlán, and Nochistlán. The supplies were almost certainly for the work force of the Zacatecas mines. In 1587 Melchor de Brito bid successfully for 522 fanegas, five almudes of maize, and 364½ chickens of the tributes due for 1586 from a number of coastal and highland towns. He was a vecino of the mines of Espíritu Santo.[10] We cannot be certain of his use of these foodstuffs, but the probability would seem to be feeding his work force, human and animal.

Provisioning expeditions for opening new territories and new mines would have led the organizers, who needed large amounts of supplies, to turn to the royal auctions. In 1558 Francisco de Ibarra, the nephew and protegé of Diego de Ibarra, one of the wealthiest men in New Spain, bought the right to 1,395 fanegas of maize, 50 fanegas six almudes of chile, 40 fanegas of frijoles, and 720 chickens due that year from Nochistlán, Teocaltiche, and Teocaltitlán–all southwest of Zacatecas City and a rich, relatively accessible source of supply for the city and its mines. The next year he bid successfully for far larger quantities from all the towns of the Zacatecas fiscal province: 2,475 fanegas of maize, 32 fanegas six almudes of chile, whatever the harvest of the tribute sowing of frijoles might be, 884½ chickens, and 60 turkeys. He may have bought the foodstuffs for workers and animals in the mines. but more likely

---

[9]Mota y Escobar, passim.

[10]See Appendix A.

he was accumulating supplies for his expeditions, which added much of what became Nueva Vizcaya to Spanish territory.[11]

Besides mining and territorial expansion, Spanish enterprises included cacao orchards on the coast, raising livestock throughout the jurisdiction, and workshops (which developed especially in the last decades of the sixteenth century) for processing wool, weaving textiles, and meeting the needs of mines and households.[12] In such enterprises, supervision tended to be Hispanic but most or all of the work force was Indian and had Indian tastes in food. Unless the estate was able to raise its own maize, chile, and beans, it had to buy the foodstuffs, either by bidding successfully for tribute commodities in the royal auctions or by purchase in private markets. Maritime transportation was yet another form of Spanish enterprise, for which supply must at times have been difficult. The successful bid in 1563 by Maese Pedro–by his title sailing master and navigator of a ship–for the 120 arrobas of dried fish, 16 arrobas of dried oysters, and 100 turkeys of tribute from Sentispac for that year looks remarkably like supply of his vessel. He was sufficiently well-known to the royal treasury officials to require no further identification. In 1569 he bid successfully for 388 fanegas six almudes of maize from Cuitzeo, due that year. Two purchases by Bartolomé Napolitano, one in January 1558 for 150 arrobas of dried fish from Sentispac and 32 fanegas of maize and 4 mantas from San Juan, and another in December 1559 for 120 arrobas of dried fish from Sentispac,[13] may also have been for supply of ships. Napolitano, meaning from Naples, was a common name among seamen in Spanish service. He may have been a ship's chandler rather than a seaman, since the quantities were large.

A prominent motive for Spanish purchase in the auctions must have been speculation and resale. The auctions coming around the New Year took place soon after the harvests at the end of the rainy season, when crops were as abundant as the year permitted and prices accordingly were low. Thereafter, as supplies were slowly consumed, prices rose until they reached the high point of the agricultural year just before the new crops were harvested. A purchaser who bought at the lowest price of the year and hoarded supplies until prices rose could make substantial gains. Spanish custom and law frowned on this sort of activity as impermissible regrating,[14] but folk and Crown came to recognize a beneficent distributive function in buying up large lots for distribution in smaller lots among other purchases–in other words, buying wholesale for disposal at retail to consumers or to middlemen who completed the distribution. A large number of the successful bidders secured such

[11]See Appendix A; Porras Muñoz, pp. 17-26; J. Lloyd Mecham, *Francisco de Ibarra and Nueva Vizcaya*, passim.

[12]Mota y Escobar, passim. The pasturing of large numbers of sheep indicates substantial production of wool, and that, in turn, spinning and weaving into cloth. The course of prices for mantas, the cotton competition for woolens, further supports this view of the development of woolen textiles.

[13]See Appendix A.

[14]As is evident in the ordinances of 15 October, 10 and 17 November, and 11 January 1583 for the Audiencia of Mexico, mss. in Archivo General de la Nación, Mexico, Reales cédulas duplicados, vol. 14, ff. 129-136.

quantities of commodities far more than they, their households, and their enterprises could possibly have consumed, and their buying activity spread over so many years that there cannot be much doubt of their function. They could hope to gain substantial profits from a distributive activity that the community needed and the Crown was forced to accept, if only to dispose of its tributes in kind. An example of people who obviously were traders would be Don Cristóbal de Ayala, a Spaniard of quality who settled in Guadalajara in the early 1560s and became a prominent citizen. He bid successfully in the auctions of 1563, 1565, 1566, 1567, 1568, and 1572 for tributes in such quantities that some of the commodities must have been resold.[15] Another would be Bernardo de Balbuena, father of the famous poet of the *Grandezas Mexicanas* and a man who, among his many activities, traded in royal tribute commodities in 1558, 1569, 1577, 1578, and 1581.[16] Another obvious trader was Bernabé García, who was successful in bidding in 1574, 1577, 1578, 1579, 1584, 1585, 1586, 1591, 1592, 1593, 1594, and 1595. The quantities of the later years were small enough to be purchases for household supply, but earlier years involved amounts that indicate resale.[17] Still another obvious trader was Juan González de Apodaca, alguacil mayor of the audiencia–an important post, notary, and obviously a trader in royal tribute commodities. He bid successfully in 1576, 1579, 1581, 1582, 1584, 1586, and 1587.[18] A full list of obvious traders would be very long. None of the traders lost social prestige by an activity that would have been frowned upon if pursued openly in the Peninsula.

Some of the purchasers may have been people acting as agents for principals who preferred to be anonymous, or whose active participation in the bidding would have been illegal. Unfortunately for the inquisitive scholar, an eye to the keyhole yields no results, for two reasons. In the first place, such transactions would have been kept secret with little or no record. In the second place, traces of administrative or judicial proceeding against transgressors and complaints of transgression, if they existed, have been lost in the general disappearance of sixteenth-century records in Guadalajara. A suspicion that such transactions may have taken place, though, must arise, since we have considerable evidence of similar transactions in land grants, in which Spaniards secured grants of land, held them for the requisite period to establish firm title, and then sold them to powerful figures who were thus creating huge holdings. The use of clients by Luis de Ahumada in acquiring much of the valley of Ameca is a well-known illustration,[19] as is any grant of land held for a short period and then transferred to another man who was creating a large holding. Since ownership of land, to be effective, had to be founded upon registered title to at least part of the

---

[15]See Appendix A; Lic. Vásquez and the royal treasury officials of Nueva Galicia to the King, Mines of Zacatecas, 10 February 1563, in Paso y Troncoso, *Epistolario*, 9: 201; Palomino y Cañedo, *Los protocolos*, pp. 201, 241-242, and 245.

[16]See Appendix A; Rojas Garcidueñas, pp. 3-7; and Mota Padilla, p. 206.

[17]See Appendix A.

[18]See Appendix A; Palomino y Cañedo, *Los protocolos*, pp. 249-253; Arregui, pp. 71-72; and Jesús Amaya Topete, *Bioteca*, pp. 71 et seq.

[19]Chevalier, pp. 186-187; Amaya Topete, *Bioteca*, pp. 6-8; and Palomino y Cañedo, *Los protocolos*, pp. 205-206.

holding, there was no effective way to keep such dealings secret, unlike dealings in tribute commodities. Of course, except when purchases involved evading the prohibition against royal treasury officials and members of the audiencia entering the bidding, or the prohibition against clerical bidding imposed by the Third Mexican Church Council, transfers of commodities bought in the royal actions would have been legal.

Thus far, enumeration of motives for dealing in royal tribute commodities has supposed that the purchasers who bid successfully for the tributes-in-kind of a town claimed the commodities within a reasonable period of time. That such was not always the case was stated by Arregui in his extensive report on Nueva Galicia early in the seventeenth century. Maize grown on the coast spoiled easily and could not be stored for long periods, so that two crops a year were needed to maintain a year long supply. According to Arregui, Spaniards purchasing the right to tribute maize would not attempt to collect the fanegas due until a scarce season or year, when they demanded delivery either in maize or the equivalent value of coin at the high prices then prevailing.[20] Such extortion was sufficiently common in the neighboring Audiencia of Mexico for the high court in 1575 to issue a stringent order that tribute maize must be collected within two months of the purchase by a successful bidder or the Indians of the town could not be held liable for any spoilage or other damage. By royal cédula issued in Madrid 4 June 1576, the order of the audiencia received Crown confirmation, with the amendment that for towns fifty leagues or more distant from Mexico City the time limit for collection of the maize was to be three months.[21] Under the custom of Spanish legislation for the Indies that royal orders for specific, local instances were held to have general application, a copy of the royal cédula of 4 June 1576 probably was sent to the Audiencia of Guadalajara and was known there. Accordingly, the practice was probably illegal in Nueva Galicia.

Again, the unfortunate loss of archives in Guadalajara thwarts general confirmation of this charge through a search of records. The one bit of confirmatory evidence in surviving documents is a complaint of 1590 against Juan Toledano by the Indians of Jocotlán that the right to their tribute in maize and chickens for 1589 had been bought by Martín Real in the royal auction, the maize for 0/5 the fanega, the right to collect the maize and chickens transferred to Juan Toledano for 0/7 for a fanega and a chicken, and that Toledano, in turn, was demanding payment in maize and chickens or in coin. At the time of the complaint, the current value of a fanega of maize plus one chicken was 1/4, the price arrieros were willing to pay. The Indians of Jocotlán petitioned for protection against such extortion.[22] Auction data for 1589 are lacking, but the two Spaniards figure prominently in other auction transactions. Martín Real, or more accurately, Martín Real de Azúa, held a number of official posts and served as mayordomo of the building of the cathedral. He bid

[20]Arregui, pp. 93-94.

[21]Autos 91 of 5 October 1575 and 92 of 14 October 1575 and 11-12 November 1577, incorporating real cédula of 4 June 1576, Madrid, in Juan de Montemayor y Córdova de Cuenca, 2nd pagination, f. 342.

[22]GBPE, Archivo de la Real Audiencia, Ramo Civil, 32-9-433, ff. 75-76.

successfully for tributes in 1584, 1587, 1593, 1597, 1598, and 1599.[23] Juan Toledano, who may have been a priest, since a man of that name was described in 1605 as parish priest of Tlaltenango, earlier served as collector of alcabala for Guadalajara. He bid successfully on royal tributes in 1576, 1585, 1591, 1592, and 1595.[24] Although the complaint was probably accurate, neither party seems to have incurred any social stigma. According to Arregui, the practice was widespread.

Let us now look at the purchasers in terms of occupation and class and examine the question of the nature of the market. As has already been stated, the European settlers in Nueva Galicia were what is best described as a motley lot. Many were adventurers led to America rather than the wars in Europe. Most were plebeians or men with a tenuous claim to *hidalguía*. Most were energetic and hard-working, although avoiding direct manual labor as fit only for Indians, *castas*, and slaves. All were searching for a livelihood in a new and hopefully easier land. Some were higher officials of royal administration and the Church, with numerous dependents. Government and Church posts might be assigned according to Old World ideas of quality, but on this raw frontier salaries and emoluments came to fairly small sums. Wealth soon became the basic standard of social value. Mining, stock-raising, and commerce became as respectable as administration and holding encomiendas. For that matter, encomiendas, held by a fortunate few early conquerors, settlers, and their descendants, shrank in yield to a point at which they could seldom support a family in what was regarded as a decent standard of living, and had to be supplemented by other activity. The bulk of settlers, accordingly, turned to stock-raising, farming, mining, trade, and occasional administrative posts, and the humbler settlers worked in crafts not known to or open to Indians. The major sources of wealth for Spaniards were mining, large-scale stock-raising and agriculture, commerce, and government, especially the higher ranks of government. Since each form of economic activity yielded small sums for most, the bulk of the settlers dealt in a variety of functions and activities simultaneously or at intervals during their lives.[25] For example, Don Bernardo de Balbuena, already mentioned, came to Nueva Galicia as secretary to the newly appointed audiencia in 1548-1549. He was a notary in Zacatecas, became a vecino of Guadalajara, and died ca. 1592. In the course of the four decades he lived in Nueva Galicia, he was an estanciero owning much land and raising livestock, participated in mining ventures, held official posts as alcalde mayor, corregidor, judge of the mercury monopoly for Chiametla, and deputy *contador* and auditor of the royal

---

[23]See Appendix A; GBPE, Archivo de la Real Audiencia, Ramo Fiscal, exp. 3, Cuentas 1598-1599, f. 127v; exp. 3a, f. 157f.

[24]See Appendix A; GBPE, Archivo de la Real Audiencia, Ramo Fiscal, exp. 3, Cuentas 1598-1599, f. 68f; exp. 3a, f. 80f; exp. 4, Cuentas 1605-1606, f. 152v.

[25]Chevalier, pp. 22-56 and passim; Rodolfo Pastor, *Campesinas y reformas*, pp. 116 and 120-121; Peter Gerhard, passim. José Durand, *La transformacion social del conquistador*, passim but esp. 2: 31-72, and "*La Grandeza Mexicana* y el ennoblecimiento del mercader."

treasury, and he dealt substantially in royal tributes in kind. He is one of the few who died wealthy.[26]

In terms of territorial scope, the royal auctions took place in two markets centered in Guadalajara and Zacatecas, Guadalajara handling the tributes of most of the Indian towns and Zacatecas restricted essentially to the towns southwest of it. To be sure, the dominance of Guadalajara in its territory nevertheless allowed some scope for bids by vecinos of Colima and Purificación and owners of local enterprises outside of the capital, but that competition slowly diminished with time.[27] The question of the extent to which there was a free market or one governed by collusion must be considered separately for each of the two great centers. As has already been stated, the estimated 160 vecinos of Guadalajara in 1592 were so bound by ties of family relationship, alliance, *compadrazgo*, clientage, and patronage that one might well question the possibility of a free market, despite royal prohibitions and precautions. If the royal treasury officials and the judges of the audiencia were forbidden to enter the bidding, their secretaries and subordinates not only were free to do so but also did, as the successful bids attest. On the other hand, inspection of the records of sales shows that most Spaniards bid successfully once or twice or sporadically. They may have bid unsuccessfully at other times, but only a few functioned as experienced traders who might buy in commodities year after year for purposes of resale. Since there was no legal impediment to resale of the purchased right to receive a commodity from an Indian town, behind the formal records may have lain the reality of purchase through intermediaries, with eventual transfer to the true purchaser, or the existence of a business agent buying for resale or extortion on behalf of a principal who did not dare or wish to have this activity made public. There may well have been some of this illegal manipulation. That it controlled the Guadalajara market we may rule out by inspecting the graphs of unit sales year by year. The auctions took place when the success or failure of the harvest was known, and show far more variation than would be likely if the bidding were under the kind of control a theory of massive collusion would envisage. Variation was wide and seems to have varied according to the rainfall and natural disasters like epidemics, or favorable growing conditions, which in turn determined the abundance or scarcity of the yield.

The Zacatecas auctions present different characteristics. The supplies from the royal towns of the Juchipila and adjacent valleys, although particularly welcome in the early history of the settlement, always formed a fairly small and steadily diminishing proportion of the total supplies that the mines of the Zacatecas area drew from Michoacán, the Bajío, and oases in newly settled territory. Moreover, the bidding in Zacatecas was dominated by the miners, merchants, and artisans of the mining center and adjacent areas. Names of Guadalajara vecinos seldom figure among the

[26]Rojas Garcidueñas, *Bernardo de Balbuena*, pp. 3-7; Mota Padilla, p. 206; Audiencia of Guadalajara to the King, Guadalajara, 10 April 1572 and Information on services of Bernardo Balbuena, Guadalajara, 4 December 1573, AGI, Audiencia of Guadalajara, leg. 5, exp. 5, and leg. 34, exp. 12, respectively.

[27]What follows is based on inspection of Appendix A.

successful bidders in Zacatecas. Success in bidding in Zacatecas tended to be concentrated in one or two people each year, who obtained relatively large amounts of foodstuffs at prices that except in unusual years failed to rise as the prices of maize and chickens did elsewhere. One has the impression that the greater abundance of supplies from alternative sources gave the Zacatecas bidders greater ability to keep down prices in the royal auctions. Moreover, concentration of successful bidding in a few names, changing each year, would indicate that dealing in tribute commodities as supplies for the mines was either controlled by agreement among the bidders or that it yielded such a low margin of profit as to discourage competition. The reaction of the royal treasury officials and the audiencia increasingly was to withdraw maize from sale in the auctions and apply it for the Indians who worked in the royal salt monopoly of Peñol Blanco, which provided salt for the patio process of ore reduction. By 1587 relatively little tribute maize from towns in the Zacatecas province entered the auctions. Chickens and turkeys continued to be sold in the royal auctions, but an unvarying sale of chickens for 0/1 for 1584 and subsequent years suggests some kind of arrangement, obviously with the acquiescence of the royal treasury officials and audiencia judges. In this connection, it is worth noting that the viceregal order authorizing the sale of royal tribute chickens in the jurisdiction for 0/1 to the *beneméritos de la república* did not apply to Zacatecas. There may well have been a similar order issued ten years earlier for Zacatecas, the record of which has been lost or has not yet come to light. In short, although the absence of information precludes our determining precisely what took place, the royal tribute auctions in Zacatecas increasingly showed features that indicate control, collusion, or a slack market–perhaps all of them–with the acquiescence of the royal administration.

When one examines the names of successful bidders in the auctions in terms of wealth, class, and occupation–three terms that were inextricably mixed in Nueva Galicia, but gave far greater prominence to wealth than was true in the Peninsula–one is struck immediately by the sparse representation of artisans and people who might be presumed *castas* or Indians. Indians might occasionally be permitted to bid in the tributes of their own town, at first through agents, the one kind of instance in which a friar entered the bidding, or in later years directly. Of possible mixed bloods, I can find only one–Juan de Colima–who bid in the 1576 tribute of Teocaltiche, consisting of 216 chickens, 9 fanegas of frijoles, and 10½ fanegas of chile. The adoption for identification of a local place-name, Colima, suggests that he was a mestizo or mulatto who, in the mines of the Zacatecas area, accumulated enough wealth to enter the bidding. Others, of course, may have been hidden under more concealing surnames. Of artisan-class people of European stock, Jorge Griego, described as a carter in the instrument of purchase, bought the tribute of Teocaltitlán for 1577, consisting of 9 fanegas of frijoles, 14½ fanegas of chile, and 216 chickens, and that of Mitic for 1578, consisting of 7 fanegas of frijoles and 11½ fanegas of chile.[28] The beans might have been for consumption in his household, but the chile and chickens must have been mostly for resale. Judging from his name, he was an immigrant from the eastern Mediterranean who was doing well in the

[28]See Appendix A.

mines of Zacatecas. Another person of lower economic status was Bartolomé de Coca, who bought the tribute of 502½ fanegas of maize due from Poncitlán for 1562. He was mentioned in the will of Doña María de Sámano, widow of Francisco Merodio de Velasco, dated 5 March 1590, as the man who built an oven, corral, and other structures in her house and married *una criada mía*, one of her servants and dependents. He apparently had connections in Guadalajara and may have been related to Simón de Coca, a notary and vecino of Guadalajara who held various official posts.[29] Bartolomé de Coca was able to convince the royal treasury officials of his credit-worthiness. Maese Pedro and other persons connected with shipping should be remembered here, too.

Virtually all other successful bidders were of the middle and upper ranges of Spanish society. Some were people of the greatest wealth known in Nueva Galicia, like Diego and Francisco de Ibarra, famous in the history of Zacatecas mining and northern exploration;[30] the two brothers Luis de Ahumada, who wound up owning much of the Valley of Ameca,[31] and Pedro de Ahumada Sámano, governor of the Cortés Estate and speculator in the mines of Zacatecas;[32] Diego de Colio el Viejo, conqueror, vecino of Guadalajara, encomendero, landowner, and holder of official posts;[33] Luis de Contreras y Guevara, son of a judge of the Audiencia of Guadalajara;[34] Diego de Porres Baranda, landowner and stock-raiser, married to a cousin of President Santiago de Vera, involved in a lucrative supply of mules to the mines of Zacatecas and adjacent areas, and one of the wealthiest men in Nueva Galicia;[35] and Andrés de Villanueva, conqueror, encomendero, vecino and regidor of Guadalajara, and wealthy landowner and stock-raiser.[36] All were involved in a number of pursuits.

A number of merchants in Guadalajara were reputed to be especially wealthy. They owned businesses that specialized in imported goods bought, in turn, from the

---

[29]See Appendix A; Palomino y Cañedo, *Los protocolos*, p. 37; Mota Padilla, p. 204; Mecham, p. 202; José Dávila Garibi, *Apuntes*, 1:251, 256, and 529-530; Lic. Vázquez and the royal treasury officials of Nueva Galicia to the King, Mines of Zacatecas, 10 February 1563, in Paso y Troncoso, *Epistolario*, 9: 200-201.

[30]Victor M. Alvarez, *Diccionario*, 1: 276; Gerhard, passim; Mota Padilla, pp. 191b, 207b, and 209c; and Mecham, pp. 48-49; Appendix A.

[31]Palomino y Cañedo, *Los protocolos*, p. 206; Chevalier, pp. 186-187; and Amaya Topete, *Bioteca*, pp. 6-8; Appendix A.

[32]Gerhard, pp. 76 and 109; Parry, p. 88; and Bakewell, pp. 26-27 and 85; Appendix A.

[33]Alvarez, *Diccionario*, 1: 138; Mecham, pp. 92-93, 113-115, and 198-200; Dávila Garibi, *Apuntes*, 1: 253-255, and *Estudio genealógico*, passim; Appendix A.

[34]Real cédula recommending Lic. Luis Contreras y Guevara, San Lorenzo, 15 May 1575, AGI, Audiencia de Méjico, leg. 1090, fascicle 8, ff. 43f-44v; Palomino y Cañedo, *Los protocolos*, p. 113; Amaya Topete, *Bioteca*, p. 42; and Eugenía Vizcarra A. de Jiménez and Miguel Jiménez y Vizcarra, *Noticias*, #5; Appendix A.

[35]Chevalier, pp. 213-214; Amaya Topete, *Bioteca*, pp. 134-135; Palomino y Cañedo, *Los protocolos*, p. 29; Appendix A.

[36]Alvarez, *Diccionario*, 2: 595; Francisco A. Icaza, *Diccionario autobiográfico*, 1: 244-245; Dávila Garibi, *Apuntes*, 1: 258, 529-535; Appendix A.

Spanish importing firms in Mexico City that distributed European and Oriental wares.[37] The names of some figure as buyers of tribute commodities. An example is Francisco de Camarena, successful bidder in 1592, 1595, 1596, and 1599, a member of a Flemish family that settled in Nueva Galicia, Hispanized its name, and prospered. In 1589 he was one of the founders of the cofradía of Nuestra Señora de la Soledad, established in the Hospital de San Miguel and restricted to thirty principal vecinos of Guadalajara.[38] Another is Cristóbal de Sandoval, born about 1558, a vecino of Guadalajara, who had extensive dealings with other citizens and ran up substantial debts.[39] Some were lesser figures like Juan Cortés, with stores dealing in such imported goods as they could buy and in local products. Juan Cortés dealt in account books, paper, and wax, both imported and local, among other items.[40] Information on the merchants resident in Guadalajara is relatively good, but on merchants in Zacatecas, as designated in the instruments of purchase, and other Zacatecas purchasers who may have been merchants but were not so described, as well as vecinos of Compostela and other lesser centers who may have kept stores, there is simply no information.

Mining is one occupation that was most likely to be mentioned in instruments of purchase. A considerable number of successful bidders in Zacatecas had at the least mining interests and may have devoted most of their economic effort to mining. Some of them have already been mentioned. Juan de Huidobro, who bought the maize and chickens of Nochistlán and Mexticacán and the maize of Teocaltiche due as tribute in 1576 figures as one of the informants for the second questionnaire on Fresnillo in 1585. He was then described as a vecino and miner of Fresnillo.[41] Miners in the western reaches of the jurisdiction apparently bid for tributes of towns near them as sources of foodstuffs and other supplies. Such were Hernando de la Peña, who in 1558 successfully bid for 24 fanegas of salt due in past tributes from Ixtapa, for 13 fanegas of maize due from Amaxaque, and 40 chickens from Zacatlán. He was described as a miner of Izatlán and continued to mine successfully for some decades.[42] Lázaro Blanco, who bought the 1584 tribute of Hostoticpac and Zapotlán of 210 fanegas 10 almudes of maize and that for 1585 of Jala and Acaponeta of 315 chickens and 173 fanegas 8 almudes of maize, is described as a vecino of Ahuacatlán and active in the mines of Chimaltitlán. He held at various times official posts as *teniente de alcalde mayor* in Compostela, where he supervised the preparation of the *relación geográfica* for that city, and alcalde mayor of Izatlán

---

[37]Mota y Escobar, p. 295.

[38]Vizcarra A. de Jiménez and Jiménez y Vizcarra, *Noticias*, #56, #77, #92, and passim; Mota Padilla, p. 235; interview with Jorge Palomino y Cañedo; Appendix A.

[39]Palomino y Cañedo, *Los protocolos*, pp. 68, 104, and 126; Appendix A.

[40]GBPE, Archivo de la Real Audiencia, Ramo Fiscal, exp. 3a, Cuentas 1599, ff. 153f. 157v, 194f.; and Dávila Garibi, *Apuntes*, I:634-635; Appendix A.

[41]Acuña, 10: 101, 119-126; Appendix A.

[42]Palomino y Cañedo, *Los protocolos*, p. 181; Lic. Vázquez and the Royal Treasury Officials of Nueva Galicia to the King, Mines of Zacatecas, 10 February 1563, in Paso y Troncoso, *Epistolario*, 9: 199; GBPE, Archivo de la Real Audiencia, Ramo Fiscal, exp. 2, Cuentas 1583-1584, 85f; Appendix A.

and administrator of the royal mercury monopoly there.[43] Another would be Pedro Narváez, who bid successfully for tribute maize and chickens, mostly from coastal towns, in 1580, 1583, and 1586. When he died early on the morning of 26 January 1590 in Guadalajara, he left extensive holdings in the form of an ore treatment plant at Chimaltitlán, ranches of cattle and sheep, interests in the mines of Tinamache, houses, and slaves. Through two marriages and business he was allied to the Estrada, Ayala Benavides, and Bracamonte families.[44]

As has already been made clear, the overwhelming majority of the purchasers on whom biographical details can be found held official posts part or all of the time. Legally, the royal treasury officials, the audiencia judges, and presumably their deputies having a role in the tribute auctions were barred from bidding, but the prohibitions apparently were construed to allow all but the highest officials entrance into the bidding. Instances were numerous. Lic. Andrés Ramírez de Alarcón, who bought the tribute in maize and chickens of Mezquituta for 1593, was fiscal, that is, crown attorney, of the audiencia, presumably a watchdog of the royal interests.[45] Juan de la Cueva, who figured in purchases of tributes in 1581, 1582, 1585, and 1595, was secretary of the audiencia.[46] Alonso Sánchez de Toledo, who bought royal tributes in kind extensively between 1562 and 1573, was Escribano de Cámara y Gobernación of the audiencia, its chief recording notary for all official acts, and one of the most powerful men in Nueva Galicia.[47] Rodrigo de Ojeda, who bid actively and successfully for tributes from 1573 to 1593, was Teniente de Contador, deputy accountant, for the royal treasury in Guadalajara, keeper of one of the three keys to the royal treasure chest, and familiar for the Inquisition.[48] Francisco Merodio de Velasco, who bought royal tributes from 1566 to 1574, in addition to various provincial posts held office as Alguacil Mayor (chief bailiff) of the audiencia. (He must have discharged some of the duties of these posts by deputy, since he could not have been in two places at the same time.)[49] Baltasar de Orozco, *Oficial Mayor de la Contaduría de Su Magestad* in Guadalajara, that is, the senior administrative official under the royal treasury officials, bid successfully for tribute in maize for 1591,

---

[43]Miguel Jiménez Vizcarra, *Indice del Archivo de Bienes de Defuntos*, p. 34; Palomino y Cañedo, *Los protocolos*, pp. 88, 90, 92, and 95; petition of Capt. Lázaro Blanco for appropriate post for past services, Guadalajara, 1602, and accompanying documents, AGI, Audiencia de Guadalajara, leg. 36, exp. 6; relación de la ciudad de Compostela, 26 November 1584, in Acuña, 10: 86-96.

[44]Appendix A; Palomino y Cañedo, *Los protocolos*, pp. 72, 84-85, 88-91, and 239; GBPE, Archivo de la Real Audiencia, Ramo Fiscal, exp. 2, Cuentas 1583-1584, f. 85f.

[45]Appendix A, Amaya Topete, *Bioteca*, p. 140; Mota Padilla, p. 258b.

[46]Appendix A, GBPE, Archivo de la Real Audiencia, Ramo Fiscal, exp. 2, Cuentas 1583-1584, f. 122v.

[47]Appendix A; Audiencia of Guadalajara to the King, Guadalajara, 26 August 1574, AGI, Audiencia de Guadalajara, leg. 34, exp. 14.

[48]Appendix A; Palomino y Cañedo, *Los protocolos*, pp. 213-215.

[49]Appendix A; Audiencia of Guadalajara to the King, Guadalajara, 21 April 1586, AGI, Audiencia de Guadalajara, leg. 6, exp. 69; Amaya Topete, *Bioteca*, p. 104.

1596, and 1597.[50] Bernardo de Balbuena, who dealt extensively in tribute commodities over the years, has already been mentioned. He served as auditor and royal inspector of the fisc in Guadalajara. To be sure, it is not certain that he served the two conflicting functions at the same time. If objection ever arose to the purchases by these people, it has not come down to us, nor did it bar their transactions.

Most of the purchasers either held subordinate posts in the royal administration or moved from one post to another in provincial government in what were one-year terms renewable for another year. Alonso de Llerena, who bought tributes in 1563 and 1571 and died in 1590, held various posts as provincial administrator and wound up as attorney for the Church and the audiencia's attorney for the poor. The first post had a salary of 50/ , which was never paid; the second post, one of 100/ , which was paid.[51] Bernabé García, who combined the offices of *balanzario* (weighmaster), *portero* (usher), and *alguacil* (bailiff) of the royal treasury in Guadalajara, the three posts combined providing a modest annual wage of slightly over 236/ , was active in purchases of royal tributes in kind from 1574 to 1595.[52] Diego Martín de Rivera, alguacil, portero, and attorney for the poor of the audiencia, was similarly active in buying royal tributes in kind from 1578 to 1595. In at least two transactions he may have acted in the royal service, when on 19 January 1581 he bought 33 mantas and 1¼ piernas due from Sentispac and 1½ mantas due from adjacent San Juan to be used for arms in royal service, that is, for the quilted armor favored in war with the Indians. In other transactions, he acted as his own agent, as far as the records suggest.[53] Francisco de Plaza, as one of the founders of the third Guadalajara (on its present site), a notary, and for a time collector of *alcabala* (sales tax) for the district of Tlajomulco as well as corregidor of the town, bought Indian tribute commodities during the years from 1571 to 1574. Since the quantities were comparatively large, he probably resold much or all of them.[54] Similarly, Antonio del Rincón, an early settler and *regidor* of Guadalajara, who held posts as corregidor and alcalde mayor of various provinces, figures in the lists of successful bidders in the years 1559 to 1584.[55] These people were representative of the large proportion of

---

[50]Appendix A; GBPE, Archivo de la Real Audiencia, Ramo Fiscal, exp. 3, Cuentas, 1598-1599, f. 112v.

[51]Appendix A; Palomino y Cañedo, *Los protocolos*, pp. 103 and 243; GBPE, Archivo de la Real Audiencia, Ramo Fiscal, exp. 2, Cuentas 1583-1584, ff. 106v and 123v.

[52]Appendix A; GBPE, Archivo de la Real Audiencia, Ramo Fiscal, exp. 3, Cuentas 1598-1599, ff. 113v and 119f; exp. 3a, ff. 154v, 159f, and 159v.

[53]Appendix A; GBPE, Archivo de la Real Audiencia, Ramo Fiscal, exp. 2, Cuentas 1583-1584, ff. 102f, 103f; and exp. 3, Cuentas 1598-1599, ff; 80f, 118v, and 146f.

[54]Appendix A; Palomino y Cañedo, *Los protocolos*, pp. 82-83 and 123; relación geográfica de Nuchistlán, 2 December 1584 and relación geográfica de Poncitlán, 9 March 1585, in Acuña, 10: 162-165 and 198, respectively; información de méritos y servicios de Francisco de Plaza, Guadalajara, 1585, AGI, Audiencia de Guadalajara, leg. 35, exp. 2.

[55]Appendix A; Lic. Vázquez and the Royal Treasury Officials of Nueva Galicia to the King, Mines of Zacatecas, 10 February 1563, in Paso y Troncoso, *Epistolario*, 9: 197; GBPE, Archivo de la Real Audiencia, Ramo Fiscal, exp. 2, Cuentas 1583-1584, f. 104f; GBPE, Archivo del Juzgado de Bienes de Difuntos, item #11, 1584.

Spanish residents, and almost all of the vecinos, who at one time or another entered the auctions of royal tribute commodities. Most bid successfully one or a few times. Others entered the auctions repeatedly, and might be dubbed traders in the royal tribute commodities. Virtually the entire upper and middle strata of the Spanish population characteristically hunted for such royal office as it could get and supplemented the revenues from royal posts by resort to stock-raising, farming, mining, speculation in land, and acting as professional agents and notaries. A single occupation seldom sufficed for a satisfactory livelihood.

One group remains to be dealt with: the clergy. The statutes of the First Mexican Provincial Church Council in 1555 forbade clergy to trade publicly or privately, to deal in any merchandise for resale, or to make usurious contracts directly or indirectly (i.e., contracts calling for illegal interest).[56] These prohibitions were restated in the statutes of the Second Mexican Provincial Church Council in 1565.[57] For almost all of our period, 1557-1598, these prohibitions governed, since the legislation of the Third Provincial Church Council of 1585 did not become binding until confirmed, almost at the end of our period.[58] As regards the prohibitions, the regular clergy presented no problem, since they did not engage in trade and entered the auctions only as clearly stated spokesmen for Indian towns. Presumably this form avoided the imputation of indirect dealing. The secular clergy were another matter, for parish and cathedral stipends in these years were low and additions to revenue in the form of tithes inadequate as supplements. Canons and other members of the cathedral chapter might seek additional revenue through discharging the offices of chantries and foundations;[59] for priests in provincial parishes, a decent revenue had to come through supplementary activity in mining, farming, and stock-raising. A number of parish priests and members of the cathedral staff resorted to the royal tribute auctions, and some bid successfully. Royal legislation set no bar to such purchases, and the legislation of the Archbishopric of Mexico was perhaps ambiguous in this respect. Father Francisco de Ángulo was already a priest when he bid in the tributes of a number of coastal towns in December 1559, the one purchase recorded for him. The quantities were larger than could be absorbed by household use. In 1572 he became parish priest of Zacatecas.[60] Father Luis Gómez de Alvarado, described as vicar of Purificación and a miner in the mines of Ocotitlán, bought the 200 chickens of tribute from Poncitlán in 1575, a number conceivably within possibilities of household use and certainly that of his work force.[61] Father Jorge Pérez, who

---

[56]Mexico (Ecclesiastical Province), *Concilios provinciales primero y segundo*, Statutes, cl. LVI, pp. 126-127.

[57]Ibid., cl. XXVII, pp. 203-205.

[58]Papal approval came on 28 October 1589 and royal on 18 September 1591. Stafford Poole, *Pedro Moya de Contreras*, pp. 199-200. Printing the decrees for effective implementation was long-delayed, ibid., pp. 200-202.

[59]Schwaller, pp. 55-147.

[60]Appendix A; José de Rivera Bernárdez, *Compendio*, p. 11.

[61]Appendix A; relación geográfica de la Villa de la Purificación, 12 January 1585, Acuña, 10: 206 and 208; GBPE, Archivo de la Real Audiencia, Ramo Fiscal, exp. 3, Cuentas 1598-1599, f. 99v; and exp. 3a, f. 114f.

was a simple priest until appointed treasurer, provisor, and ecclesiastical judge in 1564, and thus a canon, bid successfully in the royal auctions in 1559, 1560, 1566, and 1568. Some of his purchases, such as the 630 fanegas of maize from Atengoichán, would seem more than the household requirements even of a household lavish in Indian servants and domestic animals, unless he divided the purchase with the other canons.[62] Members of the cathedral chapter, such as Lorenzo de Padilla, the dean; Francisco de Morales, the treasurer; Pedro Bernardo de Quirós, the archdeacon, and Gaspar de Contreras, José de Ramírez, and Hernán Vela, canons all, figured as occasional bidders. Only Canon Francisco García de Urrieta's purchases covered a number of years (1562 to 1571), but the quantities were relatively small and were almost certainly for consumption in his household, as were those by the other members of the chapter.[63]

Although there were no legal bars to purchases by clergy, enough moral objections apparently arose so that the Third Mexican Provincial Church Council in 1585 enacted far more stringent prohibitions. Under its decrees, no clergy, secular or regular, might trade; no minister to the Indians might deal directly or indirectly in products arising in their land, including fish or game; no priest of a parish of Indians might cultivate fields within the parish or for 10 leagues (approximately 25 miles) beyond; and finally, no priest, secular or regular, in a parish of Indians might bid in auctions of royal tribute in kind for towns in his district, either directly or indirectly.[64] When confirmed by the Crown and the Vatican, these prohibitions became binding in the Archbishopric of Mexico and its suffragan bishoprics. In present-day legal jargon, the legislation was supposed to have a chilling effect.

The viceregal order of 1594 and the audiencia one of 1600, diverting maize and chickens for distribution at set prices among the *beneméritos de la república*, of course constituted a new system and effectively ended the free market except for the few amounts of other commodities still delivered as tribute. The judges of the audiencia and the royal treasury officials, previously barred from the auctions, could now apply for and receive allotments of maize and chickens at moderate prices. Whatever the prohibitions of the Third Mexican Provincial Church Council, such allotments were held to fall outside their scope, and so the cathedral chapter, particularly, could still benefit from access at low prices to foodstuffs.[65] This system of allotment partially compensated for salaries and stipends that failed to accommodate to a rising level of prices. The Crown lost revenue, but was under less pressure to raise salaries.

---

[62]Appendix A; King to the Bishop of Nueva Galicia, Madrid, 31 August 1561, AGI, Audiencia of Guadalajara, leg. 230, ff. 66-67; and Dávila Garibi, *Apuntes*, 1: 565.

[63]Appendix A.

[64]Mexico (Ecclesiastical Province), *Concilium Mexicanum Provinciale III*, *lib.* III, *titulus* XX, clauses II, IV, and V.

[65]The royal treasury accounts show payments for allocations of chickens to canons. GBPE, Archivo de la Real Audiencia, Ramo Fiscal, exp. 3, Cuentas 1598-1599, receipts of almonedas of tributes, ff. 77f-85v; and exp. 3a, ff. 90v-98f; exp. 4, Cuentas 1605-1606, ff. 90f-108v.

7

CONCLUDING REMARKS

We now examine two quite different aspects of the movement of prices in Nueva Galicia. One is the cost of unskilled labor as a gross indication of what rise in prices, measured in terms of silver coin, meant in terms of the purchasing power of labor. Economists today would call this real terms. The phraseology is distinctly less applicable to sixteenth-century western Nueva Galicia, where the Indians were essentially meeting their own needs, but they were also compelled to find silver coin for their tribute and so were drawn into the Spanish markets by sale of labor or produce. The other aspect is the influence of possible climatic change in the second half of the sixteenth century, which may add another factor determining scarcity or abundance of supply. The examination of both aspects is greatly complicated by the meagerness of firm evidence.

Let us start with the cost of unskilled labor. Our attempt at analysis may best begin by summarizing the experience of the Audiencia of Mexico as set forth in the study *Price Trends . . ., 1531-1570*, by myself and the late Professor Sherburne F. Cook. What is stated in that study on the importance of Indian labor to the Spaniards and the forms of procurement applies equally well to the Audiencia of Nueva Galicia. In the Audiencia of Mexico, unskilled labor earned, as a general rate around 1550, 2 to 3 granos a day, or 1 to 1½ reales for a week of six days. The rate rose steadily, if irregularly, until in 1590 it was set by viceregal ordinance at 12 granos or one real a day for the entire Audiencia of Mexico, that is, 6 reales for a week of six days. In 1591 a real a day was the prevailing rate in the province of Ávalos, neighboring to Nueva Galicia but still in the Audiencia of Mexico. The wage for unskilled labor continued to rise for some years thereafter until it reached a plateau in the seventeenth century. The experience of the Audiencia of Mexico is thus a fairly steady rise on the order of a sixfold increase between 1550 and 1590, and more thereafter.[1]

We shall omit from our attempt at analysis Zacatecas and the eastern part of Nueva Galicia, since we have no detailed information whatever on that area. Witnesses and Crown officials all agreed that costs there were much higher than in the Guadalajara area.[2] For Guadalajara and its hinterland, the loss of sixteenth-century records has reduced us to one important bit of indirect evidence and several bits of direct evidence. For the seventeenth century, much more information survives, some of it shedding light on earlier practice. Our one bit of sixteenth-century indirect evidence relates to the rise in prices in Guadalajara between 1547 and 1550. On 16 July 1550, Lic. Hernando Martínez de la Marcha, Alcalde Mayor of Guadalajara and Visitor-General of Nueva Galicia, received testimony from worthy citizens of the city on the sharp rise in prices in those years. All agreed that the cost of maize, wheat, and chickens had at least doubled in three years or even tripled. In Zacatecas, prices had risen even more,[3] testifying to the effect of the flood of silver from the newly discovered mines and the bidding up of prices by a mining population avid for supplies. Unfortunately, the witnesses did not comment on the cost of labor, but a comparison of the prices they gave for the three foodstuffs with those prevailing in the Audiencia of Mexico and a further comparison of tribute schedules for the two audiencias, which showed lower assessments in silver coin for Nueva Galicia, suggests that unskilled labor in Guadalajara probably earned somewhat less than two granos a day, perhaps one to one and a half. The wages of unskilled labor, being set by ordinance of the city or audiencia, usually lagged in adjusting to the rising prices of commodities.

Four of our bits of direct evidence relate to the price of convict labor, i.e., Indians sold for ten years of service—ten being the maximum term permitted by royal order. On 1 April 1598, Álvaro de Vergara, a priest, deposited 90/1/6 with the royal treasury officials, his winning bid for ten years' service by Juan Miguel, an Indian of Suchipil, convicted of killing Alonso Núñez, a Spaniard. The price works out to 2.4 granos a day, but does not include the cost of housing, feeding, and clothing the convict, whose maintenance became a charge upon his new master. In our studies of the cost of labor in sixteenth-century central Mexico, Professor Cook and I found that providing maintenance constituted on average approximately half the price bid, that is, a third of the total cost to the master. Any bid must have taken that additional cost into account. Accordingly, the 2.4 granos paid for Juan Miguel really implied a cost of at least 3.6 granos a day. That same day in 1598, the royal treasury officials entered in their ledgers 43/7/8 from Antonio de Aguayo for ten years' service by Pedro, an

---

[1]Borah and Cook, *Price Trends*, pp. 38-46 and 86-89. See also Charles Gibson, *The Aztecs under Spanish Rule*, pp. 249-252.

[2]Información hecha por el Alcalde Mayor de Guadalajara y Visitador General del Reino de la Nueva Galicia, Lic. D. Hernando Martínez de la Marcha acerca del precio de venta de varios alimentos de primera necesidad, Guadalajara, 16 July 1550, in Orozco y Jiménez, *Colección*, 5: 7-15; Lic. Vásquez and the royal treasury officials of Nueva Galicia to the King, Mines of Zacatecas, 10 February 1563, in Paso y Troncoso, *Epistolario*, 9: 205; and Chevalier, pp. 74-75.

[3]Orozco y Jiménez, 5: 7-15.

Indian of Tecomatlán, who had killed his mother-in-law. The sum was net of legal costs,[4] which already had been paid out and unfortunately are not stated in the surviving records. Legal costs, involving fees of all officials taking part in the trial, the judge included, and charges for arrest and keeping in jail, customarily absorbed a large part of the payment; we may estimate them at 50 percent, or a sum equal to the amount deposited. Accordingly, the payment by Antonio de Aguayo, with adjustments for legal costs and maintenance, would have meant a total cost of 3.51 granos a day or more. The next year, on 4 May 1599, Diego Rubio, through Francisco Covarrubias, deposited 108/2/2 for ten years' service from Sebastián Vicente, a native of Quaquala, convicted of killing another Indian.[5] Rubio's successful bid comes to 2.9 granos a day, which with calculation for maintenance works out to 4.35 granos daily. We may add to these bits of evidence for the sixteenth century one other item on convict labor of the seventeenth century, but close enough in time to be considered with them. On 8 August 1605 Diego Nieto Maldonado deposited 101/6 for ten years' service from Diego Hernández, condemned for killing a girl with an arrow (*flechazo*).[6] The sum works out to 2.7 granos a day, which after adjustment for maintenance comes to 4.05 granos daily.

These values are fairly congruent, since they occur in a range of 3.5 to 4.35 granos a day. They suggest that the cost of labor had risen perhaps threefold since 1550. However, they represent the price of convict labor, whose relation to free unskilled labor in the Guadalajara area must still be established. So-called free unskilled labor, drawn by repartimiento draft from Indian towns, was paid according to scales set by audiencia ordinance. *Tapixques*, Indians set to personal service in Spanish households and to cleaning and building in the Spanish towns, were paid 0/2 for a week of six days, that is, 4 granos a day and food, during the first decade of the seventeenth century, a rate that we may assume applied as well to the last years of the sixteenth century. Since they came from towns at relatively short distances from the Spanish settlements, they were not paid for *ida y vuelta*—time spent in traveling to and from work.[7] This rate compares well with the cost of convict labor, if the latter is considered to have meant household service, as it probably did.

A second category of Indian workers, field and harvest hands laboring in the raising of maize and wheat, earned a higher wage. Our sixteenth-century evidence is from the valley of Ameca and the province of Ávalos, both administratively in the Audiencia of Mexico but adjacent to Guadalajara and really part of its economic hinterland. The valley of Ameca was largely owned by residents of Guadalajara. According to the *relación geográfica* for the province of Tenamaztlán, dated 28 November 1579, the Indians of the province of their own free will went to the valley of Ameca for work on the Spanish-owned farms and ranches there. They earned 0/4

---

[4]Both entries in GBPE, Archivo de la Real Audiencia, Ramo Fiscal, exp. 3, Book of accounts, 1598-1599, f. 70f; Borah and Cook, *Price Trends*, pp. 38-46, esp. 46.

[5]GBPE, Archivo de la Real Audiencia, Ramo Fiscal, exp. 3a, Book of accounts, 1599, f. 70.

[6]Ibid., exp. 4, Libro de cargo y data, 1605, f. 82f.

[7]Águeda Jiménez Pelayo, "Condiciones del trabajo de repartimiento indígena en la Nueva Galicia en el siglo XVII," pp. 463-464.

for six days' work, and so in twelve days earned enough to cover their cash tribute of 1/0 in silver.[8] Presumably they were also furnished food and paid for the journey to and from the place of work. At the rate of 4 reales for a week's work, the wage comes to 8 granos a day. Approximately twelve years later, in 1591, the Viceroy of New Spain issued an order to the Alcalde Mayor of the province of Ávalos to supply Indian workmen for the raising of maize and wheat by the Jesuits on their properties in the province. The Indians were to be paid 6 silver reales a week for six days' work, or at the rate of 1 real a day.[9]

A rise in the wage of free unskilled labor from 8 granos a day in 1580 to 12 a day in 1591 records the experience of the Audiencia of Mexico, within whose administration the province of Ávalos lay. Its proximity to Guadalajara, however, suggests that a similar wage scale prevailed in that city as well, and that in those years free unskilled labor in western Nueva Galicia earned as much as in central Mexico. For the seventeenth century there can be no doubt that the wage scale of the Audiencia of Mexico for repartimiento labor prevailed also in Nueva Galicia. During the first half of the century, harvesters of wheat and maize in Nueva Galicia were paid between 0/1 and 0/1/6 a day; by 1671 they received 0/2. A lesser category of workers, called *pajareros*, were paid 0/0/6 in the earlier seventeenth century, rising to 0/1 by 1671.[10] These were as well the prevailing wage scales of the Audiencia of Mexico. Studies by Moïsés González Navarro and Eric Van Young establish that for the years after 1670, the two audiencias had a parallel wage scale for unskilled agricultural labor.[11]

The evidence adduced here indicates that wages for unskilled labor, free and convict, in the Guadalajara area rose at least as rapidly as in the Audiencia of Mexico. Since prior to 1550 they were probably lower than in the Audiencia of Mexico, they may well have risen more. If so, relative to the price of maize, they kept pace approximately in their rise (about 2.5-fold from 1557 to 1598).[12] On this somewhat fragile basis, we may say that the Indian workmen of western Nueva Galicia did not lose in terms of real wages during our period, but compared to their counterparts in the Audiencia of Mexico they gained less, or may not have gained at all.

Let us now consider the weather in Nueva Galicia during the years 1557-1598, and further, the extent to which longer-term changes affected prices. The years 1557-1598 fall within a long-term change in climate that has been relatively well charted for Europe and Anglo-America, all within the North Temperate Zone, and has been dubbed the "Little Ice Age." It was marked there by a decrease in average temperature that may have been as much as 1 degree Celsius; by colder winters,

---

[8]Acuña, 10: 291.

[9]Lesley Bird Simpson, *Studies in the Administration of the Indians in New Spain*, 3: 87.

[10]Jiménez Pelayo, "Condiciones," p. 463. *Pajareros* apparently were people, mostly boys, employed to scare off birds from the ripening grain.

[11]González Navarro, *Repartimiento de indios en Nueva Galicia*, passim; Van Young, *Hacienda and Market in Eighteenth-Century Mexico*, pp. 241-242.

[12]See section on maize, Chapter 4 above.

cooler summers, and the advance of glaciers. One of the most detailed local studies is the magnificent examination of the climate of Switzerland in recent centuries.[13] For the United States and Canada, we have the remarkable and comprehensive studies emanating from the Laboratory of Tree-Ring Research in Tucson, Arizona, which have established chronologies through sampling and comparison of tree rings reaching back thousands of years. For the Southwest of the United States–especially samples taken in southern Arizona–their reports indicate that the years 1557-1598 were characterized by lessened precipitation and lowered temperatures.[14] Stations in parts of southern Arizona and New Mexico lie in the northernmost extension of the summer rainfall zone that is characteristic of most of Mexico and all of Nueva Galicia. Unfortunately, the applicability of the data as a probable indication of weather in Nueva Galicia must be held to be unlikely. The dendrochronologies prepared in Tucson do not reach far into Mexico in space or time. The southernmost samples have been investigated in locations at high altitudes in Durango and do not go farther back than 1592.[15] They are derived from what are basically temperate-zone conifers, which add a ring a year.[16] The inquiry has not been extended to tropical-zone conifers at lower altitudes, that of the zone of agriculture in Nueva Galicia. In attempts to determine the extent to which the data for the Durango samples and those for the southern U.S. Southwest correspond, the two sets were compared by computer for the years from 1592 through the seventeenth century in various ways, including lagging one set against the other by a year to cover possible delays in effect. Correlations for the comparisons were +0.27 or less, that is, weakly positive but statistically insignificant. As far as could be determined, there is no way at this point that the impressive dendrochronological studies carried out in the United States and northern Mexico can be applied farther south.[17]

---

[13] Christian Pfister, *Das Klima der Schweiz von 1525-1800*, passim; and "Fluctuations climatiques et prix céréaliers en Europe du XVIe au XXe siècle"; Emmanuel Le Roy Ladurie, *Histoire du climat depuis l'an mil*, passim; Jean M. Grove, *The Little Ice Age*, passim; John Herman and Richard Goldberg, *Sun, Weather, and Climate*, passim; D. Justin Schove, ed. *Sunspot Cycles*, passim; Minze Stuiver, "Solar Variability and Climatic Change during the Current Millennium"; Claxton and Hecht, "Climatic and Human History in Europe and Latin America."

[14] Fritts, *Tree Rings and Climate*, passim, and "Tree Ring Evidence for Climatic Change in Western North America"; Leona M. Libby, *Past Climates: Tree Thermometers, Commodities, and People*, passim: Jeffrey S. Dean and William J. Robinson, *Expanded Tree Ring Chronologies for the Southwestern United States*, passim; Drew, *Tree-Ring Chronologies of Western America. III. California and Nevada*, passim, and *Tree Ring Chronologies of Western America. VI. Western Canada and Mexico*, passim; Schulman, *Dendroclimatic Changes in Semiarid America*, passim, esp. pp. 58-69 and Table 66; Stokes, Drew, and Stockton, *Tree Ring Chronologies of Western America. I. Selected Tree-Ring Stations*, passim.

[15] Drew, *Tree Ring Chronologies. VI. Western Canada and Mexico*, p. 30.

[16] Schulman, pp. 39-41.

[17] These conclusions differ from those of Claxton and Hecht, p. 200, who found that periods of high precipitation in Mexico City occurred during wet decades reconstructed from tree-ring variations for the U.S. Southwest. See also Susan Swan, "Mexico in the Little Ice Age"; and Dieter Klaus, "Las fluctuaciones del clima en el valle de Puebla-Tlaxcala."

Another approach is to tabulate the years of sharp rise and continuation of that rise for maize and wheat.[18] Such rises might be due to rebellion, epidemic, drought, frost, and hail during the growing season. The factor of silver inflation because of the continuing flood of silver must also be considered. It may be adjusted for, at least in part, by accounting as years of great stress in maize after 1572 those that are marked "xx" or "xxx" in Table 7.1, and placing much less emphasis on those marked "x". Rebellion we may rule out, since only local ones on the coast are reported for the period.[19] Epidemics we may identify from reports of the time, for the widespread onslaught of disease would be noticed. Enrique Florescano has reported, on evidence for central Mexico, the years 1563-1564, 1576-1581, and 1588 as years of epidemic, and has pointed to 1563-1565, 1573, and 1579-1581 as years of shortage and hunger.[20] One must be careful in extrapolating these reports to Nueva Galicia since conditions were often locally confined. Thus in 1568, Viceroy Enríquez wrote to Philip II that the maize crop in New Spain had been heavily damaged by frosts and the price of maize had risen sharply.[21] Nueva Galicia, on our evidence, shows no such price rise. Of course, its crops might be less likely to be affected by frost that would damage crops at the higher altitudes of the valleys of Mexico, Toluca, and Puebla-Tlaxcala. Epidemics were and are less likely to respect altitude, and were much more likely than frost to spread. Table 7.1, which compares what one might call the periods of stress in prices of maize and wheat, shows a common sharp rise in 1578, but stress only in the prices of maize in 1563-1564. Unfortunately, we lack data for 1588.

Our comparison of rise in prices for maize and wheat has the advantage that the requirements in moisture and temperature tolerances of the two crops differ considerably. Maize needs more water than wheat. Its needs have been estimated at 40 to 50 centimeters in the rainy season, whereas wheat grows well in areas of lower precipitation and resists periods of drought somewhat better. It was grown through irrigation in Nueva Galicia. In terms of temperature tolerance, maize requires warmer temperatures and is easily damaged by frost, whereas wheat withstands lower temperatures well and resists frost better.[22] Table 7.1, therefore, permits us to locate years of exceptional strain when prices of tribute maize and wheat both shot up, and years of lesser strain when the price of maize alone rose. We may eliminate the years 1557-1558, when the price of tribute wheat alone rose, as due to demand when Zacatecas was drawing in supplies and Spanish cultivation of wheat was not well under way. The only coincidences of stress in the prices of the two crops came in 1575, 1578, 1582, and 1586. The year 1578 must be accounted at least in part the aftermath of epidemic, since matlazáhuatl invaded Nueva Galicia in

---

[18]See Table 7.1.

[19]See Appendix A.

[20]Florescano, *Origen y desarrollo de los problemas agrarios de México*, pp. 52-53.

[21]Enríquez to Philip II, México, 29 December 1568 (AGI, México, leg. 1089), cited in García-Abasolo, p. 143.

[22]A. Landaverde, *El maís y su cultivo en México*, pp. 58-60; and Michael Y. Nuttonson, *Wheat-Climate Relationships and the Use of Phenology in Ascertaining the Thermal and Photo-Thermal Requirements of Wheat*, pp. 34-57.

October 1576 and lasted through most of 1577. Its ravages may have interfered with the cultivation of crops in 1578 but, coupled with the lack of stress in the price of tribute wheat in 1576 and 1577, one suspects difficulty in weather. The years 1582-1583 and 1586, equally years of stress in the prices of both crops, indicate unusually unfavorable weather. For the rest, our table suggests–through the many years of stress in prices of tribute maize and few in tribute wheat–that the "Little Ice Age" came to Nueva Galicia in the form of a moderate lowering of rainfall, or perhaps more irregular occurrence, and an equally moderate lowering of temperature during the growing season that placed maize at greater risk. The stress years 1560-1564 do embrace Florescano's epidemic years of 1563-1564, but form a much longer period of higher maize prices and possibly less favorable weather conditions. Similarly, the long run of stress in the prices of maize from 1572 to 1583, with a gap in 1579 because of our lack of data, indicate less favorable conditions for maize, again because of weather. The years 1576, 1578, and 1580-1582 were unusually difficult ones, but only 1576 and perhaps 1578 can be ascribed to epidemic. Trouble in the food supply in those years started long before matlazáhuatl arrived in Nueva Galicia. The years 1585-1598, with evidence lacking for 1588 and 1589, were again periods of stress in the price of tribute maize, with 1586 an especially unfavorable year, as indicated by stress in the price of wheat as well. For maize, 1586, 1591-1594, and 1596 stand out as periods of even sharper price rise. The years 1594 and 1596 were apparently the worst. There may have been an influence of epidemic in the stress of the 1590s, since an outbreak of smallpox was reported in Sinaloa in 1592–well north of Nueva Galicia proper–and central Mexico experienced a compound epidemic in 1595. The extent to which these invaded Nueva Galicia is unknown.

A further attempt to compare the data in Table 7.1 and the dendrochronology for southern Arizona[23] by comparing years of low tree-ring growth with years of stress in the prices for sales led again to an inconclusive result. Simple visual inspection indicates that years of low growth occasionally correspond to years of stress, but as often do not. In the end, we must return to the comparison of maize and wheat for clues.

Our data, to the extent that they shed light on climate, suggest that drought and lower temperatures during the growing season may have affected Nueva Galicia in the years 1557-1598. More exact determinations must await the uncovering and analysis of more precise data.

The preceding chapters have analyzed the price data in the records of Indian tributes sold at public auction in Nueva Galicia in the years 1557-1598. They contain a number of basic arguments. First, in the absence of other types of price data conventionally used for price studies, the records of royal tribute auctions afford a substitute. Despite limitation to a single annual datum for each commodity in the tribute of each town, they provide material for a clear determination of trend. They also provide evidence of what are essentially the lower levels of prevailing prices. In effect, they give us an entry into the very difficult question of movement of prices in sixteenth-century Spanish America. Second, the analysis of the royal auction data

[23]The data for southern Arizona and New Mexico are in Schulman, Table 66.

Table 7.1
Periods of Stress in Prices of Maize and Wheat[1]

Year	Maize	Wheat	Year	Maize	Wheat
1557		x	1577	x	
1558		x	1578	xx	x
1559			1579	NA	NA
1560	x		1580	xx	
1561	x		1581	xx	
1562	x		1582	xx	x
1563	x		1583	x	x
1564	x		1584		
1565			1585	x	
1566			1586	xx	x
1567			1587	x	
1568			1588	NA	NA
1569			1589	NA	NA
1570			1590	xx	
1571			1591	xx	
1572	x		1592	xx	
1573	x		1593	xxx	
1574	x		1594	xxx	
1575	x	x	1595	x	
1576	xx		1596	xxx	
			1597	xx	

1. Degree of stress shown by x, xx, or xxx.
Source: Appendix C.

demonstrates very clearly that three of the major factors determining the movement of prices in the Audiencia of Mexico–that is, basically central Mexico–also operated in the Audiencia of Nueva Galicia. They were: the requirements of the Spanish settlers; the flood of silver from the mines of Pachuca, Zacatecas, and numerous other discoveries; and the rapid decline of the Indian population.

The requirements of the Spanish settlers, real and perceived, in part set by their own culture and their wish to avoid manual labor, in part decided by the world economy and the technology of the time, determined essentially what the Spanish sought. The flood of silver that began in the 1540s and continued in increasing volume through the rest of the sixteenth century meant that a larger and larger quantity of silver confronted amounts of consumer goods that were not expanding at the same rate, and in most cases were contracting. The decline of the Indian population brought about a drop in the goods and services that could be secured by the Spaniards. However, our analyses make it very clear that these three major factors were not operating at parallel pace in the two audiencia jurisdictions. If measured in terms of maize, the basic foodstuff of the Indians, lower classes in general, and beasts, especially those used for power and transportation, prices rose faster in Nueva Galicia than in the Audiencia of Mexico. Furthermore, for purposes of comparison, we must separate Nueva Galicia into two areas: the eastern part of the jurisdiction, comprising Zacatecas and its hinterland, and the western part, comprising Guadalajara and its hinterland, for in terms of silver, the rise in the price of maize was far steeper in the western part than in the eastern part. Zacatecas and its mines very rapidly developed a network of cart roads that brought supplies from Michoacán, the Bajío, and the oases of the north, and further developed extensive stock-raising and cereal agriculture in those oases. In the last years of the sixteenth century, the prices in silver of tribute maize auctioned at Zacatecas actually fell to lower levels from the heights of earlier decades. Only in the western part of the jurisdiction, the economic territory of Guadalajara, did prices rise faster than in the Audiencia of Mexico.

If measured in terms of wheat, prices in Nueva Galicia followed a very different course from those in the Audiencia of Mexico. Whereas in New Spain proper the prices of wheat tended to rise somewhat faster than those of maize, in Nueva Galicia, after rising in the middle years of the century, prices of tribute wheat tended to move lower in the later years of the century. Clearly, the Spanish settlers were able to establish their own production of wheat on their own estates (using Indian workers, of course) and so make tribute wheat one element among several in an adequate supply. Toward the end of the sixteenth century, wheat ceased to figure in the tribute of royal towns, and probably of all towns.

Third, it follows from this discussion that New Spain, in the larger sense of the territory of the two audiencias, although under one viceroy, did not constitute a unified market. Lack of roads and adequate means of land transport for bulk commodities meant that the two audiencia jurisdictions essentially had separate, though similar, economies. Each jurisdiction, further, was subdivided into smaller market areas, like Yucatán and Oaxaca in the Audiencia of Mexico, and the eastern and western parts of the jurisdiction in Nueva Galicia. The economic history of Mexico has included the slow creation of a unified market embracing the country through the development of roads, railroads, and highways in a process that did not reach completion until the 1930s and later. In the sixteenth century, Mexico must have consisted of many small market zones, connected by the exchange of higher unit value and less bulky goods, but separated by the costs of transportation. Zacatecas and its zone stand out from this general pattern because of the rapid building of cart roads and speedy creation of stock-raising and cereal-growing haciendas. Moreover, its relatively high wage levels and free life attracted Indians and *castas* as well as Europeans, so that in an area previously inhabited by a few nomadic Indians there rose substantial settlements with an influx of workmen. Its work force increased through recruitment from all over the colony, and in the general melting-pot of the mining settlements, Indians merged with non-Indian elements to form a distinctively Mexican population attached to Hispanic culture. In contrast, the western parts of the jurisdiction of Nueva Galicia, that is, Guadalajara and its hinterland, formed a much less unified market area, where transportation moved by pack train and bearer. It probably resembled other areas in central Mexico in its more primitive transportation.

Fourth, our examination of the buyers should have made clear that the Spanish settlers in Nueva Galicia, despite their aversion to manual labor, constituted an energetic, entrepreneurial group. Since the initial size and steady decline of the Indian inhabitants made impossible fulfillment of any desire to live on income from encomiendas, nor could most Crown appointments provide more than modest salaries and fees, they rapidly sought their livelihood through a variety of undertakings in mining, stock-raising, farming, speculation, trade, and longer-range commerce. Some were eminently successful, most less so.

Fifth, the problem of longer-term climatic change, as separate from the vagaries of normal occurrence of years of drought and ample rainfall in Nueva Galicia–essentially the meaning of the concept of the "Little Ice Age" as applied to the region–must remain unresolved until more data are available.

Appendix A

Auction Data

Symbols and Abbreviations

a/m = alcalde mayor	governor of a province
@ = arroba	about 25 lb. dry measure
alg = algodon	cotton
C = cacaxtle (de fruta)	a basket (of fruit)
can = cántaro	pitcher = liq. measure
car = carga	load = ca. 100 lb.
cu = cada uno	each one
f = fanega	Sp. bushel = 54.52 liters
fr = frijoles	frijoles
g = guajolote	turkey
j = jarro (de miel)	jar = a measure for honey
lib = libra	Castilian pound (460 gr.)
m = maíz	maize
mech = mechinpuyeque	torches of mangrove wood
ost = ostiones	oysters
oz = onzas	ounces
p = pollo	chicken
pi - pierna }	{pierna = strip of cloth from
pi de m = pierna de manta}	backstrap loom}
pes = pescado	fish
prod = productos de	products of
qtla = cuartilla o 1/4 arroba	4.0325 liters
qtlo = cuartillo	Castilian quart (1/2 liter)
t, T, (t) = Todo	all
tr = trigo	wheat
v = vara	Castilian yard (33 in.)
vc = vara cuadrada	square (Castilian) yard

Date	Town	Item & Amount	Unit Price	Buyer & Remarks
?	Nochistlanejo	20 f m	0/2	Cosecha de 1554
1555?	Tequila	180 f m	1/0	1555 valuación por los oficiales reales
		8 f fr	1/0	
		22 f tr	1/4	
		9 j miel	1/0	
?	Tlajomulco	mantas	7/0	Conmutación 1555
			3/0	Conmutación en la tasación vieja
?	Temichoque	algodón de 1557	t 43/	Rodrigo Pérez, vecino de Compostela
	Tepic.-sem.	20 f tr	2/0	Cosecha de 1557
16-XI-1557	Amboquito y Atengo	2 mantas (4 pi)		
		100 car sal = 33⅓ f		
		4 tecomales miel		
		(1 @ cu)	t 53/6	?
		12 g		
		1 sem m de 1 f de invierno		
	Maito	100 car sal = 33⅓ f		
		8 pi de m		
		4 g	t 55/6	?
		1 sem m de 1½ f de invierno		
	Colique	8 pi de m		
		80 car sal		
		2 can miel = ½ @		
		10 g	t 50/2	?
		2 sem m de ½ f cu de invierno y verano		
22-XI-1557	Atetaco	8 pi de m	1/4	?
		8 g	0/1	?
		12 f m	0/6	?
16-I-1558	Analco y Tetlán	1350 f m	0/2	Lope de Cisneros
		700 p	0/0/3	Lope de Cisneros
17-I-1558	Cuitzeo	648 f m	0/2	Lope de Cisneros
		1440 p	0/0/3	Lope de Cisneros
	Tlajomulco	810 f m	0/2	Lope de Cisneros
		400 p	0/0/3	Lope de Cisneros
	Tonalá	630 f m	0/2	Lope de Cisneros
		45 6 fr	0/2	Lope de Cisneros
		22: f ají	0/2	Lope de Cisneros
		Comida	56/	Lope de Cisneros
	Tlaquepaque, San Pedro	720 f m	0/2	Lope de Cisneros
		400 p	0/0/3	Lope de Cisneros
	Atemajac	450 f m	0/2	Lope de Cisneros
		50 p	0/0/3	Lope de Cisneros
	Nochistlanejo	270 f m	0/2	Lope de Cisneros
		40 g	0/0/3	Lope de Cisneros
		30 p	0/0/3	Lope de Cisneros

Date	Town	Item & Amount	Unit Price	Buyer & Remarks
	Camotlán (Barranca)	198 f m	0/2	Lope de Cisneros
		50 p	0/0/3	Lope de Cisneros
17-I-1558	Tequila	180 f m	0/3/6	Lope de Cisneros
		22:6 f tr	1/0	Lope de Cisneros
		18 f fr	0/3/6	Lope de Cisneros
		9 j miel	1/0	Lope de Cisneros
	Copala y Quilitlán	180 f m	0/2	Lope de Cisneros
		rezago	t 20/4	Lope de Cisneros
	Amatitlán	180 f m	0/2	Lope de Cisneros
	Cuyutlán y Cajititlán	126 f m	0/2	Lope de Cisneros
		comida	12/	Lope de Cisneros
1-II-1558	Sentispac	270 f m	0/2	Alonso Valiente
		40 mantas	8/0	Rodrigo de Aranda
		150 @ pes	0/1/9	Bartólome Napolitano
		24 @ ost	0/5	Francisco Rojo
	Tepic	360 f m	0/2	Alonso Valiente
		40 f tr	1/0	Bartolomé de Balbuena
		200 p	0/0/7	Pedro Ladrón de Guevara
		Mandados diarios durante Cuaresma: 20 pes } 20 huevos}	t 13/	Bartolomé de Balbuena
	Suchipil	270 f m	0/3/6	Alonso Valiente
		13:6 f tr	1/2	Rodrigo de Aranda
		4 camas	24/	Rodrigo de Aranda
		Semanario: 5 p } 1 g } 20 huevos} 1 C fruta}	t 31/	Rodrigo Pérez
		18 f fr	0/4/6	Alonso Valiente
	Ahuacatlán	112:6 f m	0/3/4	Juan Ayllán
		8 f fr	0/4/6	Juan Ayllán
		8 f tr	1/3	Rodrigo de Aranda
		2 camas	24/3/6	Rodrigo de Aranda
		Semanario: 3 p } 1 g } 10 huevos} 1 C fruta}	t 13/	Bartolomé de Valbuena
	Jala	36 mantas	4/4	Alonso Valiente
		8 camas	18/1/6	Tomás Laso
		180 f m	0/2/6	Francisco Rojo
		Semanario: 3 p } 1 g } 20 huevos} 1 C fruta}	t 20/4	Juan de Ayllán
1-II-1558	San Juan, et al.	32 f m	0/2	Bartólome Napolitano
		4 mantas	3/0	Bartólome Napolitano

Date	Town	Item & Amount	Unit Price	Buyer & Remarks
		3 naguas	0/6	Francisco Rojo
		3 huipiles	0/6	Francisco Rojo
		3 g	t 0/4	Francisco Rojo
		3 j miel	t 1/0	Francisco Rojo
		3 car pes	0/2	Francisco Rojo
4-II-1558	Jalcocotán	27 f m	0/2	Martín de Rentería
		30 p }		
		8 g }	t 3/0	Martín de Rentería
		2 j miel }		
		de 1 @ }	t 3/0	Bartolomé de Balbuena
	Mecatán	13:6 f m	0/2	Martín de Rentería
		1 j miel	0/7	Rodrigo Pérez
		10 p }		
		4 g }	t 1/0	Rodrigo Pérez
	Jaltepec	5 f m	0/3	Rodrigo de Aranda
	Tepuzhuacán	12 mantas (5v x 4v)	4/4	Francisco Rojo
	Atengoichán	630 f m	0/2	Rodrigo de Aranda
	Jalacingo	6 mantas	4/4	Alonso Valiente
		4 p }		
		2 g }	t 0/4	Rodrigo de Aranda
	Ixtimitique	3 mantas	4/0	Alonso Valiente
		3 p }		
		1 g }	t 0/3	Rodrigo de Aranda
	Amatlán	8 mantas	4/4	Alonso Valiente
		5 p }		
		3 g }	t 1/1	Juan S^{e}, Intérprete
	Ixtapa	24 f sal	1/3	Rodrigo Pérez
		4 car pes	t 1/5	Juan de Ayllán
		12 p	t 0/4	Rodrigo de Aranda
		Rezago:		
		24 f sal	1/1	Hernando de la Peña
	Amaxaque	90 f m	t 14/4	Hernando de la Peña
		45 p	t 3/0	Bartolomé de Balbuena
9-II-1558	Temichoque	13 f m	0/1	Francisco Rojo
		2-1/3 @ alg	0/4	Rodrigo Pérez
		10 g	0/1	Rodrigo Pérez
		10 calabazas		
		de miel = }		
		10 qtlos }	t 0/4	Rodrigo Pérez
	Pontoque	18 f m	0/1	Rodrigo Pérez
		4 g	0/1	Rodrigo Pérez
	Acatispa	36 f m	0/1	Rodrigo Pérez
		4 g	0/1	Rodrigo Pérez
	Orita	18 f m	0/1	Rodrigo Pérez
		2 g	0/1	Rodrigo Pérez
	Zacatlán	20 mantas		
		(chicas)	0/4	Francisco Rojo
		20 naguas }		
		20 camisas }	0/2	Francisco Rojo

Date	Town	Item & Amount	Unit Price	Buyer & Remarks
		? f m	0/2	Bartolomé de Balbuena
		? f fr	0/2	Bartolomé de Balbuena
		? @ alg	0/2	Bartolomé de Balbuena
		40 p	t 1/1	Hernando de la Peña
		3 j miel }		
		1 car pes }	t 0/4	Bartolomé de Balbuena
3-XI-1558	Analco y Tetlán	630 f m	0/2	Luis Pérez
		700 p	0/0/3	Luis Pérez
	Tlajomulco	810 f m	0/2	Luis Pérez
		400 p	0/0/3	Luis Pérez
	Cuyutlán y Cajititlán	226 f m	0/2	Luis Pérez
		Comida	12/	Luis Pérez
	Tonalá	630 f m	0/2	Luis Pérez
		45 f fr	0/2	Luis Pérez
		22:6 f ají	0/2	Luis Pérez
		Comida	56/	Luis Pérez
13-XI-1558	Mezquituta	100 p	0/0/6	Francisco de Ibarra
		540 f m	0/3	Francisco de Ibarra
	Tlaltenango et al.	990 f m	0/4	Francisco de Ibarra
		106 g	0/2	Francisco de Ibarra
		214 p	0/0/6	Francisco de Ibarra
14-XI-1558	Nochistlan }	1395 f m	0/4/6	Francisco de Ibarra
	Teocaltiche }	50:6 f ají	1/4	Francisco de Ibarra
	Teocaltitlan}	40 f fr	1/4	Francisco de Ibarra
		(set as average, but to be checked)		
		720 p	0/1	Francisco de Ibarra
17-XII-1558	Zalatitlán	45 f m	0/2	Lope de Cisneros
		161 p	0/0/3	Lope de Cisneros
		100 huevos	t 0/4	Lope de Cisneros
	Ixtlahuacán }	94:6 f m	0/2	Lope de Cisneros
	Cozcotitán }	henequen}		
	Ixtlahuatengo }	miel }	t 30/	Lope de Cisneros
	(La Barranca)}	Comida }		
	Nochistlanejo	270 f m	0/2	Lope de Cisneros
		40 g }		
		30 p }	0/0/3	Lope de Cisneros
17-XII-1558	Zalatitlán	45 f m	0/2	Lope de Cisneros
		161 p	0/0/3	Lope de Cisneros
		100 huevos	t 0/4	Lope de Cisneros
	Ixtlahuacán }	94:6 f m	0/2	Lope de Cisneros
	Cozcotitán }	henequin }		
	Ixtlanuatengo }	miel }	t 30/	Lope de Cisneros
	(La Barranca)}	comida }		
	Nochistlanejo	270 f m	0/2	Lope de Cisneros
		40 g }		
		30 p }	0/0/3	Lope de Cisneros
	Tequila	180 f m	0/3/6	Lope de Cisneros
		22:6 f tr	1/0	Lope de Cisneros
		18 f fr	0/3/6	Lope de Cisneros
		9 j miel	1/0	Lope de Cisneros

Date	Town	Item & Amount	Unit Price	Buyer & Remarks
	Tlajomulco	310 f m	0/2	Lope de Cisneros
		400 p	0/0/3	Lope de Cisneros
3-XI-1559	Atemajac	225 f m	0/2	Luis Pérez
		50 p	0/0/3	Luis Pérez
	Nochistlanejo	90 f m	0/3	Luis Pérez
		40 p	0/0/3	Luis Pérez
	Coscotitán (La Barranca de Bargaña)	45 f m	0/2	Luis Pérez
		45 p	0/0/3	Luis Pérez
	Copala y Quilitlán	180 f m	0/2	Luis Pérez
	Camotlán	54 f m	0/2	Luis Pérez
		60 p	0/0/3	Luis Pérez
	Tlaquepaque, San Pedro	720 f m	0/2	Luis Pérez
		400 p	0/0/3	Luis Pérez
	Amatitlán	180 f m	0/2	Luis Pérez
	Cuitzeo	648 f m	0/2	Luis Pérez
		1440 p	0/0/3	Luis Pérez
	Zalatitlán	45 f m	0/2	Luis Pérez
		100 p	0/0/3	Luis Pérez
	Tequila	180 f m	0/3/6	Luis Pérez
		22:6 f tr	1/0	Luis Pérez
		18 f fr	0/3/6	Luis Pérez
		9 j miel	1/0	Luis Pérez
13-XI-1559	Nochistlán } Teocaltiche } Teocaltitlán }	1215 f m	0/4/6	Francisco de Ibarra
		570 p	0/1	Francisco de Ibarra
		60 g	0/2	Francisco de Ibarra
		32:6 f ají	1/4	Francisco de Ibarra
		cosecha de fr	1/4 f	Francisco de Ibarra
	Tlaltenango } Tachiteuca } Totatiche } Indios de Zac. }	990 f m	0/4	Francisco de Ibarra
		106 g	0/2	Francisco de Ibarra
		214 1/2 p	0/0/6	Francisco de Ibarra
	Mezquituta y Moyagua	270 f m	0/3	Francisco de Ibarra
		100 p	0/0/6	Francisco de Ibarra
29-XI-1559	Amaxaque	90 f m	0/2	Rodrigo Pérez
		45 p	0/0/4	Rodrigo Pérez
28-XII-1559	Sentispac	120 @ pes	0/4	Bartolomé Napolitano
		16 @ ost	0/4	Bartolomé Napolitano
		100 g	0/1/7	Vicario Jorge Pérez
		180 f m	0/3	Bartolomé Napolitano
	Suchipil	225 f m	0/3/6	Pedro Ruiz de Haro
		27 f tr	0/7	Rodrigo Pérez
		50 g	0/1/6	Juan Arias
		100 p	0/0/6	Rodrigo Pérez
28-XII-1559	Ahuacatlán	90 f m	0/2	Juan Arias
		9 f tr	0/7	Licenciado Vásquez
		25 g	0/1/3	Gerónimo de Orozco
		50 p	0/0/6	Rodrigo Pérez

Date	Town	Item & Amount	Unit Price	Buyer & Remarks
	Papachula, San Juan	24 f m	0/3	Rodrigo de Aranda, corregidor del Pueblo
		6 naguas }		
		6 huipiles }	0/6	Pedro Ruiz de Haro
		4 mantas	3/4	Pedro Ruiz de Haro
		1½ j miel	0/4	Rodrigo Pérez
		3 g	1/4	Francisco de Villamicar
	Jalcocotán	27 f m	0/2	Gerónimo de Orozco
		8 g	0/1/6	Gerónimo de Orozco
		30 p	0/0/6	Gerónimo de Orozco
		2 j miel	1/4	Gerónimo de Orozco
	Mecatán	12:6 f m	0/2	Gerónimo de Orozco
		4 g	0/1/6	Gerónimo de Orozco
		10 p	0/0/6	Gerónimo de Orozco
		1 j miel	1/4	Gerónimo de Orozco
	Zacatlán	20 mantas pequeñas	0/5/6	Juan Sánchez de la Torre
		20 naguas	0/5/6	Juan Sánchez de la Torre
		20 camisas	0/5/6	Juan Sánchez de la Torre
		m }		
		alg }	t 8/	Juan Sánchez de la Torre
	Atengoichán	630 f m	0/3/3	Padre Jorge Pérez
	Pontoque (diezmo quitado)	12 f m	0/2	Diego López
		4 g	0/1/6	Diego López
	Acatispa	14:6 f m	0/2	Diego López de Altapica
		6 p	0/0/6	Diego López de Altapica
		6 g	0/1/6	Diego López de Altapica
	Orita	13:6 f m	0/2	Diego López de Altapica
		12 p	0/0/6	Diego López de Altapica
		12 g	0/1/6	Diego López de Altapica
		4 @ alg	0/4	Diego López de Altapica
29-XII-1559	Jaltepec	4:6 f m	0/4	Rodrigo Pérez
	Tepuzhuacán	12 mantas	5/3	Padre Francisco de Angulo
	Jalacingo	6 mantas	5/	Padre Francisco de Angulo
		4 p }		
		2 g }	t 0/5	Padre Francisco de Angulo
	Amatitlán	8 mantas	5/	Juan Arias
		5 p }		
		3 g }	t 1/0	Padre Francisco de Angulo
29-XII-1559	Ixtimitique	3 mantas	5/	Padre Francisco de Angulo
		3 p }		
		1 g }	t 0/2	Padre Francisco de Angulo
	Temichoque	38 f m	0/3	Vicario Jorge Pérez
		2 1/3 @ alg	1/4	Juan Sánchez de la Torre
		12 p	0/0/6	Padre Jorge Pérez
29-XII-1559	Ixtapa, de Castañeda	10 f sal	1/0/6	Rodrigo Pérez
		Toda la cosecha:		
		12 @ alg	0/4	Antonio del Rincón
30-XII-1559	Tepic	360 f m	0/2	Diego López
		72 f tr	0/7	Diego López

Date	Town	Item & Amount	Unit Price	Buyer & Remarks
		Cuaresma Comida	9/0	Diego López
		200 p	0/0/6	Diego López
	Jala	157 f m	0/2	Diego López
		75 p	0/0/6	Diego López
	Ixtapa	15 f sal	1/1	Luis Alonso
		4 car pes	0/7	Simón de Coca
		12 p	0/0/7	Luis Alonso
	Ixcuintla (sin quitar el diezmo)	36 f m	0/2	Diego López de Altapica
		1 @ miel	1/4	Diego López de Altapica
		8 g	0/1/6	Diego López de Altapica
		16 p	0/0/6	Diego López de Altapica
	Matacticpac (sin quitar el diezmo)	12 f m	0/4	Antonio del Rincón
		4 f fr	0/5/6	Antonio del Rincón
		6 p } 6 g }	t 2/0	Francisco de Villamiçar
	Jocotlán y Quilitlán (menos el diezmo)	27 f m	0/1	Antonio del Rincón
		21½ @ alg	0/4	Antonio del Rincón
14-III-1560	Atengoichán	630 f m	0/3	Vicario Jorge Pérez en 1559
	Sentispac	m de 1557	t 83/5	Alonso López (vecino de Compostela)
14-V-1560	Analco y Tetlan	630 f m	0/3/6	Luis Pérez
	Tlaquepaque, San Pedro	720 f m	0/3/6	Luis Pérez
	Tlajomulco	810 f m	0/3/6	Luis Pérez
	Tonalá	630 f m	0/3/6	Luis Pérez
		45 f fr	0/3/6	Luis Pérez
		22:6 f ají	0/3/6	Luis Pérez
	Cuitzeo	648 f m	0/3/6	Luis Pérez
14-V-1560	Amaxaque	225 f m	0/3/6	Luis Pérez
	Nochistlanejo	90 f m	0/3/6	Luis Pérez
	Amatitlán	180 f m	0/3/6	Luis Pérez
	Copala	180 f m	0/3/6	Luis Pérez
	Cuyutlán y Zalatitlán	108 f m	0/3/6	Luis Pérez
		60 p	0/0/3	Luis Pérez
14-V-1560	Barranca de Borgoña (Coscotitán)	45 f m	0/3/6	Luis Pérez
	Camotlán (Barranca)	54 f m	0/3/6	Luis Pérez
25-V-1560	Sentispac	75 mantas	6/7/3	Lorenzo Vallejo
	(reservadas para velas de los buques y ahora puestas en venta)			
15-VI-1560	Sentispac	15 mantas	9/0	Juan Arias

Date	Town	Item & Amount	Unit Price	Buyer & Remarks
17-XI-1560	Tlaltenango y ptdo.	990 f m	1/0/3	Pedro de Ahumada
		214 p	0/0/6	Pedro de Ahumada
		106 g	0/2	Pedro de Ahumada
25-XI-1560	Nochistlán (4a postura)	270 f m	1/2	Pedro de Ahumada
		90 p	0/0/6	Pedro de Ahumada
		60 g	0/1	Pedro de Ahumada
25-XI-1560	Teocaltiche y Teocaltitlán	945 f m	1/2	Pedro de Ahumada
		32:6 f ají	1/0	Pedro de Ahumada
		cosecha de fr.	1/0 t	Pedro de Ahumada
		480 p	0/0/6	Pedro de Ahumada
25-XI-1560	Mezquituta y Moyagua	270 f m	1/0	Pedro García
		100 p	0/0/6	Damián de Argüello
1-XII-1560	Analco y Tetlán	630 f m	0/4/6	Pedro Sánchez Mexía
		700 p	0/0/3	Pedro Sánchez Mexía
	Tonalá	540 f m	0/4/6	Pedro Sánchez Mexía
		100 g }		
		200 p }	0/0/3	Pedro Sánchez Mexía
	Tlajomulco	810 f m	0/4/6	Pedro Sánchez Mexía
		400 p	0/0/3	Pedro Sánchez Mexía
	Cuitzeo y Poncitlán	648 f m	0/4/6	Pedro Sánchez Mexía
		1440 p	0/0/3	Pedro Sánchez Mexía
	Tlaquepaque, San Pedro	540 f m	0/4/6	Pedro Sánchez Mexía
		200 p	0/0/3	Pedro Sánchez Mexía
	Camotlán	54 f m	0/4/6	Pedro Sánchez Mexía
		60 p	0/0/3	Pedro Sánchez Mexía
	Cozcotitán	45 f m	0/4/6	Pedro Sánchez Mexía
		45 p	0/0/3	Pedro Sánchez Mexía
	Nochistlanejo	90 f m	0/4/6	Pedro Sánchez Mexía
		40 p	0/0/3	Pedro Sánchez Mexía
	Atemajac	225 f m	0/4/6	Pedro Sánchez Mexía
		50 p	0/0/3	Pedro Sánchez Mexía
	Cuyutlán	63 f m	0/4/6	Pedro Sánchez Mexía
		60 p	0/0/3	Pedro Sánchez Mexía
	Zalatitlán	45 f m	0/4/6	Pedro Sánchez Mexía
		100 p	0/0/3	Pedro Sánchez Mexía
1-XII-1560	Amatatitlán	180 f m	0/4/6	Pedro Sánchez Mexía
	Copala	90 f m	0/4/6	Pedro Sánchez Mexía
		50 p	0/0/3	Pedro Sánchez Mexía
	Tequila	180 f m	0/4/6	Pedro Sánchez Mexía
		22:6 f tr	1/0	Pedro Sánchez Mexía
		18 f fr	0/4/6	Pedro Sánchez Mexía
		9 j miel	1/0	Pedro Sánchez Mexía
15-XII-1560	Sentispac	180 f m	0/2	Fran. Rodríguez Bertanjillo
		30 mantas	7/0	Fran. Rodríguez Bertanjillo
		120 @ pes	0/4	Fran. Rodríguez Bertanjillo
		16 @ ost	0/4	Fran. Rodríguez Bertanjillo

Date	Town	Item & Amount	Unit Price	Buyer & Remarks
		100 g	0/1/7	Fran. Rodríguez Bertanjillo
	Tepic	360 f m	0/2	Fran. Rodríguez Bertanjillo
		72 f tr	0/7	Fran. Rodríguez Bertanjillo
		Comida	9/0	Fran. Rodríguez Bertanjillo
		200 p	0/0/6	Fran. Rodríguez Bertanjillo
15-XII-1560	Suchipil	225 f m	0/2	Fran. Rodríguez Bertanjillo
		27 f tr	0/7	Fran. Rodríguez Bertanjillo
		100 p	0/0/4	Fran. Rodríguez Bertanjillo
		50 g	0/1/6	Fran. Rodríguez Bertanjillo
	Ahuacatlán	90 f m	0/2	Baltasar del Río
		9 f tr	0/7	Baltasar del Río
		50 p	0/0/4	Baltasar del Río
	Amaxaque	90 f m	0/2	Fran. Rodríguez Bertanjillo
		45 p	0/0/4	Fran. Rodríguez Bertanjillo
	Jala	137:6 f m	0/2	Fran. Rodríguez Bertanjillo
		75 p	0/0/4	Fran. Rodríguez Bertanjillo
	San Juan	9 f m	0/2	Fran. Rodríguez Bertanjillo
		2½ mantas	3/4	Fran. Rodríguez Bertanjillo
		2½ huipiles }		
		2½ naguas }	0/6	Fran. Rodríguez Bertanjillo
		1 j miel	0/4	Fran. Rodríguez Bertanjillo
		3 g	0/1/6	Fran. Rodríguez Bertanjillo
	Papachula	1½ mantas	2/2/8	Fran. Rodríguez Bertanjillo
		½ nagua }		
		½ huipil }	0/7	Fran. Rodríguez Bertanjillo
		6 f m	0/2	Fran. Rodríguez Bertanjillo
	Michoacán	3 car pes	0/7	Fran. Rodríguez Bertanjillo
	Jalcocotán	27 f m	0.2	Fran. Rodríguez Bertanjillo
		30 p	0/0/4	Fran. Rodríguez Bertanjillo
		8 g	0/1/6	Fran. Rodríguez Bertanjillo
		2 j miel	1/4	Fran. Rodríguez Bertanjillo
	Mecatán	13:6 f m	0/2	Fran. Rodríguez Bertanjillo
		1 j miel	1/4	Fran. Rodríguez Bertanjillo
		10 p	0/0/4	Fran. Rodríguez Bertanjillo
		4 g	0/1/6	Fran. Rodríguez Bertanjillo
15-XII-1560	Ixtapa	15 f sal	1/1	Fran. Rodríguez Bertanjillo
		4 car pes	0/7	Fran. Rodríguez Bertanjillo
		12 p	0/0/4	Fran. Rodríguez Bertanjillo
	Jaltepec	5 f m	0/2	Fran. Rodríguez Bertanjillo
		4 p }		
		}		
		2 g }	t 0/4/4	Fran. Rodríguez Bertanjillo
	Tepuzhuacán	12 mantas	5/3	Fran. Rodríguez Bertanjillo
	Xalacingo	6 mantas	5/0	Fran. Rodríguez Bertanjillo
		4 p }		
		2 g }	t 0/4/4	Fran. Rodríguez Bertanjillo
	Amatlán	8 mantas	5/0	Fran. Rodríguez Bertanjillo
		5 p }		
		3 g	t 0/6/2	Fran. Rodríguez Bertanjillo

Date	Town	Item & Amount	Unit Price	Buyer & Remarks
15-XII-1560	Iztimitique	3 mantas	5/0	Fran. Rodríguez Bertanjillo
		2 p } 1 g }	0/2	Fran. Rodríguez Bertanjillo
	Zacatlán	60 piezas de ropa	0/5/6	Fran. Rodríguez Bertanjillo
		tr } fr } alg } p } miel } pes } etc. }	t 8/0	Fran. Rodríguez Bertanjillo
	Atengoichán	630 f m	0/2/9	Fran. Rodríguez Bertanjillo
	Temichoque	38 f m	0/2	Fran. Rodríguez Bertanjillo
		6 @ alg	0/4	Fran. Rodríguez Bertanjillo
		12 p	0/0/4	Fran. Rodríguez Bertanjillo
	Pontoque	12 f m	0/2	Fran. Rodríguez Bertanjillo
		4 g	0/1/6	Fran. Rodríguez Bertanjillo
	Acatispa	14:6 f m	0/2	Fran. Rodríguez Bertanjillo
		6 g	0/1	Fran. Rodríguez Bertanjillo
		6 p	0/0/6	Fran. Rodríguez Bertanjillo
	Orita	13:6 f m	0/2	Fran. Rodríguez Bertanjillo
		12 g	0/1/6	Fran. Rodríguez Bertanjillo
		12 p	0/0/6	Fran. Rodríguez Bertanjillo
		4 @ alg	0/4	Fran. Rodríguez Bertanjillo
	Ixcuintla	36 f m	0/2	Fran. Rodríguez Bertanjillo
		1 @ miel	1/4	Fran. Rodríguez Bertanjillo
		16 p	0/0/4	Fran. Rodríguez Bertanjillo
		8 g	0/1/6	Fran. Rodríguez Bertanjillo
	Ixtapa de Castañeda	10 f sal	1/0/6	Fran. Rodríguez Bertanjillo
		12 @ alg	0/4	Fran. Rodríguez Bertanjillo
	Matacticpac	11 f m	0/2	Fran. Rodríguez Bertanjillo
		4 f fr	0/4	Fran. Rodríguez Bertanjillo
		6 p	0/0/6	Fran. Rodríguez Bertanjillo
		6 g	0/1/6	Fran. Rodríguez Bertanjillo
15-XII-1560	Jocotlán y Quilitlán	27 f m	0/2	Fran. Rodríguez Bertanjillo
		21½ @ alg (menos el diezmo)	0/4	Fran. Rodríguez Bertanjillo
	Tomatlán y Toconis (ninguna venta--huyeron los indios en 1559 y 1560)			
30-XI-1561	Tlaltenango	990 f m	1/0/3	Pedro de Egurrola
		214 p	0/0/6	Pedro de Egurrola
		106 g	0/2	Pedro de Egurrola
30-XI-1561	Nochistlán	270 f m	1/0/3	Pedro de Egurrola
		90 p	0/0/6	Pedro de Egurrola
		60 g	0/1	Pedro de Egurrola
	Teocaltiche	360 f m	1/2	Pedro de Egurrola
	Teocaltitlán	405 f m	1/2	Pedro de Egurrola
		16 f ají	1/0	Pedro de Egurrola

Date	Town	Item & Amount	Unit Price	Buyer & Remarks
	(cosecha como del > año pasado)	12 f fr	1/0	Pedro de Egurrola
		240 p	0/0/6	Pedro de Egurrola
	Mezquituta	270 f m	1/0/6	Juan de Heredia
		100 p	0/0/6	Juan de Heredia
7-XII-1561	Analco y Tetlán	630 f m	0/4	Juan de Heredia
		700 p	0/0/3	Juan de Heredia
	Tonalá	540 f m	0/4	Juan de Heredia
		200 p }		
		100 g }	0/0/3	Juan de Heredia
	Tlajomulco	810 f m	0/4	Juan de Heredia
		400 p	0/0/3	Juan de Heredia
	Cuitzeo	146:6 f m	0/4	Juan de Heredia
		324 p	0/0/4	Juan de Heredia
	Poncitlán	502 f m	0/4	Juan de Heredia
		1116 p	0/0/3	Juan de Heredia
	Tlaquepaque, San Pedro	540 f m	0/4	Juan de Heredia
		200 p	0/0/3	Juan de Heredia
	Camotlán (Barranca)	54 f m	0/4	Juan de Heredia
		60 p	0/0/3	Juan de Heredia
	Coscocotán (Barranca)	45 f m	0/4	Juan de Heredia
		45 p	0/0/3	Juan de Heredia
	Nochistlanejo	90 f m	0/4	Juan de Heredia
		40 p	0/0/3	Juan de Heredia
7-XII-1561	Atemajac	225 f m	0/4	Juan de Heredia
		50 p	0/0/3	Juan de Heredia
	Coyutlán y } Zalatitlán }	108 f m	0/4	Juan de Heredia
		160 p	0/0/3	Juan de Heredia
	Matatlán	180 f m	0/4	Juan de Heredia
	Copala	90 f m	0/4	Juan de Heredia
		50 p	0/0/3	Juan de Heredia
	Tequila y Los Guajes	104:6 f m	0/4	Juan de Heredia
		11 f tr	1/0	Juan de Heredia
		6 p	0/0/3	Juan de Heredia
	Sentispac	180 f m	0/2/6	Juan de Heredia
		45 mantas	7/0	Juan de Heredia
		120 @ pes	0/4	Juan de Heredia
		16 @ ost	0/4	Juan de Heredia
		100 g	0/1/7	Juan de Heredia
7-XII-1561	Tepic	360 f m	0/2	Juan de Heredia
		27 f tr	0/7	Juan de Heredia
		60 p	0/0/6	Juan de Heredia
		30 g	0/1/6	Juan de Heredia
	Suchipil	225 f m	0/2/6	Juan de Heredia
		27 f tr	0/7	Juan de Heredia
		100 p	0/0/4	Juan de Heredia
		50 g	0/1/6	Juan de Heredia

Date	Town	Item & Amount	Unit Price	Buyer & Remarks
	Ahuacatlán y Amaxaque	180 f m	0/2/6	Juan de Heredia
		9 f tr	0/7	Juan de Heredia
		95 p	0/0/4	Juan de Heredia
	Jala	157:6 f m	0/2/6	Juan de Heredia
		75 p	0/0/4	Juan de Heredia
	San Juan	9 f m	0/2/6	Juan de Heredia
		2½ mantas	8/6	Juan de Heredia
		2½ naguas }		
		2½ huipiles }	0/6	Juan de Heredia
		1 j miel	0/4	Juan de Heredia
		3 g	0/1/6	Juan de Heredia
	Papachula	1½ mantas	3/4	Juan de Heredia
		6 f m	0/2/6	Juan de Heredia
		½ huipil }		
		½ nagua }	t 0/7	Juan de Heredia
		1 j miel	0/2	Juan de Heredia
	Michoacán	3 car pes	0/7	Juan de Heredia
	Jalcocotán	27 f m	0/2/6	Juan de Heredia
		30 p	0/0/4	Juan de Heredia
		8 g	0/1/6	Juan de Heredia
		2 j miel	1/4	Juan de Heredia
7-XII-1561	Mecatán	13:6 f m	0/2/6	Juan de Heredia
		1 j miel	1/4	Juan de Heredia
		10 p	0/0/4	Juan de Heredia
		4 g	0/1/6	Juan de Heredia
	Ixtapa	15 f sal	1/1	Juan de Heredia
		4 car pes	0/7	Juan de Heredia
		12 p	0/0/4	Juan de Heredia
	Jaltepec	5 f m	0/2/6	Juan de Heredia
	Tepuzhuacán	12 mantas	5/3	Juan de Heredia
	Jalacingo	6 mantas	5/0	Juan de Heredia
		4 p }		
		2 g }	t 0/4/4	Juan de Heredia
	Amatlán	8 mantas	5/	Juan de Heredia
		5 p }		
		3 g }	t 0/6/2	Juan de Heredia
	Ixtimitique	3 mantas	5/	Juan de Heredia
		2 p }		
		1 g }	t 0/2	Juan de Heredia
	Zacatlán	Todo	20/	Juan de Heredia
	Atengoichán	630 f m	0/3/6	Pedro de Céspedes
	Temichoque	38 f m	0/2/6	Juan de Heredia
		6 @ alg	0/4	Juan de Heredia
		12 p	0/0/4	Juan de Heredia
	Pontoque	12 f m	0/2/6	Juan de Heredia
		4 g	0/1/6	Juan de Heredia
	Acatispa	14:6 f m	0/2/6	Juan de Heredia
		6 p }		

Date	Town	Item & Amount	Unit Price	Buyer & Remarks
		6 g)	t 1/4	Juan de Heredia
	Orita	13:6 f m	0/2/6	Juan de Heredia
		4 @ alg	0/4	Juan de Heredia
		12 g	0/1/6	Juan de Heredia
	Ixcuintla	36 f m	0/2/6	Juan de Heredia
		1 @ miel	1/4	Juan de Heredia
		16 p	0/0/4	Juan de Heredia
		8 g	0/1/6	Juan de Heredia
	Ixtapa, de Castañeda	10 f sal	1/0/6	Juan de Heredia
		12 @ alg	0/4	Juan de Heredia
	Matacticpac	11 f m	0/2/6	Juan de Heredia
		4 f fr	0/4	Juan de Heredia
		6 p	0/0/4	Juan de Heredia
		6 g	0/1/6	Juan de Heredia
	Jocotlán y Quilitlán (menos el diezmo)	27 f m	0/2/6	Juan de Heredia
		21½ @ alg	0/4	Juan de Heredia
1-IV-1562	Opono y su partido:			
	Atengo	40 f m	0/2/6	?
	Cuyutlán Mariana	14 f m	0/2/6	?
	Amatitlán	21 f m	0/2/6	?
	Zayula	13 f m	0/2/6	?
	Jocotlán	12 f m	0/2/6	?
17-XI-1562	Camotlán (Barranca)	54 f m	0/3/3	Francisco de Nájara
		60 p	0/0/6	Francisco de Nájara
	Coscotitán (Barranca)	45 f m	0/3	Francisco de Nájara
		45 p	0/0/6	Francisco de Nájara
	Nochistlanejo	90 f m	0/5/6	Juan Guerra
		40 p	0/1	Canónigo Francisco García de Urrieta
	Atemajac	225 f m	0/4	Juan de Aguilar
		50 p	0/0/6	Juan de Aguilar
	Cuyutlán y Zalatitlán	108 f m	0/7	Juan Guerra
		150 p	0/1	Gerónimo de Orozco
	Matatatlán	130 f m	0/5	Secretario Alonso Sánchez
	Copala	90 f m	0/6	Pedro de Hubiedo (o Oviedo)
		50 p	0/1	Pedro de Hubiedo (o Oviedo)
	Tequila y Los Guajas	104:6 f m	0/4	Gerónimo de Orozco
		11 f tr	1/1	Gerónimo de Orozco
		6 p	0/0/6	Gerónimo de Orozco
24-XI-1562	Suchipil	225 f m	0/4/6	Tomás Lazo
		27 f tr	0/7	Tomás Lazo
		50 g	0/1/6	Tomás Lazo
		100 p	0/0/6	Tomás Lazo
	Ahuacatlán y Amaxaque	108 f m	0/4/6	Gerónimo de Ortega
		9 f tr	0/7	Gerónimo de Ortega
		95 p	0/0/6	Gerónimo de Ortega
	Jala	157:6 f m	0/4/6	Gerónimo de Ortega

Date	Town	Item & Amount	Unit Price	Buyer & Remarks
		75 p	0/0/6	Gerónimo de Ortega
	San Juan	Todo	17/3	Gerónimo de Ortega
	Papachula	Todo	9/0	Gerónimo de Ortega
	Michoacán	3 car pes	0/7	Gerónimo de Ortega
	Jalcocotán	Todo	14/6	Gerónimo de Orozco
	Mecatán	Todo	7/0	Gerónimo de Orozco
	Ixtapa	Todo	24/0	Gerónimo de Orozco
	Jaltepec	Todo	4/4	Gerónimo de Orozco
	Tepuzhuacán	12 mantas	6/0	Tomás Lazo
	Jalacingo	6 mantas	6/0	Tomás Lazo
		4 p } 2 g }	t 0/7	Tomás Lazo
	Amatlán	8 mantas	6/	Tomás Lazo
		5 p } 3 g }	t 1/2	Tomás Lazo
24-XI-1562	Ixtimitique	3 mantas	6/0	Tomás Lazo
		2 p } 1 g }	t 0/2/6	Tomás Lazo
	Zacatlán	27 f m	0/1/6	Gerónimo de Ortega
	Atengoichán	630 f m	0/2/6	Tomás Lazo
	Temichoque	Todo	15/3	Gerónimo de Ortega
	Pontoque	Todo	4/4	Gerónimo de Ortega
	Acatispa	Todo	6/0/3	Gerónimo de Ortega
	Orita	Todo	8/7/9	Gerónimo de Ortega
	Santiago (precio del año pasado)	Todo	15/	Gerónimo de Ortega
	Ixtapa, de Castañeda	Todo	5/0	Gerónimo de Ortega
	(ninguna otra oferta porque todos los indios ya se habían muerto o huido)			
	Sentispac	180 f m	0/3/6	Juan Guerra
		45 mantas	11/2	Juan Guerra
		120 @ pes } 16 @ ost }	0/7	Juan Guerra
		100 g	0/1/6	Juan Guerra
	Tepic	153 f m	0/4	Gerónimo de Orozco
		27 f tr	0/7	Gerónimo de Orozco
		30 g	0/1/6	Gerónimo de Orozco
		60 p	0/0/6	Gerónimo de Orozco
	Matacticpac	Todo	6/6/6	Gerónimo de Orozco
	Quilitlán y Jocotlán	Todo	19/1/6	Gerónimo de Orozco

Date	Town	Item & Amount	Unit Price	Buyer & Remarks
27-XI-1562	Analco	630 f m	0/4	Juan de Aguilar
		700 p	0/0/6	Juan de Aguilar
	Tonalá	540 f m	0/6	Pedro Sánchez Mexía
		200 p	0/1	Pedro Sánchez Mexía
		100 g	0/2/9	Juan de Aguilar
	Tlajomulco	810 f m	0/4	Vicente de Saldívar
		400 p	0/0/6	Vicente de Saldívar
	Cuitzeo y Guázcato	155:6 f m	0/3/6	Juan Gallego
		324 p	0/1	Lope de Cisneros
	Poncitlán	502:6 f m	0/4/3	Bartolomé de Coca
		1116 p	0/1	Antonio de Sandoval
27-XI-1562	Tlaquepaque, San Pedro	540 f m	0/4	Juan de Aguilar
		200 p	0/0/6	Juan de Aguilar
21-XII-1562	Tlaltenango	990 f m	0/7	Pedro de Egurrola
		106 g	0/2	Pedro de Egurrola
		214 p	0/0/6	Pedro de Egurrola
31-XII-1562	Nochistlán	270 f m	0/7	Pedro de Egurrola
		60 g	0/2	Pedro de Egurrola
		90 p	0/0/6	Pedro de Egurrola
	Teocaltiche y Teocaltitlán	745 f m	0/7	Pedro de Egurrola
		14:6 @ ají	0/7	Pedro de Egurrola
		240 p	0/0/6	Pedro de Egurrola
		12 f fr	0/7	Pedro de Egurrola
31-XII-1562	Mezquituta	270 f m	0/7	Pedro de Egurrola
		100 p	0/0/6	Pedro de Egurrola
15-XI-1563	Analco	630 f m	0/4	Juan de Aguilar
		700 p	0/0/6	Juan de Aguilar
	Tonalá	540 f m	1/2	Gerónimo de Orozco
		200 p	0/1	Gerónimo de Orozco
		100 g	0/2/6	Juan de Aguilar
	Tlajomulco	810 f m	1/	Vicente de Saldívar
		400 p	0/0/6	Vicente de Saldívar
	Cuitzeo y Guázcato	146:6 f m	0/5	Don Cristóbal de Ayala
		9 f m	0/2	Don Cristóbal de Ayala
		324 p	0/0/9	Lope de Cisneros
	Poncitlán	502 f m	0/5	Don Cristóbal de Ayala
		1116 p	0/0/3	Alonso de la Vera
	Tlaquepaque, San Pedro	540 f m	0/4	Juan de Aguilar
		200 p	0/0/6	Juan de Aguilar
	Camotlán (Barranca)	54 f m	0/5	Diego Vázquez
		60 p	0/0/6	Canónigo Francisco García de Urrieta y Lorenzo de Padilla, Decano
	Coscotitán (Barranca)	45 f m	0/4	Simón de Coca
		45 p	0/0/6	Simón de Coca
	Nochistlanejo	90 f m	1/1	Lorenzo de Padilla, Decano
		40 p	0/1	Gerónimo de Orozco

Date	Town	Item & Amount	Unit Price	Buyer & Remarks
	Atemajac	225 f m	1/2	Lorenzo de Padilla, Decano
		50 p	0/0/6	Lorenzo de Padilla, Decano
	Cuyutlán y Zalatitlán	63 f m	1/2/6	Juan Guerra
		60 p	0/1	Gerónimo de Orozco
		45 f m	1/2/6	Juan Guerra
		100 p	0/1	Gerónimo de Orozco
	Matatlán	180 f m	1/0/6	Pedro Sánchez Mexía
15-XI-1563	Copala	90 f m	1/3	Gerónimo de Orozco
		50 p	0/1	Gerónimo de Orozco
	Tequila y Los Guajes	104:6 f m	1/4/3	Lorenzo de Padilla, Decano
		11 f tr	1/4	Lorenzo de Padilla,
Decano				
		6 p	0/0/6	Lorenzo de Padilla, Decano
	Sentispac	45 mantas	13/4	Lorenzo de Padilla, Decano
		180 f m	0/7	Juan Guerra
		120 @ pes	0/7/3	Maese Pedro
		16 @ ost	1/0/3	Maese Pedro
		100 g	0/2	Maese Pedro
	Tepic	153 f m	0/5	Gerónimo de Ortega
		27 f tr	1/0	Gerónimo de Ortega
		30 g	0/1/6	Gerónimo de Ortega
		60 p	0/0/6	Gerónimo de Ortega
	Ahuacatlán y Amaxaque	180 f m	1/0	Andrés de Villanueva
		9 f tr	0/7	Gerónimo de Ortega
		95 p	0/0/9	Juan Casero
	Suchipil	225 f m	1/0	Gerónimo de Orozco
		27 f tr	0/7	Gerónimo de Ortega
		50 g	0/2/6	Gerónimo de Ortega
		100 p	0/0/6	Juan Fernández
	Jala	157:6 f m	0/7	Gerónimo de Ortega
		75 p	0/0/9	Alonso de Llerena
	San Juan	Todo	17/3	Gerónimo de Ortega
	Papachula	Todo	9/0	Gerónimo de Ortega
	Michuacán	(ninguna venta por ser despoblado)		
	Jalcocotán	Todo	15/	Gerónimo de Ortega
	Mecatán	Todo	7/	Gerónimo de Ortega
	Ixtapa	Todo	15/	Gerónimo de Ortega
	Jaltepec	Todo	5/	Gerónimo de Ortega
16-XI-1563	Tepuzhuacan	12 mantas	6/	Gerónimo de Ortega
	Jalacingo	6 mantas	6/	Gerónimo de Ortega
		4 p }		
		2 g }	t 1/	Gerónimo de Ortega
	Amatlán	8 mantas	6/	Gerónimo de Ortega
		5 p }		
		3 g }	t 1/2	Gerónimo de Ortega

Date	Town	Item & Amount	Unit Price	Buyer & Remarks
	Ixtimitique	3 mantas	6/	Gerónimo de Ortega
		2 p } 1 g }	t 0/3	Gerónimo de Ortega
	Zacatlan	27 f m	t 6/	Gerónimo de Ortega
16-XI-1563	Atengoichan	630 f m	0/2/6	Gerónimo de Ortega
	Temichoque	Todo	16/	Juan Guerra
	Pontoque	Todo	4/4	Juan Guerra
	Acatispa	Todo	6/3	Juan Guerra
	Orita	Todo	9/	Juan Guerra
	Ixcuintla	Todo	15/	Juan Guerra
	Ixtapa, de Castañeda	Todo	5/	Juan Guerra
	Matacticpac	Todo	9/	Gerónimo de Ortega
	Quilitlán y Jocotlán	Todo	19/2	Juan Guerra
	Acaponeta	Todo	30/	Juan Guerra
	Quebiquito	Todo	5/	Gerónimo de Ortega
	Totorán	Todo	6/	Juan Guerra
	Quexdaquepa	Todo	1/	Juan Guerra
	Opono } Cuyutlán } Amatitlán } Zayula } Jocotlán }	91 f m	0/2	Gerónimo de Ortega
	Zapotlán	27 f m	0/2	Gerónimo de Ortega
		5 mantas	4/	Gerónimo de Ortega
		2½ @ miel	t 3/2	Gerónimo de Ortega
	Contlá	18 f m	0/2	Gerónimo de Ortega
		3 mantas	4/	Gerónimo de Ortega
		1 @ miel	1/	Gerónimo de Ortega
		2 @ pes	0/6	Gerónimo de Ortega
	Sila	13:6 f m	0/2	Gerónimo de Ortega
		4 j miel	0/2	Gerónimo de Ortega
	Tena	Todo	6/	Gerónimo de Ortega
	Piloto	Todo	20/	Gerónimo de Ortega
	Quilapique } Apanaloa } (despoblados--por fé del escribano de Purificación, 27-XII-1563)			
16-XI-1563	Quilapique	Todo	20/	Gerónimo de Ortega
	Apeque	Todo	12/	Gerónimo de Ortega
	Apanaloa	Todo	6/	Gerónimo de Ortega

Date	Town	Item & Amount	Unit Price	Buyer & Remarks
	Maito	Todo	40/	Gerónimo de Ortega
	Maloto	Todo	30/	Gerónimo de Ortega
	Queleque [Colique?]	Todo	35/	Gerónimo de Ortega
	Hatataco	Todo	11/	Gerónimo de Ortega
15-XII-1563	Yegualtitlán	36 f m	1/2	Gerónimo de Ortega
		10 p	0/0/6	Gerónimo de Ortega
	Acatique	22:6 f m	1/2	Gerónimo de Ortega
		10 p	0/0/6	Gerónimo de Ortega
	Huelotitlán	27 f m	1/2	Gerónimo de Ortega
		10 p	0/0/6	Gerónimo de Ortega
	Inrimota	13:6 f m	1/2	Gerónimo de Ortega
		8 p	0/0/6	Gerónimo de Ortega
	Tequiltitlán	18 f m	1/2	Gerónimo de Ortega
		10 p	0/0/6	Gerónimo de Ortega
	Cuyulomitle	7:6 f m	1/2	Gerónimo de Ortega
	Mezquitlán	27 f m	1/2	Gerónimo de Ortega
		15 p	0/0/6	Gerónimo de Ortega
	Mezquititique	9 f m	1/2	Gerónimo de Ortega
		6 p	0/0/6	Gerónimo de Ortega
	Cacalotitlán	22:6 f m	1/2	Gerónimo de Ortega
		10 p	0/0/6	Gerónimo de Ortega
19-XII-1563	Tlaltenango	490 f m	0/4/9	Pedro de Egurrola
		(500 para las salinas)		
		106 g	0/2	Pedro de Egurrola
		214 p	0/0/6	Pedro de Egurrola
	Nochistlán	270 f m	0/4/9	Pedro de Egurrola
		60 g	0/2	Pedro de Egurrola
		90 p	0/0/6	Pedro de Egurrola
	Teocaltiche y Teocaltitlán	765 f m	0/4/9	Pedro de Egurrola
		9 f fr	0/4/9	Pedro de Egurrola
		14:6 f ají	0/4/9	Pedro de Egurrola
		240 p	0/0/6	Pedro de Egurrola
	Mezquituta	270 f m	0/4/6	Antonio López Adán
		100 p	0/0/6	Pedro de Madrid
6-XI-1564	Analco	630 f m	0/4	Juan de Aguilar
		700 p	0/0/6	Juan de Aguilar
	Tonalá	100 g	0/2	Juan de Aguilar
		200 p	0/0/9	Secretario Alonso Sánchez
	de Toledo			
		540 f m	0/6/6	Gerónimo de Lozada
	Tlajomulco	810 f m	0/6/6	Gerónimo de Lozada
		400 p	0/0/9	Vicente de Saldívar
	Cuitzeo y Guázcato	324 p	0/0/8	Rodrigo Gutiérrez de Baeza
		155:6 f m	0/6	Gerónimo de Lozada

Date	Town	Item & Amount	Unit Price	Buyer & Remarks
	Poncitlán	1116 p	0/0/9	Rodrigo Gutiérrez de Baeza
		502 f m	0/6	Gerónimo de Lozada
	Tlaquepaque, San Pedro	540 f m	0/4/6	Juan de Aguilar
		200 p	0/0/6	Juan de Aguilar
	Camotlán (Barranca)	54 f m	0/6	Gerónimo de Lozada
		60 p	0/0/6	Alonso de la Vera
	Coscotitán	45 p	0/0/6	Alonso de la Vera
		45 f m	0/6	Gerónimo de Lozada
	Nochistlanejo	90 f m	0/6/6	Gerónimo de Lozada
		40 p	0/0/9	Pedro de Ledesma
	Atemajac	50 p	0/0/10	Francisco de Nájera
		225 f m	0/6/6	Gerónimo de Lozada
	Cuyutlán y Zalatitlán	108 f m	0/6/6	Gerónimo de Lozada
		160 p	0/0/10	Gerónimo de Orozco
	Matatlán	180 f m	0/6/6	Gerónimo de Lozada
	Copala	90 f m	0/6/6	Gerónimo de Lozada
		50 p	0/0/10	Francisco Flores Biochero
7-XI-1564	Apozulco	141 f m	0/6/6	Vicente de Saldívar
		79 p	0/0/9	Vicente de Saldívar
	Tepacatengo (Barranca)	16:5 f m	0/6	Vicente de Saldívar
		3½ g }		
		5½ p }	t 1/	Vicente de Saldívar
	Sentispac	45 mantas	10/	Gerónimo de Ortega
		180 f m	0/5	Gerónimo de Ortega
		120 @ pes	0/5	Gerónimo de Ortega
		16 @ ost	0/5	Gerónimo de Ortega
		100 g	0/5	Gerónimo de Ortega
	(regalados a Gerónimo de Ortega para vender el maíz)			
7-XI-1564	Tepic	153 f m	0/5	Gerónimo de Ortega
		27 f tr	0/7	Gerónimo de Ortega
	(25 de rezago)	85 p	0/0/6	Gerónimo de Ortega
		30 g	0/1/6	Gerónimo de Ortega
	Suchipil	225 f m	0/6	Gerónimo de Ortega
		27 f tr	1/	Gerónimo de Ortega
		50 g	0/2	Gerónimo de Ortega
		100 p	0/0/6	Gerónimo de Ortega
	Ahuacatlán y Amaxaque	180 f m	0/6	Gerónimo de Ortega
		9 f tr	1/	Gerónimo de Ortega
		95 p	0/0/7	Gerónimo de Ortega
	Jala	157 6 f m	0/7	Gerónimo de Ortega
		75 p	0/0/8	Gerónimo de Ortega
	San Juan	Todo	18/	Rodrigo Pérez
	Papachula	Todo	9/0	Rodrigo Pérez
	Michoacán	(despoblado)		
	Tequila y	104:6 f m	1/	Cristóbal de Oñate

Date	Town	Item & Amount	Unit Price	Buyer & Remarks
	Los Guaxes	11 f tr 6 p	1/1 0/0/6	Gerónimo de Orozco Gerónimo de Orozco
	Atengoichán	630 f m	0/6	García de Chávez
8-XI-1564	Jalcocotán	Todo	15/	Gerónimo de Orozco
	Mecatán	Todo	7/	Gerónimo de Orozco
	Ixtapa	Todo	15/	Gerónimo de Orozco
	Jaltepec	Todo	5/	Gerónimo de Orozco
	Tepuzhuacán	12 mantas	5/6	García de Chavez
	Jalacingo	6 mantas 4 p } 2 g }	5/6 t 0/6	García de Chavez García de Chavez
	Zacatlán	27 f m	0/2	Rodrigo Pérez
	Temichoque	Todo	16/	Rodrigo Pérez
	Pontoque	Todo	4/	Rodrigo Pérez
	Acatispa	Todo	5/	Rodrigo Pérez
	Orita	Todo	9/	Rodrigo Pérez
	Santiago	Todo	15/	Rodrigo Pérez
	Ixtapa, de Castañeda	Todo	5/	Rodrigo Pérez
	Matacticpac	Todo	9/	García de Chavez
	Quilitlán y Jocotlán	Todo	19/2	Rodrigo Pérez
8-XI-1564	Acaponeta	Todo	30/	Cristóbal de Morales
	Quebiquito	Todo	5/	Cristóbal de Morales
	Totorán	Todo	6/	Cristóbal de Morales
	Quexdaquepa	Todo	1/	Cristóbal de Morales
9-XI-1564	Amatlán	8 mantas 5 p } 3 g }	5/6 t 1/	García de Chavez García de Chavez
	Ixtimitique	3 mantas 2 p } 1 g }	5/6 t 0/3	García de Chavez García de Chavez
	Yegualtitlán	36 f m 10 p	0/5 0/0/6	Andrés de Villanueva Gerónimo de Ortega
	Acatique	22:6 f m 10 p	0/5 0/0/6	Andrés de Villanueva Gerónimo de Ortega
	Huelotitlán	27 f m 10 p	0/5 0/0/6	Andrés de Villanueva Gerónimo de Ortega
	Inrimota	12:6 f m	0/5	Andrés de Villanueva

Date	Town	Item & Amount	Unit Price	Buyer & Remarks
		8 p	0/0/6	Gerónimo de Ortega
	Tequiltitlán	18 f m	0/5	Andrés de Villanueva
		10 p	0/0/6	Gerónimo de Ortega
	Cuyulomitle	7:6 f m	0/5	Andrés de Villanueva
		6 p	0/0/6	Gerónimo de Ortega
	Mezquitlán	27 f m	0/5	Andrés de Villanueva
		15 p	0/0/6	Gerónimo de Ortega
	Mezquititique	9 f m	0/5	Andrés de Villanueva
		6 p	0/0/6	Gerónimo de Ortega
	Cacalotitlán	22:6 f m	0/5	Andrés de Villanueva
		10 p	0/0/6	Gerónimo de Ortega
13-XII-1564	Tlaltenango	690 f m	0/6/6	Pedro de Madrid
		(300 f m para las salinas pero 60 vendidas)		
		214 p	0/0/6	Pedro de Madrid
		106 g	0/2	Pedro de Madrid
	Nochistlán	270 f m	0/6/6	Pedro de Egurrola
		60 g	0/2	Pedro de Egurrola
		90 p	0/0/6	Pedro de Egurrola
	Teocaltiche y Teocaltitlán	765 f m	0/6/6	Pedro de Egurrola
		9 f fr	0/6/6	Pedro de Egurrola
		14:6 f ají	0/6/6	Pedro de Egurrola
		240 p	0/0/6	Pedro de Egurrola
	Mezquituta	270 f m	0/4/6	Juan García de Manzanares
		100 p	0/0/6	Juan García de Manzanares
5-XI-1565	Analco	630 f m	0/4	Juan de Aguilar
		700 p	0/0/6	Juan de Aguilar
	Tonalá	540 f m	0/4	Alonso Sánchez de Toledo,
	Sec.			
		200 p	0/1	Alonso Sánchez de Toledo,
	Sec.			
		100 g	0/2	Juan de Aguilar
	Tlajomulco	810 f m	0/4/1	Gerónimo de Ortega
		400 p	0/1/2	Alonso de la Vera
	Cuitzeo y Guázcato	420 f m	0/3/6	Cristóbal de Ayala
		450 p	0/1	Alonso de la Vera
	Poncitlán	945 f m	0/3	Francisco Delgadillo
		1050 p	0/1	Alonso de la Vera
	Tlaquepaque	540 f m	0/4	Juan de Aguilar
		200 p	0/0/6	Juan de Aguilar
	Camotlán	104 f m	0/3	Cristóbal de Ayala
		60 p	0/1	Alonso de la Vera
	Coscotitán	45 f m	0/3	Cristóbal de Ayala
		45 p	0/1	Alonso de la Vera
	Nochistlanejo	90 f m	0/3	Cristóbal de Ayala
		40 p	0/1	Alonso de la Vera
	Tequila y	104:6 f m	0/6	Antonio del Rincón

Date	Town	Item & Amount	Unit Price	Buyer & Remarks
	Los Guajes	11 f tr	1/0	Gerónimo de Ortega
		6 p	0/0/9	Juan de Aguilar
	Apozulco	63 f m	0/3	Juan de Segura
		70 p	0/1	Juan de Segura
	Tepacatengo	36 f m	0/3	Cristóbal de Ayala
		12 p	0/1	Alonso de la Vera
6-XI-1565	Matatlan	180 f m	0/4/4	Juan de Aguilar
	Atemajac	225 f m	0/5	Gerónimo de Orozco
		50 p	0/1/2	Gerónimo de Orozco
	Cuyutlán y Zalatitlán	108 f m	0/4/3	Pero Sánchez Mexía
		160 p	0/1	Alonso de la Vera
	Copala	90 f m	0/5/3	Rodrigo Gutiérrez de Baeza
		50 p	0/1/2	Diego Conde
	Tepic	153 f m	0/7	Diego Ruiz
		27 f tr	1/0	Diego Ruiz
		60 p	0/0/9	Diego Ruiz
		30 g	0/2	Juan de Saldívar
	Suchipil	225 f m	1/2	Diego Ruiz
		50 g	0/2	Gerónimo de Ortega
		100 p	0/0/9	Antonio del Rincón
6-XI-1565	Ahuacatlán y Amaxaque	180 f m	0/6	Cristóbal de Ayala
		9 f tr	1/0	Gerónimo de Ortega
		95 p	0/1	Gerónimo de Ortega
	Jala	157:6 f m	1/2	Cristóbal de Ayala
		75 p	0/0/9	Antonio del Rincón
7-XI-1565	San Juan	4 f m		
		2½ mantas		
	(menos el diezmo	2½ naguas	t 18/0	Diego Ruiz, vecino de
	del maíz)	2½ huipiles		Compostela
		1 j miel--qtlo		
		3 g		
	Papachula	1½ mantas		
		½ huipil		
	(menos el diezmo	½ nagua	t 9/4	Diego Ruiz
	del maíz)	3 f m		
		½ qtlo miel		
	Jalcocotán	30 f m		
		30 p		
		8 g	t 19/0	Diego Ruiz
		2 j miel (½ @ cu)		
	Acatispa	16 f m		
		6 g	t 4/0	Diego Ruiz
		6 p		
	Mecatán	13 f m		
		1 j miel--qtlo	t 8/0	Diego Ruiz
		10 p		
		4 g		

Date	Town	Item & Amount	Unit Price	Buyer & Remarks
1565	Jaltepec	9 f m		
		11 p	t 5/2	Diego Ruiz
		1 j miel--qtlo		
	Ixtapa	15 f sal		
		4 car pes	t 16/0	Diego Ruiz
		12 p		
	Tepuzhuacán	12 mantas		
		(5 x 4v)	t 64/	Alonso Sánchez de Toledo
	Jalacingo	6 mantas		
		(4 pi de 4 x 1v)		
		4 p	t 36/	Diego Ruiz
		2 g		
	Amatlán	8 mantas		
		(4 pi de 4 x 1v)		
		3 g	t 48/	Diego Ruiz
		5 p		
	Ixtimitique	3 mantas		
		(4 pi de 4 x 1)		
		2 p	t 16/	Diego Ruiz
		1 g		
	Zacatlán	27 f m	4/0	Diego Ruiz
7-XI-1565	Temichoque	18 f m		
		5½ @ alg	t 10/	Diego Ruiz
		12 p		
	Pontoque	4 g		
		9 f m	t 4/	Diego Ruiz
	Orita	13:6 f m		
		4 @ alg		
		12 g	t 11/0	Diego Ruiz
		12 p		
	Matacticpac	11 f m		
		4 f fr		
		6 g	16/	Diego Ruiz
		6 p		
	Quilitlán y Jocotlán	18 f m		
		16½ @ alg	20/	Diego Ruiz
	Acaponeta	100 f m	0/2	Diego Ruiz
		4½ mantas		
		(4 pi - 4 x 1v cu)	1/4/3	Diego Ruiz
		20 g	0/1	Diego Ruiz
	Quebiquito	20 f m	0/2	Diego Ruiz
		1½ mantas		
		(4 pi - 4 x 1v)	1/4/3	Diego Ruiz
		7½ g	0/1	Diego Ruiz
	Totorán	25 f m	0/2	Diego Ruiz
		3 mantas		
		(4 pi - 4 x 1v)	4/4/9	Diego Ruiz
		15 g	0/1	Diego Ruiz
	Quexdaquepa	10 f m	0/2	Diego Ruiz
		7½ g	0/1	Diego Ruiz

Date	Town	Item & Amount	Unit Price	Buyer & Remarks
8-XI-1565	Sentispac	90 f m	0/5/9	Diego Ruiz, vecino de Compostela
		51 mantas	10/4	Juan de Aguilar
		120 @ pes	0/6 @	Diego Ruiz
		30 @ ost y camarrones	1/2 @	Diego Ruiz
		30 @ mech	0/6 @	Diego Ruiz
		100 g	0/1/6	Diego Ruiz
	Yegualtitlán	36 f m	1/0	Gerónimo de Ortega
		10 p	0/0/6	Gerónimo de Ortega
	Acatique	22:6 f m	1/0	Gerónimo de Ortega
		10 p	0/0/6	Gerónimo de Ortega
	Huelotitlán	27 f m	1/0	Gerónimo de Ortega
		10 p	0/0/6	Gerónimo de Ortega
	Inrimota	13:6 f m	1/0	Gerónimo de Ortega
		8 p	0/0/6	Gerónimo de Ortega
	Tequiltitlán	18 f m	1/0	Gerónimo de Ortega
		10 p	0/0/6	Gerónimo de Ortega
	Cuyulomitle	7:6 f m	1/0	Gerónimo de Ortega
		6 p	0/0/6	Gerónimo de Ortega
	Mezquitlán	27 f m	1/0	Gerónimo de Ortega
		15 p	0/0/6	Gerónimo de Ortega
	Mezquititique	9 f m	1/0	Gerónimo de Ortega
		6 p	0/0/6	Gerónimo de Ortega
	Cacalotitlán	22 f m	1/0	Gerónimo de Ortega
		10 p	0/0/6	Gerónimo de Ortega
	Acaponeta	90 f m	0/2	Diego Ruiz
		4½ mantas	1/4/3	Diego Ruiz
		20 g	0/1	Diego Ruiz
	Quebiquito	18 f m	0/2	Diego Ruiz
		1½ mantas	1/4/3	Diego Ruiz
		7½ g	0/1	Diego Ruiz
	Totorán	22:6 f m	0/2	Diego Ruiz
		3 mantas	1/4/3	Diego Ruiz
		15 g	0/1	Diego Ruiz
	Quexdaquepa	9 f m	0/2	Diego Ruiz
		7½ g	0/1	Diego Ruiz
	Ixcuintla	36 f m 1 @ miel 16 p 8 g	20/4	Gerónimo de Orozco
	Ixtapa, de Castañeda	20 car sal 3 @ alg	5/0	Diego Ruiz
14-XI-1565	Atengoichán	630 f m	0/3/6	Alonso de la Vera
6-XII-1565	Tlaltenango (de las reservadas en XII-1564)	60 f m	0/6/6	Antonio de Carmona

Date	Town	Item & Amount	Unit Price	Buyer & Remarks
16-XII-1565	Tlaltenango	400 f m	0/5	Pedro de Egurrola
		290 f m	0/5	Juan Calvo
		214 p	0/0/6	Pedro de Madrid
		106 g	0/2	Pedro de Madrid
	Nochistlán	270 f m	0/5	Pedro de Egurrola
		60 g	0/2	Pedro de Egurrola
		90 p	0/0/6	Pedro de Egurrola
	Teocaltiche y Teocaltitlán	765 f m	0/5	Pedro de Egurrola
		9 f fr	0/5	Pedro de Egurrola
		14:6 aji	0/5	Pedro de Egurrola
		240 p	0/0/6	Pedro de Egurrola
	Mezquituta	270 f m	0/4	Pedro de Madrid
		100 p	0/0/6	Pedro de Madrid
18-XII-1566	Poncitlán	945 f m	0/5	Pedro de Céspedes
		1050 p	0/0/8	Alonso de Herrera
	Camotlán	54 f m	0/4/6	Cristóbal de Ayala
		60 p	0/0/6	Cristóbal de Ayala
	Atemajac	225 f m	0/7/3	Pedro de Céspedes
		50 p	0/0/6	Francisco de León
	Cuyutlán	63 f m	0/6/3	Juan Téllez
		60 p	0/0/9	Pero Sánchez Mexía
	Zalatitlán	45 f m	0/6/3	Juan Téllez
		100 p	0/0/9	Alonso Sánchez, Secretario
	Matatlán	180 f m	0/4/6	Pero Sánchez Mexía
	Tequila	90 f m	0/6	Alonso Marín
		11 f tr	0/4	Alonso Marín
	Los Guajes	14:6 f m	0/5	Alonso Marín
		6 p	0/0/6	Alonso Marín
	Copala	90 f m	0/7	Fran. Rodríguez Bertajillo
		50 p	0/0/6	Fran. Merodio de Velasco, Alguacil Mayor
	Apozolco (27 rezago)	63 f m	0/6	Loc. López de Bergara
		97 p	0/0/6	Juan de Aguilar
	Tepacatengo	36 f m	0/3	Juan de Aguilar
		8 g	0/2	Juan de Aguilar
		12 p	0/0/6	Juan de Aguilar
19-XII-1566	Analco	630 f m	0/4	Alonso Marín
		700 p	0/0/6	Juan de Aguilar
	Tonalá	270 f m	0/4	Alonso Marín
		200 p	0/0/6	Francisco de León
		100 g	0/2	Alonso de Herrera
	Tlaquepaque, San Pedro	540 f m	0/4	Alonso Marín
		200 p	0/0/8	Juan Téllez
	Tlajomulco	810 f m	0/4	Alonso Marín
		400 p	0/0/6	Tesorero Jorge Pérez
	Cuitzeo y Guázcato	411:6 f m	0/5/9	Cristóbal de Ayala

Date	Town	Item & Amount	Unit Price	Buyer & Remarks
		450 p	0/0/9	Secretario Alonso Sánchez
	(no vendieron el maíz de Guázcato porque estaba despoblado)			
	Coscotitán, Sn. Cristobal	45 f m	0/3	Juan de Aguilar
		45 p	0/0/6	Juan de Aguilar
	Nochistlanejo	90 f m	0/5	Cristóbal de Ayala
		40 p	0/0/6	Cristóbal de Ayala
29-XII-1566	Sentispac	66 mantas	10/0	Don Alonso [Sánchez de (15 rezago) Toledo]
31-XII-1566	Sentispac	120 @ pes	0/6	Pedro de Ordaz
		15 @ camarron	0/6	Pedro de Ordaz
		15 @ ost	0/6	Pedro de Ordaz
		30 @ mech	0/6	Pedro de Ordaz
		100 g	0/2	Diego Ruiz
		90 f m	0/2/6	Diego Ruiz y Pedro de Ordaz
	Tepic	153 f m	0/7	Diego Ruiz
		27 f tr	0/6	Diego Ruiz
		30 g	0/2/3	García de Chaves
		60 p	0/1	García de Chaves
	Suchipil	225 f m	0/6/3	Diego Ruiz
		27 f tr	0/6	Diego Ruiz
		50 g	0/2/3	Diego López de Ayala
		100 p	0/1	Diego López de Ayala
	Ahuacatlán	90 f m	0/5	Juan de Aguilar
		9 f tr	0/4	Diego Ruiz
		50 p	0/1	Diego López de Ayala
	Amaxaque	10 mantas (4 pi de m)	5/2	Diego Ruiz
		25 p	0/0/6	Diego López de Ayala
	Jala	157:6 f m	0/6	Diego Ruiz
		75 p	0/1	Diego López de Ayala
31-XII-1566	San Juan	4 f m } 2½ mantas } 2½ naguas } 2½ huipiles } 1 j miel } 3 g }	t 16/0	Diego Ruiz
	Papachula	1½ mantas } ½ nagua } ½ huipil } 3 f m } ½ qtlo miel }	t 9/4	Diego Ruiz
	Jalcocotán	27 f m	0/3/3	Diego Ruiz
		30 p	0/0/6	Diego Ruiz
		8 g	0/2	Diego Ruiz
		2 j miel (½ @ cu)	1/2	Juan de Aguilar
	Mecatán	13:6 f m } 1 j miel } (1 qtlo) } 10 p } 4 g }	t 7/7	Diego Ruiz

Date	Town	Item & Amount	Unit Price	Buyer & Remarks
	Ixtapa, Santa María	15 f sal	0/5	Juan de Heredia
		4 car pes	1/4	Diego Ruiz
		12 p	0/0/6	Diego Ruiz
	Jaltepec	9 f m }		
		11 p }	t 6/4	Diego Ruiz
		1 j miel }		
		(1 qtlo)		
	Tlaltenango	106 g	0/2	Pedro de Madrid
		214 p	0/0/6	Pedro de Madrid
		882 f m	0/5	Pedro de Madrid
		(108 f m mandadas a las salinas)		
	Teocaltiche y Teocaltitlán	765 f m	0/5 }	Juanes de Tolosa, criado de Diego de Ibarra
		9 f fr	0/5 }	
		14:6 f ají	0/5 }	(tercera oferta)
		240 p	0/0/6 }	
	Nochistlán	270 f m	0/5 }	Juanes de Tolosa, criado de
		60 g	0/2 }	Diego de Ibarra
		90 p	0/0/6 }	(tercera oferta)
	Mezquituta	180 f m	0/3	Pedro de Madrid
		100 p	0/0/6	Pedro de Madrid
2-I-1567	Tepuzhuacán	12 mantas	5/0	Diego Ruiz
		(5v x 4v)		
	Jalacingo	6 mantas	4/4	Diego Ruiz
		(4 pi de m)		
		(16 vc cu) }		
		4 p }	t 0/4	Diego Ruiz
		2 g }		
	Amatlán	8 mantas	4/4	Diego Ruiz
		(4 pi de m)		
		(16 vc cu)		
		5 p }		
		3 g }	t 0/6	Diego Ruiz
	Ixtimitique	3 mantas	4/4	Diego Ruiz
		(4 pi de m)		
		2 p }		
		1 g }	t 0/2	Diego Ruiz
	Zacatlán	27 f m	t 4/0	Diego Ruiz
	Atengoichán	630 f m	0/3/6	Juan de Aguilar
	Temichoque	18 f m }		
		5½ @ alg }	t 7/0	Diego Ruiz
		12 p }		
	Pontoque	6 g	0/1	Diego Ruiz
	Acatispa	14:6 f m }		
		6 g }	t 4/0	Diego Ruiz
		6 p }		
	Orita	13:6 f m }		
		4 @ alg }		
		12 g }	t 6/0	Diego Ruiz
		12 p }		

Date	Town	Item & Amount	Unit Price	Buyer & Remarks
	Ixcuintla	36 f m	0/2	Alonso de Herrera
		1 @ miel	1/4	Alonso de Herrera
		8 g }		
		16 p }	t 2/0	Alonso de Herrera
	Quilitlán y Jocotlán	18 f m } 16½ @ alg }	t 10/0	Diego Ruiz
	Ixtapa, de Castañeda	9 car alg } 5 f sal }	t 9/0	Diego Ruiz
	Matacticpac	11 f m } 4 f fr } 6 g } 6 p }	t 8/0	Diego Ruiz
	Yegualtitlán	36 f m } 10 p }	t 18/0	Diego Ruiz
	Acatique	22 f m } 10 p }	t 10/0	Diego Ruiz
	Huelotitlán	27 f m } 10 p }	t 16/0	Alonso de Herrera
2-I-1567	Inrimota	13 f m } 8 p }	t 9/0	Alonso de Herrera
	Tequiltitlán	18 f m } 10 p }	t 10/1	Diego Ruiz
	Cuyulomitle	7:6 f m } 10 p }	t 4/0	Diego Ruiz
	Mezquitlán	27 f m } 15 p }	t 17/1	Alonso de Herrera
	Mezquititique	9 f m } 6 p }	t 5/0	Diego Ruiz
	Cacaluta	22:6 f m } 10 p }	t 12/0	Diego Ruiz
	Zanalatlán } Mayanalistlán } Chila }		t 20/0	Diego Ruiz
	Acaponeta	90 f m } 4½ mantas } (4 pi de m) } (16 vc cu) } 20 g }	t 20/0	Diego Ruiz
	Quebiquito	18 f m } 1½ mantas } (16 vc cu) } 7½ g }	t 4/0	Diego Ruiz
	Totorán	22:6 f m } 3 mantas } (16 vc cu) } 15 g }	t 2/0	Diego Ruiz
	(precio tan bajo porque indios en rebelión)			
	Quexdaquepa	9 f m }		

Date	Town	Item & Amount	Unit Price	Buyer & Remarks
		7½ g }	t 2/0	Diego Ruiz (misma razon)
5-XII-1567	Analco	530 f m	0/4	Lope de Cisneros
		700 p	0/0/6	Lope de Cisneros
	Tonalá	270 f m	0/7	Gerónimo de Ortega
		200 p	0/0/6	Juan Téllez
		100 g	0/2/1	Lope de Cisneros
	Tlaquepaque, San Pedro	540 f m	0/4	Lope de Cisneros
		200 p	0/0/6	Lope de Cisneros
	Tlajomulco	810 f m	0/6	Lope de Cisneros
		400 p	0/0/6	Francisco de León
	Cuitzeo y Guázcato	411:6 f m	0/6	Gerónimo de Ortega
		450 p	0/0/6	Lope de Cisneros
	(Guázcato--no vendieron el 9 f m porque está despoblado)			
5-XII-1567	Poncitlán	945 f m	0/6	Gerónimo de Ortega
		1050 p	0/0/6	Cristóbal Perea
	Camotlán (Barranca)	54 f m	0/6	Gonzalo de Valdenebro
		60 p	0/0/8	Gonzalo de Valdenebro
	Coscotitán, Sn. Cristobal	45 f m	0/5	Gonzalo de Valdenebro
		45 p	0/0/8	Gonzalo de Valdenebro
	Nochistlanejo	90 f m	0/7	D. Cristóbal de Ayala
		40 p	0/0/9	D. Cristóbal de Ayala
	Atemajac	225 f m	0/6/6	D. Lorenzo de Padilla
		50 p	0/0/6	Pero Sánchez Mexía
	Cuyutlán y Zalatitlán	63 f m	0/5	Pero Sánchez Mexía
		60 p	0/0/7	Pero Sánchez Mexía
		67:6 f m	0/5	Pero Sánchez Mexía
		75 p	0/0/6	Pero Sánchez Mexía
	Matatlán	129 f m	0/5	Gerónimo de Ortega
		143 p	0/0/6	Gerónimo de Ortega
	Tequila y Los Guajes	104:6 f m	0/4/6	Antonio del Rincón
		6 p	0/0/6	Antonio del Rincón
		11 f tr	0/4	Gerónimo de Ortega
	Copala	90 f m	0/6	Gerónimo de Ortega
		50 p	0/0/6	Francisco de León
	Apozolco	63 f m	0/5/6	Gonzalo de Valdenebro
		70 p	0/0/6	Gonzalo de Valdenebro
	Tepacatengo (Barranca)	36 f m	0/4	Gonzalo de Valdenebro
		12 p }		
		8 g }	t 0/2/6	Gonzalo de Valdenebro
10-XII-1567	Sentispac	34 mantas	8/0	Diego Ruiz
		90 f m	0/2	Diego Ruiz
		180 @ pes, canarrones, ost, mech }	t 0/3/6	Diego Ruiz
		100 g	0/2	Diego Ruiz
	Tepic	153 f m	0/5	Diego Ruiz
		27 f tr	0/5	Diego Ruiz

Date	Town	Item & Amount	Unit Price	Buyer & Remarks
		30 g	0/2/3	Diego Ruiz
		60 p	0/0/6	Diego Ruiz
	Suchipil	225 f m	0/5	Gerónimo de Ortega
		27 f tr	1/0	Gerónimo de Ortega
		50 g	0/2	Gerónimo de Ortega
		100 p	0/0/7	Gerónimo de Ortega
	Ahuacatlán	90 f m	0/5	Gerónimo de Ortega
		9 f tr	1/0	Gerónimo de Ortega
		50 p	0/0/7	Gerónimo de Ortega
10-XII-1567	Amaxaque	10 mantas	5/5/6	Diego Ruiz
		25 p	0/0/7	Gerónimo de Ortega
	Jala	157:6 f m	0/5	Gerónimo de Ortega
		75 p	0/0/6	Alonso de Aguiar
	San Juan	Todo	15/0	Diego Ruiz
	Papachula	Todo	9/0	Diego Ruiz
	Jalcocotán	Todo	15/0	Diego Ruiz
	Mecatán	Todo	7/	Diego Ruiz
	Ixtapa	Todo	10/1	Diego Ruiz
	Jaltepec	Todo	6/4	Diego Ruiz
	Tepuzhuacán	12 mantas	9/0	Diego Ruiz
	Jalacingo	6 mantas	5/0	Diego Ruiz
		4 p }		
		2 g }	t 0/6	Diego Ruiz
	Amatlán	8 mantas	5/0	Diego Ruiz
		5 p }		
		3 g }	t 1/0	Diego Ruiz
	Ixtimitique	3 mantas	5/	Gerónimo de Ortega
		2 p }		
		1 g }	t 0/4	Gerónimo de Ortega
	Zacatlán	27 f m	t 4/	Diego Ruiz
	Atengoichan	630 f m	0/2/9	Antonio del Rincón
	Temichoque	Todo	8/	Diego Ruiz
	Pontoque	6 g	t 1/	Diego Ruiz
	Acatispa	Todo	5/	Diego Ruiz
	Orita	Todo	7/	Diego Ruiz
	Ixcuintla	Todo	15	Diego Ruiz
	Quilitlán y Jocotlán	Todo	10/	Diego Ruiz
	Ixtapa, de Castañeda	Todo	10/	Diego Ruiz
	Matacticpac	Todo	8/4	Diego Ruiz

Date	Town	Item & Amount	Unit Price	Buyer & Remarks
	Yegualtitlán	Todo	18/	Antonio del Rincón
	Acatique	Todo	10/	Antonio del Rincón
	Huelotitlán	Todo	16/	Antonio del Rincón
	Inrimota	Todo	9/	Antonio del Rincón
10-XII-1567	Tequiltitlán	Todo	10/4	Antonio del Rincón
	Cuyulomitle	Todo	4/	Antonio del Rincón
	Mezquitlán	Todo	18/2	Antonio del Rincón
	Mezquititique en Jocotlán	9 f m } 6 p }	t 5/	Antonio del Rincón
	Cacaluta	22:6 f m } 10 p }	t 12/	Antonio del Rincón
	Zanalatlán } Mayanalistlán } Chila }		t 21/	Diego Ruiz
	Acaponeta	90 f m } 4½ mantas } (16 vc cu) } 20 g }	t 20/	Diego Ruiz
	Quebiquito	18 f m } 1½ mantas } (16 vc cu) } 7½ g }		
	(ninguna oferta porque los indios estaban en rebelión)			
	Totorán	22:6 f m } 3 mantas } (16 vc cu) } 15 g }		
	(ninguna oferta porque los indios estaban en rebelión)			
	Quexdaquepa	9 f m } 7½ g }		
	(ninguna oferta porque los indios estaban en rebelión)			
21-XII-1567	Tlaltenango	690 f m	0/5	Juan de Rentería
		(300 f m--reservadas para los recogedores de sal)		
		106 g	0/2	Juan de Rentería
		214 p	0/0/6	Juan de Rentería
	Nochistlán	270 f m	0/5	Diego de Ibarra
		60 g	0/2	Diego de Ibarra
		90 p	0/0/6	Diego de Ibarra
	Teocaltiche y Teocaltitlán	765 f m	0/5	Diego de Ibarra
		9 f fr	0/5	Diego de Ibarra
		14:6 f ají	0/5	Diego de Ibarra
		240 p	0/0/6	Diego de Ibarra
	Mexticacán	171 f m	0/5	Juan Vicente
		60 p	t 4/	Juan Vicente
9-I-1568	Mezquituta	180 f m	0/4	Pedro de Madrid
		100 p	0/0/6	Pedro de Madrid

Date	Town	Item & Amount	Unit Price	Buyer & Remarks
10-XII-1568	Analco y Tetlán	630 f m	0/4	Juan Téllez
		630 p	0/0/6	Juan Téllez
	Tonalá	270 f m	0/4/7	Juan Téllez
	Tlaquepaque, San }	410:6 f m	0/4	Juan Téllez
	Pedro y Toluquilla}	462 p	0/0/6	Juan Téllez
	Tlajomulco	810 f m	0/4	Lope de Cisneros
		360 p	0/0/6	Lope de Cisneros
	Cuitzeo	388:6 f m	0/4/9	Gonzalo de Valdenebro
		377 p	0/0/9	Tesorero Jorge Pérez
	Poncitlán	945 f m	0/4/9	Lope de Cisneros
		945 p	0/0/10	Lope de Cisneros
	Camotlán (Barranca)	54 f m	0/4	Juan de Segura
		54 p	0/0/7	D. Cristóbal de Ayala
	Coscotitán (Barranca)	45 f m	0/4	Juan de Aguilar
		41 p	0/0/7	Juan de Aguilar
	Nochistlanejo	90 f m	0/6	Cristóbal Pérea
		36 p	0/0/9	D. Cristóbal de Ayala
	Atemajac (con ajuste de 24 pollos)	114:6 f m	0/4	Juan Téllez
		206 p	0/0/6	Juan Téllez
11-XII-1568	Cuyutlán	63 f m	0/6	Juan de Leiva
		54 p	0/0/9	Gonzalo de Valdenebro
	Zalatitlán	67:6 f m	0/7	Fran. Meredio de Velasco
		68 p	0/0/10	Fran. Meredio de Velasco
	Matatlán	129 f m	0/6/3	Francisco de Cepeda
		129 p	0/0/6	Diego Vázquez
	Tequila y Los Guajes	104:6 f m	0/4/6	Gonzalo de Valdenebro
		11 f tr	0/7	Francisco de Cepeda
		6 p	0/0/6	Gonzalo de Valdenebro
	Copala y Quilitlán	90 f m	0/6/6	Juan de Segura
		45 p	0/0/11	Pedro de Céspedes
	Apozolco y Otala	63 f m	0/6	Fran. Meredio de Velasco
		63 p	0/0/9	Pedro de Céspedes
	Tepacatengo (Barranca)	36 f m	0/5/9	Francisco de Cepeda
		7 g	0/2	Francisco de Cepeda
		11 p	0/0/6	Francisco de Cepeda
14-XII-1568	Sentispac	90 f m	0/2/6	Diego Ruiz
		180 @ pes (productos de)	0/3/3	Rodrigo Pérez
	(oferta única)	51 mantas	9/4	Diego Ruiz
		90 g	0/1/6	Diego Ruiz
	Atengoichán	630 f m	0/3	Juan de Segura
	Jocotlán, Prov. }			
	Jegualtitlán }			
	Acatique }			
	Huelotitlán }			

Date	Town	Item & Amount	Unit Price	Buyer & Remarks
	Inrimota }	182:6 f m	0/7/6	Gonzalo de Valdenebro
	Tequiltitlán }	76½ p	0/1	Canónigo Francisco García de Urrieta
	Cuyolomitle }			
	Mezquitlán }			
	Mezquititique }			
	Cacalutla }			
	Zanalatlán, }			Tesorero Jorge Pérez
	Mayanalistlán y }	Todo	23/4	(única oferta--22/ de
el 1/4)	Chila }			mismo. Pero por fin la levantó
15-XII-1568	Piloto	15 @ pes	0/4	Marcos Galindo
		8 f m	0/4	Pedro Hurtado
		3 @ henequén	0/4	Pedro Hurtado
		16 f sal	1/0	Pedro Hurtado
	Amboquito y Atengo	2 mantas (4 pi cu)	1/4 cada pi	Pedro de Trujillo
		33:3 f sal	1/0	Pedro Hurtado
		1 @ miel	1/0	Pedro Hurtado
		12 g	0/1	Pedro Hurtado
		12 f m	0/4	Pedro Hurtado
	Maito	33:3 f sal	1/0	Pedro Hurtado
		8 pi de mantas	1/4 cada pi	Pedro de Trujillo
		4 g	0/1	Pedro Hurtado
		20 f m	0/4	Pedro Hurtado
	Colique	8 pi de mantas	1/4	Pedro de Trujillo
		½ @ miel	1/0 @	Pedro Hurtado
		26:6 f sal	1/0 f	Pedro Hurtado
		10 g	0/1	Pedro Hurtado
		20 f m (incluye el m de Atelaco)	0/4	Pedro Hurtado
	Atelaco	8 pi de mantas	1/4	Pedro de Trujillo
		8 g	0/1	Pedro Hurtado
	Opono (ptdo)	90 f m	0/2/6	Marcos Galindo
	Zapotlán	9 f m	0/2/6	Pedro Hurtado
		4 pi de mantas	1/0	Pedro Hurtado
		1 @ miel	1/0	Pedro Hurtado
15-XII-1568	Panpuchín	6 pi de mantas	1/0	Pedro Hurtado
		20 g	0/4	Pedro Hurtado
		1½ @ miel	1/0	Pedro Hurtado
		14:6 f m	0/2/6	Pedro Hurtado
	Contlan	18 f m	0/2	Pedro Hurtado
		12 pi de mantas	1/0	Pedro Hurtado
		1 @ miel	1/0	Pedro Hurtado
		2 @ pes salado	0/4	Pedro Hurtado
	Sila	13:6 f m	0/2	Pedro Hurtado
		1 @ miel	1/0	Pedro Hurtado
	Tepic	153 f m	0/5	D. Cristóbal de Ayala
		27 f tr	0/6	D. Cristóbal de Ayala
		27 g	0/2/3	Diego Ruiz
		63 p	0/0/7	Diego Ruiz
	Suchipil	225 f m	0/5/6	D. Cristóbal de Ayala

Date	Town	Item & Amount	Unit Price	Buyer & Remarks
		27 f tr	0/6/3	Diego Ruiz
		90 p	0/0/7	Diego Ruiz
		45 g	0/2/3	Diego Ruiz
	Ahuacatlán	90 f m	0/5/6	Diego Ruiz
		9 f tr	0/6/3	Diego Ruiz
		45 p	0/0/7	Diego Ruiz
	Amaxaque	10 mantas	6/3/6	Diego Ruiz
		23 p	0/0/8	Diego Ruiz
	Jala	157:6 f m	0/5/6	Diego Ruiz
		68 p	0/0/7	Diego Ruiz
	San Juan	Todo	16/4	Diego Ruiz
	Papachula	Todo	10/1	Diego Ruiz
	Jalcocotán	Todo	16/6	Diego Ruiz
	Mecatán	Todo	7/6	Diego Ruiz
	Ixtapa	2 car pes)		
		11 p)	t 1/6/5	Diego Ruiz
	Jaltepec	Todo	7/1	Diego Ruiz
	Tepuzhuacán	12 mantas	5/6	Diego Ruiz
	Jalacingo	6 mantas	5/6	Diego Ruiz
		3 p)		
		2 g)	t 0/6	Diego Ruiz
	Amatlán	8 mantas	5/6	Diego Ruiz
		4 p)		
		3 g)	t 1/0	Diego Ruiz
	Iximitique	3 mantas	5/6	Diego Ruiz
		2 p)		
		1 g)	t 0/4	Diego Ruiz
15-XII-1568	Zacatlán	27 f m	t 5/5/6	Diego Ruiz
	Temichoque	Todo	9/1	Diego Ruiz
	Pontoque	5½ g	t 1/0	Diego Ruiz
	Acatispa	Todo	5/7	Diego Ruiz
	Orita	Todo	6/0	Diego Ruiz
		(menos 2:6 f m de ajuste para 1559)		
	Ixcuintla	Todo	17/	Diego Ruiz
	Quilitlán y Jocotlán	Todo	11/1	Diego Ruiz
	Ixtapa, de C.	Todo	10/	Diego Ruiz
	Matacticpac	Todo	8/5	Diego Ruiz
	Acaponeta	Todo	28/5	Don Cristóbal de Ayala
	Quebiquito			
	(ninguna oferta--pueblo despoblado y indios en guerra)			

Date	Town	Item & Amount	Unit Price	Buyer & Remarks
	Totorán (ninguna oferta--pueblo despoblado y indios en guerra)			
	Quexdaquepa (ninguna oferta--pueblo despoblado y indios en guerra)			
27-XII-1568	Tlaltenango	690 f m	0/5	Gerónimo de Rojas
		(300 f m reservadas para los indios, recogedores de sal)		
		193 p	0/0/6	Gerónimo de Rojas
		95 g	0/2	Gerónimo de Rojas
	Teocaltiche y Teocaltitlán	720 f m	0/5	Martín de Eguiguren
		9 f fr	0/5	Martín de Eguiguren
		14:6 f ají	0/5	Martín de Eguiguren
		396 p	0/0/6	Martín de Eguiguren
	Nochistlán (ya pagaron el diezmo de aves)	270 f m	0/5/6	Pedro de Madrid
		54 g	0/2	Pedro de Madrid
		81 p	0/0/6	Pedro de Madrid
	Mezquituta	180 f m	0/5	Juan Díaz de Alfaro
		90 p	0/0/6	Juan Díaz de Alfaro
	Mexticacán	71 f m	0/4/3	Juan Díaz de Alfaro
		54 p	0/0/6	Juan Díaz de Alfaro
15-I-1569	Sentispac	51 mantas	10/2	Pero Núñez de Silva
		90 f m	0/3	Bernardo de Balbuena
		180 @ prod pes	0/3	Bernardo de Balbuena
		90 g	0/2	Fran. Merodio de Velasco, Alguacil Mayor
	Yegualtitlán } Acatique } Huelotitlán } Inrimota } Tequiltitlán } Cuyolomitle } Mezquitlán } Mezquititique } Cacaluta }	182:6 f m 76½ p	0/6 0/1	Canónigo Francisco García de Urrieta
16-I-1569	Zanalatitlán } Mayanalistlán } Chila }	Todo	23/4	Diego Ruiz
	Acaponeta	90 f m } 3½ mantas } (16 vc cu) } 18 g }	t 30/0	Diego Ruiz
	Quebiquito	18 f m } 1½ mantas } (16 vc cu) } 6 g }		
	(no hubo almoneda porque los indios están en rebelión)			
	Totorán	22:6 f m } 3 mantas } (16 vc cu) } 13 g }		
	(no hubo almoneda porque los indios están en rebelión)			
	Quexdaquepa	9 f m }		

Date	Town	Item & Amount	Unit Price	Buyer & Remarks
		6 g }		
	(no hubo almoneda porque los indios están en rebelión)			
	Tepic	153 f m	0/4/6	Pero Núñez de Silva
		27 f tr	0/7	Pero Núñez de Silva
		27 g	0/2/3	Rodrigo Pérez
		63 p	0/0/7	Rodrigo Pérez
	Suchipil	27 f tr	0/6/3	Pero Núñez de Silva
		90 p	0/0/7	Pero Núñez de Silva
		45 g	0/2/3	Pero Núñez de Silva
		225 f m	0/5	Diego Ruiz
	Ahuacatlán	45 p	0/0/7	Rodrigo Pérez
		9 f tr	0/6	Pero Núñez de Silva
		90 f m	0/5	Diego Ruiz
13-V-1569	Cuyutlán	63 f m	0/4/9	Francisco de Céspedes
		54 p	0/1	Secretario Alonso Sánchez
	Zalatitlán	67:6 f m	0/5	Pero Vázquez
		67 p	0/1/3	Pero Vázquez
13-V-1569	Matatlán	129 f m	0/5	Pero Sánchez Mexía
		129 p	0/1/1	Pero Sánchez Mexía
	Tequila y Los Guajes	104:6 f m	0/6	Pero Vázquez
		11 f tr	0/6/6	Francisco de Céspedes
		5 p	t 0/3	Pero Vázquez
	Copala y Quilitlán	68 f m	0/5	Secretario Alonso Sánchez
		68 p	0/1	Secretario Alonso Sánchez
	Apozolco y Tala	63 f m	0/4	Gonzalo de Valdenebro
		63 p	0/1	Francisco de Céspedes
	Ahuisculco	22 p	0/1	Secretario Alonso Sánchez
		11 f m	0/4	Gonzalo de Valdenebro
	Tepacatengo	36 f m	0/4/3	Francisco de Céspedes
		7 g	0/2	Francisco de Céspedes
		11 p	0/0/6	Francisco de Céspedes
12-XII-1569	Analco y Tetlán	630 f m	0/3/6	Antonio Díaz, Alguacil
		630 p	0/0/6	Antonio Díaz, Alguacil
	Tonalá	270 f m	0/3/6	Antonio Díaz, Alguacil
		180 p	0/0/6	Antonio Díaz, Alguacil
		90 g	0/2	Antonio Díaz, Alguacil
	Tlaquepaque, Sn. Pedro y Toluquilla }	410:6 f m	0/3/6	Antonio Díaz, Alguacil
		461 p	0/0/6	Antonio Díaz, Alguacil
	Tlajomulco	810 f m	0/4/6	Gonzalo de Valdenebro
		360 p	0/0/6	Antonio Díaz, Alguacil
	Cuitzeo	388:6 f m	0/4	Maese Pedro
		457 p	0/0/9	Juan Téllez
	Poncitlán	727 f m	0/4	Bernardo de Balbuena
		812 p	0/0/9	Pero Sánchez Mexía
	Camotlán	54 f m	0/4	Alonso de Rubalcava
		54 p	0/1	Alonso de Rubalcava

Date	Town	Item & Amount	Unit Price	Buyer & Remarks
	Coscotitán	45 f m	0/3/9	Juan de Segura
		40 p	0/0/10	Juan de Segura
	Nochistlanejo	90 f m	0/5	Juan Téllez
		36 p	0/0/10	Juan Téllez
	Atemajac	114:6 f m	0/3/6	Antonio Díaz, Alguacil
		229 p	0/0/6	Antonio Díaz, Alguacil
16-XII-1569	Nochistlán	330:6 f m	0/4/6	Vicente de Saldívar
		374 p	0/0/6	Vicente de Saldívar
	Teocaltiche y Teocaltitlán	766 f m, fr, ají }	0/4/6	Vicente de Saldívar
		396 p	0/0/6	Vicente de Saldívar
16-XII-1569	Mexticacán	171 f m	0/4/6	Vicente de Saldívar
		54 p	0/0/6	Vicente de Saldívar
	Mezquituta	180 f m	0/4	Bernardo de Balbuena
		90 p	0/0/6	Bernardo de Balbuena
	Amaxaque	22 p	0/0/7	Rodrigo Pérez
		10 mantas (16 vc cu)	6/0	Diego Ruiz
	Jala	68 p	0/0/7	Rodrigo Pérez
		157:6 f m	0/5	Diego Ruiz
	San Juan	3 g } 3:6 f m } 2½ mantas } 2½ naguas } 2½ huipiles } 1 j miel-qtlo}	t 15/5	Diego Ruiz
	Papachula	1½ mantas } ½ huipil } ½ nagua } 3 f m } ½ qtlo miel }	t 10/1	Diego Ruiz
	Jalcocotán	27 p	0/0/7	Rodrigo Pérez
		7 g	0/2	Rodrigo Pérez
		27 f m } 2 j miel--½ @ cu}	t 12/6/6	Diego Ruiz
	Mecatán	9 p	0/0/7	Rodrigo Pérez
		4 g	0/2/3	Rodrigo Pérez
		13:6 f m } 1 j miel-qtlo}	t 5/7/9	Diego Ruiz
	Ixtapa	11 p	0/0/7	Rodrigo Pérez
		15 f sal } 2 car pes }	t 5/0	Diego Ruiz
	Jaltepec	10 p	0/0/7	Rodrigo Pérez
		9 f m } 1 j miel-qtlo}	t 6/3/2	Diego Ruiz
	Tepuzhuacán	12 mantas (20 vc cu)	6/0	Diego Ruiz
	Jalacingo	3 p	0/0/7	Rodrigo Pérez

Date	Town	Item & Amount	Unit Price	Buyer & Remarks
		2 g	0/2/3	Rodrigo Pérez
		6 mantas (16 vc cu)	6/0	Diego Ruiz
	Amatlán	4 p	0/0/7	Rodrigo Pérez
		3 g	0/2/3	Rodrigo Pérez
		8 mantas (16 vc cu)	6/0	Diego Ruiz
	Ixtimitique	1 g	0/2/3	Rodrigo Pérez
		2 p	0/0/7	Rodrigo Pérez
		3 mantas (16 vc cu)	6/0	Diego Ruiz
16-XII-1569	Zacatlán	27 f m	t 5/5/6	Diego Ruiz
	Atengoichán	630 f m	0/2	Cristóbal de Oñete
	Temichoque	11 p	0/0/7	Rodrigo Pérez
		18 f m }		
		5½ @ alg }	t 8/2/7	Diego Ruiz
	Pontoque	5 g	0/2/3	Rodrigo Pérez
	Acatispa	5 g }		
		6 p }	t 1/6/9	Rodrigo Pérez
		14:6 f m	t 4/0/3	Diego Ruiz
	Orita	11 g }		
		11 p }	t 3/7/9	Rodrigo Pérez
		13:6 f m }		
		3½ @ alg }	t 3/0/3	Diego Ruiz
	Ixcuintla	7 g }		
		15 p }	t 3/0/6	Rodrigo Pérez
		36 f m }		
		1 j miel-1 @}	t 14/0	Diego Ruiz
	Quilitlán y Jocotlán	18 f m }		
		16½ @ alg }	t 11/1	Diego Ruiz
	Ixtapa	7 f sal	t 2/0	Diego Ruiz
	Matacticpac	6 p }		
		5 g }	t 1/6/9	Rodrigo Pérez
		11 f m }		
		3:6 f fr }	t 6/6/3	Diego Ruiz
20-XII-1569	Piloto	100 f sal	0/7/6	Manuel Salgado
		36 f m	0/2	Marcos Galindo
21-XII-1569	Maito	50 sal	0/7/6	Manuel Salgado
		27 f m	0/2	Marcos Galindo
	Panpuchín	6 pi de m	1/0	Domingo Alvarez
		20 p	0/0/6	Domingo Alvarez
		1½ @ miel	3/0	Domingo Alvarez
		16 f m	0/3	Domingo Alvarez
	Zapotlán	4 pi de m	1/0	Domingo Alvarez
		1 @ miel	4/4	Domingo Alvarez
		14:6 f m	0/3	Domingo Alvarez
	Sila	13:6 f m	0/3	Domingo Alvarez
		1 @ miel	4/4	Domingo Alvarez

Date	Town	Item & Amount	Unit Price	Buyer & Remarks
	Contlan	3 pi de m	1/0	Domingo Alvarez
		6 f m	0/2	Marcos Galindo
8-I-1570	Tlaltenango	551 f m	0/3	Hortuño de Areylça,
	(300 f m reservadas para recogedores de sal)			Alguacil
		905 p	0/0/6	Hortuño de Areylça, Alguacil
12-XII-1570	Mezquituta	180 f m	0/3/6	Rodrigo Gutiérrez de Baeza
		90 p	0/0/6	Rodrigo Gutiérrez de Baeza
	Analco y Tetlán	530 f m	0/3/6	Antonio Díaz
		530 p	0/0/6	Antonio Díaz
	Tonalá	270 f m	0/3/6	Antonio Díaz
		180 p	0/0/6	Antonio Díaz
		90 g	0/2	Antonio Díaz
	Tlaquepaque, Sn. Pedro y Toluquilla	410:6 f m	0/3/6	Antonio Díaz
		461 p	0/0/6	Antonio Díaz
	Tlajomulco	810 f m	0/5/2	Alonso de la Vera
		360 p	0/0/11	Alonso de la Vera
	Cuitzeo	388 f m	0/3	Alonso de la Vera
		457 p	0/0/8	Alonso de la Vera
	Poncitlán	727 f m	0/3/6	Alonso de la Vera
		812 p	0/0/6	Alonso de la Vera
	Camotlán (Barranca)	54 f m	0/4/9	Alonso de la Vera
		54 p	0/0/8	Alonso de la Vera
	Coscotitán (Barranca)	45 f m	0/4/9	Alonso de la Vera
		40 p	0/0/8	Alonso de la Vera
	Nochistlanejo	90 f m	0/5	Gonzalo de Valdenebro
		36 p	0/0/9	Gonzalo de Valdenebro
	Atemajac	1146 f m	0/3/6	Antonio Díaz
		229 p	0/0/6	Antonio Díaz
	Cuyutlán	63 f m	0/5	Gerónimo de Ortega
		54 p	0/0/10	Fran. Merodio de Velasco
	Zalatitlán	67:6 f m	0/5/3	Secretario Alonso Sánchez
		67 p	0/0/10	Secretario Alonso Sánchez
	Matatlán	129 f m	0/4	Pero Sánchez Mexía
		129 p	0/0/6	Pero Sánchez Mexía
13-XII-1570	Tequila y Los Guajes	104:6 f m	0/6	Rodrigo Pérez
		11 f tr	0/6	Gerónimo de Ortega
		5 p	0/0/6	Rodrigo Pérez
	Copalá y Quilitlán	68:6 f m	0/6	Gerónimo de Ortega
		68 p	0/0/8	Gerónimo de Ortega
	Apozolco y Tala	63 f m	0/6	Fran. Merodio de Velasco
	Ahuisculco	29 f m	0/5/3	Rodrigo Pérez
		29 p	0/0/9	Alonso de la Vera
	Tepacatengo	36 f m	0/5	Rodrigo de Baeza
		7 g	0/2/9	Francisco de Cepeda

Date	Town	Item & Amount	Unit Price	Buyer & Remarks
		11 p	0/0/6	Francisco de Cepeda
13-XII-1570	Sentispac	51 mantas	10/1	Diego Ruiz
		90 f m	0/2/9	Fran. Merodio de Velasco
		180 @ pro de pes	0/4/3	Fran. Merodio de Velasco
		90 g	0/2	Fran. Merodio de Velasco
	Tepic	153 f m	0/4	Diego Ruiz
		27 f tr	0/6	Diego Ruiz
		27 g	0/2	Diego Ruiz
		63 p	0/0/7	Diego Ruiz
	Suchipil	225 f m	0/4	Diego Ruiz
		27 f tr	0/6	Diego Ruiz
		90 p	0/1	Diego Ruiz
		45 g	0/2	Diego Ruiz
	Ahuacatlán	90 f m	0/4	Diego Ruiz
		9 f tr	0/6	Diego Ruiz
		45 p	0/1	Diego Ruiz
	Amaxaque	10 mantas	8/1	Diego Ruiz
		22 p	0/0/6	Diego Ruiz
	Jala	157:6 f m	0/6	Diego Ruiz
		68 p	0/0/6	Diego Ruiz
14-XII-1570	San Juan	Todo	16/4	Diego Ruiz
	Papachula	Todo	10/1	Diego Ruiz
	Jalcocotán	Todo	16/1	Diego Ruiz
	Mecatán	Todo	7/7	Diego Ruiz
	Ixtapilla	Todo	6/	Diego Ruiz
	Jaltapec	Todo	7/1	Diego Ruiz
	Tepuzhuacán	12 mantas	5/2	Diego Ruiz
	Jalacingo	6 mantas	5/2	Diego Ruiz
		3 p } 2 g }	t 0/6	Diego Ruiz
	Amatlán	8 mantas	5/2	Diego Ruiz
		4 p } 3 g }	t 1/0	Diego Ruiz
	Ixtimitique	3 mantas	5/	Diego Ruiz
		2 p } 1 g }	t 0/3	Diego Ruiz
	Zacatlán	27 f m	0/2	Diego Ruiz
	Atengoichán	630 f m	0/3	Francisco de Estrada
	Temichoque	Todo	9/1	Diego Ruiz
	Pontoque	5 g	0/2	Diego Ruiz
	Acatispa	Todo	6/	Diego Ruiz
14-XII-1570	Orita	Todo	7/	Diego Ruiz

Date	Town	Item & Amount	Unit Price	Buyer & Remarks
	Ixcuintla	Todo	17/	Diego Ruiz
	Quilitlán y Jocotlán	Todo	11/1	Diego Ruiz
	Ixtapa, de C.	7 f sal	t 2/0	Diego Ruiz
	Matacticpac	Todo	8/5	Diego Ruiz
	Jocotlán--Provincia 9 pueblos como antes (sin cambio de tasación)	180 f m	0/5	Gerónimo de Ortega
		76 p	0/0/9	Diego Ruiz
	Jalisco	35:3 f m	0/4	Diego Ruiz
		1 f fr	0/4	Diego Ruiz
		1½ oz miel } 1 g }	t 1/	Diego Ruiz
	Mascota	17:6 f m	0/2	Deigo Ruiz
		8 p } 2 oz miel }	t 1/0	Diego Ruiz
	Zanalatlán } Mayanalistlán } Chila }	Todo	23/4	Diego Ruiz
	Acaponeta	Todo	30/	Diego Ruiz
	Quebiquito	Todo	3/	Diego Ruiz
	Totorán	Todo	5/	Diego Ruiz
	Quexdaquepa	Todo	2/	Diego Ruiz
17-XII-1570	Tlaltenango	351 f m	0/4	Francisco de Hoz
	(500 f m reservadas para los indios, recogedores de sal)			
		905 p	0/0/6	Francisco de Hoz
	Nochistlán	330:6 f m	0/6/7	Diego Gutiérrez Carcaja
		374 p	0/0/6	Diego Gutiérrez Carcaja
	Teocaltiche y Teocaltitlán	766 f m, fr, ají	0/6/7	Diego Gutiérrez Carcaja
		396 p	0/0/6	Diego Gutiérrez Carcaja
	Mexticacán	171 f m	0/6/7	Diego Gutiérrez Carcaja
		54 p	0/0/6	Diego Gutiérrez Carcaja
28-XII-1570	Piloto	100 f sal	0/6/6	Antonio Griego
		36 f m	0/1	Francisco de Burgos
	Maito	50 f sal	0/6/6	Antonio Griego
		27 f m	0/1	Francisco de Burgos
28-XII-1570	Zapotlán	4 pi de m	1/4	Domingo Alvarez
		1 @ miel	3/0	Domingo Alvarez
		16 f m [sic]	0/4	Domingo Alvarez
	Pampuchín	6 pi de m	1/4	Domingo Alvarez
		20 p	0/1	Domingo Alvarez
		1½ @ miel	3/0	Domingo Alvarez
		16 f m	0/4	Domingo Alvarez
	Contla	3 pi de m	1/4	Domingo Alvarez

Date	Town	Item & Amount	Unit Price	Buyer & Remarks
		7 f m	0/4	Domingo Alvarez
	Sila	15 f m	0/4	Domingo Alvarez
		1 @ miel	3/0	Domingo Alvarez
	Opono	69 f m	0/4	Antonio Griego
		58 p	0/0/6	Antonio Griego
11-XII-1571	Mezquituta	180 f m	0/4	Alonso de la Vera
		90 p	0/1	Canónigo Francisco García de Urrieta
	Analco y Tetlán	509:2 f m	0/3	Antonio Díaz, Alguaríl
		572 p	0/0/6	Antonio Díaz, Alguaríl
	Tonalá	270 f m	0/3	Antonio Díaz, Alguaril
		180 p	0/0/6	Antonio Díaz, Alguaril
		90 g	0/2	Antonio Díaz, Alguaril
	Tlaquepaque, San Pedro y Toluquilla	410:6 f m	0/3	Antonio Díaz, Alguaril
		461 p	0/0/6	Antonio Díaz, Alguaril
	Tlajomulco	865 f m	0/5	Rodrigo de Balcázar
		949 p	0/1	Lope de Cisneros
	Cuitzeo	388:6 f m	0/4	Gonzalo de Valdenebro
		457 p	0/0/9	Luis Infante Balderrama
	Poncitlán	727 f m	0/4/10	Rodrigo de Balcázar
		812 p	0/0/7	Francisco de Plaza
	Atemajac	114:6 f m	0/3	Antonio Díaz, Alguaril
		229 p	0/0/6	Antonio Díaz, Alguaril
12-XII-1571	Camotlán	54 f m	0/3	Canónigo José Ramírez
		54 p	0/0/10	Canónigo José Ramírez
	Coscotitán	45 f m	0/3	Canónigo José Ramírez
		40 p	0/0/10	Canónigo José Ramírez
	Nochistlanejo	90 f m	0/4/6	Alonso de la Vera
		36 p	0/0/9	Alonso de la Vera
	Cuyutlán	63 f m	0/4/1	Secretario Alonso Sánchez
		54 p	0/0/3	Secretario Alonso Sánchez
	Zalatitlán	67:6 f m	0/5/8	Secretario Alonso Sánchez
		67 p	0/0/9	Secretario Alonso Sánchez
13-XII-1571	Matatlán	129 f m	0/3/6	Alonso de la Vera
		129 p	0/0/6	Alonso de la Vera
	Tequila y Los Guajes	104:6 f m	0/6	Rodrigo de Balcázar
		11 f tr	0/5/6	Diego de Colio, el Viejo
		5 p	0/0/6	Diego de Colio, el Viejo
	Copala y Quilitlán	68:6 f m	0/4	Pedro de Céspedes
		68 p	0/0/3	Pedro de Céspedes
	Apozolco y Tala	63 f m	0/4	Diego de Colio, el Viejo
		63 p	0/1	Diego de Colio, el Viejo
	Ahuisculco	29 f m	0/4	Francisco Narváez
		29 p	0/1	Francisco Narváez

Date	Town	Item & Amount	Unit Price	Buyer & Remarks
	Tepacatengo	36 f m	0/4	Diego de Colio, el Viejo
		7 g	0/2/9	Diego de Colio, el Viejo
		11 p	0/0/6	Diego de Colio, el Viejo
13-XII-1571	Sentispac	90 f m	0/4	Alonso de Llerena
		51 mantas	11/	Francisco de Plaza
		180 @ prod pes	0/4/3	Rodrigo de Balcázar
		90 g	0/2	Rodrigo de Balcázar
14-XII-1571	Tepic	153 f m	0/4/6	Gonzalo de Valdenebro
		27 f tr	0/5/6	Gonzalo de Valdenebro
		27 g	0/2	Gonzalo de Valdenebro
		63 p	0/0/6	Gonzalo de Valdenebro
	Suchipil	190:6 f m	0/4/6	Alonso de Llerena
		14:6 f tr	1/	Rodrigo de Balcázar
		124 p	0/0/9	Alonso de Llerena
	Ahuacatlán	90 f m	0/5	Alonso de Llerena
		9 f tr	0/7	Rodrigo de Balcázar
		45 p	0/0/9	Alonso de Llerena
	Amaxaque	10 mantas	7/	Alonso de Llerena
		22 p	0/0/9	Alonso de Llerena
	Jala	157:6 f m	0/6	Juan de Salcedo
		58 p	0/0/9	Alonso de Llerena
	San Juan	Todo	19/	Juan de Salcedo
	Papachula	Todo	11/	Juan de Salcedo
	Jalcocotán	Todo	19/	Rodrigo de Balcázar
	Mecatán	Todo	8/4	Rodrigo de Balcázar
	Ixtapilla	Todo	13/	Rodrigo de Balcázar
	Jaltepec	Todo	8/	Rodrigo de Balcázar
	Tepuzhuacán	12 mantas	7/	Alonso de Llerena
	Jalacingo	6 mantas	6/	Alonso de Llerena
		3 p }		
		2 g }	t 0/6	Alonso de Llerena
	Amatlán	8 mantas	6/5	Juan de Salcedo
		4 p }		
		3 g }	t 1/	Juan de Salcedo
	Ixtimitique	3 mantas	6/3	Juan de Salcedo
		2 p }		
		1 g }	t 0/4	Juan de Salcedo
	Zacatlán	27 f m	0/2/9	Rodrigo de Balcázar
15-XII-1571	Atengoichán	630 f m	0/2/9	Alonso de Llerena
	Temichoque	Todo	12/2	Alonso de Llerena
	Pontoque	6 g	1/2	Alonso de Llerena
	Acatispa	Todo	7/1	Alonso de Llerena
15-XII-1571	Orita	Todo	8/	Rodrigo de Balcázar

Date	Town	Item & Amount	Unit Price	Buyer & Remarks
	Ixcuintla	Todo	21/	Rodrigo de Balcázar
	Quilitlán	Todo	11/4	Alonso de Llerena
	Ixtapa, de C.	7 f sal	t 4/	Alonso de Llerena
	Matacticpac	Todo	10/4	Rodrigo de Balcázar
	Partido de Jocotlán			
	Yegualtitlán }			
	Acatic }			
	Huelotitlán }			
	Inrimota }	182:6 f m	0/4/6	Juan de Salcedo
	Tequiltitlán }	77 p	0/0/9	Alonso de Llerena
	Cuyolomitle }			
	Mezquitlán }			
	Mezquititique }			
	Cacaluta }			
	Jalisco	156:6 f m	0/6	Gonzalo de Valdenebro
		4 f fr	0/6	Gonzalo de Valdenebro
		1 @ miel }		
		4 g }	t 6/	Alonso de Llerena
		60 p	0/0/9	Gonzalo de Valdenebro
	Mascota	90 f m	0/2/9	Alonso de Llerena
		45 p	0/0/9	Alonso de Llerena
		1 @ miel	4/4	Alonso de Llerena
	Tepetlatlauca y Chistique	86:6 f m	0/2/6	Alonso de Llerena
		40 p	0/0/9	Alonso de Llerena
	Mexcala	60 f m	0/3/9	Martín de Carranza
		30 p	0/0/8	Rodrigo de Balcázar
16-XII-1571	Zanalatitlán }			
	Mayanalistlán }	Todo	24/2	Rodrigo de Balcázar
	Chila }			
	Acaponeta	Todo	50/	Juan Rodríguez, mercador
	Quebiquito	Todo	10/	Juan Rodríguez, mercador
	Totorán	Todo	15/	Juan Rodríguez, mercador
	Quexdaquepa	Todo	4/	Juan Rodríguez, mercador
	Opono	52 f m	0/3	Alonso de Llerena
		52 p	0/0/11	Alonso de Llerena
	Piloto	36 f m	0/2/6	Antonio de Aguayo
		100 f sal	0/5	Antonio de Aguayo
	Maloto	50 f sal	0/5	Antonio Bote
		27 f m	0/2/6	Antonio Bote
	Zapotlán	9 f m	0/3	Antonio de Aguayo
		1 manta }		
		1 @ miel }	t 7/	Alonso de Llerena
16-XII-1571	Panpuchín	14:6 f m	0/3	Antonio de Aguayo
		6 pi de m	0/6/6	Alonso de Llerena
		18 p	0/0/6	Andrés Méndez
		1½ @ miel	t 5/	Alonso de Llerena

Date	Town	Item & Amount	Unit Price	Buyer & Remarks
	Tena (no hubo almoneda--despoblado, dicen Antonio de Aguayo y Antonio Bote, vecinos de Purificación)			
	Sila	13:6 f m	0/2/9	Antonio de Aguayo
		1 @ miel	1/4	Juan de Salcedo
	Contla	Todo	12/	Juan de Salcedo
21-XII-1571	Tlaltenango	517 p	0/0/6	Luis de las Doblas
		(498:6 f m reservadas para las salinas)		
30-XII-1571	Mexticacán	171 f m	0/3	Alonso de Velasco, vecino
	(ofertas muy pocas y bajas)	374 p	0/0/6	Alonso de Velasco, vecino
	Nochistlán (vea arriba)	330:6 f m	0/3	Alonso de Velasco, vecino de las minas
		374 p	0/0/6	Alonso de Velasco, vecino de las minas
	Teocaltiche (vea arriba)	298 f m	0/2	Hernando de Burgos y Alonso de Velasco
		318 p	0/0/6	
	Teocaltitlán	405 f m	0/2	
		216 p	0/0/6	
		9 f fr	0/2	
		14:6 f ají	0/2	
14-XI-1572	Tlaltenango	498:6 f m		(reservadas para las salinas)
24-XI-1572	Teocaltiche	298 f m		(reservadas para las salinas)
	Teocaltitlán	405 f m		(reservadas para las salinas)
19-XII-1572	Mezquituta	180 f m	0/4/6	Fran. Merodio de Velasco
		90 p	0/0/9	Fran. Merodio de Velasco
	Analco y Tetlán	509:2 f m	0/4	Rodrigo Gutiérrez de Baeza
		572 p	0/0/6	Rodrigo Gutiérrez de Baeza
	Tonalá	270 f m	0/4	Rodrigo Gutiérrez de Baeza
		180 p	0/0/6	Rodrigo Gutiérrez de Baeza
		90 g	0/2	Rodrigo Gutiérrez de Baeza
	Tlaquepaque, S. Pedro y Toluquilla	410:6 f m	0/4	Rodrigo Gutiérrez de Baeza
		461 p	0/0/6	Rodrigo Gutiérrez de Baeza
	Tlajomulco	875 f m	0/7/6	Gerónimo de Ortega
		949 p	0/0/10	Rodrigo Gutiérrez de Baeza
	Cuitzeo	388:6 f m	0/6/6	Fran. Merodio de Velasco
		457 p	0/0/9	Juan García del Corro
19-XII-1572	Poncitlán	727 f m	0/6/6	Fran. Merodio de Velasco
		812 p	0/0/6	Fran. Merodio de Velasco
	Camotlán	54 f m	0/5	Fran. Merodio de Velasco
		54 p	0/0/8	Fran. Merodio de Velasco
	Coscotitán	45 f m	0/5	Rodrigo Gutiérrez de Baeza
		40 p	0/0/8	Francisco de Cepeda
	Atemajac	114:6 f m	0/4	Rodrigo Gutiérrez de Baeza
		229 p	0/0/6	Rodrigo Gutiérrez de Baeza

Date	Town	Item & Amount	Unit Price	Buyer & Remarks
	Cuyutlán	63 f m	0/5/6	Juan de Salcedo
		54 p	0/0/9	Francisco de Cepeda
	Zalatitlán	67:6 f m	0/7	Secretario Alonso Sánchez
		67 p	0/0/9	Secretario Alonso Sánchez
	Mexcala	90 f m	0/4	Fran. Merodio de Velasco
		45 p	0/0/6	Fran. Merodio de Velasco
	Tequila y Los Guajes	104:6 f m	0/7/9	Juan de Salcedo
		11 f tr	0/6/6	Juan de Salcedo
20-XII-1572	Tepacatengo	36 f m	0/4	Diego de Colio
		7 g	0/2	Diego de Colio
		11 p	0/0/6	Diego de Colio
21-XII-1572	Tlaltenango	517 p	0/0/6	Mensio García
22-XII-1572	Nochistlán	330:6 f m	1/1/6	Martín de Eguiguren
		374 p	0/1/2	Martín de Eguiguren
	Teocaltiche	318 p	0/1/2¼	Martín de Eguiguren
	Teocaltitlán	216 p	0/1/2¼	Martín de Eguiguren
		9 f fr	1/1/6	Martín de Eguiguren
		14:6 f ají	1/1/6	Martín de Eguiguren
	Mexticacán	171 f m	1/1/6	Martín de Eguiguren
		54 p	0/1/2¼	Martín de Eguiguren
23-XII-1572	Nochistlanejo	90 f m	0/7	Diego Ramírez Barrionuevo
		36 p	0/0/9	Alonso de la Vera
	Matatlán	129 f m	0/5/3	Rodrigo Gutiérrez de Baeza
		129 p	0/0/9	Rodrigo Gutiérrez de Baeza
	Copala y Quilitlán	68:6 f m	0/6/6	Pedro de Céspedes
		68 p	0/0/10	Pedro de Céspedes
	Apozolco y Tala	63 f m	0/4	Diego de Colio
		63 p	0/0/9	Diego de Colio
	Ahuisculco	29 f m	0/6/3	Diego de Colio
		29 p	0/0/7	Alonso de la Vera
	Sentispac	90 g	0/2	Fran. Merodio de Velasco
		51 mantas	9/	Gerónimo de Ortega
		90 f m	0/5/6	Gerónimo de Ortega
		180 @ prod pes	0/5/6	Juan de Salcedo
23-XII-1572	Tepic y Analco Tepic	123 f m	0/7/6	García de Chávez
		45 g	0/2/6	Fran. Merodio de Velasco
		46 p	0/1	García de Chávez
		2 @ miel	3/5	Fran. Merodio de Velasco
	Jalisco	92:6 f m	0/7/6	García de Chávez
		224 p	0/1	Juan de Salcedo
	Mascota	90 f m	0/3/1	García de Chávez
		45 p	0/0/6	Juan de Salcedo
		1 @ miel	4/4	Juan de Salcedo
	Tepetlatlauca y Chistique	36:6 f m	0/2	Juan de Salcedo
		36 p	0/0/6	Juan de Salcedo

Date	Town	Item & Amount	Unit Price	Buyer & Remarks
30-XII-1572	Suchipil	148:6 f m	0/6/9	Fran. Merodio de Velasco
		168 p	0/0/6	Fran. Merodio de Velasco
	Ahuacatlán	90 f m	0/7	Fran. Merodio de Velasco
		9 f tr	1/	Don Cristóbal de Ayala
		45 p	0/0/6	Don Cristóbal de Ayala
	Amaxaque	8 mantas	6/	Gerónimo de Ortega
		23 p	0/1	Fran. Merodio de Velasco
		5 g	0/2	Fran. Merodio de Velasco
	Jala	157:6 f m	0/7/6	Juan de Salcedo
		58 p	0/1	Juan de Salcedo
	San Juan	9 p		
		6 f m	t 6/6	Juan de Salcedo
		1½ mantas		
	Papachula	7 f m		
		7 p		
		1½ mantas	t 5/4	Juan de Salcedo
		½ j miel		
	Jalcocotán	27 f m	0/4	Don Cristóbal de Ayala
		27 p	0/0/6	Antonio del Rincón
		7 g	0/2	Antonio del Rincón
		2 j miel	1/5	Antonio del Rincón
	Mecatán	13:6 f m	0/4	Don Cristóbal de Ayala
		9 p	0/0/6	Don Cristóbal de Ayala
		4 g	0/2	Don Cristóbal de Ayala
		1 j miel-qtla	1/	Don Cristóbal de Ayala
	Ixtapa	11 p		
		15 f sal	t 12/	Don Cristóbal de Ayala
		2 car pes		
30-XII-1572	Jaltepec	9 f m		
		10 p	t 8/	Antonio del Rincón
		1 j miel-qtla		
	Tepuzhuacán	12 mantas	6/5	Gerónimo de Ortega
	Jalacingo	6 mantas	6/	Gerónimo de Ortega
		3 p		
		2 g	t 0/6	Gerónimo de Ortega
	Amatlán	8 mantas	6/	Gerónimo de Ortega
		4 p		
		3 g	t 1/	Gerónimo de Ortega
	Ixtimitique	3 mantas	6/	Gerónimo de Ortega
		2 p		
		1 g	t 0/4	Gerónimo de Ortega
	Zacatlán	27 f m	0/2/6	Fran. Merodio de Velasco
	Atengoichán	630 f m	0/4/1	Juan de Salcedo
	Temichoque	18 f m		
		4½ @ alg	t 8/4	Juan de Salcedo
		11 p		
	Pontoque	5 g	t 1/	Juan de Salcedo

Date	Town	Item & Amount	Unit Price	Buyer & Remarks
	Acatispa	14:6 f m } 5 g } 6 p }	t 7/2	Antonio del Rincón
	Jocotlán, ptdo. (9 pueblos)	182:6 f m	0/6	Gerónimo de Ortega
		77 p	0/0/9	Gerónimo de Ortega
31-XII-1572	Orita	13:6 f m } 3½ @ alg } 11 g } 11 p }	t 8/	Juan de Salcedo
	Ixcuintla	36 f m	1/0	Rodrigo Gutiérrez de Baeza
		1 @ miel	4/	Rodrigo Gutiérrez de Baeza
		7 g	0/2/6	Rodrigo Gutiérrez de Baeza
		15 p	0/0/9	Antonio de Rincón
	Quilitlán	18 f m	0/3	Antonio del Rincón
		1 @ miel	2/	Antonio del Rincón
	Ixtapa, de C.	7 f sal	0/5/6	Fran. Merodio de Velasco
	Matacticpac	11 f m	0/6/6	Fran. Merodio de Velasco
		3:6 f fr	0/6/6	Fran. Merodio de Velasco
		6 p } 5 g }	t 1/5	Antonio del Rincón
31-XII-1572	Zanalatitlán } Mayanalistlán } Chila }	Todo	24/2	Antonio del Rincón
	Acaponeta	90 f m	0/6/3	Fran. Merodio de Velasco
		4½ mantas	5/3	Juan Rodríguez
		18 g	0/2/4	Fran. Merodio de Velasco
	Quebiquito	18 f m	0/5	Juan Rodríguez
		1½ mantas	5/3	Juan Rodríguez
		7 g	0/2	Juan Rodríguez
	Totorán	22:6 f m	0/6/6	Juan Rodríguez
		3 mantas	5/4	Juan Rodríguez
		13 g	0/2	Juan Rodríguez
	Quexdaquepa	9 f m	0/6/1	Juan Rodríguez
		7 g	0/2	Juan Rodríguez
	Opono	52 f m	0/2	Antonio de Aguayo
		52 p	0/0/6	Antonio de Aguayo
	Zapotlán	9 f m	0/2	Antonio de Aguayo
		1 manta	2/	Antonio de Aguayo
		1 @ miel	2/	Antonio de Aguayo
	Panpuchín	14:6 f m	0/2	Antonio de Aguayo
		18 p	0/0/6	Antonio de Aguayo
		6 pi de m	0/4	Antonio de Aguayo
		1 @ miel	3/	Antonio de Aguayo
	Tena	(Despoblado)		
9-IV-1573	Piloto	100 f sal	0/5	Francisco de Cepeda
		36 f m	0/2/6	Rodrigo Gutiérrez de Baeza
	Maloto	50 f sal	0/5	Francisco de Cepeda
		27 f m	0/2/6	Rodrigo Gutiérrez de Baeza

Date	Town	Item & Amount	Unit Price	Buyer & Remarks
	Sila	13:6 f m	0/2/9	Antonio de Aguayo
		4 j miel-@ cada j	2/	Antonio de Aguayo
	Contla	6 f m }		
		3 pi de m}	t 4/	Antonio de Aguayo
4-XII-1573	Mezquituta	180 f m	0/4	Juan Dávalos
		90 p	0/0/9	Rodrigo de Ojeda
	Analco y Tetlán	200 f m	1/	Juan Ruiz
		200 f m	1/	Secretario Alonso Sánchez
		109:9 f m	1/	Secretario Alonso Sánchez
		200 p	0/1	Secretario Alonso Sánchez
		200 p	0/1	Gerónimo de Ortega
		172 p	0/0/11	Martín de Carranza
4-XII-1573	Tonalá	270 f m	0/7	Rodrigo Gutiérrez de Baeza
		180 p	0/0/8	Juan Rodríguez
		90 g	0/2/6	Rodrigo Gutiérrez de Baeza
	Tlaquepaque, S. Pedro y Toluquilla	200 f m	1/	Gerónimo de Ortega
		187 f m	1/	Gonzalo de Valdenebro
		200 p	0/1	Francisco de Cepeda
		227 p	0/0/11	Gonzalo de Valdenebro
	Toluquilla	23:6 f m	0/7/6	Juan Dávalos
		34 p	0/0/10	Rodrigo Gutiérrez de Baeza
	Tlajomulco	875 f m	0/7/6	Juan de Aguilar
		949 p	0/0/9	Juan Rodríguez
	Cuitzeo	266:6 f m	0/5/6	Secretario Alonso Sánchez
		286 p	0/0/8	Rodrigo Gutiérrez de Baeza
	Poncitlán	727 f m	0/5	Gerónimo de Ortega
		812 p	0/0/8	Juan Dávalos
	Camotlán	54 f m	0/5/6	Juan Téllez
		54 p	0/0/11	Juan Téllez
	Coscotitán	45 f m	0/5	Fran. Rodríguez Bertavillo
		40 p	0/0/9	Fran. Rodríguez Bertavillo
	Nochistlanejo	90 f m	0/7	Francisco de Estrada
		36 p	0/0/10	Pero Sánchez Mexía
	Atemajac	114:6 f m	0/7/6	Secretario Alonso Sánchez
		229 p	0/0/10	Alonso Cordero
	Cuyutlán	63 f m	0/7	Francisco de Estrada
		54 p	0/0/9	Pero Sánchez Mexía
	Zalatitlán	67:6 f m	0/7	Francisco de Estrada
		67 p	0/0/10	Pero Sánchez Mexía
	Matatlán	129 f m	0/5/3	Juan Dávalos
		129 p	0/0/9	Juan Dávalos
5-XII-1573	Tequila y Los Guajes	104:6 f m	0/5/6	Diego de Aguilar
		11 f tr	1/0/6	Antonio de Aguayo
		5 p	0/0/6	Diego de Aguilar
	Copala y Quilitlán	68:6 f m	0/6/9	Antonio de Aguayo
		68 p	0/0/11	Lope de Cisneros

Date	Town	Item & Amount	Unit Price	Buyer & Remarks
	Ahuisculco	29 f m	0/5/6	Gregorio Ruiz
		29 p	0/1	Juan de Aguilar
	Sentispac	51 mantas	9/	Gerónimo de Ortega
		90 f m	0/3/6	Gerónimo de Ortega
		180 @ prod pes	0/4	Rodrigo Gutiérrez de Baeza
		90 g	0/1/6	Rodrigo Gutiérrez de Baeza
5-XII-1573	Jalisco	92:6 f m	0/4/8	Martín de Carranza
		224 p	0/0/7	Martín de Carranza
10-XII-1573	Tepic y Analco Tepic	123 f m	0/5/1	Secretario Alonso Sánchez
		45 g	0/2	Secretario Alonso Sánchez
		46 p	0/0/6	Secretario Alonso Sánchez
		2 @ miel	3/1	Martín de Carranza
	Suchipil	148:6 f m	0/6/6	Secretario Alonso Sánchez
		168 p	0/0/9	Gerónimo de Ortega
	Ahuacatlán	70 f m	0/6	Secretario Alonso Sánchez
		4:8 f tr	0/6	Secretario Alonso Sánchez
		52 p	0/0/8	Gregorio Ruiz
	Amaxaque	8 mantas	6/1	Gerónimo de Ortega
		23 p	0/0/6	Gregorio Ruiz
		5 g	0/2	Gregorio Ruiz
	Jala	157:6 f m	0/5	Secretario Alonso Sánchez
		68 p	0/0/8	Secretario Alonso Sánchez
	Papachula	7 f m } 7 p } 1½ mantas } 1 j miel }	t 5/4	Gerónimo de Ortega
	Mascota	90 f m	0/3	Francisco Xuárez
		5 p	0/0/6	Antonio de Aguayo
		1 @ miel	3/4	Gregorio Ruiz
	Tepetlatlauca y Chistique	36:6 f m	0/3/3	Canónigo Ramírez
		37 p	0/0/6	Francisco Xuárez
15-XII-1573	Jalcocotán	27 f m	0/3	Gerónimo de Ortega
		27 p	0/0/6	Gerónimo de Ortega
		7 g	0/1/6	Gerónimo de Ortega
		2 j miel-½ @ cu	1/5	Gerónimo de Ortega
	Mecatán	13:6 f m	0/3	Gerónimo de Ortega
		9 p	0/0/6	Gerónimo de Ortega
		4 g	0/1/6	Gerónimo de Ortega
		1 j miel-qtla	1/	Gerónimo de Ortega
	Jaltepec	9 f m } 10 p } 1 j miel-qtla }	t 8/	Gerónimo de Ortega
	Tepuzhuacán	12 mantas	6/5	Secretario Alonso Sánchez
17-XII-1573	Teocaltitlán	(405 f m mandadas a las salinas)		
	Matatlán	129 f m	0/5/3	Rodrigo Gutiérrez de Baeza
		129 p	0/0/9	Rodrigo Gutiérrez de Baeza
3-I-1574	Nochistlán	330:6 f m	0/4	Domingo de Gorraunz
		374 p	0/0/6	Domingo de Gorraunz

Date	Town	Item & Amount	Unit Price	Buyer & Remarks
	Teocaltitlán	216 p	0/0/6	Domingo de Gorraunz
		9 f fr	0/4	Domingo de Gorraunz
		14:6 f ají	0/4	Domingo de Gorraunz
		(405 f m para los indios de las salinas)		
	Tlaltenango	404 p	0/0/6	Martín de Eguiguren
		(405 f m para los indios de las salinas)		
	Mexticacán	171 f m	0/4	Domingo de Gorraunz
		54 p	0/0/6	Domingo de Gorraunz
	Teocaltiche	298 f m	0/4	Domingo de Gorraunz
		318 p	0/0/6	Domingo de Gorraunz
7-XII-1574	Tlaquepaque, San Pedro y Toluquilla	387 f m	0/4/7	Rodrigo Gutiérrez de Baeza
		427 p	0/0/8	Rodrigo Gutiérrez de Baeza
		23:6 f m	0/4/7	Rodrigo Gutiérrez de Baeza
		34 p	0/0/8	Rodrigo Gutiérrez de Baeza
	Tonalá	270 f m	0/4	Rodrigo Gutiérrez de Baeza
		180 p	0/0/8	Rodrigo Gutiérrez de Baeza
		90 g	0/2	Rodrigo Gutiérrez de Baeza
	Atemajac	114:6 f m	0/4/7	Rodrigo Gutiérrez de Baeza
		229 p	0/0/10	Lope de Cisneros
	Tlajomulco	200 f m	0/4	Francisco de Plaza
		200 f m	0/4	Juan Dávalos
		200 f m	0/4/6	Lope de Cisneros
		200 f m	0/4/9	Pero Sánchez Mexía
		65 f m	0/4/6	Juan de Salcedo
		400 p	0/1/1	Gerónimo de Ortega
		549 p	0/1	Lope de Cisneros
	Cuitzeo	265:6 f m	0/4/1	Juan Rodríguez
		285 p	0/0/9	Diego Navarro
	Poncitlán	200 f m	0/4/1	Francisco de Plaza
		200 f m	0/4/1	Lope de Cisneros
		100 f m	0/4/9	Francisco de Plaza
		100 f m	0/4/9	Lope de Cisneros
		127 f m	0/4/5	Francisco de Plaza
		200 p	0/0/9	Diego Navarro
		200 p	0/0/9	Lope de Cisneros
		412 p	0/0/9	Rodrigo Gutiérrez de Baeza
	Camotlán (Barranca)	54 f m	0/4	Diego Navarro
		54 p	0/0/9	Francisco de Cepeda
	Coscotitán (Barranca)	45 f m	0/3	Rodrigo Gutiérrez de Baeza
		40 p	0/0/9	Francisco de Cepeda
9-XII-1574	Mezquituta	180 f m	0/4/6	Francisco de Plaza
		90 p	0/1/2	Vicente de Saldívar
	Analco y Tetlán	509 9 f m	0/4/7	Rodrigo Gutiérrez de Baeza
		572 p	0/0/10	Francisco de Plaza
	Nochistlanejo	90 f m	0/5/6	Juan Rodríguez
		36 p	0/1	Francisco de Cepeda
	Cuyutlán	63 f m	0/5/1	Antonio de Aguayo
		54 p	0/1	Pero Sánchez Mexía
	Zalatitlán	67:6 f m	0/6	Gregorio Ruiz

Date	Town	Item & Amount	Unit Price	Buyer & Remarks
		67 p	0/1	Francisco de Cepeda
	Suchipil	148:6 f m	0/7/9	Bernabé García
		168 p	0/1	Bernabé García
	Matatlán	60 f m	0/4/7	Gonzalo de Valdenebro
		69 f m	0/4/7	Gerónimo de Ortega
		129 p	0/0/9	Gonzalo de Valdenebro
	Mexcala	90 f m	0/3/6	Gonzalo de Valdenebro
		45 p	0/0/10	Gonzalo de Valdenebro
	Tequila y Los Guajes	104:6 f m	0/5/9	Gregorio Ruiz
		11 f tr	0/7/6	Diego de Colio
		5 p	0/0/6	Diego de Colio
	Copala y Quilitlán	68:6 f m	0/5/1	Gerónimo de Ortega
		68 p	0/1	Gerónimo de Ortega
	Ahuisculco	29 f m	0/4	Francisco de Saldívar
		29 p	0/0/9	Francisco de Saldívar
	Jalcocotán, ptdo. (9 pueblos)	182:6 f m	0/7/6	Juan de Salcedo
		77 p	0/0/10	Juan de Salcedo
	Ahuacatlán	49:6 f m	1/0/5	Bernabé García
		49 p	0/1/1	Bernabé García
	Amaxaque	8 mantas	5/6	Gregorio Ruiz
		23 p	0/0/6	Gregorio Ruiz
		5 g	0/2	Gregorio Ruiz
	Jala	137:6 f m	1/1	Francisco de Saldívar
		156 p	0/1	Juan Cortés
10-XII-1574	Sentispac	25 mantas	9/4	Bernabé García
		26 mantas	9/2	Bernabé García
		90 f m	1/0/1	Bernabé García
		60 @ pes	0/5/2	Bernabé García
		60 @ pes	0/5/1	Juan de Salcedo
		30 @ mech	0/6	Juan de Salcedo
		15 @ camarrón	1/0/2	Bernabé García
		15 @ ost	1/2	Rodrigo Gutiérrez de Baeza
		90 g	0/2/6	Bernabé García
	Jalisco	92:6 f m	1/0/1	Bernabé García
		224 p	0/1	Bernabé García
	Mascota	90 f m	0/2/9	Fran. Merodio de Velasco
		45 p	0/0/9	Alonso de la Vera
		1 @ miel	3/	Juan de Salcedo
	Tepetlatlauca y Chistique	36: f m	0/3/1	Fran. Merodio de Velasco
		37 p	0/0/6	Fran. Merodio de Velasco
	Atengoichán	200 f m	0/2/9	Fran. Merodio de Velasco
		200 f m	0/2/9	Gerónimo de Ortega
		230 f m	0/3/1	Gerónimo de Ortega
	Tepic y Analco Tepic	123 f m	1/0	Bernabé García
		45 g	0/2/6	Juan de Salcedo
		46 p	0/0/10	Juan de Salcedo
		2 @ miel	3/	Juan de Salcedo
12-XII-1574	Tlaltenango	(405 f m mandadas a las salinas)		

Date	Town	Item & Amount	Unit Price	Buyer & Remarks
	Nochistlán	330 f m	0/5/6	Pedro de Chalas
		374 p	0/1	Pedro de Chalas
	Teocaltiche	298 f m	0/5/6	Pedro de Chalas
		318 p	0/1	Pedro de Chalas
	Teocaltitlán	(405 f m mandadas a las salinas)		
		216 p	0/1	Diego Sánchez Quadrado
		9 f fr	0/5/6	Pedro de Chalas
		14:6 f ají	0/5/6	Pedro de Chalas
	Mexticacán	171 f m	0/5/6	Pedro de Chalas
		54 p	0/1	Pedro de Chalas
	Jalcocotán	27 f m	0/4/9	García de Chávez
		27 p	0/0/6	García de Chávez
		7 g	0/2	García de Chávez
		2 j miel	t 3/2	Alonso de la Vera
13-XII-1574	Mecatán	13:6 f m	0/3/1	García de Chávez
		9 p	t 1/	García de Chávez
		4 g	t 0/6	García de Chávez
		1 j miel	1/	García de Chávez
	Tepuzhuacán	12 mantas	6/	Juan de Salcedo
	Jalacingo	4 mantas y 1 pierna	5/	Juan de Salcedo
	Amatlán	9½ mantas	5/	Juan de Salcedo
	Ixtimitique	1½ mantas	5/	Juan de Salcedo
	Zacatlán	27 f m	0/3	Gerónimo de Ortega
	Pontoque	5 g	t 0/6	Bernabé García
	Acatispa	Todo	6/	Bernabé García
	Orita	Todo	8/	Bernabé García
	Ixtapilla	Todo	12/	Bernabé García
	Jaltapec	Todo	8/	García de Chávez
	Ixcuintla	36 f m	0/5	García de Chávez
		1 @ miel	3/	García de Chávez
		7 g	0/2	García de Chávez
		15 p	0/0/6	García de Chávez
	Matacticpac	Todo	10/4	García de Chávez
	Zanalatitlán } Mayanalistlán } Chila } San Miguel }	29 f m	0/3	García de Chávez
		32 g	0/1/6	Juan de Salcedo
		7 p	0/0/6	Juan de Salcedo
13-XII-1574	Papachula	Todo	7/	Juan de Salcedo
	San Juan	Todo	7/4	Juan de Salcedo
	Temichoque	Todo	10/	Bernabé García
	Quilitlán	Todo	10/4	Bernabé García

Date	Town	Item & Amount	Unit Price	Buyer & Remarks
	Ixtapa, de Castañeda	7 f sal	t 4/0	Bernabé García
	Acaponeta	90 f m	1/3	Don Luis de los Ríos
		18 g	0/2	Don Luis de los Ríos
		4½ mantas	5/	Juan de Salcedo
	Quebiquito	18 f m	1/0	Gerónimo de Ortega
		1½ mantas	4/	Gerónimo de Ortega
		7 g	0/2	Gerónimo de Ortega
	Totorán	22 f m	1/	Gerónimo de Ortega
		3 mantas	4/	Gerónimo de Ortega
		13 g	0/2	Gerónimo de Ortega
	Quexdaquepa	9 f m	1/	Gerónimo de Ortega
		7 g	0/2	Gerónimo de Ortega
	Opono	52 f m	1/	Juan de Salcedo
		52 p	0/1	Juan de Salcedo
	Piloto	36 f m	0/6/3	Juan de Salcedo
14-XII-1574	Maloto	27 f m	0/6/6	Juan de Salcedo
	Zapotlán	9 f m	4/4	Francisco de Cepeda
		1 manta	4/4	Francisco de Cepeda
		1 @ miel	4/	Francisco de Cepeda
	Panpuchín	14:6 f m	0/5/1	Francisco de Cepeda
		18 p	0/1	Francisco de Cepeda
		1½ @ miel	6/	Francisco de Cepeda
		6 pi de m	1/	Francisco de Cepeda
	Tena	(Despoblado)		
	Sila	13:6 f m	0/6	Francisco de Cepeda
		4 j miel	t 3/	Juan de Salcedo
	Contla	6 f m	0/4	Francisco de Cepeda
		3 pi de m	1/	Francisco de Cepeda
22-XII-1574	Tlaltenango	404 p	0/0/6	Pedro de Madrid
5-XII-1575	Tlaltenango	(450 f m mandadas a las salinas)		
20-XII-1575	Mezquituta	180 f m	0/3/3	Juan de Aguilar
		90 p	0/1	Alonso de Morales
	Analco y Tetlán	509:9 f m	0/7/6	Francisco Lopez
		572 p	0/1	Gerónimo de Ortega
	Tlaquepaque, S. Pedro y Toluquilla	387 f m	0/7/1	Miguel de Medina
		427 p	0/1/2	Rodrigo Gutiérrez de Baeza
		23:6 f m	0/7/1	Rodrigo Gutiérrez de Baeza
		34 p	0/1/2	Rodrigo Gutiérrez de Baeza
	Tonalá	260 f m	0/7	Alonso Cordero
		180 p	0/1	Lic. Sotomayor
		90 g	0/2/8	Francisco de León
	Atemajac	114:6 f m	1/	Gerónimo de Ortega
		229 p	0/1/2	Francisco de León
	Tlajomulco	200 f m	0/7/6	Gerónimo de Ortega

Date	Town	Item & Amount	Unit Price	Buyer & Remarks
		100 f m	0/7/8	Rodrigo Gutiérrez de Baeza
		100 f m	0/7/6	Francisco de León
		100 f m	0/7/7	Rodrigo Gutiérrez de Baeza
		100 f m	0/7/8	Tomás López
		100 f m	0/7/7	Rodrigo Gutiérrez de Baeza
		83:6 f m	0/7/6	Francisco Xuárez
		200 p	0/1	Alonso Cordero
		200 p	0/1/1	Gerónimo de Ortega
		200 p	0/1/1	Rodrigo Gutiérrez de Baeza
		200 p	0/1/1	Alonso Cordero
		139 p	0/1	Francisco Xuárez
	Cuitzeo	266:6 f m	0/7/1	Juan de Vega
		286 p	0/0/9	Alonso Cordero
	Poncitlán	200 f m	0/5/9	Francisco de León
		200 f m	0/5/6	Francisco de León
		200 f m	0/5/6	Diego Navarro
		127 f m	0/5/8	Lic. Sotomayor
		200 p	0/1	Lope de Segura
		200 p	0/1	Rodrigo Gutiérrez de Baeza
		200 p	0/1	Gómez de Alvarado
		212 p	0/1/1	Alonso Cordero
	Camotlán	54 f m	0/6/2	Francisco Xuárez
		54 p	0/1	Francisco Xuárez
	Coscotitán	45 f m	0/6	Miguel de Medina
		40 p	0/1	Francisco Xuárez
	Nochistlanejo	90 f m	0/6/3	Alonso Cordero
		36 p	0/1	Alonso Cordero
	Cuyutlán	63 f m	0/6/6	Luis de Ahumada
		54 p	0/1/4	Francisco de Cepeda
	Zalatitlán	67 6 f m	0/7/2	Luis de Ahumada
		67 p	0/1/3	Diego Navarro
20-XII-1575	Matatlán	129 f m	0/5/6	Alonso de la Vera
		129 p	0/1/3	Alonso de la Vera
	Mexcala	90 f m	0/3/1	Andrés de Castro
		45 p	0/0/9	Miguel de Medina
	Tequila y Los Guajes	104:6 f m	0/5/8	Francisco Xuárez
		11 f tr	1/1	Alonso Cordero
		5 p	t 0/4	Alonso Cordero
	Copala y Quilitlán	68:5 f m	0/7	Juan Sánchez
		68 p	0/1/3	Alonso de la Vera
	Ahuisculco	29 f m	0/6	Juan de Saldívar
		29 p	0/1/1	Juan de Saldívar
22-XII-1575	Jocotlán, ptdo. (9 pueblos)	217 f m	0/6/3	Francisco Pérez
		130 p	0/0/9	Gerónimo López
	Mochiltitic	28 f m	0/4	Gerónimo de Ortega
		27 p	0/0/9	Gerónimo de Ortega
	Sentispac	51 mantas	9/	Gerónimo de Chávez
		120 @ pes	0/6/1	Rodrigo Gutiérrez de Baeza
		30 @ mech	0/4/6	Gerónimo de Ortega
		15 @ camarrón	1/1	Antonio Vélez de Vargas

Date	Town	Item & Amount	Unit Price	Buyer & Remarks
		90 f m	0/6/3	Alonso Sánchez Gonzalez
		15 @ ost	1/2	Antonio Vélez de Vargas
		90 g	0/2	Francisco de Estrada
	Jalisco	93:6 f m	1/4	Gerónimo de Chavez
		224 p	0/1/2	Francisco de Estrada
	Mascota	90 f m	0/3	Francisco Xuárez
		45 p	0/0/6	Francisco Xuárez
		1 @ miel	t 2/6	Francisco de Estrada
	Tepetlatlauca y Chistique	36:6 f m	0/3	Francisco Xuárez
		37 p	0/0/6	Francisco Xuárez
	Atengoichán	88:6 f m	0/3	Francisco Xuárez
		88 p	0/0/6	Francisco de Estrada
	Tepic y Analco Tepic	108:6 f m	1/5	García de Chávez
		14:6 f m	1/4	García de Chávez
		45 g	0/3/2	Francisco de Estrada
		46 p	0/1/6	García de Chávez
		2 @ miel	3/	Alonso Cordero
	Suchipil	148:6 f m	1/	Francisco de Estrada
		168 p	0/1/2	Francisco de Estrada
	Ahuacatlán	49:6 f m	1/0	García de Chávez
		49 p	0/1/1	Alonso Cordero
	Tetitlán y sujetos	77 f m	1/1	Francisco de Estrada
		77 p	0/1/1	Francisco de Estrada
	Amaxaque	8 mantas	5/1	Francisco de Estrada
		23 p	0/1	Francisco de Estrada
		5 g	0/2	Francisco de Estrada
22-XII1575	Jala	137:6 f m	1/1/6	García de Chávez
		156 p	0/0/6	Francisco de Estrada
	Jalcocotán	27 f m	1/2/1	García de Chávez
		27 p	0/1	Francisco de Estrada
		7 g	0/2	Francisco de Estrada
		2 j miel	0/2	García de Chávez
23-XII-1575	Mecatán	13:6 f m	1/0/3	García de Chávez
		9 p	0/0/9	Francisco de Estrada
		4 g	0/0/9	Francisco de Estrada
		1 j miel-qtla	0/6/6	Francisco de Estrada
	Tepuzhuacán	12 mantas	7/	Gerónimo de Ortega
	Jalacingo	2 mantas } 1 pi de m }	5/	Francisco de Estrada
	Amatlán	9½ mantas	6/1/6	Francisco de Estrada
	Ixtimitique	1½ mantas	5/	Francisco de Estrada
	Zacatlán	27 f m	0/4/7	Francisco de Estrada
	Pontoque	5 g	t 0/6	Francisco de Estrada
	Acatispa	14:6 f m	0/4	Francisco de Estrada
		5 g } 6 p }	t 1/	Francisco de Estrada

Date	Town	Item & Amount	Unit Price	Buyer & Remarks
	Orita	13:6 f m	0/3	Francisco de Estrada
		3½ @ alg	1/	Francisco de Estrada
		11 g }		
		11 p }	0/1	Francisco de Estrada
	Ixtapilla	15 f sal }		
		10 p }	t 14/2	García de Chávez
		2 car pes }		
	Jaltepec	9 f m	1/4	Alonso Sánchez González
		10 p	0/1/3	Alonso Sánchez González
		1 j miel-qtla	1/	Alonso Sánchez González
	Ixcuintla	36 f m	1/4	Alonso Sánchez González
		1 @ miel	5/2	Alonso Sánchez González
		7 g	0/2/6	Francisco de Estrada
		15 p	0/1/3	Alonso Sánchez González
	Matacticpac	11 f m	1/0/3	García de Chávez
		3:6 f fr	0/5	Francisco de Estrada
		6 p }		
		5 g }	t 2/1	Francisco de Estrada
	Zanalatitlán }			
	Mayanalistlán }	39:9 f m	0/4	Francisco de Estrada
	Chila }	32 g	0/1	Francisco de Estrada
	San Miguel }	7 p	t 0/4	Francisco de Estrada
23-XII-1575	Papachula	7 f m }		
		7 p }		
		1½ mantas }	t 8/4	Francisco de Estrada
		½ j miel }		
	San Juan	9 p }		
		6 f m }	t 8/4	Francisco de Estrada
		1½ mantas }		
	Temichoque	18 f m	0/4/4	Francisco de Estrada
		5½ @ alg	0/4	Francisco de Estrada
		11 p	0/0/6	Francisco de Estrada
	Quilitlán	18 f m	0/5	García de Chávez
		1 @ miel	2/	García de Chávez
	Ixtapa, de C.	7 f sal	t 4/1	Francisco de Estrada
	Acaponeta	90 f m	1/6	Alonso Sánchez González
		4½ mantas	6/	Francisco de Estrada
		18 g	0/2/9	Alonso Sánchez González
	Quebiquito	18 f m	0/2	Francisco de Estrada
		1½ mantas	2/	Francisco de Estrada
		7 g	0/1/6	Francisco de Estrada
	Totorán	22:6 f m	0/2	Francisco de Estrada
		13 g	0/1/6	Francisco de Estrada
		3 mantas	2/	Francisco de Estrada
	Quexdaquepa	9 f m	0/2	Francisco de Estrada
		7 g	0/1/6	Francisco de Estrada
29-XII-1575	Opono	52 f m	0/6	José de León
		52 p	0/1/1	José de León
	Piloto	35 f m	0/6	José de León

Date	Town	Item & Amount	Unit Price	Buyer & Remarks
	Maloto	27 f m	0/6	José de León
	Panpuchín	14:6 f m	0/6	José de León
		18 p	t 2/6	José de León
		1½ @ miel	t 7/6	José de León
		6 pi de m	t 4/2	José de León
	Zapotlán	1 manta	3/	José de León
		1 @ miel	5/	José de León
		9 f m	0/6	José de León
	Sila	13:6 f m	0/6	José de León
		4 j miel	t 5/2	José de León
	Contla	6 f m	0/6	José de León
		3 pi de m	1/	José de León
30-XII-1575	Tlaltenango	404 p	0/1	Luis de las Doblas
	Nochistlán	330 f m	0/3/3	Domingo de Gorraunz
		74 p	0/1	Domingo de Gorraunz
	Teocaltiche	298 f m	0/3/3	Domingo de Gorraunz
		318 p	0/1	Domingo de Gorraunz
	Teocaltitlán	(405 f m mandadas a las salinas)		
		206 p	0/1	Luis de las Doblas
		9 f fr	0/3/3	Luis de las Doblas
		14:6 f ají	0/3/3	Luis de las Doblas
	Mexticacán	171 f m	0/3/3	Domingo de Gorraunz
		54 p	0/1	Domingo de Gorraunz
5-XII-1576	Mezquituta y	94½ p	0/0/10	Alonso de Morales
	Moyagua	174:2 f m	0/5/6	Francisco de Plaza
	Analco y Tetlán	250 f m	0/7/3	Lope de Cisneros
		50 f m	0/7/3	Licenciado Vázquez
		100 f m	0/7/3	Gerónimo de Ortega
		109:9 f m	0/7/3	Lope de Cisneros
		200 p	0/1/2	Francisco de Plaza
		100 p	0/1/2	Antonio Vélez
		100 p	0/1/2	Tomé López
		162 p	0/1/2	Alonso de Morales
	Atemajac	114:6 f m	1/	Gerónimo de Ortega
		229 p	0/1/1	Gerónimo de Ortega
	Tlajomulco	200 f m	0/6/9	Alonso de Morales
		200 f m	0/7	Alonso de Rubalcava
		200 f m	0/6/6	Francisco de Plaza
		100 f m	0/6/6	Francisco de Plaza
		100 f m	0/6/6	Francisco de Plaza
		120 f m	0/6/6	Melchor Ruiz
		300 p	0/1/1	Alonso de Morales
			+ 0/6	(de premio en toda la oferta)
		300 p	0/1/3	Diego Navarro
		320 p	0/1/2	Alonso de Morales
6-XII-1576	Tlaquepaque, San	100 f m	0/7	Tomé López
	Pedro y Toluquilla	310:6 f m	0/7	Melchor Ruiz
		200 p	0/1/3	Licenciado Vázquez
		100 p	0/1/3	Francisco de Cepeda
		161 p	0/1/3	Lope de Cisneros

Date	Town	Item & Amount	Unit Price	Buyer & Remarks
	Tonalá	60 f m	0/7	Lope de Cisneros
		100 f m	0/7	Alonso de Morales
		180 p	0/1	Lope de Cisneros
		90 g	0/2/7	Alonso de Morales
	Nochistlanejo	90 f m	0/7/2	Tomé López
		36 p	0/1/1	Alonso de Morales
	Cuitzeo y sujetos	148:10 f m	0/7	Alonso de Morales
		279½ p	0/1	Alonso de Morales
			+1/ (de premio en toda la oferta)	
	Cuyutlán	63 f m	0/7	Tomé López
		54 p	0/1/3	Francisco de Cepeda
	Zalatitlán	67½ f m	1/0/1	Alonso de Morales
		67 p	0/1/3	Tomé López
	Poncitlán	100 f m	0/5/1	Alonso de Morales
		100 f m	0/5/2	Lope de Cisneros
		100 f m	0/5/2	Francisco de Plaza
		100 f m	0/5/2	Diego Navarro
		100 f m	0/5/2	Lic. Sotomayor
		100 f m	0/5/2	Alonso de Soria
		127 f m	0/6/7	Alonso de Morales
		200 p	0/1	Alonso de la Vera
		200 p	0/1/1	Alonso de la Vera
		200 p	0/1	Lic. Sotomayor
		112 p	0/1	Alonso de Morales
6-XII-1576	Matatlán	129 f m	0/6	Diego Navarro
		129 p	0/1/1	Francisco de Cepeda
			+1/ (de premio)	
7-XII-1576	Mexcala	90 f m	0/5	Rodrigo Goite
		45 p	0/1	Rodrigo Goite
	Tequila y Los Guajes	90 f m	1/	Gerónimo de Ortega
		11 f tr	1/	Gerónimo de Ortega
		14:6 f m	0/6/3	Gerónimo de Ortega
		5 p	t 0/4	Gerónimo de Ortega
	Copala y Quilitlán	68:6 f m	0/6/4	Alonso Martín
		68 p	0/1	Francisco de Plaza
	Ahuisculco	29 f m	0/7/6	Alonso Martín
		29 p	0/1	Alonso de la Vera
	Sentispac	118:10 f m	0/5	Juan González de Apodaca
		6:14 @ camarron	1/	Martín Vélez
		6:14 @ ost	1/	Alonso de la Vera
		13:3 @ mech	1/	Alonso de la Vera
		39½ g	0/2	Rodrigo de Ojeda
	Mascota	90 f m	0/3/6	Juan Rodríguez
		45 p	0/0/9	Juan Rodríguez
		1 @ miel	3/	Alonso de la Vera
	Tepetlatlauca y Chistique	36:6 f m	0/3	Rodrigo de Ojeda
		37 p	0/0/6	Rodrigo de Ojeda
	Suchipil	148:6 f m	1/1	Antonio Vélez de Vargas
		168 p	0/1/4	Rodrigo Goite
	Ahuacatlán	49:6 f m	1/1/1	Antonio Vélez de Vargas

Date	Town	Item & Amount	Unit Price	Buyer & Remarks
		68 p	0/1/3	Rodrigo Goite
	Jala	137:6 f m	1/1/1	Juan Toledano
		156 p	0/1/3	Rodrigo Goite
7-XII-1576	Camotlán	54 f m	0/6	Alonso de Morales
		54 p	0/1	Alonso de Morales
	Coscotitán	45 f m	0/6/2	Alonso de Morales
		40 p	0/1	Alonso de Morales
10-XII-1576	Jalisco	156:7 f m	1/	Tomé López
		213 p	0/1	Juan Toledano
	Atengoichán	47½ f m	0/3/3	Juan Gonzalez
		47 p	0/0/9	Juan Gonzalez
	Tetitlán	80:4 f m	1/0/7	Tomé López
		75½ p	0/1	Alonso Vélez de Vargas
	San Pedro	26:1 f m	1/0/7	Tomé López
		30 p	0/1	Tomé López
	Tepequexpa	66:9 f m	1/2/6	Diego de Monrroy
		69 p	0/1	Diego de Monrroy
	Camotlán	42:10 f m	1/	Diego de Monrroy
		44 p	0/1	Diego de Monrroy
	Amaxaque	8 mantas	4/4	Gerónimo de Ortega
		23 p	0/1	Gerónimo de Ortega
		5 g	0/2	Gerónimo de Ortega
11-XII-1576	Sentispac	53 @ pes	0/6	Rodrigo de Ojeda
		40 mantas + } 3 5/8 pi de m }	9/manta	Gerónimo de Ortega
		118:10 f m	0/5	Juan González de Apodaca
	Tepic y Analco Tepic	133:10 f m	1/1/2	Melchor Ruiz
		100 p	0/1/2	Antonio Vélez
		19 g	0/2/3	Antonio Vélez
		3 qtlas + 1 } qtlo miel }	t 3/	Juan Toledano
	Tepuzhuacán	12 mantas	6/6/6	Juan González
	Jalacingo	2 mantas } 1 pi de m }	6/1 manta	Juan González
	Amatlán	9½ mantas	6/1	Juan González
	Ixtimitique	1½ mantas	6/1	Juan González
	Zacatlán	27 f m	0/4/6	Juan González
	Pontoque	5 g	t 0/5	Rodrigo de Ojeda
	Ixcuintla	36 f m	1/1	Gerónimo de Ortega
		15 p	0/1/1	Gerónimo de Ortega
		7 g	0/2/6	Gerónimo de Ortega
		1 @ miel	7/3	Juan Toledano
	Jocotlán, ptdo. (9 pueblos)	330:9 f m	1/2/10	Diego de Monrroy
		329 p	0/1/3	Diego de Monrroy

Date	Town	Item & Amount	Unit Price	Buyer & Remarks
	Mochitiltic }			
	Hostipaquillo }			
	Tecamatlán }	128:3 f m	1/2/10	Diego de Monrroy
	Talistaque }	129 p	0/1/2	Gerónimo de Ortega
	Amaxaque }			
	San Francisco }			
12-XII-1576	Acaponeta }	419:7 f m	0/7/6	Juan González de Apodaca
	Quebiquinto }	9 mantas	6/5	Juan González de Apodaca
	Totorán }	34 g	0/2/1	Juan González de Apodaca
	Quexdaquepa }	281 p	0/1/3	Juan Gonzálex de Apodaca
	Opono	52 f m	0/6	Rodrigo de Ojeda
		52 p	0/1	Rodrigo de Ojeda
	Panpuchín	18:2 f m	0/5/6	Rodrigo de Ojeda
		18 p	0/1	Rodrigo de Ojeda
		2 @ + 1 qtlo} miel}	4/ @	Gerónimo de Ortega
		8 pi 5/12 pi de m	1/pi de m	Gerónimo de Ortega
	Zapotlán	11 f m	0/5	Rodrigo de Ojeda
		5½ p	t 0/4	Rodrigo de Ojeda
		4 oz + 3 qtlas} miel}	t 1/6	Alonso de Morales
		2 3/4 pi de m	1/ pi de m	Gerónimo de Ortega
12-XII-1576	Sila	9:3 f m	0/5	Rodrigo de Ojeda
		3 p	t 0/2	Rodrigo de Ojeda
		½ @-3 qtlos } miel }	t 1/4	Alonso de Morales
	Contla	9:1 f m	0/5	Rodrigo de Ojeda
		1 3/4 pi de m	1/pi de m	Gerónimo de Ortega
13-XII-1576	Jalcocotán	27 f m } 37 p } 7 g } 1 @ miel}	t 25/4	Rodrigo de Ojeda
	Mecatán	13:6 f m	0/3/1	Rodrigo de Ojeda
		9 p	t 1/	Rodrigo de Ojeda
		4 g	t 0/6	Rodrigo de Ojeda
		1 j miel-1 qtla	1/0/2	Rodrigo de Ojeda
	Acatispa	14:6 f m } 5 g } 6 p }	t 6/2	Rodrigo de Ojeda
	Orita	13:6 f m } 3½ @ alg } 11 g } 11 p }	t 8/	Rodrigo de Ojeda
	Ixtapilla	10 p } 15 f sal } 2 car pes }	t 12/	Rodrigo de Ojeda
	Jaltepec	9 f m } 10 p } 1 j miel-1} qtla }	t 8/4	Tomé López

Date	Town	Item & Amount	Unit Price	Buyer & Remarks
13-XII-1576	Matacticpac	11 f m	0/5	Tomé López
		3:6 f fr	0/5	Tomé López
		6 p	0/0/6	Tomé López
		5 g	0/1/6	Tomé López
	Zanalatlán } Mayanalistlán} Chila } San Miguel }	39:9 f m	0/5/1	Diego de Monrroy
		32 g	0/1/6	Rodrigo de Ojeda
		7 p	0/0/6	Rodrigo de Ojeda
	Papachula	7 f m } 7 p } 1½ mantas } ½ j miel }	t 8/	Rodrigo de Ojeda
	San Juan	5:6 f m } 9 p } 1½ mantas }	t 8/0	Rodrigo de Ojeda
	Temichoque	18 f m } 5½ @ alg } 11 p }	t 12/4	Rodrigo de Ojeda
	Quilitlán	18 f m } 1 @ miel }	t 11/1	Rodrigo de Ojeda
	Ixtapa	7 f sal	t 4/	Rodrigo de Ojeda
2-I-1577	Nochistlán	330 f m	0/6/6	Juan de Huidobro
		374 p	0/1	Juan de Huidobro
	Teocaltitlán	216 p	0/1	Juan de Colima
		9 f fr	0/6/6	Juan de Colima
		10:6 f ají	0/6/6	Juan de Colima
	Teocaltiche	318 p	0/1	Juan de Colima
		298 f m	0/6/6	Juan de Huidobro
	Mextiticacan	171 f m	0/6/6	Juan de Huidobro
		54 p	0/1	Juan de Huidobro
19-XII-1577	Tepic y Analco	141:9 f m	1/0/2	Bernabé García
		141½ p	0/1	Alonso de la Vera
	Suchipil	148:6 f m	1/	Tomé López
20-XII-1577	Jalisco	203:10 f m	0/4	Bernardo de Balbuena
		204 p	0/1/2	Bernabé García
2-I-1578	Sentispac	158 p (de 1576)	0/0/10	Lope de Cisneros
		33 mantas } 1¼ pi de m }	8/1	Bernabé García
		129:9 f m	0/8/4	Bernabé García
		279 p	0/0/9	Martín de Carranza
	Jalcocotán	27 f m	0/6/4	Bernabé García
		27 p	0/0/9	Bernabé García
		7 g	0/1/6	Bernabé García
		1 @ miel	0/4/7	Bernardo de Balbuena
	Mecatán	Todo	9/	Bernardo de Balbuena
	Acatispa	14:6 f m	0/4	Bernabé García
		6 p } 5 g }	t 1/3	Bernabé García

Date	Town	Item & Amount	Unit Price	Buyer & Remarks
	Ixtapa	Todo	15/1	Bernabé García
	Zanalatitlán	16 f m	0/4	Bernabé García
		14 g	0/1	Bernabé García
	Mayanalistlán	12:6 f m	0/4	Bernabé García
		13 g	0/1	Bernabé García
	Chila y San Miguel	10:9 f m	0/4	Bernabé García
		5 g	0/1	Bernabé García
		7 p	0/0/6	Bernabé García
	Papachula	7 f m	0/4	Bernabá García
		7 p	0/0/6	Bernabé García
		1½ mantas	4/	Bernabé García
		½ j miel	t 1/	Bernabé García
2-I-1578	San Juan	5:6 f m	0/4	Bernabé García
		9 p	0/0/6	Bernabé García
		1½ mantas	4/	Bernabé García
	Quilitlán	18 f m	0/4	Bernabé García
		1 @ miel	2/	Lope de Cisneros
	Ixtapa, de C.	7 f sal	t 4/	Bernabé García
3-I-1578	Tlaltenango	404 p	0/1	Gerónimo de Medina
	Nochistlán	330 f m	0/3	Antonio Rodríguez
		374 p	0/1	Pedro de Murga
	Teocaltiche	298 f m	0/3	Antonio Rodríguez
		318 p	0/1	Antonio Rodríguez
	Teocaltitlán	9 f fr	0/3	Jorge Griego
		14½ f ají	0/3	Jorge Griego
		216 p	0/1	Jorge Griego
	Mexticacán	171 f m	0/3	Antonio Rodríguez
		54 p	0/1	Antonio Rodríguez
8-I-1578	Mochitiltic	30:2 f m	0/4/6	Diego Martín de Rivera
		31 p	0/0/9	Gerónimo de Ortega
	Tetitlán	76:1 f m	0/6	Bernardo de Balbuena
		76 p	0/0/9	Bernardo de Balbuena
	San Pedro	27:11 f m	0/6	Bernardo de Balbuena
		28 p	0/0/9	Bernardo de Balbuena
	Tepequexpan	67:6 f m	0/6	Bernardo de Balbuena
		67½ p	0/0/9	Bernardo de Balbuena
	Camotlán	42:4 f m	0/6	Bernabé García
		42½ p	0/0/8	Bernardo de Balbuena
	Tepetlatlauca y Chistique	36:6 f m	0/4	Bernabé García
		37 p	0/0/8	Bernabé García
	Mascota	28:4 f m	0/6/2	Francisco López
		44 p	0/0/9	Francisco López
		1 @ miel	5/4	Bernardo de Balbuena
	Atengoichán	47:6 f m	0/3/3	Bernardo de Balbuena
		47 p	0/0/6	Bernardo de Balbuena

Date	Town	Item & Amount	Unit Price	Buyer & Remarks
	Suchipil	168	0/0/9	Bernardo de Balbuena
	Amaxaque	8 mantas 23 p 5 g	5/ 0/1 0/1	Bernardo de Balbuena Bernardo de Balbuena Bernardo de Balbuena
	Tepuzhuacán	12 mantas	5/	Bernardo de Balbuena
	Jalacingo	2 mantas, } 1 pi de m }	4/	Bernardo de Balbuena
	Amatlán	9½ mantas	5/	Gerónimo de Ortega
	Zacatlán	27 f m	0/4/6	Bernabé García
	Pontoque	5 g	0/1	Bernabé García
	Orita	Todo	8/	Bernabé García
	Jaltepec	Todo	8/5	Bernabé García
	Ixcuintla	37:6 f m 24½ p 5½ g 3/4 @ miel	0/6 0/0/9 0/1/6 t 3/	Bernardo de Balbuena Bernardo de Balbuena Bernardo de Balbuena Gerónimo de Ortega
8-I-1578	Matacticpac	Todo	11/1	Bernabé García
	Temichoque	Todo	12/4	Bernabé García
9-I-1578	Jala	137:6 f m 156½ p	0/7/1 0/0/11½	Rodrigo de Ojeda Rodrigo de Ojeda
	Ixtimitique	1½ mantas	4/	Bernabé García
10-I-1578	Ahuacatlán	49:6 f m 59½ p	1/ 0/1	Alonso de la Vera Alonso de Cuellar
	Ahuisculco	29 f m 29 p	0/4 0/0/7	Alonso Martín Rodrigo de Ojeda
	Hostotipaquillo } Tecamatlán } San Francisco } Talistaque }	93:8 f m 94 p	0/6/1 0/0/9	Bernabé García Bernabé García
10-X-1578	Piloto, Maito y Maloto	8 mantas } 3 pi de m }	6/4	Gonzalo de Valdenebro
11-I-1578	Amaxaque	14:5 f m 14 p	0/4/6 0/0/6	Bernabé García Bernabé García
	Jocotlán, ptdo. (muchos remates antes de obtener oferta)	330:9 f m 329 p	1/ 0/0/9	Martín de Carranza Martín de Carranza (a crédito-la mejor oferta de dinero contante: 0/6)
	Tequila y Los Guajes (al empiezo, ninguna oferta)	104:6 f m 11 f tr 5 p	0/7 0/6 0/0/6	Gerónimo de Ortega Gerónimo de Ortega Gerónimo de Ortega
	Acaponeta y Sujetos	200 f m	0/6/1	Juan de Segovia
11-I-1578	Matatlán	107:4 f m	0/5	Rodrigo de Ojeda

Date	Town	Item & Amount	Unit Price	Buyer & Remarks
	(ninguna oferta el primer dia)	107½ p	0/0/8	Rodrigo de Ojeda
	Teocaltiche	252 p	0/1	Francisco Ruano
4-XI-1578	Nochistlán	374 p	0/1	Pedro de Murga
13-XI-1578	Teocaltiche	(252 f m mandadas a las salinas)		
2-XII-1578	Tlaltenango	404 p	0/1	Gonzalo de Hermosillo
		405 f m	0/3/6	Hernando de Burgos
4-XII-1578	Teocaltitlán	(371 f m mandadas a las salinas)		
4-XII-1578	Mitic	7 f fr }		
		1½ f ají}	0/3/6	Jorge Griego, Carretero
5-XII-1578	Teocaltiche	258 p	0/1	Pedro de Murga
5-I-1579	Mexticacán	371 f m	0/3/6	Hernando de Burgos
		54 p	0/1	Hernando de Burgos
6-I-1579	Nochistlán	330 f m	0/3/6	Hernando de Burgos
6-I-1579	Teocaltiche	256 f m	0/3/6	Hernando de Burgos
18-I-1578	Opono (semana para obtener oferta decente)	52 f m	0/3/3	Martín de Carranza
		52 p	0/0/6	Martín de Carranza
	Panpuchín (semana también)	20:3 f m	0/3	Martín de Carranza
		20 p	0/0/6	Martín de Carranza
		11½ pi de m	2/ cada pierna	Martín de Carranza
		2 @ 3 qtlas }		
		2 qtlos de miel}	2/ @	Martín de Carranza
	Zapotlán	14 f m	0/3	Martín de Carranza
		14 p	0/0/6	Martín de Carranza
	Sila	3:7 f m	0/3	Martín de Carranza
		7 p	0/0/6	Martín de Carranza
	Contla	11:8 f m	0/3	Martín de Carranza
	Mexcala (ninguna oferta por 1 semana)	90 f m	0/3	Rodrigo de Ojeda
		45 p	0/0/6	Rodrigo de Ojeda
	Copala y Quilitlán	60 f m	0/4	Diego Martín de Ribera
		60 p	0/0/11	Gerónimo de Valdenebro
9-I-1579	Tonalá	146:5 f m	1/	Tomé López
		238½ p	0/1/6	Juan del Castillo Villafaña
		7½ g	0/3/2	Juan del Castillo Villafaña
	Tlaquepaque, San Pedro y Toluquilla	100 f m	1/0/9	Juan del Castillo Villafaña
		193:5 f m	1/0/6	Lope de Cisneros
		293½ p	0/1/6	Juan González
	Tlajomulco	451:10 f m	0/7	Martín de Carranza
		452 p	0/1/4	Martín de Carranza
	Cuitzeo	80 f m	1/0/1	Rodrigo de Ojeda

Date	Town	Item & Amount	Unit Price	Buyer & Remarks
		180 p	0/1/3	Gaspar Vaca
		(100 f m reservadas para el convento de Cuitzeo)		
	Poncitlán	200 f m	0/7/3	Juan de Ataún Oñate
		200 f m	0/7/3	Rodrigo de Ojeda
		216:7 f m	0/7/3	Rodrigo de Ojeda
		620 p	0/1/5	Canónigo José Ramírez
10-I-1579	Analco y Tetlán	476:6 f m	0/8/6	Martín de Carranza
		509 p	0/1/3	Tomé López
	Camotlán y Cuyutlán	36 f m	0/5	Martín de Carranza
		36 p	0/1/1	Francisco Rodríguez
	Coscotitán	38 p	0/1/3	Andrés de Castro
	Atemajac	112:6 f m	1/0/8	Francisco Rodríguez
		112½ p	0/1/6	Francisco Rodríguez
	Nochistlanejo	31:6 f m	1/	Francisco Rodríguez
		31½ p	0/1/3	Francisco Rodríguez
	Cuyutlán	109:10 f m	0/7/8	Don Pedro Bernardo de Quirós, Archidiácono
		110½ p	0/1/6	Don Pedro Bernardo de Quirós, Archidiácono
	Zalatitlán	37 p	0/1/6	Bernabé García
	-37:4 f m reservadas	para los religiosos (parte de las 50 f m)		
	Tequila y Los Guajes	104:6 f m	0/6/6	Martín de Carranza
		5 p	0/1/3	Martín de Carranza
		11 f tr	1/6/1	Martín de Carranza
	Matatlán	43:2 f m	0/6	Cristóbal de Sandoval
		43½ p	0/1/3	P. Diego Ruiz Jurado
	Copala y Quilitlán	30:7 f m	0/6/6	Cristóbal de Sandoval
		31 p	0/1/3	Pedro Xuárez de Aguilera
	Ahuisculco	29:5 f m	0/6/3	P. Diego Ruiz Jurado
		29½ p	0/1/3	Canónigo José Ramírez
	Mochitiltic	30:2 f m	0/6/3	Juan González
		31 p	0/1/2	Juan González
	Amaxaque	14:5 f m	0/4/4	Juan González
		14 p	0/1	Juan González
12-I-1579	Tetitlán	76:1 f m	1/3/4	Tomé López
		76½ p	0/1/11	Rodrigo de Ojeda
	San Pedro	27:11 f m	1/3	Tomé López
		28 p	0/1/11	Rodrigo de Ojeda
	Tepequexpán	67:6 f m	1/3/4	Tomé López
		67½ p	0/1/11	Rodrigo de Ojeda
	Camotlán	42:4 f m	1/3/4	Tomé López
		42½ p	0/1/4	Rodrigo de Ojeda
	Analco Tepic	141:9 f m	1/6/11	Bernabé García
		141½ p	0/1/3	Tomé López
	Amaxaque	8 mantas	6/6	Martín de Carranza

Date	Town	Item & Amount	Unit Price	Buyer & Remarks
		23 p	0/1	Rodrigo de Ojeda
		5 g	0/2/1	Rodrigo de Ojeda
	Jalcocotán	27 f m	1/2	Tomé López
		27 p	0/1	Cristóbal de Sandoval
		7 g	0/2	Cristóbal de Sandoval
		1 @ miel	5/4/2	Tomé López
	Mecatán	13:6 f m	1/2	Tomé López
		9 p	0/1	Tomé López
		4 g	0/2	Tomé López
		1 qtlo miel	t 1/0/8	Juan de Ataún
	Tepuzhuacán	12 mantas	6/5/1	Tomé López
	Jalacingo	2 mantas }		
		1 pi de m }	6/3/11	Juan de Ataún
	Amatlán	9½ mantas	6/4	Martín de Carranza
	Ixtimitique	1½ mantas	6/	Martín de Carranza
	Zacatlán	27 f m	0/6/1	Bernabé García
	Pontoque	5 g	0/2	Tomé López
	Acatispa	14:6 f m	1/2/1	Tomé López
		6 p	0/1	Tomé López
		5 g	0/2	Tomé López
	Orita	13:6 f m	1/1/2	Tomé López
		3½ @ alg	5/1/6	Rodrigo de Ojeda
		11 g	0/2	Tomé López
		11 p	0/1	Tomé López
	Ixtapa, Santa María	6:3 f sal }		
		8½ p }		
		11/12 car alg }	t 12/	Tomé López
		46 lib pes }		
	Jaltepec	10 f m	1/2/6	Tomé López
		10 p	0/1	Tomé López
		1 qtla miel	1/2	Tomé López
12-I-1579	Ixcuintla	41:5 f m	1/6	Tomé López
		41½ p	0/1/3	Tomé López
13-I-1579	Matacticpac	11 f m	1/6/3	Bernabé García
		3:6 f fr	1/7/11	Tomé López
		6 p	0/1/3	Tomé López
		5 g	0/2/6	Tomé López
	Zanalatlán	16 f m	1/3/11½	Tomé López
		14 g	0/2/11½	Tomé López
	Mayanalistlán	12:6 f m	1/2/9	Tomé López
		13 g	0/2/6	Tomé López
	Chila y San Miguel	10:9 f m	1/2/8	Tomé López
		5 g	0/2/6	Tomé López
		7 p	0/1	Tomé López
	Papachula	7 f m	1/1/3	Tomé López
		1½ mantas	6/	Tomé López
		7 p	0/0/9	Tomé López

Date	Town	Item & Amount	Unit Price	Buyer & Remarks
		½ j miel	t 2/	Tomé López
	San Juan	5:6 f m	1/2	Tomé López
		1½ mantas	6/	Juan de Ataún
		9 p	0/1	Tomé López
	Temichoque	18 f m	1/3	Tomé López
		5½ @ alg	1/2/11½	Tomé López
		11 p	0/1/0½	Tomé López
	Quilitlán	18 f m	1/3/1	Tomé López
		1 @ miel	4/	Tomé López
	Ixtapa, de C.	7 f sal	t 11/	Tomé López
	Sentispac	33 mantas }		
		1½ pi de m }	10/6/6	Tomé López
		129:9 f m	1/3	Tomé López
		269 p	0/1/2½	Tomé López
	Jalisco	203:10 f m	1/2/2	Bernabé García
		204 p	0/1/2	Bernabé García
	Tepetlatlauca y Chistique	36:6 f m	0/4	Bernabé García
		37 p	0/1	Bernabé García
	Mascota	34:2 f m	0/6	Bernabé García
		34½ p	0/0/9	Bernabé García
	Atengoichán	47:6 f m	0/5	Bernabé García
		47 p	0/0/9	Bernabé García
	Suchipil	102:1 f m	1/6/1	Tomé López
		113½ p	0/1/10	Rodrigo de Ojeda
13-I-1579	Ahuacatlán	40 f m	1/6	Tomé López
		45 p	0/1/11	Rodrigo de Ojeda
	Jala	133:8 f m	1/6/7	Tomé López
		133 p	0/2/0½	Rodrigo de Ojeda
14-I-1579	Hostotipaquillo }			
	Tecomatlán }	104:10 f m	1/1	Juan González
	San Francisco }	104½ p	0/1	Cristóbal de Sandoval
	Talistaque }			
	Jocotlán, ptdo. }	330:9 f m	0/7	Juan González
	(9 pueblos }	329½ p	0/1	Juan González
	Mezquituta y Mayagua	100:3 f m	0/6	Cristóbal de Sandoval
		100 p	0/1	Cristóbal de Sandoval
	Acaponeta y partido	200 f m	1/1/8	Tomé López
		200 p	0/1	Tomé López
	Pueblos en rebelión y tributos atrasados en pago. Solamente:			
	de 1577 y 1578 }	100 f m	0/6/6	Tomé López
	1578 }	50 p	0/1	Tomé López
	Opono	52 f m	0/3/6	Martín de Carranza
		52 p	0/0/9	Martín de Carranza
	Pampuchín	20:3 f m	0/3/6	Martín de Carranza

Date	Town	Item & Amount	Unit Price	Buyer & Remarks
		20 p	0/0/9	Martín de Carranza
		11½ pi de m	1/	Martín de Carranza
		2 @ 3 qtlas, }		
		2 qtlos de miel}	2/4 @	Francisco Rodríguez
	Zapotlán	14 f m	0/3/6	Martín de Carranza
		14 p	0/0/9	Martín de Carranza
	Sila	3:7 f m	0/3/6	Martín de Carranza
		7 p	0/0/9	Martín de Carranza
	Contla	11:8 f m	0/3	Martín de Carranza
	Piloto	13 f m	0/3	Diego de Morales
	-2 años-1577 y 1578	14½ pi de m	1/	Rodrigo de Ojeda
		13 f m	0/3	Rodrigo de Ojeda
		27 p	0/0/9	Rodrigo de Ojeda
4-II-1579	Atengo	30½ pi de m	1/	Rodrigo de Ojeda
	-1577 y 1578	27:8 f m	0/3	Rodrigo de Ojeda
		55 p	0/0/9	Rodrigo de Ojeda
	Colique	13½ pi de m	1/	Rodrigo de Ojeda
		34 p	0/0/9	Rodrigo de Ojeda
		16:8 f m	0/3	Rodrigo de Ojeda
	Maito	23½ pi de m	1/	Rodrigo de Ojeda
	-1577 y 1578	21:2 f m	0/3	Rodrigo de Ojeda
		43 p	0/0/9	Rodrigo de Ojeda
9-I-1581	Analco y Tetlán	441:11 f m	0/7/8	P. Lázaro Vallejo
		442 p	0/1	Baltasar de Rueda
	Tonalá	144:4 f m	0/6/1	Juan González
		244 p	0/1	Baltasar de Rueda
		(100 f m para el convento)		
	Tlaquepaque, San Pedro y Toluquilla	293:5 f m	1/	Pedro de Naso
		293½ p	0/1	Pedro de Naso
	Tlajomulco	451:10 f m	0/7/4	Juan de Arriaga
		453 p	0/1	Francisco Rodríguez
	Poncitlán	611:6 f m	0/7/1	Martín Vélez
		611 p	0/1	Martín Vélez
	Cuitzeo	80 f m	0/7/2	Rodrigo de Ojeda
		180 p	0/0/11	Rodrigo de Ojeda
		(100 f m para el convento)		
	Camotlán y Cuyutlán	36 f m	0/6	P. Lázaro Vallejo
		36 p	0/0/9	Juan González
	Coscotitán	38 p	0/0/9	Rodrigo de Ojeda
	Atemajac	112:6 f m	1/	P. Lázaro Vallejo
		112½ p	0/1/1	Jaime Pérez
	Nochistlanejo	31:6 f m	0/7	Rodrigo de Ojeda
		31½ p	0/1	Juan González
	Cuyutlán y Cajetitlán	109:10 f m	0/7/9	Gonzalo de Valdenebro
		110 p	0/1	Francisco de Plaza
	Zalatitlán	37 p	0/1	Andrés de Castro

Date	Town	Item & Amount	Unit Price	Buyer & Remarks
		(37:4 f m a los religiosos		)
	Matatlán	43:2 f m	0/6	Francisco de Cepeda
		43½ p	0/1	Francisco de Cepeda
	Tequila y San Francisco	122:5 f m	0/6	Diego Rubio
		32½ p	0/0/10	Diego Rubio
		11 f tr	1/	Diego Rubio
	Ahuisculco	29:3 f m	0/6	Rodrigo de Ojeda
		29½ p	0/1	Rodrigo de Ojeda
10-I-1581	Copala y Quilitlán	30:7 f m	0/6	Francisco de Plaza
		31 p	0/1	Rodrigo de Ojeda
	Mochitiltic	30:2 f m	0/7/1	Juan de la Cueva
		31 p	0/1	Juan de la Cueva
	Yegualtitlán	22:6 f m	1/1	Juan de la Cueva
		22 p	0/1	Juan de la Cueva
	Acatique	37:4 f m	1/1	Juan de la Cueva
		37½ p	0/1	Juan de la Cueva
10-I-1581	Huelotitlán	29:8 f m	1/1	Juan de la Cueva
		30 p	0/1	Juan de la Cueva
	Inrimota	23:10 f m	1/1	Juan de la Cueva
		26 p	0/1	Juan de la Cueva
	Tequiltitlán	27 f m	1/1	Juan de la Cueva
		27 p	0/1	Juan de la Cueva
	Cuyolomitle	5:10 f m	1/1	Juan de la Cueva
		5 p	0/1	Juan de la Cueva
	Mezquitlán	59:5 f m	1/1	Juan de la Cueva
		59 p	0/1	Juan de la Cueva
	Mezquititique y Terequita	29:3 f m	1/1	Juan de la Cueva
		29 p	0/1	Juan de la Cueva
	Cacaluta	25:2 f m	1/1	Juan de la Cueva
		25½ p	0/1	Juan de la Cueva
	Tetitlán	76:1 f m	0/5	Juan de Riego
		76½ p	0/0/10	Juan de Riego
	San Pedro, sujeto de Tetillán	16:2 f m	0/5	Juan de Riego
		16½ p	0/0/10	Juan de Riego
	Tepequexpan	34:8 f m	0/5	Juan de Riego
		35 p	0/0/10	Juan de Riego
	Camotlán	42:4 f m	0/5	Juan de Riego
		42½ p	0/0/10	Juan de Riego
	Acuitlapilco y Zapotlán	56:8 f m	0/5	Juan de Riego
		57 p	0/0/10	Juan de Riego
	Jalisco	159:3 f m	1/0/7	Tomé López
		160 p	0/1	Tomé López
	Tepic	89:7 f m	1/1/9	Rodrigo de Ojeda
		89½ p	0/1	Rodrigo Gutiérrez Cordero

Date	Town	Item & Amount	Unit Price	Buyer & Remarks
	Analco Tepic	12:2 f m	1/2/2	Juan de Riego
		12 p	0/1	Rodrigo Hernández Cordero
	Suchipil	49:2 f m	1/	Andrés de Castro
		49 p	0/1	Andrés de Castro
	Ahuacatlán	31:8 f m	1/	Andrés de Castro
		32 p	0/1	Andrés de Castro
	Jala	133:2 f m	1/0/1	Andrés de Castro
		133½ p	0/1	Andrés de Castro
11-I-1581	Ixtapa, Santa María	5:3 f m	1/2	Rodrigo Hernández Cordero
		9½ p	t 0/6	Rodrigo Hernández Cordero
		1 car alg	2/	Rodrigo Hernández Cordero
		2 @ pes	0/4	Rodrigo Hernández Cordero
	Jalcocotán	49:11 f m	1/1/6	Antonio del Rincón
		50 p	0/1	Antonio del Rincón
	Mecatán	63:7 f m	1/1/9	Antonio del Rincón
		53½ p	0/0/11	Rodrigo Hernández Cordero
	Ixcuintla	41:5 f m	1/0/6	Rodrigo Hernández Cordero
		41½ p	0/1	Rodrigo Hernández Cordero
	Sentispac	129:9 f m	0/5	Bernardo de Balbuena "para los indios de Sentispac"
		269 p	0/0/9	Bernardo de Balbuena
13-I-1581	Suchitlán	179:8 f m	0/3/3	Gaspar Vaca
	-1578-80	119½ p	0/0/9	Gaspar Vaca
	Hostotipaquillo }			
	Talistac }	72:6 f m	0/7	Juan de la Cueva
	Tecomatlán }	72½ p	0/1/2	Juan de la Cueva
	Opono	52 f m	0/3/7	Bernardo de Balbuena
		52 p	0/0/9	Bernardo de Balbuena
	Mezquituta y Moyagua	75:7 f m	1/5/3	Rodrigo de Ojeda
		75½ p	0/0/9	Rodrigo de Ojeda
	Guastla ó Los Guajes	5:5 f m	0/7	Diego Martín de Rivera
		5½ p	t 0/4	Diego Martín de Rivera
	Mexcala	30:2 f m	0/2	Rodrigo de Ojeda
		30 p	0/0/6	Rodrigo de Ojeda
14-I-1581	Amaxaque	14:5 f m	0/6	Juan González
		14 p	0/0/6	Juan González
	Tepetlatlauca y Chistique	36:6 f m	0/4	Hernando Gallegos
		37 p	0/0/9	Hernando Gallegos
	Mascota	34:2 f m	0/3/6	Juan González
		34½ p	0/0/9	Juan González
	Atengoichán	18:3 f m	0/3/6	Juan González
		18½ p	0/0/6	Juan González
	San Juan	5:6 f m	1/	Antonio del Rincón
		9½ p	0/0/6	Antonio del Rincón

Date	Town	Item & Amount	Unit Price	Buyer & Remarks
	Papachula	7 f m	1/	Antonio del Rincón
		7 p	0/0/6	Antonio del Rincón
		½ j miel	t 1/	Rodrigo de Ojeda
		1½ mantas	t 6/	D. Martín de Rendón
	Tepuzhuacán	9:3 f m	1/6/6	Juan González
		9½ p	0/0/6	Juan González
	Amatlán }			
	Jalacingo }	24:4 f m	1/	Antonio del Rincón
	Ixtimitique }	24½ p	0/0/6	Antonio del Rincón
14-I-1581	Zacatlán	27 f m	0/4/2	Hernando Gallegos
	Pontoque	6:9 f m	1/	Antonio del Rincón
		7 p	0/0/6	Antonio del Rincón
	Acatispa	13:6 f m	1/	Antonio del Rincón
	Contla	13½ p	0/0/6	Antonio del Rincón
	Ixtapa, de Castañeda	7 f sal	1/2	Rodrigo de Ojeda
	Matacticpac	11 f m	1/	Antonio del Rincón
		6 p	0/0/6	Antonio del Rincón
		5 g	0/1	Antonio del Rincón
	Quilitlán	18 f m	1/	Antonio del Rincón
		1 @ miel	2/	Rodrigo de Ojeda
	Jaltepec	9 f m	1/	Antonio del Rincón
		10 p	0/0/6	Antonio del Rincón
		1 j miel	1/	Rodrigo de Ojeda
	San Miguel y Zanatlán	21:2 f m	1/	Antonio del Rincón
		21½ p	0/0/6	Antonio del Rincón
	Mayanalistlán	12:6 f m	1/	Antonio del Rincón
		13 g	0/1	Antonio del Rincón
	Chila	4 f m	1/	Antonio del Rincón
		5 g	0/1	Antonio del Rincón
	Temichoque	18 f m	1/	Antonio del Rincón
		11 p	0/0/6	Antonio del Rincón
		(5½ @ alg--ninguna oferta--así se empleó en armas para usar contra los chichimecas)		
	Acaponeta }			
	Tehuala }	250 f m	1/	Juan de la Cueva
	Tetitlán }	250 p	0/1	Baltasar de Rueda
	Ixtapa }			
	San Francisco Zayula }	(4 pueblos en rebelión; solamente podían recoger esto)		
	Quebiquito }			
	Panpuchín	21:1 f m	0/3/7	Bernardo de Balbuena
		21½ p	0/0/9	Bernardo de Balbuena
	Zapotlán	14 f m	0/3/7	Bernardo de Balbuena
		14 p	0/0/9	Bernardo de Balbuena
	Sila	3:7 f m	0/3/7	Bernardo de Balbuena
		7 p	0/0/9	Bernardo de Balbuena

Date	Town	Item & Amount	Unit Price	Buyer & Remarks
14-I-1581	Contla	11:8 f m	0/3/7	Bernardo de Balbuena
	Piloto	6:6 f m	0/3/7	Bernardo de Balbuena
		13½ p	0/0/9	Bernardo de Balbuena
		7¼ pi de m	1/	Bernardo de Balbuena
	Maito	19:7 f m	0/3/7	Bernardo de Balbuena
		21½ p	0/0/9	Bernardo de Balbuena
		11 3/4 pi de m	1/	Bernardo de Balbuena
	Colique	8:4 f m	0/3/7	Bernardo de Balbuena
		17 p	0/0/6	Bernardo de Balbuena
		9¼ pi de m	1/	Bernardo de Balbuena
	Atengo	13:10 f m	0/3/7	Bernardo de Balbuena
		28 p	0/0/9	Bernardo de Balbuena
		15¼ pi de m	1/	Bernardo de Balbuena
16-I-1581	Matacticpac	3:6 f fr	1/7	Rodrigo de Ojeda
	Amaxaque	17:10 f m	0/5	Pedro Narváez
		18 p	0/0/9	Pedro Narváez
	Ocotique } Amaxaque } Tetetlique } Huehuetitlán } Coyonatatlán }	252:2 f m 136 p 22 g	0/3 0/0/6 0/1	Rodrigo de Ojeda Rodrigo de Ojeda Rodrigo de Ojeda
19-I-1581	Sentispac	33 mantas		
		1¼ pi de m	8/1	Diego Martín de Rivera "por armas de su Magestad"
	San Juan (después de una semana)	1½ mantas	t 6/	Diego Martín de Rivera "por armas de su Magestad"
	Papachula	1½ mantas	t 6/	D. Martín de Rendón
10-XI-1581	Tlaltenango	341 p (341 f m a las salinas)	0/1	Juan de Caberio
13-XI-1581	Nochistlán	252 p	0/1	Juan de Caberio
	Teocaltiche	253 p (253 f m a las salinas)	0/1	Juan de Caberio
	Mitic	120 p (120:6 f m a las salinas)	0/1	Juan de Caberio
	Teocualtitlán	91 p (91 f m a las salinas)	0/1	Juan de Caberio
	Mexticacán	132 p	0/1	Juan de Caberio
2-I-1582	Nochistlán (varias ofertas)	252 f m	0/2/9	Gerónimo de la Cueva
	Mexticacán	132 f m	0/2/9	Gerónimo de la Cueva
9-I-1582	Jala	133:2 f m	1/5	Francisco Xuárez
		133½ p	0/1/3	Francisco Xuárez
	Analco y Tetlán	441:10 f m	1/1	Lázaro Vallejo
		442 p	0/1	Juan González

Date	Town	Item & Amount	Unit Price	Buyer & Remarks
	Tonalá	140:4 f m	0/7/10	García de Chávez
		244 p	0/1	Diego Martín de Rivera
		(100 f m a los frailes agustinos)		
	Tlaquepaque, San Pedro y Toluquilla	260:2 f m	1/0/6	Lázaro Vallejo
		260 p	0/1	Juan Gonzáles
	Tlajomulco	451:10 f m	0/7/6	Lázaro Vallejo
		252 p	0/1	Rodrigo de Ojeda
	Poncitlán	611:6 f m	0/7	Lázaro Vallejo
		611 p	0/0/9	Rodrigo de Balcázar
	Cuitzeo	80 f m	0/7	Lázaro Vallejo
		180 p	0/0/10	Juan González
		(100 f m al convento)		
	Atemajac	112:6 f m	1/	García de Chávez
		112½ p	0/1	García de Chávez
	Zalatitlán	(37:4 f m a los frailes agustinos)		
		37 p	0/1	Antonio del Rincón
	Cuyutlán y Cajetitlán	109:10 f m	0/7/4	Antonio del Rincón
		110½ p	0/1	Antonio del Rincón
10-I-1582	Suchitlán	38:3 f m	0/3/3	Rodrigo de Ojeda
		38½ p	0/0/6	Rodrigo de Ojeda
	Camotlán y Cuyutlán	36 f m	0/5/6	Pedro de Naso
		36 p	0/0/9	Pedro de Naso
	Coscotitán	38 p	0/0/9	Pedro de Naso
	Nochistlanejo	31:6 f m	0/6/9	Juan González
		31½ p	0/1	Juan de Villafaña
	Matatlán	43:2 f m	0/6/6	Juan González
		43½ p	0/1	Juan González
	Tequila	90 f m	0/7/11	Juan González
		11 f tr	1/	Juan González
	Guastla ó Los Guajes	5:5 f m	0/7/11	Juan González
		5½ p	0/0/6	Juan González
	Copala y Quilitlán	30:7 f m	0/7	Pedro de Enciso
		31 p	0/1	Pedro de Enciso
	Ahuisculco	29:3 f m	0/6/6	Juan de Villafaña
		29½ p	0/1	Juan de Villafaña
	Mochitiltic	30:2 f m	1/0/8	Antonio del Rincón
		31 p	0/1/1	Luis Moreno de Monroy
	Amaxaque	14:5 f m	1/0/8	Antonio del Rincón
		14 p	0/1/1	Luis Moreno de Monroy
	Hostotipaquillo - incluye San Francisco	104:10 f m	1/0/4	Antonio del Rincón
		105 p	0/1/1	Luis Moreno de Monroy
	Yegualtitlán	21:2 f m	1/0/4	Antonio del Rincón
		21 p	0/1	Luis Moreno de Monroy

Date	Town	Item & Amount	Unit Price	Buyer & Remarks
	Acatique	37:4 f m	1/0/4	Antonio del Rincón
		37½ p	0/1/1	Luis Moreno de Monroy
	Huelotitlán	29:8 f m	1/0/4	Antonio del Rincón
		30 p	0/1/1	Luis Moreno de Monroy
	Inrimota	23:10 f m	1/0/4	Antonio del Rincón
		26 p	0/1/1	Luis Moreno de Monroy
	Tequiltitlán	27 f m	1/0/4	Antonio del Rincón
		27 p	0/1/1	Luis Moreno de Monroy
	Cuyolomitle	5:5 f m	1/0/4	Antonio del Rincón
		5 p	0/1/1	Luis Moreno de Monroy
	Mezquitlán	595 f m	1/0/4	Antonio del Rincón
		59 p	0/1/1	Luis Moreno de Monroy
10-I-1582	Mezquititique	29:3 f m	1/0/4	Antonio del Rincón
	y Terequita	29 p	0/1/1	Luis Moreno de Monroy
	Cacaluta	25:2 f m	1/0/4	Antonio del Rincón
		25½ p	0/1/1	Luis Moreno de Monroy
	San Miguel y	21:2 f m	1/1/6	García de Chávez
	Zanatlán	21½ p	0/0/6	García de Chávez
	Tetitlán	76:1 f m	0/5	Rodrigo de Ojeda
		76½ p	0/1	Rodrigo de Ojeda
	Tepequexpan	34:8 f m	0/5	Rodrigo de Ojeda
		35 p	0/1	Rodrigo de Ojeda
	Camotlán	42:4 f m	0/5	Rodrigo de Ojeda
		42½ p	0/1	Rodrigo de Ojeda
	San Pedro, sujeto	16:2 f m	0/5	Rodrigo de Ojeda
	de Tetitlán	16½ p	0/1	Rodrigo de Ojeda
	Acuitlapilco y	65:2 f m	0/5	Rodrigo de Ojeda
	Zapotlán	65 p	0/1	Rodrigo de Ojeda
11-I-1582	San Pedro y	10:5 f m	1/1/6	García de Chávez
	Mayanalistlán	8 p	0/1	García de Chávez
	Acaponeta y su	298:10 f m	1/0/1	Diego Martín de Rivera
	partido-	299 p	0/1	Diego Martín de Rivera
	Acaponeta }		(ningún diezmo de m ó pollo)	
	Tecuela }	Nota:		
	Tetitlán }	No entraron el trigo; comprador no pagó		
	Ixtapa }	porque toda la región está medio alzado		
	San Francisco }			
	Zayula }	Los alzados incluyen:	{Zapotlán	
	Quebiquito }		{Tlachichilpa	
			{Totorami	
			{Guaxecoremi	
	Sentispac	206:4 f m	1/1/6	Diego Martín de Rivera
		212 p	0/0/8	Diego Martín de Rivera
		3 mantas }		
		2¼ pi de m}	8/2	García de Chávez
	Jalisco	159:3 f m	1/4/3	García de Chávez
		160 p	0/1/2	Diego Martín de Rivera

Date	Town	Item & Amount	Unit Price	Buyer & Remarks
	Tepic	89:7 f m	1/4/4	García de Chávez
		89½ p	0/1/2	Diego Martín de Rivera
	Analco Tepic	12:2 f m	1/4/4	García de Chávez
		12 p	0/1/2	Diego Martín de Rivera
	Suchipil	49:2 f m	1/4/7	Diego Martín de Rivera
		49 p	0/1/2	Francisco Xuárez
	Amaxaque	17:10 f m	1/4/7	Diego Martín de Rivera
		18 p	0/1/2	Francisco Xuárez
	Ahuacatlán	31:8 f m	1/4/7	Diego Martín de Rivera
		32 p	0/1/2	Francisco Xuárez
	San Juan	5:6 f m	1/0/1	García de Chávez
		9 p	0/4	García de Chávez
		1½ mantas	4/	García de Chávez
	Papachula	7 f m	1/0/6	García de Chávez
		7 p	0/0/6	García de Chávez
		1½ mantas	t 4/1	García de Chávez
		½ j miel	t 0/7	García de Chávez
	Ixtapa, Santa María	5:3 f m	1/0/6	García de Chávez
		9½ p	0/0/6	García de Chávez
		1 car alg	1/0/6	García de Chávez
		2 @ pes	0/2/6	García de Chávez
	Jalcocotán	49:11 f m	1/1	García de Chávez
		50 p	0/0/11	García de Chávez
	Mecatán	53:7 f m	1/1	García de Chávez
		53½ p	0/0/11	García de Chávez
	Jaltepec	9 f m }		
		10 p }	t 12/	García de Chávez
		1 j miel-qtla }		
	Temichoque	18 f m	1/0/6	García de Chávez
		5½ @ alg	t 3/0/6	García de Chávez
		11 p	0/0/6	García de Chávez
	Pontoque	6:9 f m	1/0/6	García de Chávez
		7 p	0/0/6	García de Chávez
	Acatispa y Canala	13:6 f m	1/0/6	García de Chávez
		13½ p	0/0/6	García de Chávez
	Ixtapa de Castañeda	7 f sal	1/0/6	García de Chávez
	Quilitlán	18 f m	1/0/6	García de Chávez
		1 @ miel	1/2	García de Chávez
	Matacticpac	11 f m	1/0/6	García de Chávez
		6 p	0/0/6	García de Chávez
		5 g	0/5	García de Chávez
		3:6 f fr	1/0	García de Chávez
	Ixcuintla	41:5 f m	1/3/10	García de Chávez
		41½ p	0/1	Diego Martín de Rivera
12-I-1582	Tepuzhuacán	9:3 f m	0/5	Juan González
		9½ p	0/0/9	Juan González

Date	Town	Item & Amount	Unit Price	Buyer & Remarks
	Amatlán, Jalacingo, Ixtimitique	24:4 f m	0/5	Juan González
		24½ p	0/0/9	Juan González
	Zacatlán	27 f m	0/5	Juan González
	Atengoichán	18:3 f m	0/5	Juan González
		18½ p	0/0/9	Juan González
	Panpuchín	21:1 f m	0/4	Pedro Hurtado
		21½ p	0/0/9	Pedro Hurtado
	Opono	52 f m	0/4	Pedro Hurtado
		52 p	0/0/9	Pedro Hurtado
	Contla	11:8 f m	0/4	Pedro Hurtado
	Zapotlán	14 f m	0/4	Pedro Hurtado
		14 p	0/0/9	Pedro Hurtado
	Sila	3:7 f m	0/4	Pedro Hurtado
		7 p	0/0/9	Pedro Hurtado
	Piloto	7 pi de m	0/7	Pedro de Naso
		5:6 f m	0/3	Pedro Hurtado
		13½ p	0/0/9	Pedro Hurtado
	Maito	11 3/4 pi de m	0/7	Pedro de Naso
		10:7 f m	0/3	Pedro Hurtado
		21½ p	0/0/9	Pedro Hurtado
	Colique	9¼ pi de m	0/7	Pedro de Naso
		3:4 f m	0/3	Pedro Hurtado
		17 p	0/0/9	Pedro Hurtado
	Atengo	15¼ pi de m	0/7	Pedro de Naso
		13:10 f m	0/3	Pedro Hurtado
		28 p	0/0/9	Pedro Hurtado
	Chila	(Despoblado)		
	Mexcala	30:2 f m	0/2	Gonzalo de Valdenebro
		30 p	0/0/6	Gonzalo de Valdenebro
	Mascota	34:2 f m	0/5/2	Juan González
		34½ p	0/0/9	Juan González
	Tepetlatlauca y Chistique	36:6 f m	0/5/2	Juan González
		37 p	0/0/9	Juan González
	Mezquituta y Moyagua	75:7 f m	0/4/11	Rodrigo de Ojeda
		75½ p	0/0/9	Rodrigo de Ojeda
15-XI-1582	Teocaltiche	(252 f m a las salinas)		
		252 p	0/1	Francisco Ruano
	Tecoaltitlán	(91 f m a las salinas)		
		91 p	0/1	Francisco Ruano
	Mitic	(120:6 f m a las salinas)		
		120 p	0/1	Francisco Ruano
17-XI-1582	Mexticacán	133 f m	0/4	Francisco Ruano
		133 p	0/1	Francisco Ruano
	Tlaltenango	341 p	0/1	Francisco Ruano

Date	Town	Item & Amount	Unit Price	Buyer & Remarks
	Nochistlán	252 f m	0/4	Francisco Ruano
		252 p	0/1	Francisco Ruano
22-XI-1582	Tlaltenango	(341 f m a las salinas)		
10-XII-1582	Analco y Tetlán	427:1 f m	1/	Juan de la Cueva
		427 p	0/1/3	Diego Martín de Rivera
	Tonalá	131:8 f m	0/7	Juan de la Cueva
		(112:8 f m para el convento)		
		244 p	0/1	Francisco de la Plaza
	Tlaquepaque y Toluquilla	243:4 f m	1/	Juan de la Cueva
		253 p	0/1/2	Rodrigo de Balcázar
	Tlajomulco	451:10 f m	0/7	Juan de la Cueva
		452 p	0/1	Rodrigo de Balcázar
	Poncitlán	611:6 f m	1/0/6	Juan de la Cueva
		611 p	0/1	Licenciado Sánchez
	Cuitzeo	80 f m	1/0/1	Juan López Tavera
		(100 f m para el convento)		
		180 p	0/0/9	Juan González
	Camotlán y Cuyutlán	36 f m	0/7/6	Andrés de Castro
		36 p	0/0/9	Andrés de Castro
	Coscotitán	38 p	0/0/10	Gerónimo Mexía
	Nochistlanejo	31:6 f m	0/7	Juan de la Cueva
		31½ p	0/1	Juan González
	Atemajac	112:6 f m	1/	Juan de la Cueva
		112½ p	0/1/2	Gabriel López
	Zalatitlán	37 p	0/1	Alonso Ramírez
		(37:4 f m para los frailes)		
	Cuyutlán y Cajetitlán	109:10 f m	0/7	Juan de la Cueva
		110½ p	0/1	Andrés de Castro
	Matatlán	43:2 f m	1/	Francisco de Cepeda
		43½ p	0/1	Francisco de Cepeda
	Tequila	90 f m	1/2/9	Andrés de Castro
		11 f tr	1/4	Juan González
	Guastla ó Los Guajes	5:5 f m	1/2/9	Andrés de Castro
		5½ p	0/0/6	Juan González
	Copala y Quilitlán	30:7 f m	0/7	Juan de la Cueva
		31 p	0/1	Cánonigo Hernán Vela
11-XII-1582	Suchitlán	35:10 f m	0/5	Francisco De Plaza
		36 p	0/1	Francisco de Plaza
	Mezquituta y Moyagua	75:7 f m	0/5	Francisco de Plaza
		75½ p	0/1	Francisco de Plaza
	Ahuisculco	29:3 f m	1/1	Gonzalo de Valdenebro
		29½ p	0/1/3	Gerónimo Mexía
	Mochitiltic	30:2 f m	1/3	García de Chávez
		31 p	0/1	García de Chávez

Date	Town	Item & Amount	Unit Price	Buyer & Remarks
	Amaxaque	14:5 f m	1/3	García de Chávez
		14 p	0/1	García de Chávez
	Hostotipaquillo	104:10 f m	1/3	García de Chávez
		105 p	0/1	García de Chávez
	Sentispac	204:4 f m	1/3	Juan González
		204½ p	0/1	Juan González
	Jalisco	109:3 f m	1/6	García de Chávez
		(50 f m para el convento de Huaynamota--recién restabecido)		
		160 p	0/1/3	Alvaro de Figueroa
	Tepic	89:7 f m	1/7/6	Juan Antonio de Carmona
		89½ p	0/1/6	Juan Antonio de Carmona
	Analco Tepic	12:2 f m	1/7/6	Juan Antonio de Carmona
		12 p	0/1/6	Juan Antonio de Carmona
	Suchipil	49:2 f m	1/3/6	Juan Vélez de Vargas
		49 p	0/1	Juan Vélez de Vargas
	Amaxaque	17 f m	1/3/6	Juan Vélez de Vargas
		18 p	0/1	Juan Vélez de Vargas
	Ahuacatlán	31:8 f m	1/3/6	Juan Vélez de Vargas
		32 p	0/1	Juan Vélez de Vargas
	Jala	133:2 f m	1/2/2	García de Chávez
		133½ p	0/1	García de Chávez
	Jalcocotán	49:11 f m	1/4/3	Juan Antonio de Carmona
		50 p	0/1/6	Juan Antonio de Carmona
	Mecatán	53:7 f m	1/4/3	Juan Antonio de Carmona
		53½ p	0/1	Juan Antonio de Carmona
	Jaltepec	9 f m	0/7	García de Chávez
		10 p	0/1/3	Alvaro de Figueroa
		1 qtlo miel	0/5/6	Juan Antonio de Carmona
	Temichoque	18 f m	1/1/5	Gonzalo de Valdenebro
		5½ @ alg	t 4/	Rodrigo de Ojeda
		11 p	0/1	Juan Antonio de Carmona
	Pontoque	6:9 f m	1/1/5	Gonzalo de Valdenebro
		7 p	0/1/3	Juan Antonio de Carmona
	Acatispa y Canala	13:6 f m	1/1/5	Gonzalo de Valdenebro
		13½ p	0/1/3	Juan Antonio de Carmona
	Ixtapa de Castañeda	7 f sal	0/7	Rodrigo de Ojeda
	Quilitlán	18 f m	0/7	García de Chávez
		1 @ miel	2/	Juan Antonio de Carmona
	Matacticpac	11:4 f m	0/7	García de Chávez
		1:11 f fr	1/	García de Chávez
		9 p }		
		3 g }	0/1/3	Alvaro de Figueroa
	Ixcuintla	41:5 f m	0/7	García de Chávez
		41½ p	0/1	Andrés de Castro

Date	Town	Item & Amount	Unit Price	Buyer & Remarks
	Yegualtitlán	20:8 f m	1/3	García de Chávez
		21 p	0/1	García de Chávez
	Acatique	37:4 f m	1/3	García de Chávez
		37½ p	0/1	García de Chávez
	Huelotitlán	29:8 f m	1/3	García de Chávez
		30 p	0/1	García de Chávez
	Inrimota	23:10 f m	1/3	García de Chávez
		26 p	0/1	García de Chávez
	Tequiltitlán	27 f m	1/3	García de Chávez
		27 p	0/1	García de Chávez
	Cuyolomitle	5:10 f m	1/3	García de Chávez
		5 p	0/1	García de Chávez
	Mezquitlán	59:5 f m	1/3	García de Chávez
		59 p	0/1	García de Chávez
	Mezquititique	29:3 f m	1/3	García de Chávez
		29 p	0/1	García de Chávez
	Cacaluta	25:2 f m	1/3	García de Chávez
		25½ p	0/1	García de Chávez
	San Miguel y Zanatlán	21:2 f m	1/1/5	Gonzalo de Valdenebro
		21½ p	0/1	Juan Antonio de Carmona
	Mayanalistlán, San Pedro	6:4 f m	1/1/5	Gonzalo de Valdenebro
	Tetitlán	76:1 f m	1/0/1	Rodrigo de Ojeda
		76½ p	0/0/9	Andrés de Castro
	Tepequexpan	34:8 f m	1/0/1	Andrés de Castro
		35 p	0/0/9	Andrés de Castro
	Camotlán	42:4 f m	1/0/1	Rodrigo de Ojeda
		42½ p	0/0/9	Andrés de Castro
	San Pedro, sujeto de Camotlán	16:2 f m	1/0/1	Rodrigo de Ojeda
		16½ p	0/0/9	Andrés de Castro
	Acuitlapilco y Zapotlán	47:8 f m	1/0/1	Rodrigo de Ojeda
		48 p	0/0/9	Andrés de Castro
12-XII-1582	Mascota	34:2 f m	0/7	Pedro de Enciso
		34½ p	0/0/9	Pedro de Enciso
	Tepetlatlauca y Chistique	36:6 f m	0/7	Pedro de Enciso
		37 p	0/0/9	Pedro de Enciso
	San Juan	5:6 f m	0/6	Gonzalo de Valdenebro
		9 p	0/0/8	Gonzalo de Valdenebro
		1½ mantas	3/4	Gonzalo de Valdenebro
	Papachula	7 f m	0/6	Gonzalo de Valdenebro
		7 p	0/0/8	Gonzalo de Valdenebro
		1½ mantas	3/4	Gonzalo de Valdenebro
		½ j miel	t 0/5/4	Gonzalo de Valdenebro
	Ixtapa, Santa María	5:3 f m	0/5/4	Gonzalo de Valdenebro
		9½ p	0/0/8	Gonzalo de Valdenebro

Date	Town	Item & Amount	Unit Price	Buyer & Remarks
		1 car alg	1/1/4	Gonzalo de Valdenebro
		2 @ pes	0/4/8	Gonzalo de Valdenebro
	Tepuzhuacán	9:3 f m	0/7	Pedro de Enciso
		9½ p	0/0/9	Pedro de Enciso
	Amatlán }			
	Jalacingo }	24:4 f m	0/7	Pedro de Enciso
	Ixtimitique }	24½ p	0/0/9	Pedro de Enciso
	Zacatlán	27 f m	0/7	Pedro de Enciso
	Atengoichán	18:3 f m	0/7	Pedro de Enciso
		18 p	0/0/9	Pedro de Enciso
	Acaponeta	248:10 f m	0/5	Luis Moreno de Monroy
	-como 1581 ningún diezmo de pollo	299 p	0/0/6	Rodrigo de Ojeda
	Panpuchín	21:1 f m	0/3	Andrés de Castro
		21½ p	0/0/6	Andrés de Castro
	Opono	49:9 f m	0/3	Andrés de Castro
		50 p	0/0/6	Andrés de Castro
	Contla	11:8 f m	0/3	Andrés de Castro
	Zapotlán	14 f m	0/3	Andrés de Castro
		14 p	0/0/6	Andrés de Castro
	Sila	3:7 f m	0/3	Andrés de Castro
		7 p	0/0/6	Andrés de Castro
	Piloto	7¼ pi de m	0/6	Andrés de Castro
		6:6 f m	0/3	Andrés de Castro
		13½ p	0/0/6	Andrés de Castro
	Maito	11 3/4 pi de m	0/6	Andrés de Castro
		10:7 f m	0/3	Andrés de Castro
		21½ p	0/0/6	Andrés de Castro
	Atengo	15¼ pi de m	0/6	Andrés de Castro
		13:10 f m	0/3	Andrés de Castro
		28 p	0/0/6	Andrés de Castro
	Colique	9¼ pi de m	0/6	Andrés de Castro
		8 4 f m	0/3	Andrés de Castro
		17 p	0/0/6	Andrés de Castro
17-IV-1583	Hostipaquillo y Zapotlán	201:11 f m	0/5	Bartolomé Pérez de Colio
		202 p	0/0/9	Bartolomé Pérez de Colio
4-XI-1583	Tlaltenango	(341 f m a las salinas)		
		341 p	0/1	Juan Alvarez, vecino de las minas
	Teocaltiche	(253 f m a las salinas)		
	Mitic	(120:6 f m a las salinas)		
	Teocaltitlán	(91 f m a las salinas)		
5-XI-1583	Nochistlán	252 f m	0/4/6	Juan Alvarez, vecino de las minas
		252 p	0/1/3	Juan Alvarez, vecino de las

Date	Town	Item & Amount	Unit Price	Buyer & Remarks
				minas
	Teocaltiche	252 p	0/1/3	Juan Alvarez, vecino de las minas
	Mitic	120 p	0/1/3	Juan Alvarez, vecino de las minas
	Teocaltitlán	91 p	0/1/3	Juan Alvarez, vecino de las minas
	Mexticacán	132 f m	0/4/6	Juan Alvarez, vecino de las minas
		132 p	0/1/3	Juan Alvarez, vecino de las minas
10-I-1584	Analco y Tetlán	335:8 f m	0/6/9	Antonio de Rincón
		336 p	0/1/4	Gabriel López
	Tonalá	131:8 f m	0/5/4	Juan González
		244 p	0/1/6	Lucas Ruiz
		(112:8 f m para el convento)		
	Tlaquepaque y Toluquilla	253:4 f m	0/6	Rodrigo de Ojeda
		253 p	0/1/3	Pedro de Naso
	Tlajomulco	451:10 f m	0/5/3	Licenciado Sánchez
		452 p	0/1/3	Pedro de Naso
11-I-1584	Mezquituta y Moyagua	75:7 f m	0/7	Francisco Rodriguez
		75½ p	0/1/6	Francisco Rodriguez
	Poncitlán	611:6 f m	0/5/6	Licenciado Sánchez
		611 p	0/1/2	Rodrigo de Ojeda
	Cuitzeo	80 f m	0/6	Martín Real
		(100 f m para el convento)		
		180 p	0/1/6	Can. Gaspar de Contreras
	Suchitlán	22:6 f m	0/7	Can. Gaspar de Contreras
		22½ p	0/1/6	Can. Gaspar de Contreras
	Camotlán y Cuyutlán	36 f m	0/6/9	Juan González
		36 p	0/1/5	Francisco Xuárez
	Coscotitán	38 p	0/1/3	Luis Moreno de Monroy
	Nochistlanejo	31:6 f m	0/6	Pedro de Céspedes
		31½ p	0/1/6	Pedro de Céspedes
	Atemajac	112:6 f m	0/6/7	Licenciado Sánchez
		112½ p	0/1/6	Bernabé García
	Zalatitlán	37 p	0/1/10	Francisco Xuárez
		(37:4 f m para los religiosos)		
	Cuyutlán y Cajetitlán	109:10 f m	0/6	Pedro de Naso
		110½ p	0/1/7	Francisco Xuárez
	Matatlán	43:2 f m	0/6	Francisco de Cepeda
		43½ p	0/1	Francisco de Cepeda
	Tequila	90 f m	0/6	Diego Rubio
		11 f tr	1/4	Luis Moreno de Monroy

Date	Town	Item & Amount	Unit Price	Buyer & Remarks
	Guastla o Los Guajes	5:5 f m	0/6	Diego Rubio
		5½ p	0/1	Diego Rubio
	Copala y Quilitlán	30:7 f m	0/5/6	Diego Martín de Rivera
		31 p	0/1/7	Hernando Navarrete
	Ahuisculco	29:3 f m	0/6	Pedro de Céspedes
		29½ p	0/1/3	Pedro de Céspedes
12-I-1584	Jalisco	159:3 f m	0/6/1	Juan González
		160 p	0/1/9	Hernando Navarrete
	Tepic	89:7 f m	0/6	Juan González
		89½ p	0/1	Pedro Narváez
	Analco Tepic	12:2 f m	0/6	Juan González
		12 p	0/1	Pedro Narváez
	Suchipil	49:2 f m	0/6	Pedro Narváez
		49 p	0/1/10	Hernando Navarrete
	Amaxaque	1710 f m	0/6	Pedro Narváez
		18 p	0/1/10	Hernando Navarrete
	Ahuacatlán	31:8 f m	0/6	Pedro Narváez
		32 p	0/1/10	Hernando Navarrete
	Jala	133:2 f m	0/7	Pedro Narváez
		133½ p	0/1/7	Pedro Narváez
	Camotlán	42:4 f m	0/5/7	Rodrigo de Ojeda
		42½ p	0/1	Rodrigo de Ojeda
	San Pedro	162 f m	0/5/7	Rodrigo de Ojeda
		16½ p	0/1	Rodrigo de Ojeda
	Acuitlapilco y Zapotlán	47:8 f m	0/5/7	Rodrigo de Ojeda
		48 p	0/1	Rodrigo de Ojeda
13-I-1584	Mochitiltic	30:2 f m	0/6	Juanes de Arrotia
		31 p	0/1/3	Juanes de Arrotia
	Amaxaque	14:5 f m	0/6	Juanes de Arrotia
		14 p	0/1/3	Juanes de Arrotia
	Hostotipaquillo y San Francisco	104:10 f m	0/6	Juanes de Arrotia
		105 p	0/1/3	Juanes de Arrotia
	Sentispac	204:4 f m	0/6/1	Sebastián Muñoz
		204½ p	0/1	Pedro Narváez
	Hostoticpac y Zapotlán	133:4 f m	0/4/3	Sebastián Muñoz
		133½ p	0/1	Pedro Narváez
	Mascota	34:2 f m	0/5/2	Diego de Morales
		34½ p	0/1	Juan González
	Tepetlatlauca y Chistique	36:6 f m	0/5/2	Diego de Morales
		37 p	0/1	Juan González
	Yegualtitlán	20:8 f m	0/6	Juanes de Arrotia
		21 p	0/1/3	Juanes de Arrotia
	Acatique	37:4 f m	0/6	Juanes de Arrotia
		37½ p	0/1/3	Juanes de Arrotia

Date	Town	Item & Amount	Unit Price	Buyer & Remarks
	Huelotitlán	29:8 f m	0/6	Juanes de Arrotia
		30 p	0/1/3	Juanes de Arrotia
	Inrimota	23:10 f m	0/6	Juanes de Arrotia
		26 p	0/1/3	Juanes de Arrotia
	Tequiltitlán	27 f m	0/6	Juanes de Arrotia
		27 p	0/1/3	Juanes de Arrotia
	Cuyolomitle	5:10 f m	0/6	Juanes de Arrotia
		5 p	0/1/3	Juanes de Arrotia
	Mezquitlán	59:5 f m	0/6	Juanes de Arrotia
		59 p	0/1/3	Juanes de Arrotia
	Mezquititique	29:3 f m	0/6	Juanes de Arrotia
		29 p	0/1/3	Juanes de Arrotia
	Cacaluta	25:2 f m	0/6	Juanes de Arrotia
		25½ p	0/1/3	Juanes de Arrotia
	San Juan	5:6 f m	0/4/7	Juan González
		9 p	0/0/9	Juan González
		1½ mantas	2/	Juan González
	Papachula	7 f m	0/4/7	Juan González
		7 p	0/0/9	Juan González
		1½ mantas	2/	Juan González
		½ j miel	t 0/4	Juan González
	Ixtapa, Santa María	5:3 f sal	0/4	Juan González
		9 p	0/0/9	Juan González
		1 car alg	1/	Juan González
		2 @ pes	0/4	Juan González
	Jalcocotán	49:11 f m	0/4/7	Juan González
		50 p	0/0/9	Juan González
	Mecatán	53:7 f m	0/4/7	Juan González
		53½ p	0/0/9	Juan González
	Jaltepec	9 f m	0/4/7	Juan González
		10 p	0/0/9	Juan González
		1 j miel--qtla	0/4	Juan González
	Tepuzhuacán	9:3 f m	0/4	Diego López de Velasco
		9½ p	0/1	Pedro Narváez
	Amatlán }			
	Jalacingo }	24:4 f m	0/4	Diego López de Velasco
	Ixtimitique }	24½ p	0/1	Pedro Narváez
	Zacatlán	27 f m	0/4	Diego López de Velasco
	Atengoichán	18:3 f m	0/4	Diego López de Velasco
		18½ p	0/1	Pedro Narváez
	Temichoque	18 f m	0/4/7	Juan González
		5½ @ alg	t 3/	Juan González
		11 p	0/0/9	Juan González
	Pontoque	6:9 f m	0/4/7	Juan González
		7 p	0/0/9	Juan González
	Acatispa y Canala	13:6 f m	0/4/7	Juan González

Date	Town	Item & Amount	Unit Price	Buyer & Remarks
		13½ p	0/0/9	Juan González
	Ixtapa, de Castañeda	7 f sal	0/4	Juan González
	Quilitlán	18 f m	0/4/7	Juan González
		1 @ miel	2/	Juan González
	Matacticpac	11:8 f m	0/4/7	Juan González
		12 p	0/0/9	Juan González
	Ixcuintla	41:5 f m	0/6	Juan González
		41½ p	0/1	Juan González
	San Miguel y Zanatlán	21:2 f m	0/4/7	Juan González
		21½ p	0/0/9	Juan González
	San Pedro Mayanalistlán	6:4 f m	0/4/7	Juan González
	Acaponeta } Quebiquito } Tetitlán } (después del diezmo)	173:8 f m	0/3	Rodrigo de Ojeda
		174 p	0/0/6	Rodrigo de Ojeda
	Tetitlán	67:6 f m	0/5/7	Rodrigo de Ojeda
		68 p	0/1	Rodrigo de Ojeda
	Tepequexpan	34:8 f m	0/5/7	Rodrigo de Ojeda
		35 p	0/1	Rodrigo de Ojeda
	Zapotlán	11 f m	0/3/6	Pedro de Naso
		11 p	0/0/9	Pedro de Naso
	Sila	3:7 f m	0/3/6	Pedro de Naso
		7 p	0/0/9	Pedro de Naso
	Panpuchín	19:3 f m	0/3/6	Pedro de Naso
		19 p	0/0/9	Pedro de Naso
	Contla	11:8 f m	0/3/6	Pedro de Naso
	Opono	47:8 f m	0/3/6	Pedro de Naso
		48 p	0/0/9	Pedro de Naso
	Piloto y sujetos:			
	Maito }	47 f m	0/3/3	Pedro de Naso
	Colique }	64 p	0/0/9	Pedro de Naso
	Atengo }	21 pi de m	0/6	Gonzalo de Valdenebro
3-XI-1584	Tlaltenango	341 p	0/1	Antonio López de Cepeda
		341 f m	---a las salinas	
	Nochistlán	252 f m	0/2/6	Antonio López de Cepeda
		252 p	0/1	Antonio López de Cepeda
	Teocaltiche	253 p	0/1	Antonio López de Cepeda
		253 f m	---a last salinas	
	Teocaltitlán	91 p	0/1	Antonio López de Cepeda
		91 f m	---a las salinas	
	Mitic	120 p	0/1	Antonio López de Cepeda
		120 f m	---a las salinas	
	Mexticacán	132 f m	0/2/6	Antonio López de Cepeda

Date	Town	Item & Amount	Unit Price	Buyer & Remarks
		132 p	0/1	Antonio López de Cepeda
8-I-1585	Poncitlán	534:11 f m	0/6	Francisco de Plaza
		535 p	0/1/6	Juan de la Cueva
	Cuitzeo	80 f m	0/8/7	Juan González de Apodaca
		180 p	0/1	Juan González de Apodaca
		(100 f m para el convento)		
	Nochistlanejo	31:6 f m	0/6	Alonso de Céspedes
		31½ p	0/2	Alonso de Céspedes
	Ahuisculco	29:3 f m	0/5	Pedro de Céspedes
		29½ p	0/1/6	Pedro de Céspedes
10-I-1585	Mezquituta y Moyagua	75:7 f m	0/3	Juan Toledano
		75½ p	0/1	Juan Toledano
	Matatlán	43:2 f m	0/6	Francisco de Cepeda
		43½ p	0/1/6	Francisco de Cepeda
11-I-1585	Atemajac	112:6 f m	0/4	Diego Martín de Rivera
		112½ p	0/1/3	Diego Muñoz
	Zalatitlán	37 p	0/1/5	Diego Martín de Rivera
		(37:4 f m para los religiosos)		
	Cuyutlán y Cajetitlán	109:10 f m	0/4/6	Gonzalo de Valdenebro
		110½ p	0/1/6	Diego Martín de Rivera
	Tequila	90 f m	0/3/3	Gaspar Vaca
		11 f tr	0/6	Gaspar Vaca
	Guastla o Los Guajes	5:5 f m	0/3/3	Gaspar Vaca
		5½ p	0/0/6	Gaspar Vaca
	Copala y Quilitlán	30:7 f m	0/3	Gaspar Vaca
		31 p	0/1	Gaspar Vaca
	Analco y Tetlán	335:8 f m	0/5/6	Indios de Analco
		336 p	0/1/6	Gaspar Vaca
	Tonalá	131:8 f m	0/5/3	Gonzalo de Valdenebro
		244 p	0/1/3	Gaspar Vaca
		(112 f m para el convento)		
	Tlaquepaque y Toluquilla	253:4 f m	0/5	Gerónimo Mexía
		253 p	0/1/5	Gaspar Vaca
	Tlajomulco	451:10 f m	0/4/3	Pedro de Naso
		452 p	0/1/6	Pedro de Naso
12-I-1585	Suchitlán	22:6 f m	0/2	Gaspar Vaca
		22½ p	0/1	Gaspar Vaca
	Camotlán y Cuyutlán	36 f m	0/3	Bernabé García
		36 p	0/1	Bernabé García
	Coscotitán	38 p	0/1	Bernabé García
	Jalisco	159:3 f m	0/3	Diego Martín de Rivera
		160 p	0/1	Diego Martín de Rivera
	Mascota	34:2 f m	0/2/6	Antonio de Aguayo
		34½ p	0/1	Antonio de Aguayo

Date	Town	Item & Amount	Unit Price	Buyer & Remarks
	Tepic	39:7 f m	0/3	Diego Martín de Rivera
		39½ p	0/1	Diego Martín de Rivera
	Analco Tepic	12:2 f m	0/3	Diego Martín de Rivera
		12 p	0/1	Diego Martín de Rivera
	San Juan	5:6 f m	0/2	Diego Martín de Rivera
		9 p	0/0/9	Diego Martín de Rivera
		1½ mantas	2/	Diego Martín de Rivera
	Papachula	7 f m	0/2	Diego Martín de Rivera
		7 p	0/0/9	Diego Martín de Rivera
		1½ mantas	2/	Diego Martín de Rivera
		½ j miel	t 0/4	Diego Martín de Rivera
	Ixtapa, Santa María	5:3 f sal	0/4	Diego Martín de Rivera
		9½ p	0/0/9	Diego Martín de Rivera
		1 car alg	1/	Diego Martín de Rivera
		2 @ pes	0/4	Diego Martín de Rivera
	Jalcocotán	49:11 f m	0/2	Diego Martín de Rivera
		50 p	0/0/9	Diego Martín de Rivera
	Mecatán	53:7 f m	0/2	Diego Martín de Rivera
		53½ p	0/0/9	Diego Martín de Rivera
	Jaltepec	9 f m	0/2	Diego Martín de Rivera
		10 p	0/0/9	Diego Martín de Rivera
		1 j miel--qtla	0/4	Diego Martín de Rivera
	Atengoichán	18:3 f m	0/2	Antonio de Aguayo
		18½ p	0/1	Antonio de Aguayo
	Temichoque	18 f m	0/2	Diego Martín de Rivera
		5½ @ alg	t 3/	Diego Martín de Rivera
		11 p	0/0/9	Diego Martín de Rivera
	Pontoque	6:9 f m	0/2	Diego Martín de Rivera
		7 p	0/0/9	Diego Martín de Rivera
	Acatispa y Canala	13:6 f m	0/2	Diego Martín de Rivera
		13½ p	0/0/9	Diego Martín de Rivera
	Ixtapa, de Castañeda	7 f sal	0/4	Diego Martín de Rivera
	Quilitlán	18 f m	0/2	Diego Martín de Rivera
		1 @ miel	2/	Diego Martín de Rivera
	Matacticpac	11:8 f m	0/2	Diego Martín de Rivera
		12 p	0/0/9	Diego Martín de Rivera
	Ixcuintla	41:5 f m	0/2	Diego Martín de Rivera
		41½ p	0/0/9	Diego Martín de Rivera
	San Miguel y Zanatlán	21:2 f m	0/2	Diego Martín de Rivera
		21½ p	0/0/9	Diego Martín de Rivera
	Mayanalistlán, San Pedro	6:4 f m	0/2	Diego Martín de Rivera
	Acaponeta	173:8 f m	0/2/6	Juan Vélez de Vargas
		174 p	0/1	Diego Martín de Rivera
15-I-1585	Panpuchín	16:9 f m	0/2	Diego Martín de Rivera

Date	Town	Item & Amount	Unit Price	Buyer & Remarks
		17 p	0/0/9	Diego Martín de Rivera
	Zapotlán	5:5 f m	0/2	Diego Martín de Rivera
		5½ p	0/0/9	Diego Martín de Rivera
	Sila	3:7 f m	0/2	Diego Martín de Rivera
		7 p	0/0/9	Diego Martín de Rivera
	Contla	11:8 f m	0/2	Diego Martín de Rivera
	Opono	47:8 f m	0/2	Diego Martín de Rivera
		48 p	0/0/9	Diego Martín de Rivera
	Piloto y sujetos:			
	Maito }	53:1 f m	0/2	Diego Martín de Rivera
	Colique }	53 p	0/0/9	Diego Martín de Rivera
	Atengo }			
	Yegualtitlán	20:8 f m	0/4/6	Juanes de Arrotia
		21 p	0/1/1	Diego Rubio
	Acatique	37:4 f m	0/4/6	Juanes de Arrotia
		37½ p	0/1/1	Diego Rubio
	Huelotitlán	29:8 f m	0/4/6	Juanes de Arrotia
		30 p	0/1/1	Diego Rubio
	Inrimota	23:10 f m	0/4/6	Juanes de Arrotia
		26 p	0/1/1	Diego Rubio
	Tequiltitlán	27 f m	0/4/6	Juanes de Arrotia
		27 p	0/1/1	Diego Rubio
	Cuyolomitle	5:10 f m	0/4/6	Juanes de Arrotia
		5 p	0/1/1	Diego Rubio
	Mezquitlán	59:5 f m	0/4/6	Juanes de Arrotia
		59 p	0/1/1	Diego Rubio
	Mezquititique	29:3 f m	0/4/6	Juanes de Arrotia
		29 p	0/1/1	Diego Rubio
	Cacaluta	25:2 f m	0/4/6	Juanes de Arrotia
		25½ p	0/1/1	Diego Rubio
	Mochitiltic	30:2 f m	0/4/6	Juanes de Arrotia
		31 p	0/1/1	Diego Rubio
	Amaxaque	14:5 f m	0/4/6	Juanes de Arrotia
		14 p	0/1/1	Diego Rubio
	Hostotipaquillo	104:10 f m	0/3	Pedro Alvarez
	y San Francisco	105 p	0/0/9	Pedro Alvarez
	Sentispac	204:4 f m	0/3/7	Diego Rubio
		204½ p	0/1	Diego Martín de Rivera
16-I-1585	Tepuzhuacán	9:3 f m	0/2/6	Diego de Morales
		9½ p	0/0/9	Diego de Morales
	Amatlán }			
	Jalacingo }	24:4 f m	0/2/6	Diego de Morales
	Ixtimitique }	24 p	0/0/9	Diego de Morales
	Zacatlán	27 f m	0/2/6	Diego de Morales

Date	Town	Item & Amount	Unit Price	Buyer & Remarks
	Tetitlán	55:8 f m	0/2/6	Diego Martín de Rivera
		56 p	0/1	Diego Martín de Rivera
	Tepequexpan	34:8 f m	0/2/6	Diego Martín de Rivera
		35 p	0/1	Diego Martín de Rivera
	Camotlán	42:4 f m	0/2/6	Diego Martín de Rivera
		42½ p	0/1	Diego Martín de Rivera
	San Pedro	16:2 f m	0/2/6	Diego Martín de Rivera
		16½ p	0/1	Diego Martín de Rivera
	Acuitlapilco y Zapotlán	47:8 f m	0/2/6	Diego Martín de Rivera
		48 p	0/1	Diego Martín de Rivera
	Hostoticpac y Zapotlán	201:10 f m	0/3	Lázaro Blanco
		202 p	0/1	Diego Martín de Rivera
	Tepetlatlauca y Chistique	36:6 f m	0/2/6	Diego de Morales
		37 p	0/0/9	Diego de Morales
	Suchipil	49 f m	0/2/6	Diego de Morales
		49 p	0/1	Diego de Morales
	Amaxaque	17:10 f m	0/2/6	Diego de Morales
		18 p	0/1	Diego de Morales
	Ahuacatlán	31:8 f m	0/2/6	Diego de Morales
		32 p	0/1	Diego de Morales
	Jala	133:2 f m	0/2/6	Diego de Morales
		133½ p	0/1	Diego de Morales
24-X-1585	Tlaltenango de las minas	301 p	0/1	Alonso de Herrera, vecino
		301 f m	---a las salinas	
	Nochistlán	252 f m	0/3	Alonso de Herrera
		252 p	0/1	Alosno de Herrera
	Mitic	120:6 f m	---a las salinas	
		120 p	0/1	Alonso de Herrera
	Teocaltiche	253 f m	---a las salinas	
		253 p	0/1	Alonso de Herrera
	Teocaltitlán	91 f m	---a las salinas	
		91 p	0/1	Alonso de Herrera
	Mexticacán	117 f m	0/3	Alonso de Herrera
		117 p	0/1	Alonso de Herrera
9-I-1586	Analco y Tetlán	335:8 f m	0/6	Oficiales del pueblo de Analco y Tetlán
		336 p	0/1/3	Gaspar Vaca de Ayala
	Tonalá	131:8 f m	0/6	Pedro de Naso
		(112:8 f m para el convento)		
		244 p	0/1	Juan González de Apodaca
	Atemajac	112:6 f m	0/6/6	Francisco de Plaza
		112½ p	0/1/3	Diego Rubio
	Tlajomulco	451:10 f m	0/6/9	Juan González
		452 p	0/1/1	Andrés Venegas

Date	Town	Item & Amount	Unit Price	Buyer & Remarks
	Poncitlán	364:6 f m	0/6/8	Juan González
		364½ p	0/1	Alvaro de Figueroa
	Cuitzeo	78:4 f m	0/7	Juan González de Apodaca
		(100 f m para el convento)		
		178½ p	0/0/9	Juan González de Apodaca
	Suchitlán	22:6 f m	0/3	Francisco de Plaza
		22½ p	0/0/8	Francisco de Plaza
	Camotlán y Cuyutlán	36 f m	0/5	Bernabé García
		36 p	0/1	Bernabé García
	Coscotitán	38 p	0/1	Bernabé García
	Nochistlanejo	31:6 f m	0/7	Pedro de Céspedes
		31½ p	0/2	Pedro de Céspedes
10-I-1586	Zalatitlán	37 p	0/1/3	Francisco Xuárez
		(37:4 f m para los religiosos)		
	Cuyutlán y Cajetitlán	109:10 f m	0/6/10	Francisco Xuárez
		110½ p	0/1/3	Francisco Xuárez
	Matatlán	37:10 f m	0/6	Francisco de Cepeda
		38 p	0/1	Francisco de Cepeda
	Copala y Quilitlán	30:7 f m	0/6	Bernabé García
		31 p	0/1	Bernabé García
	Tequila	90 f m	0/6	Gonzalo de Valdenebro
		11 f tr	1/	Gonzalo de Valdenebro
	Guastla o Los Guajes	5:5 f m	0/5	Gaspar Vaca
		5½ p	0/1	Gaspar Vaca
	Ahuisculco	29:3 f m	0/6	Gaspar Vaca
		29½ p	0/1/3	Pedro de Céspedes
	Mochitiltic	30:2 f m	0/5/11	Juan González
		31 p	0/0/9	Juan González
	Amaxaque	14:5 f m	0/5/11	Juan González
		14 p	0/0/9	Juan González
	Hostotipaquillo y San Francisco	104:10 f m	0/5/11	Juan González
		105 p	0/0/9	Juan González
	Yegualtitlán	20:8 f m	0/5/11	Juan González
		21 p	0/0/9	Juan González
	Acatique	37:4 f m	0/5/11	Juan González
		37½ p	0/0/9	Juan González
	Huelotitlán	29:8 f m	0/5/11	Juan González
		30 p	0/0/9	Juan González
	Inrimota	23:10 f m	0/5/11	Juan González
		24 p	0/0/9	Juan González
	Tequiltitlán	27 f m	0/5/11	Juan González
		27 p	0/0/9	Juan González
	Cuyolomitle	5:10 f m	0/5/11	Juan González
		5 p	0/0/9	Juan González

Date	Town	Item & Amount	Unit Price	Buyer & Remarks
	Mezquitlán	59:5 f m	0/5/11	Juan González
		59 p	0/0/9	Juan González
	Mezquititique	29:3 f m	0/5/11	Juan González
		29 p	0/0/9	Juan González
	Cacaluta	25:2 f m	0/5/11	Juan González
		25½ p	0/0/9	Juan González
	Mascota	34:2 f m	0/5	Lic. Sotomayor
		34½ p	0/1	Lic. Sotomayor
	Tepetlatlauca y Chistique	36:6 f m	0/5	Lic. Sotomayor
		37 p	0/1	Lic. Sotomayor
	Hostoticpac y Zapotlán	201:10 f m	0/6	Juan de Ledesma
		202 p	0/0/9	Juan de Ledesma
	Jalisco	159:3 f m	0/6/4	Diego de Morales
		160 p	0/1	Diego de Morales
	Tepic	89:7 f m	0/6/2	Gaspar Vaca
		89½ p	0/1	Gaspar Vaca
	Analco Tepic	12:2 f m	0/6/2	Gaspar Vaca
		12 p	0/1	Gaspar Vaca
	Sentispac	204:4 f m	0/7/6	Juan de Ledesma
		204½ p	0/1	Diego Nieto
	Suchipil	75:8 f m	0/6/6	Francisco Rodríguez
		76 p	0/1/3	Francisco Rodríguez
11-I-1586	Mezquituta y Moyagua	75:7 f m	0/4/6	Gaspar Vaca de Ayala
		75½ p	0/1	Gaspar Vaca de Ayala
	Amaxaque	17:10 f m	0/6/6	Francisco Rodríguez
		18 p	0/1/3	Francisco Rodríguez
	Ahuacatlán	31:3 f m	0/6/6	Francisco Rodríguez
		31½ p	0/1/3	Francisco Rodríguez
	Jala	140:7 f m	0/6/6	Gaspar Vaca de Ayala
		141 p	0/1/3	Lázaro Blanco
	Tetitlán	65:8 f m	0/5/6	Gaspar Vaca de Ayala
		66 p	0/1	Gaspar Vaca de Ayala
	Tepequexpan	34:8 f m	0/5/6	Gaspar Vaca de Ayala
		35 p	0/1	Gaspar Vaca de Ayala
	Camotlán	42:4 f m	0/5/6	Gaspar Vaca de Ayala
		42½ p	0/1	Gaspar Vaca de Ayala
	San Pedro	15:2 f m	0/5/6	Gaspar Vaca de Ayala
		15½ p	0/1	Gaspar Vaca de Ayala
	Acuitlapilco y Zapotlán	47:8 f m	0/5/6	Gaspar Vaca de Ayala
		43 p	0/1	Gaspar Vaca de Ayala
	Tlaquepaque y Toluquilla	253:4 f m	0/6/7	Juan González de Apodaca
		253 p	0/1/2	Francisco Rodríguez
	San Juan	5 6 f m	0/7/6	Juan de Ledesma
		9 p	0/1	Juan de Ledesma

Date	Town	Item & Amount	Unit Price	Buyer & Remarks
		1½ mantas	t 3/0/9	Juan de Ledesma
	Papachula	7 f m	0/7/6	Juan de Ledesma
		7 p	0/1	Juan de Ledesma
		1½ mantas	t 3/0/9	Juan de Ledesma
		½ j miel	t 0/5	Juan de Ledesma
	Ixtapa, Santa María	5:3 f sal	0/4/6	Juan de Ledesma
		9½ p	0/1	Juan de Ledesma
		1 car alg	1/0/6	Juan de Ledesma
		2 @ pes	0/4/6	Juan de Ledesma
	Jalcocotán	49:11 f m	0/7/6	Juan de Ledesma
		50 p	0/1	Juan de Ledesma
	Mecatán	53:7 f m	0/7/6	Juan de Ledesma
		53½ p	0/1	Juan de Ledesma
	Jaltepec	9 f m	0/7/6	Juan de Ledesma
		10 p	0/1	Juan de Ledesma
		1 j miel--qtla	0/5/1½	Juan de Ledesma
	Temichoque	18 f m	0/4/6	Juan de Ledesma
		5½ @ alg	0/4/6	Juan de Ledesma
		11 p	0/1	Juan de Ledesma
	Pontoque	6:9 f m	0/7/6	Juan de Ledesma
		7 p	0/1	Juan de Ledesma
	Acatispa y Canala	13:6 f m	0/7/6	Juan de Ledesma
		13½ p	0/1	Juan de Ledesma
	Ixtapa, de Castañeda	7 f sal	0/4/6	Juan de Ledesma
	Quilitlán	18 f m	0/7/6	Juan de Ledesma
		1 @ miel	2/4/6	Juan de Ledesma
	Matacticpac	11:8 f m	0/7/6	Juan de Ledesma
		12 p	0/1	Juan de Ledesma
	Acaponeta	173:8 f m	1/0/3	Lázaro Blanco
		174 p	0/1/3	Lázaro Blanco
13-I-1586	San Miguel y Zanatlán	21:2 f m	0/7/6	Juan de Ledesma
		21½ p	0/1	Juan de Ledesma
	Ixcuintla	24:4 f m	0/7/6	Juan de Ledesma
		24 p	0/1	Juan de Ledesma
	Mayanalistlán, San Pedro	6:4 f m	0/7/6	Juan de Ledesma
	Atengoichán	18:3 f m	0/4/11	Lic. Sotomayor
		18½ p	0/1/1	Lic. Sotomayor
	Zacatlán	27 f m	0/4/11	Lic. Sotomayor
	Amatlán) Jalacingo) Iximitique)	24:4 f m	0/4/11	Lic. Sotomayor
		24½ p	0/1/1	Lic. Sotomayor
	Tepuzhuacán	9:3 f m	0/4/11	Lic. Sotomayor
		9½ p	0/1/1	Lic. Sotomayor

Date	Town	Item & Amount	Unit Price	Buyer & Remarks
	Jaltemba, Santa María (1580-1585)	58:8 f m	0/2	Juan de Ledesma
		59½ p	0/0/6	Juan de Ledesma
		5½ j miel blanca	0/6	Juan de Ledesma
	Panpuchín	16:9 f m	0/4/1	Francisco Xuárez
		17 p	0/0/10	Francisco Xuárez
	Zapotlán	5:5 f m	0/4/1	Francisco Xuárez
		5½ p	0/0/10	Francisco Xuárez
	Sila	3:7 f m	0/4/1	Francisco Xuárez
		7 p	0/0/10	Francisco Xuárez
	Contla	11:8 f m	0/4/1	Francisco Xuárez
	Opono	47:8 f m	0/4/1	Francisco Xuárez
		48 p	0/0/10	Francisco Xuárez
	Piloto y sujetos: Maito } Colique } Atengo }	53:1 f m	0/4/1	Francisco Xuárez
		53 p	0/0/10	Francisco Xuárez
9-I-1587	Atemajac	112:6 f m	1/	Antonio Vélez de Vargas
		112½ p	0/1/2	Diego Rubio
10-I-1587	Huelotitlán	29:8 f m	1/0/2	Martín de Mendizábal
		30 p	0/1	Martín de Mendizábal
13-I-1587	Analco y Tetlán	335:8 f m	1/	Antonio Vélez de Vargas
		336 p	0/1/3	Martín de Mendizábal
	Tonalá	131:8 f m	1/0/4	Pedro Narváez
		(112:8 f m para el convento)		
		244 p	0/1	Pedro Narváez
	Tlaquepaque y Toluquilla	253:4 f m	1/1	Antonio Vélez de Vargas
		253 p	0/1/1	Andrés Venegas
	Tlajomulco	451:10 f m	1/0/2	Antonio Vélez de Vargas
		452 p	0/1/1	Francisco de Saldívar
	Poncitlán	364:6 f m	1/1/7	Diego de Porres
		364½ p	0/1	Juan González
	Cuitzeo	46:8 f m	1/1/9	Diego de Porres
		(100 f m para el convento)		
		147 p	0/0/9	Juan González
	Suchitlán	22:6 f m	0/3	Francisco de Plaza
		22½ p	0/1	Francisco de Plaza
14-I-1587	Tesistán	44:6 f m	1/	Antonio Vélez de Vargas
		45 p	0/1	Francisco de Plaza
	Epatlán	18:5 f m	1/	Antonio Vélez de Vargas
		18½ p	0/1	Antonio Vélez de Vargas
	Tepeaca	23 5 f m	1/	Antonio Vélez de Vargas
		23½ p	0/1	Antonio Vélez de Vargas
	Camotlán y Cuyutlán	36 f m	1/	Juan Rodríguez
		36 p	0/1	Juan Rodríguez

Date	Town	Item & Amount	Unit Price	Buyer & Remarks
	Coscotitán	40½ p	0/1	Juan Rodríguez
	Nochistlanejo	31:6 f m 31½ p	1/0/6 0/1	Francisco Ridríguez Pedro de Céspedes
	Zalatitlán	37 p (36:4 f m para el convento)	0/1/2	Rodrigo de Ojeda
	Cuyutlán y Cajititlán	109:10 f m 110½ p	1/1/6 0/1/2	Francisco Rodríguez Rodrigo de Ojeda
	Matatlán	36 f m 36 p	1/1/6 0/1	Francisco de Cepeda Francisco de Cepeda
	Copala y Quilitlán	23 f m 23 p	0/7/6 0/1	Diego Martín de Rivera Diego Martín de Rivera
	Tequila	90 f m 11 f tr	1/0/6 1/1	Antonio Vélez de Vargas Antonio Vélez de Vargas
	Guastla o Los Guajes	5:5 f m 5½ p	1/0/6 0/1	Antonio Vélez de Vargas Antonio Vélez de Vargas
	Ahuisculco	29:3 f m 29½ p	1/0/7 0/1	Francisco Rodríguez Juan González
19-I-1587	Mochitiltic	30:2 f m 31 p	1/0/2 0/1	Martín de Mendizábal Martín de Mendizábal
	Hostotipaquillo y San Francisco	104:10 f m 105 p	1/0/2 0/1	Martín de Mendizábal Martín de Mendizábal
	Amaxaque	14:5 f m 14½ p	1/0/2 0/1	Martín de Mendizábal Martín de Mendizábal
	Yegualtitlán	20:8 f m 21 p	1/0/2 0/1	Martín de Mendizábal Martín de Mendizábal
	Acatique	37:4 f m 37½ p	1/0/2 0/1	Martín de Mendizábal Martín de Mendizábal
	Inrimota	23:10 f m 24 p	1/0/2 0/1	Martín de Mendizábal Martín de Mendizábal
	Tequiltitlán	27 f m 27 p	1/0/2 0/1	Martín de Mendizábal Martín de Mendizábal
	Cuyolomitle	5:10 f m 5½ p	1/0/2 0/1	Martín de Mendizábal Martín de Mendizábal
	Mezquitlán	59:5 f m 59½ p	1/0/2 0/1	Martín de Mendizábal Martín de Mendizábal
	Mezquititique o Sta. María Terequita	29:3 f m 25½ p	1/0/2 0/1	Martín de Mendizábal Martín de Mendizábal
	Cacaluta	25:2 f m 25½ p	1/0/2 0/1	Martín de Mendizábal Martín de Mendizábal
	Hostotipac y Zapotlán	201:10 f m 202 p	0/6 0/1/1	Juan de Ledesma Juan de Ledesma
	Jalisco	159:3 f m 160 p	1/2 0/1	Melchor de Brito Melchor de Brito

Date	Town	Item & Amount	Unit Price	Buyer & Remarks
	Tepic	89:7 f m	1/3	Antonio de Alcega
		89½ p	0/1	Antonio de Alcega
	Analco Tepic	12:2 f m	1/3	Antonio de Alcega
		12 p	0/1	Antonio de Alcega
	Sentispac	204:4 f m	1/0/6	Melchor de Brito
		204½ p	0/1	Melchor de Brito
	Acaponeta	173:8 f m	1/1	Juan Salado
		174 p	0/1	Juan Salado
19-I-1587	Suchipíl	112:6 f m	1/	Antón Martín
		113 p	0/1/5	Antón Martín
	Amaxaque	17:10 f m	1/	Antón Martín
		18 p	0/1/5	Antón Martín
	Ahuacatlán	30:7 f m	1/	Antón Martín
		30½ p	0/1/5	Antón Martín
	Jala	161:4 f m	0/6/7	Pedro Narváez
		161½ p	0/1	Francisco de Saldívar
	Tetitlán	65:8 f m	0/6/9	Melchor de Brito
		66 p	0/1	Francisco de Saldívar
	Tepequexpan	34:8 f m	0/6/9	Melchor de Brito
		35 p	0/1	Francisco de Saldívar
	Camotlán	42:4 f m	0/6/9	Melchor de Brito
		42½ p	0/2	Francisco de Saldívar
	San Pedro	16:2 f m	0/6/9	Melchor de Brito
		16½ p	0/1	Francisco de Saldívar
	Acuitlapilco y Zapotlán	47:8 f m	0/6/1	Pedro Narváez
		48 p	0/1	Pedro Narváez
	Jaltemba, Sta. María	10:10 f m	0/6/1	Pedro Narváez
		11 p	0/1	Pedro Narváez
		1 j miel blanca	1/	Pedro Narváez
	Tosmotoc, San Miguel	38:11 f m	1/0/3	Antonio de Alcega
		39 p	0/1	Juan de Ledesma
	San Juan	5:6 f m	1/0/3	Antonio de Alcega
		9 p	0/1	Juan de Ledesma
		1½ mantas	5/	Juan de Ledesma
	Papachula	7 f m	1/0/3	Antonio de Alcega
		7 p	0/1	Juan de Ledesma
		1½ mantas	5/	Juan de Ledesma
		½ j miel	t 0/5	Juan de Ledesma
	Ixtapa, Santa María	5:3 f sal	0/5/3	Antonio de Alcega
		9½ p	0/1	Juan de Ledesma
		1 car alg	1/	Juan de Ledesma
		2 @ pes	0/4	Juan de Ledesma
	Jalcocotán	49:11 f m	1/0/3	Antonio de Alcega
		50 p	0/1	Juan de Ledesma
	Mecatán	53:7 f m	1/0/3	Antonio de Alcega

Date	Town	Item & Amount	Unit Price	Buyer & Remarks
		53½ p	0/1	Juan de Ledesma
	Jaltepec	9 f m	1/0/3	Antonio de Alcega
		10 p	0/1	Juan de Ledesma
		1 j miel--qtla	0/5	Juan de Ledesma
	Temichoque	18 f m	1/0/3	Antonio de Alcega
		5½ @ alg	t 3/2	Juan de Ledesma
		11 p	0/1	Juan de Ledesma
	Pontoque	6:9 f m	1/0/3	Antonio de Alcega
		7 p	0/1	Juan de Ledesma
	Acatispa y Canala	13:6 f m	1/0/3	Antonio de Alcega
		13½ p	0/1	Juan de Ledesma
	Ixtapa, de Castañeda	7 f sal	0/5/3	Antonio de Alcega
	Quilitlán	18 f m	1/0/3	Antonio de Alcega
		1 @ miel	1/1	Juan de Ledesma
	Matacticpac	11:8 f m	1/0/3	Antonio de Alcega
		12 p	0/1	Juan de Ledesma
	Ixcuintla	18:11 f m	1/0/3	Antonio de Alcega
		19 p	0/1	Juan de Ledesma
	San Miguel y Zanalatitlán	21:2 f m	1/0/3	Antonio de Alcega
		21½ p	0/1	Juan de Ledesma
	Mayanalistlán, San Pedro	6:4 f m	1/0/3	Antonio de Alcega
	Tomatlán	9 f m	1/0/3	Antonio de Alcega
		2 g	0/2/6	Juan de Ledesma
		2 j miel	0/5	Juan de Ledesma
	Cusmini, San Andrés	9 f m	1/0/3	Antonio de Alcega
		2 j miel	1/	Juan de Ledesma
	Jalisquillo	18 f m	1/0/3	Antonio de Alcega
	Teocaltiche (incluido el ajuste por exceso de pago)	41:10 f m	0/4	Alvaro de Figueroa
		42 p	0/1	Alvaro de Figueroa
	Mezquituta y Moyagua	75:7 f m	0/7/1	Francisco de Plaza
		75½ p	0/1	Francisco de Plaza
24-I-1587	Mascota	34:2 f m	0/4	Juan de Ledesma
		34½ p	0/1	Juan de Ledesma
	Tepetlatlauca y Chistique	36:6 f m	0/4	Juan de Ledesma
		36 p	0/1	Juan de Ledesma
	Atengoichán	18:3 f m	0/4	Juan de Ledesma
		18½ p	0/1	Juan de Ledesma
	Zacatlán	27 f m	0/4	Juan de Ledesma
	Amatlán } Jalacingo } Iximitique}	24:4 f m	0/4	Juan de Ledesma
		24½ p	0/1	Juan de Ledesma

Date	Town	Item & Amount	Unit Price	Buyer & Remarks
	Tepuzhuacán	9:3 f m	0/4	Juan de Ledesma
		9½ p	0/1	Juan de Ledesma
	Panpuchín	16:9 f m	0/4	Martín Real
		17 p	0/1	Martín Real
	Zapotlán	5:5 f m	0/4	Martín Real
		5½ p	0/1	Martín Real
	Sila	3:7 f m	0/4	Martín Real
		7 p	0/1	Martín Real
	Contla	11:8 f m	0/4	Martín Real
	Opono	47:8 f m	0/4	Martín Real
		48 p	0/1	Martín Real
	Piloto y sujetos:			
	Maito }	53:1 f m	0/4	Martín Real
	Colique }	53 p	0/1	Martín Real
	Atengo }			
15-XI-1587	Tlaltenango	300½ p	0/1	Miguel de Figueroa
	Nota: Ninguna mención de maiz; probablemente las 300:6 fanegas se mandaron a las salinas.			
	Nochistlán	252 f m	0/3/6	Miguel de Figueroa
		252 p	0/1	Miguel de Figueroa
	Teocaltiche	253 p	0/1	Miguel de Figueroa
		253 f m	---a las salinas	
	Mitic	91½ p	0/1	Miguel de Figueroa
		91:6 f m	---a las salinas	
16-XI-1587	Teocaltitlán	91 p	0/1	Miguel de Figueroa
		91 f m	---a las salinas	
	Mexticacán	117 f m	0/3/6	Miguel de Figueroa
		117 p	0/1	Miguel de Figueroa
15-I-1591	Yahualica	(19:7 f m	0/5	Bernabé García
	1589	(19½ p	0/1	Bernabé García
		67:6 f m	0/5/1	Bernabé García
		66½ p	0/1	Bernabé García
	Analco y Tetlán	335:8 f m	1/0/4	Andrés Venegas
		336 p	0/1/7	Andrés Venegas
	Tonalá	131:8 f m	1/1/2	Jaime Pérez
		(112:8 f m para el convento)		
		244 p	0/1/9	Diego Martín de Rivera
	Tlaquepaque y Toluquilla	253:4 f m	1/1/6	Diego de Porres
		253 p	0/2/1	Francisco Martín
	Atemajac	112:6 f m	1/1	Jaime Pérez
		112½ p	0/2	P. Alvaro de Vergara
	Tlajomulco	451:10 f m	1/2	Jaime Pérez
		452 p	0/2	P. Alvaro de Vergara
	Zalatitlán	37 p	0/1/9	Diego Martín de Rivera
		(37:4 f m para el convento)		

Date	Town	Item & Amount	Unit Price	Buyer & Remarks
	Cuyutlán y Cajititlán	109:10 f m	1/2/1	Diego de Porres
		110½ p	0/2	Bernabé García
16-I-1591	Poncitlán	364:6 f m	1/4	Antonio Méndez Soldado
		364 p	0/1/4	Pedro de Cuellar
	Cuitzeo	46:8 f m	1/3	Antonio Méndez Soldado
		(100 f m para el convento)		
		147 p	0/1/3	Rodrigo Hernández Cordero
	Suchitlán	22:6 f m	0/6/2	Francisco de Cepeda
		22½ p	0/1/6	Hernando de Plasencia
	Tesistán	44:6 f m	1/	Fran. de Cepeda, Relator
		45 p	0/1/7	Andrés Venegas
	Epatlán	18:5 f m	1/0	Fran. de Cepeda, Relator
		18½ p	0/1/7	Andrés Venegas
	Tepeaca	23:5 f m	1/	Fran. de Cepeda, Relator
		23½ p	0/1/7	Andrés Venegas
	Camotlán y Cuyutlán	18½ p	0/1/6	Fran. de Morales, Tesorero de la Santa Iglesia
	Coscotitán, San Cristobal	46½ p	0/1/6	Juan Sánchez de la Palma
	Nochistlanejo	31:6 f m	1/1	Juan Toledano
		31½ p	0/1/11	Bernabé García
	Matatlán	36 f m	1/	Juan Toledano
		36 p	0/1/3	Pedro de Cuellar
	Copala y Quilitlán	18 f m	1/4	Fran. de Cepeda, Relator
		18 p	0/2/2	Fran. de Cepeda, Relator
	Tequila y San Francisco	117:11 f m	1/1	Juan de Ledesma
		118 p	0/1/6	Don Fran. de Morales, Tesorero de la Santa Iglesia
	Guastla o Los Guajes	5:5 f m	1/1	Juan de Ledesma
		5½ p	0/1/6	Don Fran. de Morales, Tesorero de la Santa Iglesia
	Ahuisculco	29:3 f m	0/7/4	Antonio Vélez de Vargas
		29½ p	0/1/2	Antonio Vélez de Vargas
	Mochitiltic	30:2 f m	0/6	Antonio de Alcega
		31 p	0/1	Antonio de Alcega
	Mezquitlán	20½ p	0/1	Antonio de Alcega
		20:8 f m	0/6	Antonio de Alcega
	Mezquituta y Moyagua	75:7 f m	0/6	Antonio Vélez de Vargas
		75½ p	0/1	Antonio Vélez de Vargas
17-I-1591	Jalisco	159:3 f m	1/1/3	Andrés Venegas
		160 p	0/1	Juan de la Cueva
	Tepic	89:7 f m	1/1/3	Antonio Vélez de Vargas
		89½ p	0/1	Antonio Vélez de Vargas

Date	Town	Item & Amount	Unit Price	Buyer & Remarks
	Analco Tepic	12:2 f m	1/1/3	Antonio Vélez de Vargas
		12½ p	0/1	Antonio Vélez de Vargas
	Sentispac	428:4 f m	1/2	Diego Rubio
		428½ p	0/1	Diego Rubio
18-I-1591	Amaxaque	14:5 f m	0/6	Antonio de Alcega
		14½ p	0/1	Antonio de Alcega
	Yegualtitlán	208 f m	0/6	Antonio de Alcega
		21 p	0/1	Antonio de Alcega
	Acatique	37:4 f m	0/6	Antonio de Alcega
		37½ p	0/1	Antonio de Alcega
	Huelotitlán	29:8 f m	0/6	Antonio de Alcega
		30 p	0/1	Antonio de Alcega
	Inrimota	23:10 f m	0/6	Antonio de Alcega
		24 p	0/1	Antonio de Alcega
	Tequiltitlán	27 f m	0/6	Antonio de Alcega
		27 p	0/1	Antonio de Alcega
	Cuyolomitle	5:10 f m	0/6	Antonio de Alcega
		5½ p	0/1	Antonio de Alcega
	Cacaluta	25:2 f m	0/6	Antonio de Alcega
		25½ p	0/1	Antonio de Alcega
	Hostotipac	165:2 f m	0/5	Antonio de Alcega
	y Zapotlán	165 p	0/0/9	Juan de Ledesma
	Ahuacatlán	30:7 f m	1/1	P. Alvaro de Vergara
		30½ p	0/1/2	Antonio de Alcega
	Suchipil	112:6 f m	1/1	P. Alvaro de Vergara
		113 p	0/1/2	Antonio de Alcega
	Amaxaque	17:10 f m	1/1	P. Alvaro de Vergara
		18 p	0/1/2	Antonio de Alcega
	Jala	161:4 f m	1/1	P. Alvaro de Vergara
		161½ p	0/1/2	Antonio de Alcega
	Tetitlán	65:8 f m	1/0/6	Antonio Vélez de Vargas
		66 p	0/1	Antonio Vélez de Vargas
	Tepequexpan	34:8 f m	1/0/6	Antonio Vélez de Vargas
		35 p	0/1	Antonio Vélez de Vargas
	Camotlán	42:4 f m	1/0/6	Antonio Vélez de Vargas
		42½ p	0/1	Antonio Vélez de Vargas
	San Pedro	16:2 f m	1/0/6	Antonio Vélez de Vargas
		16½ p	0/1	Antonio Vélez de Vargas
	Acuitlapilco	47:8 f m	1/0/6	Antonio Vélez de Vargas
	y Zapotlán	48 p	0/1	Antonio Vélez de Vargas
	Jaltemba, Sta.	6:10 f m	0/5	Antonio de Alcega
	María	7 p	0/1	Antonio de Alcega
	San Juan	5:6 f m	0/5	Antonio de Alcega

Date	Town	Item & Amount	Unit Price	Buyer & Remarks
		9 p	0/1	Antonio de Alcega
		1½ mantas	4/	Antonio de Alcega
	Mezquitititique o Santa María Terequita	8:7 f m	0/6	Antonio de Alcega
		8½ p	0/1	Antonio de Alcega
	Hostotipaquillo (junto a Tequila)	72:5 f m	0/6	Antonio de Alcega
		72½ p	0/1	Antonio de Alcega
	Papachula	7:2 f m	0/5	Antonio de Alcega
		7 p	0/1	Antonio de Alcega
		1½ mantas	4/	Antonio de Alcega
		½ j miel	t 0/2	Antonio de Alcega
	Zanatlán, San Miguel	21:2 f m	0/5	Antonio de Alcega
		21½ p	0/1	Antonio de Alcega
	Mayanalistlán, San Pedro	6:4 f m	0/5	Antonio de Alcega
	Ixtapa, Santa María	5:3 f sal	0/4	Antonio de Alcega
		9½ p	0/1	Antonio de Alcega
		1 car alg	1/	Antonio de Alcega
		2 @ pes	0/4	Antonio de Alcega
	Jalcocotán	32:4 f m	0/5	Antonio de Alcega
		32½ p	0/1	Antonio de Alcega
	Mecatán	41:4 f m	0/5	Antonio de Alcega
		41½ p	0/1	Antonio de Alcega
	Jaltepec	10 p	0/1	Antonio de Alcega
		9 f m	0/5	Antonio de Alcega
		1 j miel	0/2	Antonio de Alcega
	Temichoque	18 f m	0/5	Antonio de Alcega
		5½ @ alg	0/4	Antonio de Alcega
		11½ p	0/1	Antonio de Alcega
	Pontoque	6:9 f m	0/5	Antonio de Alcega
		7 p	0/1	Antonio de Alcega
	Tosmoto, San Miguel	36:11 f m	0/5	Antonio de Alcega
		37 p	0/1	Antonio de Alcega
	Acatispa y Canala	13:6 f m	0/5	Antonio de Alcega
		13½ p	0/1	Antonio de Alcega
	Quilitlán	18 f m	0/5	Antonio de Alcega
		1 @ miel	1/	Antonio de Alcega
	Ixtapa, de Castañeda	7 f sal	0/4	Antonio de Alcega
	Matacticpac	11:8 f m	0/5	Antonio de Alcega
		12 p	0/1	Antonio de Alcega
	Ixcuintla	18:11 f m	0/5	Antonio de Alcega
		19 p	0/1	Antonio de Alcega
	Tomatlán	9 f m	0/5	Antonio de Alcega
		2 g	0/2	Antonio de Alcega
		2 j miel	0/4	Antonio de Alcega

Date	Town	Item & Amount	Unit Price	Buyer & Remarks
	Jalisquillo	18 f m	0/5	Antonio de Alcega
	Cusmini, San Andrés	9 f m	0/5	Antonio de Alcega
		2 j miel	0/4	Antonio de Alcega
	Acaponeta	173:8 f m	0/5	Antonio de Alcega
		174 p	0/1	Antonio de Alcega
	Mascota	34:2 f m	0/5/6	Alonso de Cisneros
		34½ p	0/1	Rodrigo Hernández Cordero
	Tepetlatlauca y Chistique	36:6 f m	0/5/6	Alonso de Cisneros
		37½ p	0/1	Rodrigo Hernández Cordero
	Atengoichán	18½ p	0/1	Diego de Espinosa
		18:3 f m	0/5	Alonso de Cisneros
	Zacatlán	27 f m	0/5	Alonso de Cisneros
	Amatlán } Jalacingo } Ixtimitique }	24:4 f m	0/5	Alonso de Cisneros
		24½ p	0/1	Diego de Espinosa
	Tepuzhuacán	9:3 f m	0/5	Alonso de Cisneros
		9½ p	0/1	Diego de Espinosa
	Panpuchín	17:9 f m	0/6	Antonio Vélez de Vargas
		17 p	0/0/9	Antonio Vélez de Vargas
	Zapotlán	5:5 f m	0/6	Antonio Vélez de Vargas
		5½ p	0/0/9	Antonio Vélez de Vargas
	Sila	3:7 f m	0/6	Antonio Vélez de Vargas
		7 p	0/0/9	Antonio Vélez de Vargas
	Contla	11:8 f m	0/6	Antonio Vélez de Vargas
	Opono	47:8 f m	0/6	Alonso Vélez de Vargas
		48 p	0/0/9	Alonso Vélez de Vargas
	Piloto, Maito } Colique, Atengo }	53:1 f m	0/6	Alonso Vélez de Vargas
		53 p	0/0/9	Alonso Vélez de Vargas
	Tlacatlán y Ixtlahuacán	101:8 f m	0/6/6	Juan de Saldívar
		102 p	0/1/7	Juan de Saldívar
	Temacapulin	18 f m	0/6/6	Juan de Saldívar
		18 p	0/1/7	Juan de Saldívar
	Acatic y Tepatitlán	62½ p	0/1/7	Juan de Saldívar
		62:1 f m	0/6/6	Juan de Saldívar
	Juanacatlán, Santa Fe	72 f m	0/6/6	Juan de Saldívar
		72 p	0/1/7	Juan de Saldívar
	Zapotlán	33:8 f m	0/6/6	Juan de Saldívar
		33½ p	0/1/7	Juan de Saldívar
14-I-1592	Analco	148:10 f m	1/1	Baltasar de Orozco
		111:10 f m	1/1	Indios de Analco
		(75 f m para el convento)		
		336 p	0/1/6	Andrés Venegas
	Tlaquepaque y Toluquilla	178:4 f m	1/2	Rodrigo Hernández Cordero
		(75 f m para el convento)		

Date	Town	Item & Amount	Unit Price	Buyer & Remarks
		253 p	0/1/9	Rodrigo Hernández Cordero
	Tonalá	131:8 f m	1/1	Francisco de Plaza
		(112:8 f m para el convento)		
		244 p	0/1/9	Juan Toledano
	Atemajac	112:6 f m	1/1/7	Francisco de Camarena
		112½ p	0/1/9	Rodrigo Hernández Cordero
	Tlajomulco	351:10 f m	1/1	Lic. Enrique Tavares
		(100 f m para el convento)		
		452 p	0/2	Diego de Espinosa
15-I-1592	Yahualica	59:4 f m	0/4	Bernabé García
		59½ p	0/1	Bernabé García
	Poncitlán	264:6 f m	1/2/1	Diego Martín de Rivera
		(100 f m para el convento)		
		364 p	0/1/7	Juan Toledano
	Cuitzeo	46:8 f m	1/2/1	Diego Martín de Rivera
		(100 f m para el convento)		
		147 p	0/1/7	Juan Toledano
	Mezquituta y Moyagua	75:7 f m	0/6/2	Antonio Vélez de Vargas
		75½ p	0/1	Antonio Vélez de Vargas
16-I-1592	Tesistán	44:6 f m	1/2/1	Antonio Vélez de Vargas
		45 p	0/1/3	Juan Sánchez de la Palma
	Epatlán	18:5 f m	1/2/3	Antonio Vélez de Vargas
		18½ p	0/1/3	Juan Sánchez de la Palma
	Tepeaca	23:5 f m	1/2/1	Antonio Vélez de Vargas
		23½ p	0/1/3	Juan Sánchez de la Palma
	Suchitlán	22:6 f m	1/2/1	Antonio Vélez de Vargas
		22½ p	0/1/3	Juan Sánchez de la Palma
	Camotlán y Cuyutlán	20½ p	0/1/3	Juan Sánchez de la Palma
	Coscotitán, San Cristobal	46½ p	0/1/3	Juan Sánchez de la Palma
	Nochistlanejo	31:6 f m	1/2/1	Antonio Vélez de Vargas
		31½ p	0/1/11	Antonio Vélez de Vargas
	Zalatitlán	37 p	0/2	Francisco de Camarena
		(37:4 f m para el convento)		
	Cuyutlán y Cajititlán	109:10 f m	1/2	Juan Toledano
		110½ p	0/2	Juan de Ledesma Mexía
	Matatlán	36 f m	1/2/1	Baltasar de Orozco
		36 p	0/2	Pedro de Cuéllar
	Copala y Quilitlán	18 f m	1/	Juan de Cepeda
		18 p	0/1/6	Juan de Cepeda
	Tequila y San Francisco	117:11 f m	1/1/1	Antonio Vélez de Vargas
		118 p	0/1/6	Juan Toledano
	Guastla o Los Guajes	5:5 f m	1/1/1	Antonio Vélez de Vargas
		5½ p	0/1/6	Juan Toledano

Date	Town	Item & Amount	Unit Price	Buyer & Remarks
	Ahuisculco	19 f m	1/	Juan Toledano
		19 p	0/1/8	Juan Toledano
17-I-1592	Hostotipaquillo (cerca de Tequila)	56:11 f m	0/5/3	Antonio Vélez de Vargas
		57 p	0/1/5	Antonio Vélez de Vargas
	Amaxaque	14:5 f m	0/5/3	Antonio Vélez de Vargas
		14½ p	0/1/5	Antonio Vélez de Vargas
	Yegualtitlán	20:8 f m	0/5/3	Antonio Vélez de Vargas
		21 p	0/1/5	Antonio Vélez de Vargas
	Acatique	37:4 f m	0/5/3	Antonio Vélez de Vargas
		37½ p	0/1/5	Antonio Vélez de Vargas
	Huelotitlán	29:8 f m	0/5/3	Antonio Vélez de Vargas
		30 p	0/1/5	Antonio Vélez de Vargas
	Inrimota	23:10 f m	0/5/3	Antonio Vélez de Vargas
		24 p	0/1/5	Antonio Vélez de Vargas
	Tequiltitlán	27 f m	0/5/3	Antonio Vélez de Vargas
		27 p	0/1/5	Antonio Vélez de Vargas
	Cuyolomitle	5:10 f m	0/5/3	Antonio Vélez de Vargas
		5½ p	0/1/5	Antonio Vélez de Vargas
	Mezquitlán	20:8 f m	0/5/3	Antonio Vélez de Vargas
		20½ p	0/1/5	Antonio Vélez de Vargas
	Cacaluta	25:2 f m	0/5/3	Antonio Vélez de Vargas
		25½ p	0/1/5	Antonio Vélez de Vargas
	Hostotipac y Zapotlán	165:2 f m	0/6/1	Antonio de Alcega
		165 p	0/1/1	Juan de Ledesma
	Jalisco	148:7 f m	0/5	Antonio de Alcega
		148½ p	0/1	Antonio de Alcega
	Tepic	89:7 f m	0/6	Antonio de Alcega
		89½ p	0/1	Antonio de Alcega
	Analco Tepic	12:2 f m	0/6	Antonio de Alcega
		12 p	0/1	Antonio de Alcega
	Sentispac	378:4 f m	0/6	Antonio de Alcega
		(50 f m para el convento)		
		428½ p	0/1	Antonio de Alcega
	Ahuacatlán	30:7 f m	0/4/3	Antonio de Alcega
		30½ p	0/1/5	Pedro Alvarez
	Suchipil	112:6 f m	0/4/3	Antonio de Alcega
		113 p	0/1/5	Pedro Alvarez
	Amaxaque	17:10 f m	0/4/3	Antonio de Alcega
		18 p	0/1/5	Pedro Alvarez
	Jala	151:4 f m	0/7/1	Antonio Alcega
		151 p	0/1/4	Alvaro de Vergara
	Tetitlán	65:8 f m	0/7/1	Antonio de Alcega
		65 p	0/1/6	Antonio Vélez de Vargas
	Tepequexpan	34:8 f m	0/7/1	Antonio de Alcega

Date	Town	Item & Amount	Unit Price	Buyer & Remarks
		35 p	0/1/6	Antonio Vélez de Vargas
	Camotlán	42:4 f m	0/7/1	Antonio de Alcega
		42½ p	0/1/6	Antonio Vélez de Vargas
	San Pedro	16:2 f m	0/7/1	Antonio de Alcega
		16½ p	0/1/6	Antonio Vélez de Vargas
	Acuitlapilco y Zapotlán	47:8 f m	0/7/1	Antonio de Alcega
		48 p	0/1/6	Antonio Vélez de Vargas
	Jaltemba, Santa María	6:9 f m	0/4	Antonio de Alcega
		7 p	0/1	Antonio de Alcega
	San Juan	5:6 f m	0/4	Antonio de Alcega
		9 p	0/1	Antonio de Alcega
		1½ mantas	4/	Antonio de Alcega
	Papachula	7:2 f m	0/4	Antonio de Alcega
		7 p	0/1	Antonio de Alcega
		1½ mantas	4/	Antonio de Alcega
		½ j miel	t 0/2	Antonio de Alcega
	Zanatlán, San Miguel	21:2 f m	0/4	Antonio de Alcega
		21½ p	0/1	Antonio de Alcega
	Mayanalistlán, San Pedro	6:4 f m	0/4	Antonio de Alcega
	Ixtapa, Santa María	5:3 f sal	0/4	Antonio de Alcega
		9½ p	0/1	Antonio de Alcega
		1 car alg	1/	Antonio de Alcega
		2 @ pes	0/4	Antonio de Alcega
	Jalcocotán	32:4 f m	0/4	Antonio de Alcega
		32½ p	0/1	Antonio de Alcega
	Mecatán	41:4 f m	0/4	Antonio de Alcega
		41½ p	0/1	Antonio de Alcega
	Jaltepec	9 f m	0/4	Antonio de Alcega
		10 p	0/1	Antonio de Alcega
		1 j miel--qtla	0/2	Antonio de Alcega
	Temichoque	18 f m	0/4	Antonio de Alcega
		5½ @ alg	0/4	Antonio de Alcega
		11½ p	0/1	Antonio de Alcega
	Pontoque	6:9 f m	0/4	Antonio de Alcega
		7 p	0/1	Antonio de Alcega
	Tosmotoc, San Miguel	36:11 f m	0/4	Antonio de Alcega
		37 p	0/1	Antonio de Alcega
	Acatispa y Canala	13:6 f m	0/4	Antonio de Alcega
		13½ p	0/1	Antonio de Alcega
	Quilitlán	18 f m	0/4	Antonio de Alcega
		1 @ miel	1/	Antonio de Alcega
	Ixtapa, de Castañeda	7 f sal	0/4	Antonio de Alcega
	Matacticpac	11:8 f m	0/4	Antonio de Alcega
		12 p	0/1	Antonio de Alcega

Date	Town	Item & Amount	Unit Price	Buyer & Remarks
	Ixcuintla	18:11 f m	0/4	Antonio de Alcega
		19 p	0/1	Antonio de Alcega
	Tomatlán	9 f m	0/4	Antonio de Alcega
		2 g	0/2	Antonio de Alcega
		2 j miel	0/4	Antonio de Alcega
	Jalisquillo	18 f m	0/4	Antonio de Alcega
	Cusmismi,	9 f m	0/4	Antonio de Alcega
	San Andrés	2 j miel	0/4	Antonio de Alcega
18-I-1592	Acaponeta	123:8 f m	0/4	Antonio de Alcega
		(50 f m para el convento)		
		174 p	0/1	Antonio de Alcega
	Mascota	34:2 f m	0/4	Juan de Ruas
		34½ p	0/1	Fran. de Cepeda, Relator
	Tepetlatlauca	36½ f m	0/4	Juan de Ruas
	y Chistique	38 p	0/1	Fran. de Cepeda, Relator
	Atengoichán	18:3 f m	0/4	Juan de Ruas
		18½ p	0/1	Juan de Ruas
	Zacatlán	27 f m	0/4	Juan de Ruas
	Amatlán }			
	Jalacingo }	24:4 f m	0/4	Juan de Ruas
	Ixtimitique }	24½ p	0/1	Juan de Ruas
	Tepuzhuacán	9:3 f m	0/4	Juan de Ruas
		9½ p	0/1	Juan de Ruas
	Panpuchín	17:9 f m	0/5/1	Antonio Vélez de Vargas
		17 p	0/1	Antonio Vélez de Vargas
	Zapotlán	5:5 f m	0/5/1	Antonio Vélez de Vargas
		5½ p	0/1	Antonio Vélez de Vargas
	Sila	3:7 f m	0/5/1	Antonio Vélez de Vargas
		7 p	0/1	Antonio Vélez de Vargas
	Contla	11:8 f m	0/5/1	Antonio Vélez de Vargas
	Opono	37:8 f m	0/5/1	Antonio Vélez de Vargas
		(10 f m para los indios de las salinas)		
		48 p	0/1	Antonio Vélez de Vargas
	Piloto, }	43:1 f m	0/5/1	Antonio Vélez de Vargas
	Maloto, }	(10 f m para los indios de las salinas) (no se entregó el maiz porque se destinó a los frailes)		
	Colique, }	53 p	0/1	Antonio Vélez de Vargas
	Atengo }			
	Tlacotlán y	101:8 f m	1/1	Juan de Saldívar
	Ixtlahuacán	102 p	0/1	Juan de Saldívar
	Temacapulin	18 f m	1/1	Juan de Saldívar
		18 p	0/1	Juan de Saldívar
	Juanacatlán, Sta.	72 f m	1/1	Juan de Saldívar
	Fe, y Acatlán	72 p	0/1	Juan de Saldívar
	Acatic y	62:1 f m	1/1	Juan de Saldívar

Date	Town	Item & Amount	Unit Price	Buyer & Remarks
	Tepatitlán	62 p	0/1	Juan de Saldívar
	Zapotlán	38:8 f m	1/1	Juan de Saldívar
		38½ p	0/1	Juan de Saldcvar
12-I-1593	Analco	335 f m	1/	Alonso Guerrero
		336 p	0/1/8	Antonio Vélez de Vargas
	Tonalá	131:8 f m	1/0/6	Francisco de Plaza
		244 p	0/1/9	Antonio Vélez de Vargas
	Tlaquepaque y Toluquilla	253:4 f m	1/	Martín Real
		253 p	0/1/9	Antonio Vélez de Vargas
	Atemajac	112:6 f m	1/	Alonso Guerrero
		112½ p	0/1/9	Antonio Vélez de Vargas
13-I-1593	Tlajomulco	451:10 f m	0/7	Gaspar de Mota
		452 p	0/1	Juan Sánchez de la Palma
	Poncitlán	364:6 f m	1/0/6	Alonso Guerrero
		364½ p	0/1/6	P. Alvaro de Vergara
	Cuitzeo	46:8 f m	1/0/6	Alonso Guerrero
		(100 f m para el convento)		
		147 p	0/1/6	P. Alvaro de Vergara
	Mezquituta y Moyagua	75:7 f m	0/6	Lic. Ramírez de Alarcón
		75½ p	0/1	Lic. Ramírez de Alarcón
	Tesistán	44:6 f m	0/6	Gonzalo Núñez
		44½ p	0/1	Gonzalo Núñez
	Tepeaca y Epatlán	25:2 f m	0/6	Gonzalo Núñez
		25½ p	0/1	Gonzalo Núñez
	Suchitlán	22:6 f m	0/6/3	Francisco de Plaza
		22½ p	0/1/1	Juan Sánchez de la Palma
	Camotlán y Cuyutlán	73½ p	0/1/1	Juan Sánchez de la Palma
	Coscotitán, San Cristobal	46½ p	0/1/1	Juan Sánchez de la Palma
	Nochistlanejo	31:6 f m	0/5	Fran. de Cepeda, Relator
		31½ p	0/1	Fran. de Cepeda, Relator
	Zalatitlán	37 p	0/1/6	Antonio Vélez de Vargas
		(37:4 f m para el convento)		
	Cuyutlán y Cajititlán	109:10 f m	1/	Alonso Guerrero
		110 p	0/1/6	Bernabé García
	Matatlán	36 f m	0/7/3	Antonio Vélez de Vargas
		36 p	0/1	Antonio Vélez de Vargas
	Copala y Quilitlán	18 f m	1/	Gonzalo Núñez
		18 p	0/1	Gonzalo Núñez
	Tequila y San Francisco	117:11 f m	1/0/3	Juan Sánchez de la Palma
		118 p	0/1/3	Bernabé García
	Guastla o Los Guajes	5:5 f m	1/0/3	Juan Sánchez de la Palma
		5½ p	0/1/3	Bernabé García

Date	Town	Item & Amount	Unit Price	Buyer & Remarks
	Ahuisculco	15:3 f m	0/5	Fran. de Cepeda, Relator
		15½ p	0/1	Fran. de Cepeda, Relator
	Zapotlán	40:7 f m	0/7	Antonio Vélez de Vargas
		40½ p	0/1/6	Antonio Vélez de Vargas
	Acatique	41:6 f m	0/5	Eugenio Suárez Falero
		41½ p	0/1	Eugenio Suárez Falero
14-I-1593	Cuyolomitle	8:7 f m	0/5	Eugenio Suárez Falero
		8½ p	0/1	Eugenio Suárez Falero
	Mezquitlán	20 f m	0/5	Eugenio Suárez Falero
		20 p	0/1	Eugenio Suárez Falero
	Cacaluta	46:6 f m	0/5	Eugenio Suárez Falero
		46½ p	0/1	Eugenio Suárez Falero
	Hostotipac	109:3 f m	0/7	Antonio Vélez de Vargas
		109½ p	0/1/6	Antonio Vélez de Vargas
	Jalisco	144:11 f m	1/	Pedro de Ataún
		145 p	0/1/6	Pedro de Ataún
	Tepic	89:7 f m	1/	Eugenio Suárez Falero
		89½ p	0/1/6	Eugenio Suárez Falero
	Analco Tepic	12:2 f m	1/	Eugenio Suárez Falero
		12 p	0/1/6	Eugenio Suárez Falero
	Sentispac	428:4 f m	1/2	Eugenio Suárez Falero
		428½ p	0/1/3	Eugenio Suárez Falero
	Ahuacatlán	30:7 f m	0/6	Antonio Vélez de Vargas
		30½ p	0/1/3	Eugenio Suárez Falero y
Pedro de Ataún				
				(por mitades)
	Suchipil	112:11 f m	0/6	Antonio Vélez de Vargas
		113½ p	0/1/3	Eugenio Suárez Falero y
Pedro de Ataún				
	Amaxaque	17:10 f m	0/6	Antonio Vélez de Vargas
		18 p	0/1/3	Eugenio Suárez Falero y
Pedro de Ataún				
	Jala	161:4 f m	0/6	Antonio Vélez de Vargas
		161½ p	0/1/8	Pedro de Ataún
	Tetitlán	56:8 f m	1/0/6	P. Alvaro de Vergara
		56½ p	0/1/6	Eugenio Suárez Falero
	Tepequexpan	34:8 f m	1/0/6	P. Alvaro de Vergara
		35 p	0/1/6	Eugenio Suárez Falero
	San Pedro	16:2 f m	1/0/6	P. Alvaro de Vergara
		16½ p	0/1/6	Eugenio Suárez Falero
	Camotlán	42:4 f m	1/0/6	P. Alvaro de Vergara
		42½ p	0/1/6	Eugenio Suárez Falero
	Acuitlapilco	47:8 f m	1/	P. Alvaro de Vergara
	y Zapotlán	48 p	0/1	Eugenio Suárez Falero
	Hostotipaquillo	67 f m	0/5	Eugenio Suárez Falero

Date	Town	Item & Amount	Unit Price	Buyer & Remarks
	(cerca de Tequila)	67 p	0/1	Eugenio Suárez Falero
	Amaxaque	20 f m	0/5	Eugenio Suárez Falero
		20 p	0/1	Eugenio Suárez Falero
	Yegualtitlán	26:5 f m	0/5	Eugenio Suárez Falero
		26 p	0/1	Eugenio Suárez Falero
	Huelotitlán	36:11 f m	0/5	Eugenio Suárez Falero
		37 p	0/1	Eugenio Suárez Falero
	Inrimota	24:6 f m	0/5	Eugenio Suárez Falero
		24½ p	0/1	Eugenio Suárez Falero
	Tequiltitlán	32:5 f m	0/5	Eugenio Suárez Falero
		32½ p	0/1	Eugenio Suárez Falero
15-I-1593	Jaltemba, Santa María	6:9 f m	1/4	Eugenio Suárez Falero
		7 p	0/1	Eugenio Suárez Falero
	San Juan y Papachula	1½ mantas	4/	Eugenio Suárez Falero
		9 f m	1/4	Eugenio Suárez Falero
		11 p	0/1/3	Eugenio Suárez Falero
		1 j miel--qtla	0/2	Eugenio Suárez Falero
	Zanatlán, San Miguel	21:2 f m	1/4	Eugenio Suárez Falero
		21½ p	0/1/3	Eugenio Suárez Falero
	Mayanalistlán, San Pedro	6:4 f m	1/4	Eugenio Suárez Falero
	Ixtapa, Santa María	5:3 f m	1/4	Eugenio Suárez Falero
		9½ p	0/1/3	Eugenio Suárez Falero
		1 car alg	1/	Eugenio Suárez Falero
		2 @ pes	0/4	Eugenio Suárez Falero
	Jalcocotán	32:4 f m	1/4	Eugenio Suárez Falero
		32½ p	0/1/3	Eugenio Suárez Falero
	Mecatán	41½ p	0/1/3	Eugenio Suárez Falero
		41:4 f m	1/2	Eugenio Suárez Falero
	Temichoque	18 f m	1/4	Eugenio Suárez Falero
		5½ @ alg	0/4	Eugenio Suárez Falero
		11½ p	0/1/3	Eugenio Suárez Falero
	Pontoque	6:9 f m	1/4	Eugenio Suárez Falero
		7 p	0/1/3	Eugenio Suárez Falero
	Acatispa y Canala	13:6 f m	1/4	Eugenio Suárez Falero
		13½ p	0/1/3	Eugenio Suárez Falero
	Ixcuintla	16:11 f m	1/4	Eugenio Suárez Falero
		17 p	0/1/3	Eugenio Suárez Falero
	Ixtapa, de Castañeda	7 f sal	0/4	Eugenio Suárez Falero
	Matacticpac	11:8 f m	1/4	Eugenio Suárez Falero
		10 p	0/1/3	Eugenio Suárez Falero
	Quilitlán	18 f m	1/4	Eugenio Suárez Falero
		1 @ miel	1/	Eugenio Suárez Falero
	Jaltepec	9 f m	1/4	Eugenio Suárez Falero

Date	Town	Item & Amount	Unit Price	Buyer & Remarks
		10 p	0/1/3	Eugenio Suárez Falero
		1 j miel--qtla	0/2	Eugenio Suárez Falero
	Tomatlán	9 f m	1/4	Eugenio Suárez Falero
		2 g	0/2	Eugenio Suárez Falero
		2 j miel	0/4	Eugenio Suárez Falero
	Jalisquillo	18 f m	1/4	Eugenio Suárez Falero
	Cusmini, San Andrés	9 f m	1/4	Eugenio Suárez Falero
		2 j miel	0/4	Eugenio Suárez Falero
	Tosmotoc, San			
	Miguel o Sta.	32:7 f m	1/4	Eugenio Suárez Falero
	María Atlaco	32½ p	0/1/3	Eugenio Suárez Falero
	Acaponeta	173:8 f m	1/	Miguel de Funes
		174 p	0/1	Miguel de Funes
	Mascota	34:2 f m	0/7	Cristóbal de Sandoval
		34½ p	0/1	Cristóbal de Sandoval
	Tepetlatlauca	36:2 f m	0/7	Cristóbal de Sandoval
	y Chistique	38 p	0/1	Cristóbal de Sandoval
	Atengoichán	13:3 f m	0/5	Cristóbal de Sandoval
		13½ p	0/1	Cristóbal de Sandoval
	Zacatlán	27 f m	0/5	Cristóbal de Sandoval
	Amatlán y sujetos	24:4 f m	0/5	Cristóbal de Sandoval
		24½ p	0/1	Cristóbal de Sandoval
	Tepuzhuacán	9 3 f m	0/5	Cristóbal de Sandoval
		9½ p	0/1	Cristóbal de Sandoval
	Panpuchín	17:9 f m	0/4	Juan del Castillo
		17 p	0/1	Juan del Castillo
	Zapotlán	5:5 f m	0/4	Juan del Castillo
		5½ p	0/1	Juan del Castillo
	Sila	3:7 f m	0/4	Juan del Castillo
		7 p	0/1	Juan del Castillo
	Contla	11:8 f m	0/4	Juan del Castillo
	Opono	47:8 f m	0/4	Juan del Castillo
		48 p	0/1	Juan del Castillo
	Piloto }			
	Maloto }	53:1 f m	0/4	Juan del Castillo
	Colique }	53 p	0/1	Juan del Castillo
	Atengo }			
	Guamuchol y }	40:5 f m	0/4	Juan del Castillo
	Chamela }	40½ p	0/1	Juan del Castillo
18-I-1594	Analco	335:8 f m	1/	Indios de Analco
		336 p	0/1/3	Alonso Guerrero
	Tonalá	131:8 f m	1/0/3	Nicolás Pereyra
		(112:8 f m para el convento)		
		244 p	0/1/6	Antonio Vélez de Vargas
	Tlaquepaque y	253:4 f m	1/0/9	Juan Sánchez de la Palma

Date	Town	Item & Amount	Unit Price	Buyer & Remarks
	Toluquilla	(no es claro--precio total para maiz = 261/2/6)		
		(150 f m a los frailes, por fin)		
		253 p	0/1/3	Alonso Guerrero
	Atemajac	112:6 f m	1/0/6	Alonso Guerrero
		112½ p	0/1/6	Rodrigo Hernández Cordero
	Tlajomulco	451:10 f m	0/7/1	Don Luis de Contreras y Guevara
		100 f m por fin al convento)		
		452 p	0/1/3	Don Luis de Contreras y Guevara
	Mezquituta y Moyagua	75:7 f m	0/6	Diego Ruiz
		75½ p	0/1	Diego Ruiz
	Poncitlán y Cuitzeo	411:2 f m	1/0/6	Don Luis de Contreras y Guevara
		(100 f m para el convento y otro tanto por fin)		
		511½ p	0/1/4	Alonso Guerrero
	Copala y Quilitlán	18 f m	0/7	Alonso Guerrero
		18 p	0/1/3	Alonso Guerrero
	Tesistán } Tepeaca } Epatlán }	66:1 f m	0/7	Juan Sánchez de la Palma
		66 p	0/1/2	Alonso Guerrero
	Suchitlán	22:6 f m	0/5/6	Francisco de Plaza
		22½ p	0/1/3	Juan Sánchez de la Palma
	Camotlán, San } Cristóbal, y } Cuyutlán }	83½ p	0/1/1	Juan Sánchez de la Palma
		(incluye Coscotitán)		
	Nochistlanejo	31:6 f m	0/7	Fran. de Cepeda, Relator
		31½ p	0/1/6	Fran. de Cepeda, Relator
	Zalatitlán	37 p	0/1/6	Bernabé García
		(37:4 f m para el convento)		
	Tepic y Analco	101:9 f m	1/4/6	Antonio de Alcega
		101½ p	0/1/6	Francisco de Balbuena
19-I-1594	Cuyutlán y Cajititlán	109:10 f m	0/7/1	Diego de Porres
		110 p	0/1/6	Diego Martín de Rivera
	Matatlán	36 f m	0/7/3	Francisco de Plaza
		36 p	0/1	Francisco de Plaza
	Tequila y Guastla	123:4 f m	0/7/4	Alonso Guerrero
		123½ p	0/1/1	Don Juan de Tovar
	Ahuisculco	15:3 f m	0/6	Fran. de Cepeda, Relator
		15½ p	0/1	Fran. de Cepeda, Relator
	Jocotlán, Part. } Hostotipac } Amaxaque } Yegualtitlán } Acatique } Huejotitlán } Inrimota } Tequiltitlán } Cuyolomitle }	341:1 f m	0/6	Alvaro de Figueróa
		340½ p	0/1	Alvaro de Figueróa

Date	Town	Item & Amount	Unit Price	Buyer & Remarks
	Cacaluta }			
	Sentispac	380:3 f m	2/0/3	Don Luis de Contreras y Guevara
		419 p	0/1/4	Don Luis de Contreras y Guevara
	Hostotipaquillo y Zapotlán	120:7 f m	1/2/6	Antonio Vélez de Vargas
		120½ p	0/1/6	Francisco de Balbuena
	Jalisco	144:11 f m	1/4/6	Antonio de Alcega
		145 p	0/1/6	Francisco de Balbuena
	Ahuacatlán } Suchipil }	161:4 f m	1/4	Don Luis de Contreras y Guevara
	Amaxaque }	162 p	0/1/6	Don Luis de Contreras y Guevara
	Jala	161:4 f m	1/4/1	Don Luis de Contreras y Guevara
		161½ p	0/1/6	Francisco de Balbuena
		(al fin 50 f m al convento)		
	Tetitlán } Tepequexpan}	140 f m	1/3/6	Francisco de Balbuena
	San Pedro } Camotlán }	141 p	0/1/6	Gerónimo de Aguayo
	Acuitlapilco y Zapotlán	47:8 f m	1/3/6	Francisco de Balbuena
		48 p	0/1/6	Gerónimo de Aguayo
	Jaltemba,	6:9 f m	1/5/1	Don Luis de Contreras y Santa María Guevara
		7 p	0/1/3	Don Luis de Contreras y Guevara
	Papachula, San Juan y sujetos:			
	San Miguel } Zanatlán }	106:8 f m	1/5/1	Don Luis de Contreras y Guevara
	San Pedro } Mayanalistlán }	110½ p	0/1/3	Don Luis de Contreras y Guevara
	Santa María } Ixtapa }	5:3 f sal	0/4	Don Luis de Contreras y Guevara
	Jalcocotán } Mecatán }	1 car alg	1/0	Don Luis de Contreras y Guevara
		2 @ pes	0/4	Don Luis de Contreras y Guevara
	Temichoque	18 f m	1/5/1	Don Luis de Contreras y Guevara
		11½ p	0/1/3	Don Luis de Contreras y Guevara
		5½ @ alg	0/4	Don Luis de Contreras y Guevara
	Pontoque y sujetos:			
	San Juan Canala } San Miguel }	35:1 f m	1/5/1	Don Luis de Contreras y Guevara
	Tosmotoc }	35 p	0/1/3	Don Luis de Contreras y Guevara
	Ixcuintla y sujetos:			
	Ixtapa, de C. }	43:7 f m	1/5/1	Don Luis de Contreras y

Date	Town	Item & Amount	Unit Price	Buyer & Remarks
	Matactipac }			Guevara
	Quilitlán }	32 p	0/1/3	Don Luis de Contreras y Guevara
	Jaltepec }	7 f sal	0/4	Don Luis de Contreras y Guevara
		1 @ miel	1/	Don Luis de Contreras y Guevara
		1 j miel--qtla	0/2	Don Luis de Contreras y Guevara
	Tomatlan, } Jalisquillo }	36 f m	1/5/1	Don Luis de Contreras y Guevara
	San Andrés } Cusmini }	4 j miel	0/4	Don Luis de Contreras y Guevara
		2 g	0/2	Don Luis de Contreras y Guevara
	Acaponeta	164 p	0/1	Miguel de Funes
	Mascota y sujetos:			
	Tepetlatlauca }	70:5 f m	0/5	Gerónimo de Aguayo
	Chistique }	72½ p	0/1	Gerónimo de Aguayo
	Atengoichán y sujetos:			
	Zacatlán }			
	Tepuzhuacán }	78:10 f m	0/4	Gerónimo de Aguayo
	Amatlán, y }	52½ p	0/1	Gerónimo de Aguayo
	Jalacingo y }			
	sujetos }			
	Panpuchín }			
	Zapotlán }	37:4 f m	0/3	Antonio Vélez de Vargas
	Sila }	29½ p	0/0/9	Antonio Vélez de Vargas
	Contla }			
	Opono	47:9 f m	0/3	Antonio Vélez de Vargas
		48 p	0/0/9	Antonio Vélez de Vargas
	Piloto y sujetos:			
	Guamuchíl y }	67 f m	0/3	Antonio Vélez de Vargas
	Chamela }	67 p	0/0/9	Antonio Vélez de Vargas
11-I-1595	Analco	335:8 f m	1/2/8	Gabriel de Montenegro
		336 p	0/1/2	Diego Martín de Rivera
	Tonalá	131:8 f m	1/2	Alonso Guerrero
		(112:8 f m para el convento)		
		244 p	0/1/6	Antonio Vélez de Vargas
	Tlaquepaque y	253:4 f m	1/2	Juan Toledano
	Toluquilla	253 p	0/1/3	Diego Martín de Rivera
	Atemajac	112:6 f m	1/4/1	Rodrigo Hernández Cordero
		112½ p	0/1/3	Rodrigo Hernández Cordero
	Tlajomulco	451:10 f m	1/2	Cristóbal de Sandoval
		452 p	0/1/3	Diego de Espinosa
	Poncitlán y	511:2 f m	1/4	Gabriel de Montenegro
	Cuitzeo	511½ p	0/1/3	Gabriel de Montenegro
	Tesistán	44:6 f m	1/4	Gabriel Núñez
		44½ p	0/1/7	Gabriel Núñez

Date	Town	Item & Amount	Unit Price	Buyer & Remarks
	Tequila y Guastla	123:4 f m	1/4	Don Juan de Tovar
		123½ p	0/1/3	Pedro de Cuéllar
	Ahuisculco	15:3 f m	1/3	Hernán Gómez de Rivera
		15½ p	0/1/8	Hernán Gómez de Rivera
12-I-1595	Mezquituta y Moyagua	75:7 f m	1/0/1	Andrés de Torres
		75½ p	0/1	Andrés de Torres
	Copala y Quilitlán	18 f m	1/1/3	Gabriel Núñez
		18 p	0/1/7	Gabriel Núñez
	Tepeaca y Epatlán	21:7 f m	1/4	Gabriel Núñez
		21½ p	0/1/9	Gabriel Núñez
	Suchitlán	22:6 f m	1/1/6	Pedro de Cuéllar
		22½ p	0/1/3	Cristóbal de Sandoval
	Coscotitán, San Cristóbal	46½ p	0/1/4	Pedro de Cuéllar
	Camotlán y Cuyutlán	37 p	0/1/4	Pedro de Cuéllar
	Nochistlanejo	31:6 f m	1/4/1	Bernabé García
		31½ p	0/1/6	Bernabé García
	Zalatitlán	37 p	0/2	Francisco Camarena
		(37:4 f m para el convento)		
	Cuyutlán y Cajititlán	109:10 f m	1/2/9	Cristóbal de Sandoval
		110 p	0/2	Diego de Espinosa
	Matatlán	36 f m	1/4	Alonso Guerrero
		36 p	0/1/3	Pedro de Cuéllar
	Mexcala	9:2 f m	1/4	Alonso Guerrero
		9 p	0/1/3	Pedro de Cuéllar
	Jocotlán, Par.:			
	Hostotipac)	341:7 f m	1/1/3	Francisco Camarena
	Amaxaque)	341 p	0/1	Francisco Camarena
	Yegualtitlán)			
	Acatique)			
	Huejotitlán)			
	Inrimota)			
	Tequiltitlán)			
	Cuyolomitle)			
	Mezquitlán)			
	Cacaluta)			
	Ahuacatlán	30:11 f m	1/5/6	Gabriel de Montenegro
		30½ p	0/1/8	Francisco Camarena
	Suchipil	112:11 f m	1/5/6	Gabriel de Montenegro
		(53 f m al convento, en fin)		
		113½ p	0/1/8	Francisco Camarena
	Amaxaque	17:10 f m	1/5/3	Gabriel de Montenegro
		18 p	0/1/8	Francisco Camarena
	Jala	161:4 f m	1/6/9	Gabriel de Montenegro
		161½ p	0/1/6	Francisco Camarena
	Tetitlán	46:9 f m	2/0/2	Eugenio Suárez Falero
		47 p	0/1/7	Eugenio Suárez Falero

Date	Town	Item & Amount	Unit Price	Buyer & Remarks
	Tepequexpan	34:8 f m	2/0/2	Eugenio Suárez Falero
		35 p	0/1/7	Eugenio Suárez Falero
	San Pedro	16:2 f m	2/0/2	Eugenio Suárez Falero
		16½ p	0/1/1	Eugenio Suárez Falero
	Camotlán	42:4 f m	2/0/2	Eugenio Suárez Falero
		42½ p	0/1/7	Eugenio Suárez Falero
	Acuitlapilco y Zapotlán	47:8 f m	2/0/2	Eugenio Suárez Falero
		48 p	0/1/7	Eugenio Suárez Falero
14-I-1595	Hostotipaquillo	83:8 f m	1/5	Francisco Camarena
		83½ p	0/1/4	Eugenio Suárez Falero
	Zapotlán	36:10 f m	1/4	Francisco Camarena
		37 p	0/1/4	Eugenio Suárez Falero
	Jalisco	144:11 f m	2/0/6	Juan Tenorio
		145 p	0/1/6	Juan Tenorio
	Tepic	89:7 f m	2/0/6	Juan Tenorio
		89½ p	0/1/6	Juan Tenorio
	Analco Tepic	12:2 f m	2/0/6	Juan Tenorio
		12 p	0/1/6	Juan Tenorio
	Sentispac	297 f m	2/	Francisco Camarena
		(pero por orden de la R. Aud 14-II-1595, a causa de la necesidad de los indios, el maíz estaba vendido a ellos a 1/2, y esta almoneda hecha inválida)		
		402 p	0/1/3	Francisco Camarena
	Jaltemba, Santa María	6:9 f m	1/6/6	Francisco Camarena
		7 p	0/1	Francisco Camarena
	Papachula, San Juan	5:4 f m	1/6/6	Francisco Camarena
		5½ p	0/1	Francisco Camarena
	Zanatlán, San Miguel	21:2 f m	1/6/6	Francisco Camarena
		21½ p	0/1	Francisco Camarena
	Mayanalistlán, San Pedro	6:4 f m	2/0/6	Francisco Camarena
	Ixtapa, Santa María	5:3 f sal	0/4	Francisco Camarena
		9½ p	0/1	Francisco Camarena
		1 car alg	1/	Francisco Camarena
		2 @ pes	0/4	Francisco Camarena
	Jalcocotán	32:4 f m	1/6	Don Juan de Tovar
		32½ p	0/1/1	Don Juan de Tovar
	Mecatán	41:4 f m	1/6	Don Juan de Tovar
		41½ p	0/1/1	Don Juan de Tovar
	Canala, San Juan, y Acatispa	5:6 f m	1/6/6	Francisco Camarena
		5½ p	0/1	Francisco Camarena
	Tostomotoc, San Miguel	17:1 f m	1/6/6	Francisco Camarena
		17½ p	0/1	Francisco Camarena
	Temichoque	18 f m	1/6/6	Francisco Camarena
		5½ @ alg	0/4	Francisco Camarena

Date	Town	Item & Amount	Unit Price	Buyer & Remarks
		11½ p	0/1	Francisco Camarena
	Pontoque	69 f m	1/6/6	Francisco Camarena
		7 p	0/1	Francisco Camarena
	Ixcuintla	9:11 f m	1/6/6	Francisco Camarena
		10 p	0/1	Francisco Camarena
	Ixtapa, de Castañeda	7 f sal	0/4	Francisco Camarena
	Matacticpac	11:8 f m	1/6/6	Francisco Camarena
		12 p	0/1	Francisco Camarena
	Quilitlán	18 f m	1/6/6	Francisco Camarena
		1 @ miel	1/	Francisco Camarena
	Jaltepec	9 f m	1/6/6	Francisco Camarena
		9 p	0/1	Francisco Camarena
		1 j miel--qtla	0/2	Francisco Camarena
	Tomatlán	9 f m	1/6/6	Francisco Camarena
		2 j miel	0/4	Francisco Camarena
		2 g	0/2	Francisco Camarena
	Jalisquillo	18 f m	1/6/6	Francisco Camarena
	Cusimini, San Andrés	9 f m	1/6/6	Francisco Camarena
		2 j miel	0/4	Francisco Camarena
	Acaponeta	164 p	0/1	Francisco Camarena
	Mascota	34:2 f m	1/	Alvaro de Figueroa
		34½ p	0/1	Alvaro de Figueroa
	Tepetlatlauca	11:8 f m	1/0	Alvaro de Figueroa
		13½ p	0/1	Alvaro de Figueroa
	Chistique	24:6 f m	1/0	Alvaro de Figueroa
		24½ p	0/1	Alvaro de Figueroa
	Atengoichán	18:3 f m	1/0/9	Alvaro de Figueroa
		18½ p	0/1	Alvaro de Figueroa
	Zacatlán	27 f m	1/0/9	Alvaro de Figueroa
	Amatlán y Jalacingo	18:4 f m	1/0/9	Alvaro de Figueroa
		18½ p	0/1	Alvaro de Figueroa
	Tepuzhuacán	9:3 f m	1/0/9	Alvaro de Figueroa
		9½ p	0/1	Alvaro de Figueroa
	Panpuchín } Zapotlán } Sila } Contla }	22:4 f m	0/4	Cristóbal de Sandoval
		29½ p	0/1	Cristóbal de Sandoval
		(15 f m para el convento)		
	Opono	47:9 f m	0/4	Cristóbal de Sandoval
		48 p	0/1	Cristóbal de Sandoval
	Piloto y sujetos	28:1 f m	0/4	Cristóbal de Sandoval
		53 p	0/1	Cristóbal de Sandoval
		(25 f m para el convento)		
	Guamuchal	13:8 f m	0/4	Cristóbal de Sandoval

Date	Town	Item & Amount	Unit Price	Buyer & Remarks
	y Chamela	14 p	0/1	Cristóbal de Sandoval
	Ocotlán } Jocotlán } Santa Ana}	108:11 f m 109 p	1/3 0/1/6	Cosme López Cosme López
12-I-1596	Atixtac	8:11 f m (ninguna almoneda de pollo)	0/6	Diego de Porres
	Ocotlán } Jocotlán } Santa Ana}	108:11 f m (ninguna almoneda de pollo y lo demás abajo)	0/7/9	Cosme López
	Tonalá	131:8 f m (112:8 f m para el convento)	0/6	Antonio Vélez de Vargas
	Atemajac	112:6 f m	0/6	Rodrigo Hernández Cordero
	Tlajomulco	351:10 f m (100 f m para el convento)	0/6	Diego de Porres
	Poncitlán	164:6 f m (100 f m para el convento)	0/6	Lic. Alarcón
	Cuitzeo	46:8 f m (100 f m para el convento)	0/6	Lic. Alarcón
	Cuyutlán y Cajititlán	109:10 f m	0/6	Antonio Vélez de Vargas
	Matatlán	36 f m	0/5	Cristóbal Ordóñez
	Mexcala	14:5 f m	0/5	Cristóbal Ordóñez
	Tequila y Guastla	123:4 f m	0/5	Miguel Manuel Pimentel
	Tetitlán	46:9 f m	0/5	Tomás Pérez
	Tepequexpan	34:10 f m	0/5	Tomás Pérez
	San Pedro	16:2 f m	0/5	Tomás Pérez
	Camotlán	42:4 f m	0/5	Tomás Pérez
	Acuitlapilco y Zapotlán	47:8 f m	0/5	Tomás Pérez
13-I-1596	Ahuisculco	15:3 f m	0/6	Gonzalo Núñez
	Hostotilac y Jocotlán (partido de)	70:7 f m	0/4/3	Tomás Pérez
	Ahuacatlán	30:11 f m	0/7/7	Miguel Manuel
	Suchipil	59:11 f m (53 f m al convento)	0/7/7	Miguel Manuel
	Amaxaque	17:10 f m	0/7/7	Miguel Manuel
	Jala	93:5 f m (60 f m al convento)	0/7/7	Miguel Manuel
	Hostotipaquillo	83:8 f m	0/6	Antonio Vélez de Vargas

Date	Town	Item & Amount	Unit Price	Buyer & Remarks
	Zapotlán	36:10 f m	0/6	Antonio Vélez de Vargas
	Jalisco	44:10 f m (100 f m para el convento)	0/7	Juan Bautista de Agüero
	Tepic	39:7 f m	0/7	Juan Bautista de Agüero
	Analco Tepic	12:2 f m	0/7	Juan Bautista de Agüero
	Sentispac y San Andrés	95:3 f m (100 f m para el convento) (101:8 f m aplazadas a la proxima cosecha--van a pagar a razón de 0/6 la fanega)	0/6	Indios del pueblo
	Ixtlán	10:9 f m	0/6	Gonzalo Núñez
	Analco	260:8 f m (75 f m al convento)	0/6/6	Gonzalo Núñez
	Tlaquepaque y Toluquilla	178:4 f m (75 f m al convento)	0/6/6	Rodrigo de Balcázar
	Mezquituta y Moyagua	50:7 f m (25 f m al convento)	0/4	Tomás Pérez
	Copala y Quilitlán	18 f m	0/6	Gonzalo Núñez
	Tesistán	44:6 f m	0/6	Gonzalo Núñez
	Tepeaca y Epatlán	21:7 f m	0/6	Gonzalo Núñez
	Nochistlanejo	31:6 f m	0/6	Gonzalo Núñez
	Zalatitlán	37:4 f m	--reservadas para los frailes	
	Jalcocotán	32:4 f m	0/6	Francisco Camarena
	Mecatán	41:4 f m	0/6	Francisco Camarena
17-I-1596	Jaltemba, Santa María	6:9 f m	0/4/6	Tomás Pérez
	Papachula, San Juan	5:4 f m	0/4/6	Tomás Pérez
	Zanatlán, San Miguel	21:2 f m	0/4/6	Tomás Pérez
	Mayanalistlán, San Pedro	6:4 f m	0/4/6	Tomás Pérez
	Ixtapa, Santa María	5:3 f sal 1 car alg 2 @ pes	0/4 1/0 0/4 @	Tomás Pérez Tomás Pérez Tomás Pérez
	Canala, San Juan	5:6 f m	0/4/6	Tomás Pérez
	Tostomotoc, San Miguel	17:1 f m	0/4/6	Tomás Pérez
	Temichoque	18 f m 5½ @ alg	0/4/6 0/4	Tomás Pérez Tomás Pérez
	Pontoque	6:9 f m	0/4/6	Tomás Pérez

Date	Town	Item & Amount	Unit Price	Buyer & Remarks
	Santiago Iztapa	9:11 f m	0/4/6	Tomás Pérez
	Ixtapa	7 f sal	0/4	Tomás Pérez
	Matacticpac	11:8 f m	0/4/6	Tomás Pérez
	Quilitlán	18 f m 1 @ miel	0/4/6 1/	Tomás Pérez Tomás Pérez
	Jaltepec	9 f m 1 j miel--qtla	0/4/6 0/2	Tomás Pérez Tomás Pérez
	Tomatlán	9 f m 2 j miel 2 g	0/4/6 0/4 0/2	Tomás Pérez Tomás Pérez Tomás Pérez
	Jalisquillo	18 f m	0/4/6	Tomás Pérez
	Cusimini, San Andrés	9 f m 2 j miel	0/4/6 0/4	Tomás Pérez Tomás Pérez
	Acaponeta	Nota: No se vendieron 73:8 f m por orden de la R. Audencia, porque se destinaron a los indios "que va poblando en Acaponeta" el capitán Gerónimo Pérez de Arciniegas.		
	Apozol	62:7 f m (25 f m al convento) (ninguna almoneda de pollo)	0/4	Tomás Pérez
	Suchitlán	22:6 f m	0/4	Tomás Pérez
	Coscotitán, San Cristóbal } Camotlán y Cuyutlán }	maíz conmutado		} ningún cambio de tasación
18-I-1596	Jocotlán Par.: Huelotitlán } Acatique } Yegualtitlán } Inrimota } Tequiltitlán } Cuyolomitle } Mezquitlán } Cacaluta }	174:3 f m	0/4/3	Tomás Pérez
	Mascota	34:2 f m	0/4	Gerónimo de Aguayo
	Tepetlatlauca	11:8 f m	0/4	Gerónimo de Aguayo
	Chistique	24:6 f m	0/4	Gerónimo de Aguayo
	Atengoichán	18:3 f m	0/4	Rodrigo de Ojeda
	Zacatlán	27 f m	0/4	Rodrigo de Ojeda
	Amatlán y Jalacingo	10:10 f m	0/4	Rodrigo de Ojeda
	Tepuzhuacán	9:3 f m	0/4	Rodrigo de Ojeda
	Panpuchín, Sila, Zapotlán	25:7 f m	0/3	Antonio Vélez de Vargas

Date	Town	Item & Amount	Unit Price	Buyer & Remarks
	Opono	47:9 f m	0/3	Antonio Vélez de Vargas
	Piloto y sujetos	53:1 f m	0/3	Antonio Vélez de Vargas
	Guamuchal y Chamela	13:11 f m	0/3	Antonio Vélez de Vargas
	Chola (Purif.)	4:6 f m	0/3	Antonio Vélez de Vargas
	Jocotlán (Purif.)	15 f m	0/3	Antonio Vélez de Vargas
21-I-1597	Atixtac	16:2 f m	0/7	Pedro de Cuéllar
	Apozol	110:8 f m (50 f m al convento)	0/5/6	Juan de Ledesma
	Ocotlán } Jocotlán } Santa Ana }	108:11 f m	1/	Pedro de Cuéllar
	Ixtlán	16:2 f m	0/7	Pedro de Cuéllar
	Analco	260 f m (75 f m al convento)	1/	Indios de Analco
	Tlaquepaque y Toluquilla	178:4 f m (75 f m al convento)	1/	Lic. Alarcón
	Tonalá	130:4 f m (112:8 f m al convento)	1/0/3	Pedro de Cuéllar
	Atemajac	112:6 f m	0/6	Rodrigo Hernández Cordero
	Tlajomulco	351:10 f m (100 f m al convento)	0/7	Baltasar de Orozco
	Mezquituta y Moyagua	50:7 f m (25 f m al convento)	0/5/6	Juan de Ledesma
	Poncitlán	264:6 f m (100 f m al convento)	0/6	Lic. Alarcón
	Cuitzeo	46:8 f m (100 f m al convento)	0/6	Lic. Alarcón
	Copala y Quilitlán	18 f m	0/7	Pedro de Cuéllar
	Tesistán	44:6 f m	0/7	Pedro de Cuéllar
	Tepeaca y Epatlán	21:7 f m	0/7	Pedro de Cuéllar
	Suchitlán	22:6 f m	0/5/6	Pedro de Cuéllar
	Coscotitán } San Cristóbal } Camotlán y } Cuyutlán }	Maíz conmutado }		Ningún cambio de tasación
	Nochistlanejo	31:6 f m	0/7	Pedro de Cuéllar
	Zalatitlán	(37:4 f m al convento)		
	Cuyutlán y Cajititlán	109:10 f m	1/	Antonio Vélez de Vargas

Date	Town	Item & Amount	Unit Price	Buyer & Remarks
	Matatlán	36 f m	0/5/6	Diego López de la Cruz
	Mexcala	14:5 f m	0/5/6	Diego López de la Cruz
	Tequila y Guastla	123:4 f m	0/7	Lic. Alarcón
	Ahuisculco	15:3 f m	0/7	Pedro de Cuéllar
22-I-1597	Jocotlán Par.: Huelotitlán } Acatique } Yegualtitlán } Inrimota } Tequiltitlán } Cuyolomitle } Mezquitlán } Cacaluta y } Amaxaque }	174:3 f m	0/4	Martín Real
	Hostotipac	70:7 f m	0/4	Martín Real
	Ahuacatlán	31:6 f m	1/0/7	Cristobal de Sandoval
	Suchipil	58:8 f m (53 f m al convento)	1/0/7	Cristobal de Sandoval
	Amaxaque	17:10 f m	1/0/7	Cristobal de Sandoval
	Jala	92:9 f m (60 f m al convento)	1/0/1	Cristobal de Sandoval
	Tetitlán	46:9 f m	0/7	Juan Bautista de Agüero
	Tepequexpan	34:8 f m	0/7	Juan Bautista de Agüero
	San Pedro	16:2 f m	0/7	Juan Bautista de Agüero
	Camotlán	42:4 f m	0/7	Juan Bautista de Agüero
	Acuitlapilco y Zapotlán	47:8 f m	0/7	Juan Bautista de Agüero
	Hostotipaquillo	83:8 f m	1/1	Antonio Vélez de Vargas
	Zapotlán	36:10 f m	1/1	Antonio Vélez de Vargas
	Jalisco	44:10 f m (100 f m al convento)	1/	Lic. Alarcón
		(Al fin, por órden virreinal, dadas como parte de las 150 f m de Jalisco y Tepic para los indios de Acaponeta)		
	Tepic	89:7 f m	1/	Lic. Alarcón
		(realmente dadas a Gerónimo Pérez de Arciniegas, capitán de Acaponeta, para alimento de los indios de aquel pueblo--fue parte de las 150 f m mandadas proveer por el virrey)		
	Analco Tepic	12:2 f m (apunte como arriba)	1/	Lic. Alarcón
	Sentispac	197 f m (100 f m al convento)	0/7	Rodrigo de Ojeda

Date	Town	Item & Amount	Unit Price	Buyer & Remarks
23-I-1597	Jaltemba, Santa María	6:9 f m	1/	Don Diego de Robles
	Papachula, San Juan	5:4 f m	1/	Don Diego de Robles
	Zanatlán, San Miguel	21:2 f m	1/	Don Diego de Robles
	Mayanalistlán, San Pedro	6:4 f m	1/	Don Diego de Robles
	Ixtapa, Santa María	5:3 f sal	0/4	Don Diego de Robles
		1 car alg	1/	Don Diego de Robles
		2 @ pes	0/4	Don Diego de Robles
	Jalcocotán	32:4 f m	0/6	Lic. Alarcón
	Mecatán	41:4 f m	0/6	Lic. Alarcón
	Canala, San Juan	5:6 f m	1/	Don Diego de Robles
	Tosmotoc, San Miguel	17:1 f m	1/	Don Diego de Robles
	Temichoque	18 f m	1/	Don Diego de Robles
	Pontoque	6:9 f m	1/	Don Diego de Robles
	Santiago Iztapa	9:11 f m	1/	Don Diego de Robles
	Ixtapa, de C.	7 f sal	0/4	Don Diego de Robles
	Matacticpac	11:8 f m	1/	Don Diego de Robles
	Quilitlán	18 f m	1/	Don Diego de Robles
		1 @ miel	1/	Don Diego de Robles
	Jaltepec	9 f m	1/	Don Diego de Robles
		1 j miel	0/2	Don Diego de Robles
	Tomatlán	9 f m	1/	Don Diego de Robles
		2 j miel	0/4	Don Diego de Robles
	Jalisquillo	18 f m	1/	Don Diego de Robles
	Cusmini, San Andrés	9 f m	1/	Don Diego de Robles
		2 j miel	0/4	Don Diego de Robles
	Acaponeta	--indios sin maíz y sin cosecha.		
	Mascota	34:2 f m	0/5/1	Cristóbal de Sandoval
	Tepetlatlauca	11:8 f m	0/5/1	Cristóbal de Sandoval
	Chistique	24:6 f m	0/5/1	Cristóbal de Sandoval
	Atengoichán	18:3 f m	0/4/6	Cristóbal de Sandoval
	Zacatlán	27 f m	0/4/6	Cristóbal de Sandoval
	Amatlán y Jalacingo	10:10 f m	0/4/6	Cristóbal de Sandoval
	Tepuzhuacán	9:3 f m	0/4/6	Cristóbal de Sandoval
	Panpuchín }			

Date	Town	Item & Amount	Unit Price	Buyer & Remarks
	Sila } Zapotlán }	25:7 f m	0/4/6	Francisco de Balbuena
	Opono	47:9 f m	0/4/6	Francisco de Balbuena
	Piloto	42:5 f m	0/4/6	Francisco de Balbuena
	Guamuchal y Chamela	13:11 f m	0/4/6	Francisco de Balbuena
	Chola	6:9 f m	0/4/6	Francisco de Balbuena
	Jocotlán	22:6 f m	0/4/6	Francisco de Balbuena
13-I-1598	Atixtac	16:2 f m	1/3/6	Francisco Ruiz de Guzmán
	Ocotlán } Jocotlán } Santa Ana}	81 f m	1/3	Don Diego de Padilla
	Analco	260:8 f m (75 f m al convento)	1/2/8	Francisco Ruiz de Guzmán
	Tlaquepaque y Toluquilla	178:4 f m (75 f m al convento)	1/2	Andrés de Torres
	Tonalá	84:11 f m (112:8 f m al convento)	1/3/1	Baltasar de Orozco
	Atemajac	91:7 f m	1/2	Rodrigo Hernández Cordero
	Poncitlán	264:6 f m (100 f m al convento)	1/3/7	Don Diego de Padilla
	Cuitzeo	46:6 f m (100 f m al convento)	1/3/7	Don Diego de Padilla
	Copala y Quilitlán	18 f m	1/0/3	Juan de Ledesma, "el pertiguero"
	Tesistán	44:6 f m	1/2/6	Diego de Espinosa
	Tepeaca y Epatlán	21:7 f m	1/2/6	Diego de Espinosa
	Suchitlán	22½ f m	0/6	Pedro de Cuéllar
	Coscotitán, San Cristóbal	24 f m	0/6	Pedro de Cuéllar
	Cuyutlán y Cajititlán	109:10 f m	1/3	Francisco Ruiz de Guzmán
14-I-1598	Cuyutlán, Sta. María (barranca)	16:8 f m	0/6	Pedro de Cuéllar
	Nochistlanejo	31:6 f m	1/2/4	Pedro de Plaza
	Zalatitlán	(37:4 f m al Padre)		
	Matatlán	36 f m	1/0/6	Don Diego de Robles
	Mexcala	14:5 f m	1/0/6	Don Diego de Robles
	Tequila y San Francisco	99:2 f m	1/1	Don Diego de Robles

Date	Town	Item & Amount	Unit Price	Buyer & Remarks
	Guastla o Los Guajes	5:5 f m	1/1	Don Diego de Robles
	Ahuisculco	15:3 f m	1/2/4	Pedro de Plaza
	Jocotlán Part.:			
	Yegualtitlán }	79 f m	0/6	Juan de Ledesma, "el pertiguero"
Amaxaque	}			
	Huelotitlán }	79 p	0/1	Juan de Ledesma, "el pertiguero"
	Inrimota }			
	Tequiltitlán }			
	Mezquitlán }			
	Cacaluta }			
	Acatique }			
	Hostotipaquillo	54 f m	0/6	Juan de Ledesma, "el pertiguero"
		54 p	0/1	Juan de Ledesma, "el pertiguero"
	Ahuacatlán	29:3 f m	0/7/7	Pedro de Cuéllar
		29½ p	0/1	Pedro de Cuéllar
	Suchipil	58:8 f m	0/7/7	Pedro de Cuéllar
		(53 f m al convento)		
		112 p	0/1	Pedro de Cuéllar
	Amaxaque	17:10 f m	{ 0/7/7 { t 16/7/4	Pedro de Cuéllar
		18 p	0/1	Pedro de Cuéllar
	Apozol	78:7 f m	0/4	Andrés de Torres
		(25 f m al convento)		
	Ixtlán	16:2 f m	1/2/4	Pedro de Plaza
	Tlajomulco	341:3 f m	1/3/6	Francisco Ruiz de Guzmán
		(100 f m para los Padres)		
	Mezquituta y Moyagua	50:7 f m	1/0/1	Andrés de Torres
		(25 f m al convento)		
	Mascota	27 f m	0/4	Martín Real
		27 p	0/1	Martín Real
	Tepetlatlauca	7:10 f m	0/4	Martín Real
		8½ p	0/1	Martín Real
	Chistique	20 f m	0/4	Martín Real
		20 p	0/1	Martín Real
	Atengoichán	15:8 f m	0/4	Cristóbal de Sandoval
		15½ p	0/1	Cristóbal de Sandoval
	Zacatlán	19:2 f m	0/4	Cristóbal de Sandoval
		5½ p	0/1	Cristóbal de Sandoval
	Amatlán y Jalacingo	10:10 f m	0/4	Cristóbal de Sandoval
		11 p	0/1	Cristóbal de Sandoval
	Tepuzhuacán	7:9 f m	0/4	Cristóbal de Sandoval
		7½ p	0/1	Cristóbal de Sandoval
15-I-1598	Acaponeta	174 p	0/1	Capitán Gerónimo de Arciniegas
		(100 f m al convento)		

Date	Town	Item & Amount	Unit Price	Buyer & Remarks
	(73:8 f m reservadas por si acaso los indios de Acaponeta siguieren de necesitarlas)			
	Panpuchín	15:8 f m	0/5	Antonio Vélez de Vargas
		15½ p	0/1	Antonio Vélez de Vargas
	Opono	39:2 f m	0/5	Antonio Vélez de Vargas
		39 p	0/1	Antonio Vélez de Vargas
	Piloto	27:6 f m	0/5	Antonio Vélez de Vargas
		27½ p	0/1	Antonio Vélez de Vargas
	Guamuchal y Chamela	13:6 f m	0/5	Antonio Vélez de Vargas
		13½ p	0/1	Antonio Vélez de Vargas
	Santiago Jocotlán (en Purif.)	18:10 f m	0/5	Antonio Vélez de Vargas
		18½ p	0/1	Antonio Vélez de Vargas
	Zapotlán } Sila } Chola } Contla }	27 f m	0/5	Antonio Vélez de Vargas
		18½ p	0/1	Antonio Vélez de Vargas
	Jala	92:9 f m	0/7/7	Pedro de Plaza
		(60 f m al convento)		
		168½ p	0/1	Pedro de Plaza
	Tetitlán	46:9 f m	0/5/2	Juan Bautista de Agüero
		47 p	0/1	Juan Bautista de Agüero
	Tepequexpan	34:8 f m	0/5/2	Juan Bautista de Agüero
		35 p	0/1/1	Juan Bautista de Agüero
	San Pedro	16:2 f m	0/5/2	Juan Bautista de Agüero
		16½ p	0/1/1	Juan Bautista de Agüero
	Camotlán	42:4 f m	0/5/2	Juan Bautista de Agüero
		42½ p	0/1/1	Juan Bautista de Agüero
	Acuitlapilco y Zapotlán	47:8 f m	0/5/2	Juan Bautista de Agüero
		48 p	0/1/1	Juan Bautista de Agüero
	Hostotipaquillo	83:8 f m	0/7	Antonio Vélez de Varas
	Zapotlán	36:10 f m	0/7	Antonio Vélez de Vargas
	Jalisco	41:6 f m	0/6/6	Juan de Ledesma
		(100 f m al convento)		
	Tepic	89:7 f m	0/6/6	Gerónimo Montesmías
	Analco Tepic	12:2 f m	0/6/6	Gerónimo Montesmías
	Sentispac	92:2 f m	0/6/6	Martín Real de Azúa
		(100 f m al convento)		
		298 p	0/1/1	Antonio Vélez de Vargas
	Jaltemba, Sta. María	6:9 f m	1/6	Gonzalo Núñez
		7 p	0/1	Gonzalo Núñez
	Papachula, San Juan	5:4 f m	1/6	Gonzalo Núñez
		5½ p	0/1	Gonzalo Núñez
	Zanatlán, San Miguel	21:2 f m	1/6	Gonzalo Núñez
		21 p	0/1	Gonzalo Núñez

Date	Town	Item & Amount	Unit Price	Buyer & Remarks
	Mayanalistlán, San Pedro	5:4 f m	1/6	Gonzalo Núñez
	Ixtapa, Sta. María	5:3 f sal	0/4	Gonzalo Núñez
		9½ p	0/1	Gonzalo Núñez
		1 car alg	1/	Gonzalo Núñez
		2 @ pes	0/4	Gonzalo Núñez
	Jalcocotán	32:4 f m	0/4	Miguel Manuel
		32½ p	0/1	Miguel Manuel
	Mecatán	41:4 f m	0/4	Miguel Manuel
		41½ p	0/1	Miguel Manuel
	Canala, San Juan	5:6 f m	1/6	Miguel Manuel
		5½ p	0/1	Miguel Manuel
	Tosmotoc, San Miguel	17:1 f m	1/6	Miguel Manuel
		17½ p	0/1	Miguel Manuel
	Temichoque	18 f m	1/6	Miguel Manuel
		5½ @ alg	0/4	Miguel Manuel
		11 p	0/1	Miguel Manuel
	Pontoque	6:9 f m	1/6	Miguel Manuel
		7 p	0/1	Miguel Manuel
	Santiago Iztlapa	9:11 f m	1/6	Miguel Manuel
		10 p	0/1	Miguel Manuel
	Ixtapa	7 f sal	0/4	Miguel Manuel
	Matacticpac	11:8 f m	1/6	Miguel Manuel
		12 p	0/1	Miguel Manuel
	Quilitlán	18 f m	1/6	Miguel Manuel
		1 @ miel	1/	Miguel Manuel
	Jaltepec	9 f m	1/6	Miguel Manuel
		9 p	0/1	Miguel Manuel
		1 j miel	0/2	Miguel Manuel
	Tomatlán	9 f m	1/6	Miguel Manuel
		2 g	0/2	Miguel Manuel
		2 j miel	0/4	Miguel Manuel
	Jalisquillo	18 f m	1/6	Miguel Manuel
	Cusmini, San Andrés	9 f m	1/6	Miguel Manuel
		2 j miel	0/4	Miguel Manuel
18-I-1599	Contla y Jala	45 f m	0/4	Andrés de Torres
	Apozol	68:7 f m (25 f m al convento)	0/4	Andrés de Torres
	Atixtac	16:2 f m	0/7/1	Juan Bautista de Agüero
	Ocotlan } Jocotlán } Santa Ana }	81 f m	0/7/1	Cosme López
	Ixtlán	13:2 f m	0/5	Pedro de Cuéllar
	Analco	260:8 f m	0/6	Pedro de Cuéllar

Date	Town	Item & Amount	Unit Price	Buyer & Remarks
		(75 f m al convento)		
	Tlaquepaque y Toluquilla	178:4 f m (75 f m al convento)	0/6	Andrés de Torres
	Tonalá	82:7 f m (115 f m al convento y al Padre)	0/6	Pedro de Cuéllar
	Atemajac	89:7 f m	0/6	Andrés de Torres
	Tlajomulco	307:3 f m (100 f m al convento)	0/7/3	Juan Bautista de Agüero
	Mezquituta y Moyagua	50:7 f m (25 f m al convento)	0/4	Andrés de Torres
	Poncitlán	264:6 f m (100 f m al convento)	1/	Pedro de Cuéllar
	Cuitzeo	46:8 f m (100 f m al convento)	1/	Pedro de Cuéllar
	Copala y Quilitlán	18 f m	0/6	Pedro de Cuéllar
	Tesistán	44:6 f m	0/6	Pedro de Cuéllar
	Tepeaca y Epatlán	21:7 f m	0/6	Pedro de Cuéllar
	Suchitlán	22:6 f m	0/4	Andrés de Torres
	Coscotitán, San Cristóbal (en la barranca)	24 f m	0/6/8	Pedro de Cuéllar
	Cuyutlán, Santa María (en la barranca)	16:8 f m	0/6/8	Pedro de Cuéllar
	Nochistlanejo	31:6 f m	0/5	Pedro de Cuéllar
	Zalatitlán	(35 f m al convento)		
	Cuyutlán y Cajititlán	109:10 f m	0/6/8	Andrés de Torres
	Matatlán	36 f m	0/4	Cristóbal de Sandoval
	Mexcala	14:5 f m	0/4	Cristóbal de Sandoval
	Tequila y San Francisco	97:10 f m	0/7	Domingo de Lizarraras
	Guastla o Los Guajes	5:5 f m	0/7	Domingo de Lizarraras
	Ahuisculco	13:6 f m	0/5/11	Pedro de Cuéllar
19-I-1599	Jocotlán Par.: Amaxaque } Yegualtitlán} Acatique } Huelotitlán } Inrimota } Tequiltitlán} Mezquitlán }	79 f m	0/4	Juan de Ledesma

Date	Town	Item & Amount	Unit Price	Buyer & Remarks
	Cacaluta }			
	Hostotipac	35:1 f m	0/4	Juan de Ledesma
	Ahuacatlán	29:3 f m	0/6	Juan Bautista de Agüero
	Suchipil	58:8 f m (53 f m al convento)	0/6	Juan Bautista de Agüero
	Amaxaque	17:10 f m	0/6	Juan Bautista de Agüero
	Jala	92:9 f m (60 f m al convento)	0/6/6	Juan Bautista de Agüero
	Tetitlán	46:9 f m	0/6/1	Juan Bautista de Agüero
	Tepequexpan	34:8 f m	0/6/1	Juan Bautista de Agüero
	San Pedro	16:2 f m	0/6/1	Juan Bautista de Agüero
	Camotlán	42:4 f m	0/6/1	Juan Bautista de Agüero
	Acuitlapilco y Zapotlán	47:8 f m	0/6/1	Juan Bautista de Agüero
	Hostotipaquillo y sujetos	72:10 f m	0/7/2	Antonio Vélez de Vargas
	Zapotlán	36:10 f m	0/7/2	Antonio Vélez de Vargas
	Jalisco	(61:10 f m al convento)		
	Tepic	50:10 f m (38:9 f m al convento)	1/0/2	Juan de Ledesma
	Analco Tepic	12:2 f m	1/0/2	Juan de Ledesma
	Sentispac	92:2 f m (100 f m al convento)	0/7	Francisco Camarena
	Jaltemba, Santa María	4:6 f m	0/5	Juan de Cepeda
	Papachula, San Juan	3:4 f m	0/5	Juan de Cepeda
	Zanatlán, San Miguel	7:2 f m	0/5	Juan de Cepeda
	Mayanalistlán, San Pedro	3:2 f m	0/5	Juan de Cepeda
	Jalcocotán	32:4 f m	0/4	Juan de Ledesma
	Mecatán	41:4 f m	0/4	Juan de Ledesma
	Canala, San Juan	2:8 f m	0/5	Juan de Cepeda
	Tosmotoc, San Miguel	17:1 f m	0/5	Juan de Cepeda
	Temichoque, Santiago	7:8 f m	0/5	Juan de Cepeda
	Pontoque	3:2 f m	0/5	Juan de Cepeda

Date	Town	Item & Amount	Unit Price	Buyer & Remarks
	Santiago Ixtapa	9:11 f m	0/5	Juan de Cepeda
	Ixtapa	0:11 f m	0/5	Juan de Cepeda
	Matacticpac	11:8 f m	0/5	Juan de Cepeda
	Quilitlán	7:2 f m	0/5	Juan de Cepeda
	Jaltepec	9 f m	0/5	Juan de Cepeda
		1 j miel	0/2	Juan de Cepeda
	Jalisquillo	18 f m	0/5	Juan de Cepeda
	Acaponeta	73:8 f m (100 f m al convento)	0/4	Martín Real
	Mascota	18:11 f m	0/4	Bachiller Juan Jiménez Calderón, Relator
	Tepetlatlauca	3:8 f m	0/4	Bachiller, Juan Jiménez Calderón, Relator
	Chistique	14:10 f m	0/4	Bachiller Juan Jiménez Calderón, Relator
	Guauchinango, Naborías	9:4 f m	0/4	Bachiller Juan Jiménez Calderón, Relator
	Atengoichán	12:10 f m	0/4	Bachiller Juan Jiménez Calderón, Relator
	Zacatlán	10:4 f m	0/4	Bachiller Juan Jiménez Calderón, Relator
	Amatlán y Jalacingo	10:10 f m	0/4	Bachiller Juan Jiménez Calderón, Relator
	Tepuzhuacán	5:11 f m	0/4	Bachiller Juan Jiménez Calderón, Relator
	Panpuchín	15:9 f m	0/3	Miguel Dientes
	Opono	38:3 f m	0/3	Miguel Dientes
	Piloto	--27:6 f m reservadas para los indios que trabajan en las salinas de Purificación.		
	Guamuchal y Chamela	12:2 f m	0/3	Miguel Dientes
	Jocotlán, Santiago (en la Purificación)	15:4 f m	0/3	Miguel Dientes
	Zapotlán, Sila, Chola, Contla	26:9 f m	0/3	Miguel Dientes

Fuentes:

AGI, Contaduría, legs. 853, 856, 857, 858, 859A, 859B, 860, 861A, 861B, 867B, 869A

Appendix B

Auctions of Tributes in Zacatecas, 1580

3-XII-1580	Tlaltenango	341 p	0/1	?
		m to salinas de Peñol Blanco		
	Nochistlán	252 p	0/1	?
		252 fm	0/3	?
	Teocaltiche	253 p	0/1	?
		m to salinas of Peñol Blanco		
	Teocaltitlán	91 p.	0/1	?
		m to salinas of Peñol Blanco		
	Mitic	120 p	0/1	?
		m to salinas of Peñol Blanco		
	Mexticacán	132 p	0/1	?
		132 fm	0/3	?

Source: Biblioteca Público del Estado, Guadalajara, Archivo de la Real Audiencia, Ramo Fiscal, exp. 1, Cargo de Reales Tributos de Zacatecas, año 1580, 3-XII-1580

Appendix C

Annual Weighted Averages Used in Calculations

	Maize: Nueva Galicia				Maize: Coast			
Year	Number Towns	Total Fanegas	Total Granos	Av Value Granos	Number Towns	Total Fanegas	Total Granos	Av Value Granos
1557	27	7812.0	194592	25	16	2273.0	58416	26
1558	8	4324.5	179118	41				
1559	48	13640.0	518196	38	21	2290.0	73158	32
1560	36	8380.0	543210	65	19	1819.0	52836	29
1561	37	8305.0	507000	61	19	1999.0	66342	33
1562	26	7950.0	474469	60	9	1634.5	65883	40
1563	39	8259.0	587335	71	21	1939.0	124665	64
1564	38	8066.9	572717	71	18	1834.5	127362	69
1565	38	8647.0	465414	54	19	1825.5	125538	69
1566	31	8134.5	455188	56	10	1489.5	75438	51
1567	29	7572.0	448413	59	8	1376.5	58596	43
1568	38	7937.5	438301	55	17	1800.5	92019	51
1569	38	7031.5	326650	46	17	1811.5	76741	42
1570	39	6923.2	344518	50	18	1845.2	82752	45
1571	41	7484.1	337435	45	18	2059.5	94975	46
1572	50	7582.1	499255	66	27	2118.5	132659	63
1573	31	5651.7	404092	71	11	902.5	52221	58
1574	53	7001.5	415564	59	28	2173.5	147664	68
1575	59	6377.9	483764	76	35	1664.2	143875	86
1576	52	6942.6	587796	85	27	2292.5	222384	97
1577	41	3276.7	221661	68	33	2086.0	168238	81
1578	62	6224.8	554678	89	42	2200.7	255178	116
*								
1580	75	5807.8	536435	92	57	2303.3	188295	82
1581	74	5379.9	483603	90	54	2379.7	235511	99
1582	75	5209.4	501226	96	56	2275.7	244120	107
1583	71	5003.6	331005	66	52	2169.8	137516	63
1584	71	5046.6	236424	47	52	2239.5	78031	35
1585	72	4869.1	351461	72	53	2308.5	171271	74
1586	78	4863.1	466417	96	57	2580.2	235580	91
1587	2	369.0	27594	75				
*								
1590	83	5055.0	499227	99	57	2447.8	215163	88
1591	80	4474.0	386791	86	55	2259.6	143455	63
1592	75	4661.3	430681	92	57	2464.8	227457	92
1593	35	4343.4	481004	111	20	2149.7	276278	129
1594	62	4413.7	627448	142	44	2002.0	313352	157
1595	69	3560.0	242148	68	47	1535.9	96792	63
1596	69	3717.0	304847	82	47	1635.0	129384	79
1597	72	3336.2	356107	107	47	1368.4	113774	83
1598	72	3169.8	229452	72	46	1210.6	78786	65

	Maize: Plateau				Maize: Zacatecas			
Year	Number Towns	Total Fanegas	Total Granos	Av Value Granos	Number Towns	Total Fanegas	Total Granos	Av Value Granos
1557	11	5539.0	136176	25				
1558	8	4324.5	179118	41	3	2925.0	142290	49
1559	27	11350.0	445038	39	3	2475.0	152010	61
1560	17	6561.0	490374	75	4	2475.0	269730	109
1561	18	6306.0	440658	70	5	2295.0	248130	108
1562	17	6315.5	408586	65	4	2295.0	192780	84
1563	18	6320.0	462670	73	4	2295.0	130005	57
1564	20	6232.4	445355	71	5	2055.0	153810	75
1565	19	6821.5	339876	50	4	1995.0	116460	58
1566	21	6645.0	379750	57	4	2097.0	121500	58
1567	21	6195.5	389817	63	5	2076.0	122400	59
1568	21	6137.0	346282	56	5	1931.0	116841	61
1569	21	5220.0	249909	43	4	1232.5	55557	45
1570	21	5078.0	261766	52	4	1032.5	64026	62
1571	23	5424.6	242460	45	5	1384.5	43566	31
1572	23	5463.6	366596	67	5	1384.5	83763	60
1573	20	4749.2	351871	74	4	979.5	47016	48
1574	25	4828.0	267900	55	4	979.0	62454	64
1575	24	4713.7	339889	72	4	979.0	38181	39
1576	25	4650.1	365412	79	4	973.1	73816	76
1577	8	1190.7	53423	45	3	799.0	28764	36
1578	20	4024.1	299500	74	5	1462.2	64422	44
*								
1580	18	3504.5	348140	99	1	751.5	119501	159
1581	20	3000.2	248092	83	3	459.5	17131	37
1582	19	2933.7	257106	88	3	460.5	23014	50
1583	19	2833.8	193489	68	3	459.5	27084	59
1584	19	2807.1	158393	56	3	459.5	14240	31
1585	19	2560.6	180190	70	3	444.5	17365	39
1586	21	2282.9	230837	101	2	117.3	8431	72
1587	2	369.0	27594	75	2	369.0	27594	75
*								
1590	26	2607.2	284064	109	3	162.5	10732	66
1591	25	2214.4	243336	110	2	134.8	8440	63
1592	18	2196.5	203224	93	1	75.5	5441	72
1593	15	2193.7	204726	93	1	75.5	5441	72
1594	18	2411.7	314096	130	1	75.5	7331	97
1595	22	2024.1	145356	72	2	113.0	5430	48
1596	22	2082.0	175463	84	2	161.1	10641	66
1597	25	1967.8	242333	123	2	128.6	8657	67
1598	26	1959.2	150666	77	2	119.0	5718	48

	Chickens: Nueva Galicia				Chickens: Coast			
Year	Number Towns	Total Fowls	Total Granos	Av Value Granos	Number Towns	Total Fowls	Total Granos	Av Value Granos
1557	8	3275.0	10760	3	3	285.0	1790	6
1558	7	1667.0	12435	7	2	72.0	228	3
1559	25	4747.5	21942	5	13	628.0	3510	6
1560	28	4603.0	17483	4	14	634.0	2924	5
1561	26	4201.0	15385	4	11	466.0	1924	4
1562	21	4325.0	37290	9	5	390.0	2340	6
1563	31	4410.0	27294	6	14	475.0	3360	7
1564	31	4514.0	34522	8	14	500.0	3245	6
1565	32	4552.0	45127	10	14	475.0	4485	9
1566	27	4511.0	33106	7	8	412.0	4182	10
1567	26	4613.0	28243	6	6	370.0	2515	7
1568	27	4666.5	34732	7	7	419.5	3342	8
1569	39	6010.5	44075	7	17	567.5	4553	8
1570	31	5946.0	41055	7	9	496.0	4305	9
1571	36	6429.0	49625	8	12	668.0	5927	9
1572	37	6633.0	56909	9	14	862.0	7722	9
1573	36	6086.0	51669	8	11	713.0	5516	8
1574	42	6425.0	65925	10	16	1007.0	10927	11
1575	51	6371.0	77490	12	21	1273.0	14088	11
1576	56	6858.0	90437	13	25	1984.0	26841	14
1577	38	3779.5	39733	11	28	2167.0	21211	10
1578	59	6214.0	92514	15	39	2392.5	34995	15
*								
1580	72	5248.0	58056	11	53	2329.5	24064	10
1581	76	5982.5	67837	11	52	2222.5	25695	12
1582	73	6081.0	71937	12	50	2174.5	23608	11
1583	74	6183.0	89040	14	51	2382.0	30648	13
1584	73	5956.0	82021	14	50	2230.0	25406	11
1585	74	5796.0	71060	12	51	2302.5	26553	12
1586	73	4794.5	60335	13	53	2387.0	29653	12
1587	6	1105.0	13260	12				
*								
1590	80	5294.5	86149	16	57	2682.5	34110	13
1591	77	5192.0	87056	17	55	2617.0	35639	14
1592	71	4933.5	78830	16	51	2438.5	36328	15
1593	37	4797.5	73517	15	21	2353.0	35428	15
1594	61	4886.0	75848	16	42	2386.0	36261	15

	Chickens: Plateau				Chickens: Zacatecas			
Year	Number Towns	Total Fowls	Total Granos	Av Value Granos	Number Towns	Total Fowls	Total Granos	Av Value Granos
1557	5	2990.0	8970	3				
1558	5	1595.0	12207	8	3	1034.0	10524	10
1559	12	4119.5	18432	4	3	884.5	8727	10
1560	14	3969.0	14559	4	4	884.0	5304	6
1561	15	3735.0	13461	4	4	644.0	3864	6
1562	16	3935.0	34950	9	4	644.0	3864	6
1563	17	3935.0	23934	6	4	644.0	3864	6
1564	17	4014.0	31277	8	4	644.0	3864	6
1565	18	4077.0	40642	10	4	644.0	3864	6
1566	19	4099.0	28924	7	4	644.0	3864	6
1567	20	4243.0	25728	6	5	704.0	4224	6
1568	20	4247.0	31390	7	5	814.0	4884	6
1569	22	5443.0	39522	7	5	1819.0	10914	6
1570	22	5450.0	36750	7	5	1819.0	10914	6
1571	24	5761.0	43698	8	6	1569.0	9954	6
1572	23	5771.0	49187	9	6	1569.0	17380	11
1573	25	5373.0	46153	9	6	1456.0	9006	6
1574	26	5418.0	54998	10	6	1456.0	15228	10
1575	30	5098.0	63402	12	6	1146.0	13752	12
1576	31	4874.0	63596	13	5	1056.5	12489	12
1577	10	1612.5	18522	11	5	1366.0	16392	12
1578	20	3821.5	57519	15	5	1190.0	14280	12
*								
1580	19	2918.5	33992	12	1	75.5	679	9
1581	24	3760.0	42142	11	7	1264.5	14947	12
1582	23	3906.5	48329	12	7	1264.5	15174	12
1583	23	3801.0	58392	15	7	1263.5	18156	14
1584	23	3726.0	56615	15	7	1264.5	15174	12
1585	23	3493.5	44507	13	7	1209.5	14514	12
1586	20	2407.5	30682	13	1	75.5	906	12
1587	6	1105.0	13260	12	6	1105.0	13260	12
*								
1590	23	2612.0	52039	20	1	75.5	906	12
1591	22	2575.0	51417	20	1	75.5	906	12
1592	20	2495.0	42502	17	1	75.5	906	12
1593	16	2444.5	38089	16	1	75.5	906	12
1594	19	2500.0	39587	16	1	75.5	906	12

	Turkeys: Nueva Galicia				Turkeys: Coast			
Year	Number Towns	Total Fowls	Total Granos	Av Value Granos	Number Towns	Total Fowls	Total Granos	Av Value Granos
1557	4	20.0	240	12	4	20.0	240	12
1558	1	106.0	2544	24				
1559	12	386.0	7963	21	10	220.0	3979	18
1560	12	367.0	6982	19	10	201.0	3718	18
1561	12	391.0	7414	19	10	225.0	4150	18
1562	6	446.0	10524	24	3	180.0	3240	18
1563	6	446.0	11424	26	3	180.0	4440	25
1564	5	346.0	8124	23	2	80.0	1740	22
1565	10	496.0	10704	22	7	230.0	4320	19
1566	9	468.0	11400	24	5	194.0	4824	25
1567	7	452.0	10990	24	4	186.0	4506	24
1568	12	377.5	8775	23	9	221.5	5031	23
1569	12	284.0	7077	25	10	187.0	4749	25
1570	6	264.0	6399	24	4	167.0	4008	24
1571	5	219.0	5319	24	3	122.0	2928	24
1572	13	305.0	7679	25	11	208.0	5351	26
1573	6	241.0	5718	24	5	151.0	3018	20
1574	13	330.0	8469	26	12	240.0	6309	26
1575	13	330.0	8878	27	12	240.0	5998	25
1576	10	240.5	6229	26	9	150.5	3439	23
1577	8	59.5	859	14	8	59.5	859	14
1578	11	81.5	2372	29	10	74.0	2087	28
*								
1580	4	45.0	540	12	4	45.0	540	12
*								
1586	1	2.0	60	30	1	2.0	60	30
*								
1590	1	2.0	48	24	1	2.0	48	24
1591	1	2.0	48	24	1	2.0	48	24
1592	1	2.0	48	24	1	2.0	48	24
1593	1	2.0	48	24	1	2.0	48	24
1594	1	2.0	48	24	1	2.0	48	24
1595	1	2.0	48	24	1	2.0	48	24
*								
1597	1	2.0	48	24	1	2.0	48	24

	Turkeys: Plateau				Turkeys: Zacatecas			
Year	Number Towns	Total Fowls	Total Granos	Av Value Granos	Number Towns	Total Fowls	Total Granos	Av Value Granos
1558	1	106.0	2544	24	1	106.0	2544	24
1559	2	166.0	3984	24	2	166.0	3984	24
1560	2	166.0	3264	20	2	166.0	3264	20
1561	2	166.0	3264	20	2	166.0	3264	20
1562	3	266.0	7284	27	2	166.0	3984	24
1563	3	266.0	6984	26	2	166.0	3984	24
1564	3	266.0	6384	24	2	166.0	3984	24
1565	3	266.0	6384	24	2	166.0	3984	24
1566	4	274.0	6576	24	2	166.0	3984	24
1567	3	266.0	6484	24	2	166.0	3984	24
1568	3	156.0	3744	24	2	149.0	3576	24
1569	2	97.0	2328	24				
1570	2	97.0	2391	25				
1571	2	97.0	2391	25				
1572	2	97.0	2328	24				
1573	1	90.0	2700	30				
1574	1	90.0	2160	24				
1575	1	90.0	2880	32				
1576	1	90.0	2790	31				
*								
1578	1	7.5	285	38				

	Wheat: Nueva Galicia				Wheat: Coast			
Year	Number Towns	Total Fanegas	Total Granos	Av Value Granos	Number Towns	Total Fanegas	Total Granos	Av Value Granos
1555	1	22.0	3168	144				
*								
1557	5	106.0	13416	127	4	83.5	11256	135
1558	1	22.5	2160	96				
1559	4	130.5	11232	86	3	108.0	9072	84
1560	4	130.5	11232	86	3	108.0	9072	84
1561	4	74.0	6348	86	3	63.0	5292	84
1562	4	74.0	6480	88	3	63.0	5292	84
1563	4	74.0	7200	97	3	63.0	5616	89
1564	4	74.0	6912	93	3	63.0	5724	91
1565	3	47.0	4512	96	2	36.0	3456	96
1566	4	74.0	4848	66	3	63.0	4320	69
1567	4	74.0	5604	76	3	63.0	5076	81
1568	8	148.0	11367	77	6	126.0	9585	76
*								
1570	4	74.0	5328	72	3	63.0	4536	72
1571	4	61.5	4656	76	3	50.5	3930	78
1572	2	20.0	1776	89	1	9.0	918	102
1573	2	15.6	1453	93	1	4.6	331	72
1574	1	11.0	990	90				
1575	1	11.0	1188	108				
1576	1	11.0	1056	96				
1577	1	11.0	792	72				
1578	1	11.0	1859	169				
*								
1580	1	11.0	1056	96				
1581	1	11.0	1056	96				
1582	1	11.0	1584	144				
1583	1	11.0	1584	144				
1584	1	11.0	792	72				
1585	1	11.0	1056	96				
1586	1	11.0	1188	108				

	Wheat: Plateau			
Year	Number Towns	Total Fanegas	Total Granos	Av Value Granos
1555	1	22.0	3168	144
*				
1557	1	22.5	2160	96
1558	1	22.5	2160	96
1559	1	22.5	2160	96
1560	1	22.5	2160	96
1561	1	11.0	1056	96
1562	1	11.0	1188	108
1563	1	11.0	1584	144
1564	1	11.0	1188	108
1565	1	11.0	1056	96
1566	1	11.0	528	48
1567	1	11.0	528	48
1568	2	22.0	1782	81
*				
1570	1	11.0	792	72
1571	1	11.0	726	66
1572	1	11.0	858	78
1573	1	11.0	1122	102
1574	1	11.0	990	90
1575	1	11.0	1188	108
1576	1	11.0	1056	96
1577	1	11.0	792	72
1578	1	11.0	1859	169
*				
1580	1	11.0	1056	96
1581	1	11.0	1056	96
1582	1	11.0	1584	144
1583	1	11.0	1584	144
1584	1	11.0	792	72
1585	1	11.0	1056	96
1586	1	11.0	1188	108

	Frijoles: Nueva Galicia				Frijoles: Coast			
Year	Number Towns	Total Fanegas	Total Granos	Av Value Granos	Number Towns	Total Fanegas	Total Granos	Av Value Granos
1555	1	8.0	768	96				
*								
1557	4	89.0	3240	36	2	26.0	1404	54
1558	2	58.0	6516	112				
1559	4	107.0	7860	73	1	4.0	264	66
1560	2	22.0	1164	53	1	4.0	192	48
1561	2	16.0	1344	84	1	4.0	192	48
1562	1	12.0	1008	84				
1563	1	9.0	513	57				
1564	1	9.0	702	78				
1565	1	9.0	540	60				
1566	1	9.0	540	60				
1567	1	9.0	540	60				
1568	1	9.0	540	60				
*								
1570	1	1.0	48	48	1	1.0	48	48
1571	2	13.0	504	39	1	4.0	288	72
1572	1	9.0	1026	114				
1573	1	9.0	432	48				
1574	1	9.0	594	66				
1575	2	12.5	561	45	1	3.5	210	60
1576	2	12.5	912	73	1	3.5	210	60
1577	1	9.0	324	36				
1578	1	3.5	668	191	1	3.5	668	191
*								
1580	1	3.5	630	180	1	3.5	630	180
1581	1	3.5	336	96	1	3.5	336	96

	Frijoles: Plateau				Frijoles: Zacatecas			
Year	Number Towns	Total Fanegas	Total Granos	Av Value Granos	Number Towns	Total Fanegas	Total Granos	Av Value Granos
1555	1	8.0	768	96				
*								
1557	2	63.0	1836	29				
1558	2	58.0	6516	112	1	40.0	5760	144
1559	3	103.0	7596	74	1	40.0	5760	144
1560	1	18.0	972	54				
1561	1	12.0	1152	96	1	12.0	1152	96
1562	1	12.0	1008	84	1	12.0	1008	84
1563	1	9.0	513	57	1	9.0	513	57
1564	1	9.0	702	78	1	9.0	702	78
1565	1	9.0	540	60	1	9.0	540	60
1566	1	9.0	540	60	1	9.0	540	60
1567	1	9.0	540	60	1	9.0	540	60
1568	1	9.0	540	60	1	9.0	540	60
*								
1571	1	9.0	216	24	1	9.0	216	24
1572	1	9.0	1026	114	1	9.0	1026	114
1573	1	9.0	432	48	1	9.0	432	48
1574	1	9.0	594	66	1	9.0	594	66
1575	1	9.0	351	39	1	9.0	351	39
1576	1	9.0	702	78	1	9.0	702	78
1577	1	9.0	324	36	1	9.0	324	36

	Chile: Nueva Galicia				Chile: Zacatecas			
Year	Number Towns	Total Fanegas	Total Granos	Av Value Granos	Number Towns	Total Fanegas	Total Granos	Av Value Granos
1558	1	50.5	7272	144	1	50.5	7272	144
1559	2	66.0	5618	85	1	32.5	4680	144
1560	1	32.5	3120	96	1	32.5	3120	96
1561	1	16.0	1536	96	1	16.0	1536	96
1562	1	14.5	1218	84	1	14.5	1218	84
1563	1	14.5	826	57	1	14.5	826	57
1564	1	14.5	1131	78	1	14.5	1131	78
1565	1	14.5	870	60	1	14.5	870	60
1566	1	14.5	870	60	1	14.5	870	60
1567	1	14.5	870	60	1	14.5	870	60
1568	1	14.5	870	60	1	14.5	870	60
*								
1571	1	14.5	348	24	1	14.5	348	24
1572	1	14.5	1653	114	1	14.5	1653	114
1573	1	14.5	783	54	1	14.5	783	54
1574	1	14.5	957	66	1	14.5	957	66
1575	1	14.5	565	39	1	14.5	565	39
1576	1	14.5	1131	78	1	14.5	1131	78
1577	1	14.5	522	36	1	14.5	522	36

	Honey: Nueva Galicia				Honey: Coast			
Year	Number Towns	Total Arrobas	Total Granos	Av Value Granos	Number Towns	Total Arrobas	Total Granos	Av Value Granos
1555	4	4.0	1200.0	300	3	3.0	816.0	272
*								
1557	1	1.0	384.0	384				
1558	1	1.0	384.0	384				
1559	4	4.0	816.0	204	3	3.0	432.0	144
1560	4	4.0	816.0	204	3	3.0	432.0	144
1561	3	3.0	432.0	144	3	3.0	432.0	144
*								
1563	3	3.0	317.0	106	3	3.0	317.0	106
*								
1566	2	2.0	384.0	192	2	2.0	384.0	192
*								
1568	5	5.0	480.0	96	5	5.0	480.0	96
1569	4	4.0	1248.0	312	4	4.0	1248.0	312
1570	3	3.0	864.0	288	3	3.0	864.0	288
1571	3	3.0	936.0	312	3	3.0	936.0	312
1572	8	8.0	2412.0	302	8	8.0	2412.0	302
1573	4	4.0	1332.0	333	4	4.0	1332.0	333
1574	8	8.0	2616.0	327	8	8.0	2616.0	327
1575	10	10.0	3472.0	347	10	10.0	3472.0	347
1576	6	6.0	2175.2	363	6	6.0	2175.2	363
1577	4	4.0	967.0	242	4	4.0	967.0	242
1578	5	5.0	2050.0	410	5	5.0	2050.0	410
*								
1580	2	2.0	576.0	288	2	2.0	576.0	288
1581	1	1.0	120.0	120	1	1.0	120.0	120
1582	2	2.0	444.0	222	2	2.0	444.0	222
1583	1	1.0	192.0	192	1	1.0	192.0	192
1584	1	1.0	192.0	192	1	1.0	192.0	192
1585	3	3.0	780.0	260	3	3.0	780.0	260
1586	5	5.0	1068.0	214	5	5.0	1068.0	214
*								
1590	4	4.0	576.0	144	4	4.0	576.0	144
1591	4	4.0	576.0	144	4	4.0	576.0	144
1592	4	4.0	576.0	144	4	4.0	576.0	144
1593	2	2.0	288.0	144	2	2.0	288.0	144
1594	4	4.0	576.0	144	4	4.0	576.0	144
1595	4	4.0	576.0	144	4	4.0	576.0	144
1596	4	4.0	576.0	144	4	4.0	576.0	144
1597	4	4.0	576.0	144	4	4.0	576.0	144
1598	1	1.0	96.0	96	1	1.0	96.0	96

	Cotton: Coast				Cloth: Coast			
Year	Number Towns	Total Arrobas	Total Granos	Av Value Granos	Number Towns	Total Sq. Vara	Total Granos	Av Value Granos
1558					6	6.0	144.600	24
1559	3	37.5	1800.0	48	5	5.0	136.800	27
1560	4	43.5	2088.0	48	6	6.0	150.800	25
1561	4	43.5	2088.0	48	6	6.0	157.800	26
1562					3	3.0	100.800	34
1563					6	6.0	184.800	31
1564					4	4.0	131.100	33
1565					3	3.0	110.250	37
1566					5	5.0	136.500	27
1567					5	5.0	167.325	33
1568					12	12.0	356.900	30
1569					8	8.0	244.800	31
1570					8	8.0	276.450	35
1571					6	6.0	50.250	8
1572					9	9.0	285.800	32
1573					2	2.0	68.900	34
1574					11	11.0	306.300	28
1575	2	9.0	600.0	67	11	11.0	288.950	26
1576					9	9.0	281.700	31
1577					8	8.0	204.000	26
1578	2	9.0	1178.2	131	13	13.0	417.280	32
*								
1580	1	2.0	192.0	96	6	6.0	144.000	24
1581	2	7.5	395.7	53	6	6.0	116.500	19
1582	2	7.5	497.0	66	6	6.0	114.000	19
1583	2	7.5	382.0	51	3	3.0	42.000	14
1584	2	7.5	382.0	51	2	2.0	24.000	12
1585	2	7.5	399.0	53	2	2.0	24.750	12
1586	2	7.5	407.8	54	2	2.0	60.000	30
*								
1590	2	7.5	360.0	48	2	2.0	48.000	24
1591	2	7.5	360.0	48	2	2.0	48.000	24
1592	2	7.5	360.0	48	1	1.0	24.000	24
1593	2	7.5	360.0	48				
1594	2	7.5	360.0	48				
1595	2	7.5	360.0	48				
1596	2	7.5	360.0	48				
1597	2	7.5	360.0	48				

	Fish: Coast				Oysters: Coast			
Year	Number Towns	Total Arrobas	Total Granos	Av Value Granos	Number Towns	Total Arrobas	Total Granos	Av Value Granos
1558	2	128.0	2676.0	21	1	16.0	336.0	21
1559	2	128.0	6096.0	48	1	16.0	768.0	48
1560	3	134.0	6348.0	47	1	16.0	768.0	48
1561	3	134.0	6348.0	47	1	16.0	768.0	48
1562	2	126.0	10332.0	82	1	16.0	1344.0	84
1563	2	124.0	10728.0	87	1	16.0	1584.0	99
1564	1	120.0	7200.0	60	1	16.0	960.0	60
1565	1	120.0	8640.0	72	1	16.0	1568.0	98
1566	2	128.0	9216.0	72	1	15.0	1080.0	72
1567	1	120.0	5040.0	42	1	15.0	630.0	42
1568	3	137.0	5496.0	40	1	15.0	585.0	39
*								
1570	1	120.0	6120.0	51	1	15.0	765.0	51
1571	1	120.0	6120.0	51	1	15.0	765.0	51
1572	1	120.0	7920.0	66	1	15.0	990.0	66
1573	1	120.0	5760.0	48	1	15.0	720.0	48
1574	1	60.0	3660.0	61	1	15.0	1470.0	98
1575	1	60.0	4380.0	73	1	15.0	1470.0	98
1576	1	53.0	3816.0	72	1	15.0	1440.0	96
*								
1580	1	2.0	96.0	48				
1581	1	2.0	60.0	30				
1582	1	2.0	112.0	56				
1583	1	2.0	96.0	48				
1584	1	2.0	96.0	48				
1585	1	2.0	108.0	54				
1586	1	2.0	96.0	48				
*								
1590	1	2.0	96.0	48				
1591	1	2.0	96.0	48				
1592	1	2.0	96.0	48				
1593	1	2.0	96.0	48				
1594	1	2.0	96.0	48				
1595	1	2.0	96.0	48				
1596	1	2.0	96.0	48				
1597	1	2.0	96.0	48				

	Salt: Coast			
Year	Number Towns	Total Fanegas	Total Granos	Av Value Granos
1558	2	48.0	5760.0	120
1559	2	25.0	2640.0	106
1560	2	25.0	2640.0	106
1561	2	25.0	2640.0	106
*				
1566	1	15.0	900.0	60
*				
1568	4	109.0	10464.0	96
1569	3	157.0	13787.0	88
1570	3	157.0	11889.0	76
1571	3	157.0	9350.0	60
1572	3	157.0	9462.0	60
*				
1574	1	7.0	385.0	55
1575	1	7.0	395.5	56
1576	1	7.0	385.0	55
1577	1	7.0	385.0	55
1578	1	7.0	1057.0	151
*				
1580	1	7.0	840.0	120
1581	1	7.0	714.0	102
1582	1	7.0	588.0	84
1583	2	12.2	588.0	48
1584	2	12.2	588.0	48
1585	2	12.2	661.5	54
1586	2	12.2	820.7	67
*				
1590	2	12.2	588.0	48
1591	2	12.2	588.0	48
1592	1	7.0	336.0	48
1593	2	12.2	588.0	48
1594	2	12.2	588.0	48
1595	2	12.2	588.0	48
1596	2	12.2	588.0	48
1597	2	12.2	588.0	48

Bibliography

Abbreviations

AGI Spain. Archivo General de Indias, Seville
AGN Mexico. Archivo General de la Nación, Mexico City
GBPE Universidad de Guadalajara. Biblioteca Pública del Estado.

Archives

Archivo General de Indias, Seville (AGI):
Audiencia de Guadalajara
Audiencia de Méjico
Contaduría

Archivo General de la Nación, Mexico City (AGN):
Reales Cédulas, Duplicados

Universidad de Guadalajara, Biblioteca Pública del Estado (GBPE):
Archivo de la Real Audiencia de Guadalajara
Ramo Fiscal
Exp. 1. 1580, Zacatecas. Libro general de mi, Francisco Covarrubias, contador de la real hacienda de Su Majestad de este Nueva Reino de Galicia de la Nueva España del cargo y descargo que hago al tesorero, Francisco López de Ibarra, de los pesos de oro y minas de plata que se meten a la caja de Su Magestad pertenecientes y tributos y penas de cámara y otras cosas en todo el año de 1580. 95 ff.

Exp. 2. 1583, Guadalajara. Libro de cargo y data de todos los ramos de hacienda. Cargo de lo procedido de la renta de alcabala, de tributos, de almonedas, de los dos novenos, de la sal, de caudillos y soldados, de tributos de mulatos y negros libres. Descargo por libranzas, de penas de cámara, de la venta de alcabalas, de la sal, de los dos novenos. 192 ff.
Exp. 3. 1598-1599, Guadalajara. Libro que asienta los pesos de oro que entran en la real caja de esta ciudad y de los pesos de oro que se pagan por libranza. El contador Covarrubias. 154 ff.
Exp. 3a. 1599-1600, Guadalajara. Libro que asienta los pesos de oro que entran en la real caja de esta ciudad y de los pesos de oro que se pagan por libranza. El contador Covarrubias. . . . 240 ff.
Exp. 4. 1605, Guadalajara. Libro y cargo y data de todos los ramos de hacienda. . . . 214 ff.
Exp. 5. 1607, Guadalajara. Libro de cargo y data de todos los ramos de hacienda. . . . 225 ff.
Ramo Civil
Ramo Criminal
Archivo del Juzgado de Bienes de Difuntos

Jalisco (state). Archivo de Instrumentos Públicos, Guadalajara.

Printed Materials

Acuña, René, ed. *Relaciones geográficas del siglo XVI.* 10 vols. Universidad Nacional Autónoma de México, Instituto de Investigaciones Antropológicas, Etnohistoria, Serie Antropológica, Mexico City, 1982-1988.

Alvarez, Víctor M. *Diccionario de conquistadores.* (Cuadernos de Trabajo del Departamento de Investigaciones Históricas, 8.) 2 vols. Mexico City, Instituto Nacional de Antropología e Historia, 1975. (Mimeographed)

Amaya Topete, Jesús. *Ameca, protofundación mexicana,* together with *Bioteca del Occidente.* Mexico City, 1951.

_____________. *Los conquistadores Fernández de Híjar y Bracamonte. Ensayo bio-geneográfico.* Guadalajara, Jalisco, Gráfica Editorial, 1952.

Arregui, Domingo Lázaro de. *Descripción de la Nueva Galicia, edición y estudio por François Chevalier.* Sevilla, 1946.

Bakewell, Peter J. *Silver Mining and Society in Colonial Mexico: Zacatecas, 1546-1700.* Cambridge, England, 1971.

Beltrán, Ulises. "Evolución de los sistemas de trabajo en la Nueva España, 1521-1640: Un ensayo en nueva historia económica." N.p., n.d. (Mimeographed)

Belveder, Juan de. *Libro general de las redvciones de plata, y oro de diferentes leyes y pesos, de menor à mayor cantidad, y de sus intereses à tanto por ciento, con otras reglas, y auisos muy necessarios para estos reynos del piru. . . .* Lima, 1597.

Benítez, Ing. José R. "Conquistadores de la Nueva Galicia," *Boletín de la Junta Auxiliar Jalisciense de la Sociedad Mexicana de Geografía y Estadística*, 7 (1941-1942):277-312.

_____________. "II. Fundadores de la ciudad de Guadalajara," *Boletín de la Junta Auxiliar Jalisciense de la Sociedad Mexicana de Geografía y Estadística*, 7 (1941-1942):289-312.

_____________. "III. Primeros vecinos pobladores [de Guadalajara]," *Boletín de la Junta Auxiliar Jalisciense de la Sociedad Mexicana de Geografía y Estadística*, 7 (1941-1942):313-322.

Borah, Woodrow, coord. *El gobierno provincial en la Nueva España, 1570-1787.* (Universidad Nacional Autónoma de México, Instituto de Investigaciones Históricas, Serie Historia Novohispana/ 33.) Mexico City, 1985.

_____________. "Los tributos y su recaudación en la Audiencia de la Nueva Galicia durante el siglo XVI," *Historia y sociedad en el mundo de habla español. Homenaje a José Miranda*, Bernardo García Martínez et al., eds., (Mexico City, 1970), pp. 27-47.

_____________ and Sherburne F. Cook. *Price Trends of Some Basic Commodities in Central Mexico, 1531-1570.* (Ibero-Americana: 40.) Berkeley and Los Angeles, 1958.

_____________. *The Aboriginal Population of Central Mexico on the Eve of the Spanish Conquest.* (Ibero-Americana: 45.) Berkeley and Los Angeles, 1963.

Braudel, H. P., and F. Spooner. "Prices in Europe from 1450 to 1750," *The Cambridge Economic History of Europe*, IV, *The Economy of Expanding Europe in the Sixteenth and Seventeenth Centuries*, E. E. Rich and C. H. Wilson, eds. (Cambridge, 1967), pp. 374-486.

Calvo, Thomas. "Un extraño señor de ganados: El Maese de Campo don Francisco de Pareja y Rivera," Revista Encuentro (El Colegio de Jalisco), 3:3 (abril-junio 1986, or núm. 11):5-19.

Campos, Carlos-Alberto. "The Atlantic Islands and the Development of Southern Castile at the Turn of the Fifteenth Century," *The International History Review* (Simon Fraser University, British Columbia), 9:2 (May 1987):173-194.

Carletti, Francisco. *Razonamientos de mi viaje alrededor del mundo (1594-1606). Estudio preliminar, traducción y notas de Francisca Perujo.* Mexico City, 1976.

Carmagnani, Marcello. *Les mécanismes de la vie economique dans une société coloniale. Le Chili (1680-1830).* Paris, 1973.

_____________. "La producción agropecuario chilena. Aspectos cuantitativos, 1680-1830," *Cahiers des Amériques Latines, Série Sciences de l'Homme* (Paris), 3 (1969):3-21.

Chávez Hayhoe, Arturo. "Guadalajara de 1542 a 1560," *Boletín de la Junta Auxiliar Jalisciense de la Sociedad Mexicana de Geografía y Estadística*, 7 (1941-1942):239-262.

_____________. "Guadalajara de 1560 a 1600," *Boletín de la Junta Auxiliar Jalisciense de la Sociedad Mexicana de Geografía y Estadística*, 8 (1943-1945):13-49 and 63.

_____________. *Guadalajara en el siglo XVI*. 2 vols. Guadalajara, 1953-1954.

_____________. "Las Guadalajaras pre-Atemajaquenses," *Boletín de la Junta Auxiliar Jalisciense de la Sociedad Mexicana de Geografía y Estadística*, 7 (1941-1942):13-67.

Chevalier, François. *La formation des grands domaines au Mexique. Terre et société aux XVIe-XVIIe siècles.* (Université de Paris, Travaux et Mémoires de l'Institut d'Ethnologie, 56.) Paris, 1952.

[Ciudad Real, Fray Antonio de]. *Relación breve y verdadera de algunas cosas de las muchas que sucedieron al Padre Fray Alonso Ponce en las provincias de la Nueva España, siendo comisario general de aquellas partes. . . .* 2 vols. Madrid, 1873; Kraus Facsimile, Vaduz, 1966.

Claxton, Robert H., and Alan D. Hecht. "Climatic and Human History in Europe and Latin America: An Opportunity for Comparative Study," *Climatic Change*, 1 (1978):195-203.

Coatsworth, John H. "Economic History and the History of Prices in Colonial Latin America," *Essays on the Price History of Eighteenth-Century Latin America*, Lyman L. Johnson and Enrique Tandeter, eds., pp. 21-33.

Cook, Sherburne F., and Woodrow Borah. *Essays in Population History: Mexico and the Caribbean*. 3 vols. Berkeley and Los Angeles, 1970-1979.

Dávila Garibi, José Ignacio Paulino. *Apuntes para la historia de la Iglesia en Guadalajara*, 5 vols. in 7. Guadalajara, 1957-1977.

_____________. *Estudio genealógico-biográfico del Capitán D. Diego de Colio, conquistador de Nueva España, particularmente de la Nueva Galicia, de Guatemala y de Tejuantepec*. Guadalajara, 1927-1928.

_____________. "Juan de Ojeda," *Historia Mexicana*, 1:4 (abril-junio 1952):629-634.

_____________. *La sociedad de Zacatecas en los albores del régimen colonial: Actuación de los principales fundadores y primeros funcionarios públicos de la ciudad*. Mexico City, 1939.

Dean, Jeffrey S., and William J. Robinson. *Expanded Tree-Ring Chronologies for the Southwestern United States.* (University of Arizona, Laboratory of Tree-Ring Research, Chronology Series 3.) Tucson, Arizona, 1978.

DeVries, Jan. "Measuring the Impact of Climate on History: The Search for Appropriate Methodology," *Journal of Interdisciplinary History*, 10 (1980):599-630.

Drew, Linda G. *Tree-Ring Chronologies of Western America. III. California and Nevada.* (University of Arizona, Laboratory of Tree-Ring Research, Chronology Series 1). Tucson, Arizona, 1972.

_____________, ed. *Tree-Ring Chronologies of Western America, VI. Western Canada and Mexico.* (University of Arizona, Laboratory of Tree-Ring Research, Chronology Series 1.) Tucson, Arizona, 1975.

Durand, José. "*La Grandeza Mexicana* y el ennoblecimiento del mercader," *Homenaje a Eugenio Asensio*, pp. 159-170. Madrid, 1988.

_____________. *La transformación social del Conquistador.* 2 vols. Mexico City, 1953.

Eddy, John A., Peter A. Gilman, and Dorothy E. Trotter. "Anomalous Solar Rotation in the Early 17th Century," *Science*, (vol. 198, no. 4319), 25 Nov. 1977, pp. 824-829.

Encinas, Diego de, comp. *Cedulario indiano. . . . .* ed. Alfonso García Gallo. 4 vols. Madrid, 1946.

Escobedo Mansilla, Ronald. *El tributo indígena en el Perú: siglos XVI y XVII.* Pamplona, 1979.

Fisher, R. A., and F. Yates. *Statistical Tables for Biological, Agricultural and Medical Research.* Edinburgh, 1918.

Florescano, Enrique. "El abasto y legislación de granos en el siglo XVI," *Historia Mexicana*, 14 (1965):567-630.

_____________. "Una historia olvidada: la sequía en México," Nexos, 32 (1980):9-18.

_____________. Origen y desarrollo de los problemas agrarios de México [1500-1821], 2nd ed. rev. Mexico City, 1976.

_____________. *Precios del maíz y crisis agrícolas en México, 1708-1810.* Mexico City, 1969.

Fritts, H. C. "Tree Ring Evidence for Climatic Change in Western North America," *Monthly Weather Review*, 93 (1965):421-443.

_____________. *Tree Rings and Climate.* London, New York, San Francisco, 1976.

García-Abasolo, Antonio F. *Martín Enríquez y la reforma de 1568 en Nueva España.* Sevilla, 1983.

Garner, Richard L. "Prices and Wages in Eighteenth-Century Mexico," *Essays on the Price History of Eighteenth-Century Latin America*, Lyman L. Johnson, and Enrique Tandeter, eds., pp. 73-108.

_____________. "Price Trends in Eighteenth-Century Mexico," *Hispanic American Historical Review*, 65 (1985):279-325.

Gerhard, Peter. *The North Frontier of New Spain.* Princeton, N. J., 1982.

Gibson, Charles. *The Aztecs under Spanish Rule. A History of the Indians of the Valley of Mexico, 1519-1810.* Stanford, Calif., 1964.

González Navarro, Moïsés. *Repartimiento de indios en Nueva Galicia.* Mexico City, 1953.

Granger, O. E. "Secular Fluctuations in Lowland California," *Monthly Weather Review*, 105 (1977):386-397.

_____________. "Toward Predictability in Agro-Climatology," *Unasylva, An International Journal of Forestry and Forest Industries*, 30 (1978):11-17.

Grove, Jean M. *The Little Ice Age.* London, 1988.

Guadalajara. Ayuntamiento Constitucional. *Actas de cabildos de la ciudad de Guadalajara. Volumen primero, 1607-1635.* Guadalajara, 1970.

Guthrie, Chester L. "Colonial Economy: Trade, Industry and Labor in the Seventeenth Century," *Revista de Historia de América*, No. 7 (December 1939):103-134.

Hamilton, Earl J. *American Treasure and the Price Revolution in Spain, 1501-1650.* Cambridge, Mass., 1934.

____________. *War and Prices in Spain, 1651-1800.* Cambridge, Mass., 1947.

Hardoy, Jorge E., and Carmen Aranovich. "Escalas y funciones urbanas en América Hispánica hacia el año 1600--primeras conclusiones," *El proceso de urbanización en América desde sus orígenes hasta nuestros días*, Jorge Enrique Hardoy and Richard P. Schaedel, eds., (Buenos Aires, 1969), pp. 171-208.

Hassig, Ross. *Trade, Tribute, and Transportation: The Sixteenth-Century Political Economy of the Valley of Mexico.* Norman, Oklahoma, 1985.

Herman, John R., and Richard A. Goldberg. *Sun, Weather, and Climate.* Washington, D.C., 1978.

Himmerich, Robert Theron. *The Encomenderos of New Spain, 1521-1555.* Ph.D. thesis, University of California, Los Angeles, 1984.

Icaza, Francisco A. *Diccionario autobiográfico de conquistadores y pobladores de Nueva España, sacado de los textos originales.* 2 vols., Madrid, 1923; facsimile, Editorial Aviña Levy, Mexico City, 1969.

Jáuregui, O. E. "Algunos aspectos de las fluctuaciones pluviométricos en México en los últimos cien años," *Boletín del Instituto de Geografía* (Universidad Nacional Autónoma de México), 9 (1979):39-64.

Jiménez Pelayo, Agueda. "Condiciones del trabajo de repartimiento indígena en la Nueva Galicia en el siglo XVII," *Historia Mexicana*, 38:3 (151, enero-marzo 1989):455-470.

____________. *Haciendas y comunidades indígenas en el sur de Zacatecas.* Instituto Nacional de Antropología e Historia (Colección Científica). Mexico City, 1990.

Jiménez Vizcarra, Miguel Claudio. *Indice del Archivo del Juzgado General de Bienes de Difuntos de Nueva Galicia, siglos XVI y XVII.* (Instituto Nacional de Antropología e Historia, Cuadernos de los Centros Regionales: Occidente.) Mexico City, 1978.

____________. *Indice y extractos del protocolo de Francisco Guerrero Vela, escribano público de Guadalajara.* Guadalajara, 1984. (Typescript.)

Johnson, Lyman L. and Enrique Tandeter, eds. *Essays on the Price History of Eighteenth-Century Latin America.* Albuquerque, New Mexico, 1990.

Klaus, Dieter. "Las fluctuaciones del clima en el valle de Puebla-Tlaxcala," *Comunicaciones*, 7 (1972):59-62.

Klein, Herbert S. and Stanley L. Engerman. "Methods and Meaning in Price History," *Essays on the Price History of Eighteenth-Century Latin America*, Lyman L. Johnson and Enrique Tandeter, eds., pp. 9-20.

Landaverde, A. *El maíz y su cultivo en México.* Mexico City, 1949.

Larraín, José Manuel. "Gross National Product and Prices: The Chilean Case in the Seventeenth and Eighteenth Centuries," *Essays on the Price History of Eighteenth-Century Latin America*, Lyman L. Johnson and Enrique Tandeter, eds., pp. 109-136.

_____________. "Movimiento de precios en Santiago de Chile durante 1749-1808: Una interpretación metodológica," *Jahrbuch für Geschichte von Staat, Wirtschaft und Gesellschaft Lateinamerikas*, 17 (1980):199-259.

Le Roy Ladurie, Emmanuel. *Histoire du climat depuis l'an mil.* Paris, 1967.

Libby, Leona Marshall. *Past Climates: Tree Thermometers, Commodities, and People.* Austin, Texas, 1983.

Lima. *Libros de cabildo de Lima.* 16 vols. Lima, 1935-1948.

Lohmann Villena, Guillermo. "Apuntaciones sobre el curso de los precios de los artículos de primera necesidad en Lima durante el siglo XVI," *Revista Histórica, Organo de la Academia Nacional de la Historia*, 19 (1966):79-104.

López de Velasco, Juan. *Geografía y descripción universal de las Indias,* 3d ed. (Biblioteca de Autores Españoles, vol. 248.) Madrid, 1971.

López-Portillo y Weber, José. *La rebelión de Nueva Galicia.* Tacubaya, D. F., 1939.

Mecham, J. Lloyd. *Francisco de Ibarra and Nueva Vizcaya.* Durham, N.C., 1927; facsimile ed., New York, 1968.

Melis, F. *Las fuentes específicas de la historia económica y otros estudios.* Valladolid, 1977.

Mexico (City). *Actas de cabildo del ayuntamiento de México.* 54 vols. Mexico City, 1884-1916.

Mexico (Ecclesiastical Province). *Concilio III mexicano*, ed. Mariano Galván Rivera. Mexico City, 1859.

_____________. *Concilios provinciales primero, y segundo celebrados en . . . los años de 1555, y 1565. . . .* Mexico City, 1769.

_____________. *Concilium Mexicanum Provinciale III. Celebratum Mexici Anno MDLXXXV. . . .* Mexico City, 1770.

Mexico (Viceroyalty). *Svmarios de las cedvlas, ordenes, y provisiones reales, que se han despachado por Su Magestad, para la Nueva-España, y otras partes . . . Que juntò, y dispvso, el doctor d. Iuan Francisco Montemayor, y Cordova, de Cuenca.* Mexico City, 1678.

Michaelsen, Joel Christian. *Large-Scale, Long-Period Ocean-Atmosphere Interactions in the North Pacific Region.* Ph.D. thesis, University of California, Berkeley, 1981.

Miranda, José. *El tributo indígena en la Nueva España durante el siglo XVI.* Mexico City, 1952.

Montemayor y Córdova de Cuenca, Juan de. See Mexico (Viceroyalty).

Mota Padilla, Matías Angel de la. *Historia del reino de Nueva Galicia en la América Septentrional*, new ed. Guadalajara, 1973.

Mota y Escobar, Alonso de la. "Descripción geográphica de los reynos de Galicia, Vizcaya y León," 3d ed. *Anales del Instituto Nacional de Antropología e Historia*, 4a ep., 16 (1963):287-364; vol. 45 of collection.

Noticias varias de Nueva Galicia, intendencia de Guadalajara. Guadalajara, 1878.

Nuttonsen, Michael Y. *Wheat-Climate Relationships and the Use of Phenology in Ascertaining the Thermal and Photo-Thermal Requirements of Wheat, Based on Data of North America and of Some Thermally Analogous Areas of North America, in the Soviet Union and in Finland.* Washington, D.C., 1955.

Orozco y Jiménez, Francisco, publ. *Colección de documentos históricos inéditos y muy raros, referentes al Arzobispado de Guadalajara.* 6 vols. Guadalajara, 1922-1927.

Otte, Enrique, comp. *Cartas privadas de emigrantes a Indias, 1540-1616.* Sevilla [1988].

Palomino y Cañedo, Jorge. *Cuatro memoriales mendocinos e información de Francisco Tellez, 1541.* Guadalajara, 1986.

____________. *Los protocolos de Rodrigo Hernández Cordero, 1585-1591, escribano público de Guadalajara.* Guadalajara, 1972.

Parry, John H. *The Audiencia of New Galicia in the Sixteenth Century: A Study in Spanish Colonial Government.* Cambridge, England, 1948.

Paso y Troncoso, Francisco del, ed. Epistolario de Nueva España. 16 vols. Mexico City, 1939-1942.

____________. *Papeles de la Nueva España: Relaciones geográficas de la diócesis de Michoacán, 1579-1580.* 2 vols. Guadalajara, 1958.

____________. *Papeles de Nueva España: Segunda serie, geografía y estadistica.* 9 vols. Madrid and Mexico City, 1905-1948.

Pastor, Rodolfo. *Campesinos y reformas: La Mixteca, 1700-1856.* Mexico City, 1987.

Pérez Herrero, Pedro. "Commercio y precios en la Nueva España. Presupuestos teóricos y materiales para una discusión," *Revista de Indias*, 46, no. 174 (julio-diciembre 1984):465-488.

Pfister, Christian. "Fluctuations climatiques et prix céréaliers en Europe du XVIe au XXe siècle," *Annales: Economies, Sociétés, Civilisations*, 43 (jan.-fév. 1988):25-53.

____________. *Das Klima der Schweiz von 1525-1800 und seine Bedeutung in der Geschichte von Bevölkerung und Landwirtschaft.* 2 vols. Bern, 1984.

Poole, Stafford. *Pedro Moya de Contreras: Catholic Reform and Royal Power in New Spain, 1571-1591.* Berkeley and Los Angeles, 1987.

Porras Muñoz, Guillermo. *El nuevo descubrimiento de San José del Parral* (Universidad Nacional Autónoma de México, Instituto de Investigaciones Históricas, Serie Historia Novohispana 39.) Mexico City, 1988.

Portig, W. "Klimapendelungen in San Salvador," *Annalen der Meteorologie*, 8 (1958):145-148.

Powell, Philip Wayne. *Soldiers, Indians, and Silver: The Northward Advance of New Spain, 1550-1600.* Berkeley and Los Angeles, 1952.

Ramón, Armando de, and José Manuel Larraín. *Orígenes de la vida económica chilena, 1659-1808.* Santiago, Chile, 1982.

Rivera Bernárdez, José de, conde de Santiago de la Laguna, ed. *Compendio de las cosas mas notables contenidas en los libros del cabildo de esta ciudad de Nuestra Señora de los Zacatecas desde el año de su descubrimiento, 1546 hasta 1730*. Mexico City, 1945.

Rojas Garcidueñas, José. *Bernardo de Balbuena: La vida y la obra*, 2nd ed. Mexico City, 1982.

Romano, Ruggiero. "Algunas consideraciones sobre la historia de precios en América colonial (y una nota complementaria)," *HISLA, Revista Latinoamericana de Historia Económica y Social*, 7 (1st sem. 1986):65-103.

_____________. *Una economía colonial: Chile en el siglo XVIII*. Buenos Aires, 1965.

_____________. "Problèmes et méthodes d'histoire économique de l'Amérique Latine," *Revue Européenne des Sciences Sociales*, 15 (1977):49-75.

_____________, ed., *I prezzi in Europa dal XIII secolo a oggi*. Turin, 1967.

_____________. "Some Considerations on the History of Prices in Colonial Latin America," *Essays on the Price History of Eighteenth-Century Latin America*, Lyman L. Johnson and Enrique Tandeter, eds., pp. 35-71.

Sánchez-Bella, Ismael. *La organización financiera de las Indias (siglo XVI)*. Sevilla, 1968.

Santamaría, Francisco J. *Diccionario de mejicanismos*. Mexico City, 1959.

Schove, D. Justin, ed. *Sunspot Cycles*. Stroudsburg, PA, 1983.

Schulman, Edmund. *Dendroclimatic Changes in Semiarid America*. Tucson, Arizona, 1956.

Schwaller, John Frederick. *Origins of Church Wealth in Mexico: Ecclesiastical Revenues and Church Finances, 1523-1600*. Albuquerque, New Mexico, 1985.

Simpson, Lesley Byrd. *Studies in the Administration of the Indians in New Spain. III. The Repartimiento System of Native Labor in New Spain and Guatemala*. (Ibero-Americana: 13.) Berkeley and Los Angeles, 1938.

Spain. Laws. *Recopilación de leyes de los reynos de las Indias,* facsimile of 4th ed. 3 vols. Madrid, 1943.

Stokes, M. A., Linda G. Drew, and C. W. Stockton. *Tree Ring Chronologies of Western America. I. Selected Tree-Ring Stations*. (University of Arizona, Laboratory of Tree-Ring Research, Chronology Series 1.) Tucson, Arizona, 1973.

Stuiver, Minze. "Solar variability and Climatic Change during the Current Millenium," *Nature*, 286 (August 1950):868-871.

Swan, Susan L. "Mexico in the Little Ice Age," *Journal of Interdisciplinary History*, 11 (1981):633-648.

Tandeter, Enrique, and Nathan Wachtel. "Conjonctures inverses: Le mouvement des prix à Potosi pendant le XVIIIe siècle," *Annales: Economies, Sociétés, Civilisations*, 38 (1983):549-613.

_____________. "Prices and Agricultural Production: Potosí and Charcas in the Eighteenth Century," *Essays on the Price History of Eighteenth-Century Latin America*, Lyman L. Johnson and Enrique Tandeter, eds., pp. 201-276.

TePaske, John J., and Herbert S. Klein. *Ingresos y egresos de la real hacienda de Nueva España*. (Instituto Nacional de Antropología e Historia, Colección Fuentes.) 2 vols. Mexico City, 1986-1988.

Van Young, Eric. *Hacienda and Market in Eighteenth-Century Mexico: The Rural Economy of the Guadalajara Region, 1675-1820*. Berkeley and Los Angeles, 1981.

Vásquez de Espinosa, Fray Antonio. *Descripción de la Nueva España en el siglo XVII . . .* Mariano Cuevas, S. J., ed. Mexico City, 1944.

Vizcarra A. de Jiménez, Eugenia Irma, and Miguel Claudio Jiménez y Vizcarra. *Noticias biográficas contenidas en las partidas de entierro del primer libro mixto del Archivo del Sagrario Metropolitano de la Ciudad de Guadalajara, 1610-1634*. [Guadalajara], n. d.

Index

Made in the USA
Monee, IL
14 September 2026

63198317R00155